TRUST BASICS

AN INTRODUCTION TO THE PRODUCTS AND SERVICES OF THE TRUST INDUSTRY

MONTY P. GREGOR, CTFA

This publication is designed to provide accurate and authoritative information in regard to the subject matter covered. It is sold with the understanding that the publisher is not engaged in rendering legal, accounting, or other professional service. If legal advice or other expert assistance is required, the services of a competent professional person should be sought.

From a Declaration of Principles jointly adopted by a Committee of the American Bar Association and a Committee of Publishers and Associations.

The American Bankers Association is committed to providing innovative, high-quality products and services that are responsive to its members' critical needs.

To comment about this product, or to learn more about the American Bankers Association and the many products and services it offers, please call 1-800-BANKERS or visit our Web site: www.aba.com.

This textbook has been approved by the American Institute of Banking for use in courses for which AIB certificates or diplomas are granted. The American Institute of Banking is the 102-year-old professional development and training affiliate of the American Bankers Association. Instructional materials endorsed by AIB have been developed by bankers, for bankers.

American Institute *of* Banking

AMERICAN **BANKERS** ASSOCIATION ®

CONTENTS

Exhibits

About the Author

Monty P. Gregor is a member of Bank One's Private Client Services Education Group. Previously he served as a vice president and business development officer in the Personal Trust and Investment Management Department of the former American National Bank and Trust Company of Chicago, now a Bank One company. He served similarly with the Harris Trust and Savings Bank of Chicago.

Gregor's past experience includes ten years as an insurance consultant with the Minnesota Mutual Life Insurance Company. He is a member of the Chicago Estate Planning Council and a faculty member of the Center for Financial Training (formerly the Chicagoland American Institute of Banking), where he teaches the Trust Basics and Estate Planning courses. In addition to this book, Gregor is the author of the American Bankers Association's *Trust Operations* textbook and of several articles for the ABA's *Trust and Investments* magazine. Gregor assisted in the ABA's recent revision of its "Building Trust Expertise" and "Personal Trust Resource Series" training material.

Gregor received his B.S. degree from Loyola University Chicago and is currently enrolled in a Masters in Adult Education program at National-Louis University. His professional designations are Chartered Life Underwriter (CLU), Certified Financial Planner (CFP™), and Certified Trust and Financial Advisor (CTFA).

REVISED INTRODUCTION

When *Trust Basics* was published in 1998, the opening pages included the following introduction. I have not changed my thinking . . . but much else has changed.

Every aspect of the trust industry has been affected by tax law changes (most notably the Economic Growth and Tax Relief Reconciliation Act of June 2001), e-commerce, and the Internet. Securities processing activities are approaching the speed of light, the stock market is a roller-coaster ride, and contemporary investment products are labeled *spiders, cubes,* and *diamonds.*

Financial services providers have blended and remolded their boundaries: banks are buying or merging with insurance companies and investment advisory firms, and vice-versa. Bankers are becoming financial planners and registered investment advisors. Huge, well-known companies are going bankrupt and restructuring. Pension reform and the Social Security system are under microscopic scrutiny. Advice is coming from—and going to—everyone.

Some things will never change, and trust professionals cannot and should not forget this, although customers and providers tend to do so. Taxes have not disappeared (despite reform), illness has not gone away (despite advances in medicine), and death still happens (despite increased longevity). Therefore, customers need our help today perhaps more than ever. We need to remind them—and ourselves—that the basics don't change and that our customers need us to help them wade through that which *has* changed.

Recently I went to my cell phone provider to buy an accessory. The store rep asked to see my phone. Her eyes showed surprise when I handed the phone to her. "Wow, this is an old one," she exclaimed. I was surprised at *her* surprise—I had bought the phone only a year earlier. Technology!

If we are so sophisticated, advanced, and knowledgeable, why are so many people unaware of what an estate is, of how large an estate must be before it is subject to transfer taxes, and even of whether they *have* an estate?

An American demographics study conducted by Professor Edward Wolff of New York University shows that 2.4 million American households in 1983 had a net worth of at least $1 million and that this number grew to 5 million households in 2000. American households with a net worth more than $10 million grew from 68,000 in 1983 to 350,000 in 2000.

Regardless of technology, investment performance, and tax law changes, a large potential market for wealth management services still stares us in the face . . . and it begins with the fundamentals. Our challenge as trust professionals is to recognize it, learn it, and do something about it.

INTRODUCTION

"Being good in business is the most fascinating kind of art. . . .
Making money is art and working is art
and good business is the best art."

Andy Warhol (1928–1987)

WHAT YOU ARE GETTING YOURSELF INTO

In the past 10 years the trust industry has traveled at warp speed: Tax laws have been modified, deleted, and added; terminology and technology have expanded and advanced; products and services have proliferated; government regulation and deregulation have changed; and marketing and selling have moved to the forefront. A decade of soul-searching has brought us to new and improved ways of analyzing our business, preparing for it, moving it into the new millennium, and meeting internal and external competitors.

This text is only a beginning. The chapters are steps leading into the world of estate and financial planning. Therefore, the primary objective of this text is to introduce trust and banking professionals at all levels to the trust industry, how we affect potential and existing customers, what we have to offer, and how we can help.

The chapters are designed to build knowledge and expertise step by step. The text presents an overview of a trust department, including how it fits into a bank's overall operations and how trust services are delivered; some brief historical happenings that have positively and negatively affected the trust environment; the importance of accumulating, preserving, and disposing of an estate; the living and dying sides of the coin; the dual significance of planning for self and others; and the competition we face.

THE PLAYERS AND SOME RULES OF THE ROAD

There are many players in the financial services industry: attorneys, actuaries, stockbrokers, trust officers, Certified Public Accountants (CPAs), Chartered Financial Analysts (CFAs), Chartered Life Underwriters (CLUs), Chartered Financial Consultants (ChFCs), Certified Financial Planners (CFPs), and Certified Trust and Financial Advisors (CTFAs). Where do the responsibilities of one stop and those of the other start? Should the client place trust in one type of advisor or turn to several? When does a suggestion become a recommendation? When does advice border on legal judgment?

Clear boundaries are established in certain circumstances when defining professional responsibility. For example, the writing of wills and trusts or documents involving legal rights is indeed the practice of law. But when a planner steps beyond this clear line, matters sometimes become fuzzy. What aspects of the legalities of a trust is the trust officer or CLU not allowed to discuss? When should an attorney not discuss the client's life insurance portfolio and its tax ramifications? Can the investment counselor objectively assess a customer's tax bracket?

It is a given that no one should heed advice from the untrained and unlicensed; there is no substitute for knowledge and experience. Clients should seek the proper direction from the appropriate sources: professionals with their own special and necessary skills.

Therefore, read the stories and take the discussion of concepts as guidelines only. This text is an information piece, not a source of financial advice. We do not assume any responsibility for the results of using the contents in individual planning circumstances. A presentation such as this cannot be a substitute for providing customers with proper legal, tax, insurance, and investment direction. Also, trust professionals should work as part of a team—a transdisciplinary interplay of several advisors with individual and group strengths—to lead the client down the proper path. Remember, planning doesn't come from the words of a book.

SETTING THE TONE

In 1940, author, psychologist, scholar, and philosopher Mortimer J. Adler wrote the book How to Read a Book. Many people have asked, "How can I read Adler's book if I don't know how to read a book?" A catch-22? What Adler assumed is that we knew how to read. With the ability to read, we could read his words in order to learn how to "properly and effectively" read others' words.

This book in your hands doesn't require that you read Adler's book first. But it is filled with thoughts, definitions, and stories and a hope that you will appreciate, and be moved to seek, more specific and advanced information on a subject rich in history and possibilities: trusts.

In this text we will explore the origins of our business, what we provide, who our customers are, why people seek us, and the way each segment of the trust industry builds on other aspects.

WHAT WE PROVIDE

The unknowing person envisions the trust business as mysterious, concocted in a dark laboratory, designed for the wealthy and the elderly and for widows and orphans. The "T-word" is avoided because it isn't understood. If customers don't know what it is, they stay away from it; if it is avoided, they don't know what it can provide and how badly they need our products and services. The following true-life drama illustrates this point.

It was Wednesday, 4:45 P.M. Mike, a trust officer, was on his way out the door as his phone rang. "Do I take the call, miss my regular train, and arrive late for cocktails with the neighbors?" he thought. "Should I have someone take a message? I can always return the call tomorrow."

"Mike? May I call you Mike?" The caller spoke in a rush. "John Philbin said I should call you. He said you would be able to help me. I'm at his office now and I can be at the bank in 10 minutes. I trust John so I know I'll trust you. John said you could help me like a father helps a daughter. I don't know which way to turn. Which floor are you on? Is 10 minutes from now okay?"

The part about "how a father helps a daughter" intrigued Mike. He called home to say he would be late, cleared a conference room, and waited for Joan. Mike never made it for cocktails and supper; Joan's needs turned out to be more important than exchanging political jokes with the neighbors.

On Monday, 2 weeks ago, Joan had begun her job as a travel agent after 15 years of staying home to raise her children. She and her husband, Bill, had always traveled; now was their chance to continue doing it while getting paid. On Wednesday, as she drove Bill to the train station for his commute to his office, they talked about going to the north woods summer house over the weekend—just the two of them away from the kids.

New travel agents do not have many customers by their third day of work, so Joan was thrilled to hear her phone ring later in the morning. But the caller was Bill's partner, and the news was the worst: Bill had suffered a massive heart attack at his desk. By the time Joan reached the hospital, Bill was dead, at 53.

Not knowing where to start or what to do, she turned to John Philbin, a close family friend. John's will and trust named Mike's bank as executor and trustee. John's first thought was to direct Joan to Mike.

What Mike, the trust department, and the bank did for Joan in the subsequent months—and to this day, 10 years later—is described in the chapters of this book: Bill's will and trust, Joan's will and trust planning for the kids, probate, investments, tax arrangement, employee benefits, and overall estate and financial planning. Today Joan is smiling again. She's a successful travel agent. Her kids are college graduates. The summer house in the north woods is beautiful and paid for.

There will be many anecdotal stories like Joan's to accompany terms, definitions, and direction in each chapter. From them we can appreciate the challenges we face each day to provide our customers with high-quality products and services, effective investment programs, and sound estate planning.

WHERE THE ACKNOWLEDGMENTS AND CREDITS BELONG

A small yet extremely impressive group of people assisted in the completion of this text. Most important is my family. Pat, Andrea, Paul: Thank you for prodding me along through your interest in what I was doing, through the happy thoughts and successes, and the frustrating times you lived through. Without your encouragement the mechanical connection of nouns, verbs, adjectives, and adverbs would have been insurmountable. I am convinced that without you I would have fallen by the wayside. And, Faye, thank you deeply for dogging me along. The great American novel is on the horizon.

Next, thank you to the members of the American Bankers Association advisory committee who were so generous with their time in reviewing this work for accuracy, clarity, and intent. Thank you to

Chris Dally, First Union National Bank, St. Petersburg, Florida
Pledger Monk, Merrill Lynch, Little Rock, Arkansas
James P. Sullivan, III, John W. Christie, P.A., Shrewsbury, New Jersey

Third, sincere appreciation is extended for the support provided by the American Bankers Association staff in molding this work. Thank you, Terry Martin, Howard Robinson, Jenny Kletzin DiBiase, and Lee Fleming. Your comments, direction, and criticisms were the best.

Fourth, thank you so very much to my coworkers, past and present (Marcia Fry, Chris Page, Leslye Mueller, Ruth Schaumberger, and Bob Garro), my coeducators (Veronica West and Jack Heyden), and my friend Barb. Thank you all for your professional help and continued encouragement.

I picked the brains of several others along the writing path—a question-and-answer here, a suggestion-and-direction there, words of confidence, inspiration, influence, interest, belief, and motivation. Thank you, Hunt Hamill, Bob Levitz, Verdean Anderson, Gera-Lind Kolarik, Harlan Burgess, Bob Potempa, Ted Gertz, and, most of all, my students. You will never know how much your encouragement sustained me.

1

TYPES OF ASSETS
AND HOW THEY ARE OWNED

"No man acquires property without acquiring with it a little arithmetic also."

Ralph Waldo Emerson (1803–1882)

As we wind our way through the world of financial products and services, the core of it all is **property,** also called **assets,** resources, principal, wealth, and capital. It comes in different sizes, shapes, and amounts. Some have a lot of it, others not so much. Different people amass varying types of assets, but how they are owned and managed determines their effective use and eventual distribution. Regardless of the size and makeup of one's estate, there is no room for error when planning the estate for today and tomorrow, for self and family. Our role as trust professionals is to assist customers in learning the basics and to keep them from making mistakes in planning how their assets are owned.

LEARNING OBJECTIVES

What customers own is important to them and to the trust personnel who help them plan their estates. It is vital in the estate planning process to know what type of property exists, how it can be owned, and what to do with it.

Upon completion of this chapter, you will be able to

- Distinguish between personal and real property and describe their respective subclassifications and conversion
- Compare the forms of property ownership
- List the methods of property transfer
- Explore the process of gathering and using financial data
- Explain the differences between common law and community property states with respect to owning assets
- Contrast the forms of business ownership
- Define and use the terms that appear in bold in the text

TYPES OF PROPERTY/ASSETS

All property is categorized as either **real property** or **personal property.** Regardless of what type of asset it is, it is either real or personal. As a trust professional, you may be called on to assist customers in classifying their assets as real or personal.

Real Property	Personal Property
Residential	Tangible
Commercial	Intangible
Rental	
Agricultural	
Vacant	
Improved	
Unimproved	

Real Property

Real property is land and anything permanently attached to it or considered a permanent structure. The land and its fixtures and attachments denote permanency. Also included in this category is anything immovable on the land. Many people equate the words *real property* with the words *real estate*, although there is a crucial difference. Real property is the physical asset itself; real estate is the owner's interest (or title) in the property.

Land can be improved. In other words, additions or changes can be made to the land. If the improvement or addition is meant to be permanent or immovable, it is categorized as real property. Examples of improvements are a bridge over the creek on the land, a parking lot in a mini-mall, and a tall wall or fence around a house.

A plot of land with a house on it is real property. Although a garage may be separate from the house (unattached), it is also real property. If an in-ground swimming pool is added, it is real property. A concrete patio behind the house is also real property. Some additional examples of real property are an oil derrick constructed beyond the pool and six cherry trees planted around the derrick. However, the oil in the well in many jurisdictions is not real property because it's not permanent or immovable. (Some states consider mineral interests, such as oil, as real property.) Neither are the barrels, stored in the garage, that will hold the oil when it comes out of the well.

If the patio had been constructed with weatherproof wood, would it be real property? Yes, because it is a permanent structure, but is it immovable? Some might say the wooden pieces could be dismantled and hauled away, which makes it seem nonpermanent. Similarly, the concrete patio could be broken apart by a jackhammer. Other examples of things attached (but possibly impermanently) are built-in kitchen appliances, electrical fixtures attached to walls and ceilings, and landscaping. When dealing with such items and structures, we must consider the "permanent intent" of the improvement.

Residential Real Property

Residential real property is a primary, temporary, or vacation residence or any other permanent structure used as a dwelling. What about a motor home? Or a house trailer? A house trailer can be hitched to the back of an auto and moved anywhere. It also can have its wheels removed and be placed on blocks in a trailer park. This property may be classified as real property or personal property, depending on how it is being used.

Note: When an individual **(debtor)** borrows money from a bank **(creditor)** for the purchase of a house, the bank provides a **mortgage** loan. The house (as real property) is the **collateral** for the loan. Banks, as a general practice, do not provide mortgage loans for motor homes, meaning a bank will not accept the motor home as collateral for the loan. For this reason, banks (as lenders) do not consider motor homes as real property.

Commercial Real Property

Commercial real property is property used for business purposes. An example of this is a place of business, such as an office building or a factory, that a business owns.

Rental Real Property

There is a fine distinction between commercial real property and **rental real property.** Rental property is commercial if business takes place there, but it is considered noncommercial to the owner who collects rents from the tenants. If a property owner owns a factory and conducts his business there, the property is categorized as commercial. If he rents the property to someone, the property can be categorized as rental property. A more distinctive example of rental property is an apartment building.

Agricultural Real Property

Agricultural real property is land used for growing crops or raising animals (horses, cattle, etc.). Interestingly, the crops are real property while in the ground; once harvested they are not real property. The animals are not real property.

Vacant Real Property

Vacant real property is empty land owned solely for investment purposes with the hope that it will increase in value. Although many investors hold vacant land for resale, it can be converted into any of the previously mentioned classifications, which are commonly called improved real property.

Some real estate professionals further classify vacant land into **improved property** and **unimproved property**. If the vacant land has access to roads and has utilities (water, gas, electricity, phone, sewer system), it is called improved vacant land. Unimproved vacant land does not have these amenities. For example, five acres of vacant land, bordered by a gravel road, beside a small lake in rural northwest Wisconsin is unimproved vacant property. However, if the land has a roadway into it, a well for water, a sewage system, and phone and electric lines leading into it, then it is classified as improved vacant land.

Personal Property

Personal property is any property that is not real property. Personal property is not permanent or immovable. It is classified as either **tangible property** or **intangible property.**

Tangible Personal Property

Tangible means that something has physical substance. It has a value of itself and can be sensed and defined for what it actually is, not for what it represents. Examples include

- Autos
- Boats
- Household goods
- Furniture
- Tools
- Business inventory
- Jewelry
- This book
- Crops

Crops are an interesting example of personal property. As mentioned earlier, when they are in the ground growing, they are real property. Once they are harvested, they become tangible personal property. Corn growing in the field is real property; when it's picked, it becomes tangible personal property.

Another term for tangible personal property is **goods and chattels.** The word *chattel* derived from the Latin and old French words for cattle, a visible type of property ownership. Over the years the term broadened to include goods (merchandise, wares, freight) and any other form of personal property, as opposed to real property. This term is not used very often today except in legal descriptions. Yet another term is **personal effects,** which is used more in the context of death. In essence, it is property of a personal nature, such as clothes and jewelry.

Intangible Personal Property

This type of personal property has value, but of itself it is only evidence of value. In essence, you cannot touch it or realize it with the human senses. Consider 50 shares of International Business Machines (IBM) stock. They have value, and the stock certificates can be touched, but the certificates aren't the asset; what they represent is. The certificates are ink-on-paper evidence of ownership in the IBM company. A stockholder owns a piece of the company. The stock is intangible. The same holds true for government securities such as Treasury bills (T-bills). The piece of paper represents indebtedness in the form of an IOU from the government. The government borrowed money, and it has to repay it at some stipulated time in the future.

A rose is a rose is a rose. A sofa is a sofa is a sofa. Roses and sofas are tangible. They do not represent anything else. Yes, the rose may signify love, and the sofa represents a great place to catch a Sunday afternoon nap. But they are what they are: roses and sofas. If the sofa is destroyed because the water pipes in the ceiling leaked onto it, it's gone. If a stock certificate is lost, the certificate is gone, but the asset itself is not. The paper called a stock certificate is reissued. A stock or bond does indeed represent something else, so it is intangible. That piece of paper is not the asset; the asset is what the paper represents.

Here are other examples of intangible personal property.

- Employee benefit plans (pension, profit sharing, deferred compensation)
- Insurance contracts (life, disability, homeowner)
- Accounts receivable
- Patents, royalties, and copyrights
- Interests in partnerships
- Cash in the bank (certificates of deposit, savings, and checking accounts)
- Stock options

We cannot leave this topic without talking a bit more about the gray areas between tangible and intangible property; coins, stamps, antiques, artwork,

and jewelry are appropriate examples. To an extent, whether an asset is tangible or intangible depends on the eye (or the pocketbook) of the beholder.

Consider stamp collecting. This is a popular hobby throughout the world, yet some people look at it as a way of investing. A stamp collector can pay $1,800 for a rare nineteenth-century stamp that has an original face value of 5¢. Could he or she put it on an envelope and use it for postage? Yes. Would he? Certainly not—that would be an expensive letter! But is the stamp a tangible or an intangible asset? This is not an instance of "a stamp is a stamp is a stamp." This is an asset that represents something else: a lot of money. Losing a present-day 5¢ stamp is like the sofa being destroyed by a leaking water pipe: When it's gone, it's gone. It can be replaced. Even IBM stock can be reissued. But the rare stamp can be replaced only by insurance coverage. Thus, this rare stamp represents something other than a piece of paper used for postage and can easily be considered intangible property.

What about antiques, artwork, and jewelry? Are they worth something? A King Louis XIV sofa? A valuable painting of a deceased artist? A diamond ring from the Medicis of the fourteenth century?

These distinctions are important for trust professionals to ponder. Although 80 to 90 percent of the assets held by most trust departments are intangible personal property (stocks, bonds, cash), as trust professionals we cannot ignore the importance and worth of these gray assets to trust customers. These assets may have a substantial worth because of their rareness. Depending on the trust or investment management relationship, the trust professional may be faced with a difficult decision. Should she sell the asset and convert it into cash to be reinvested in income-producing vehicles such as stocks and bonds? Should the physical asset be held with hope that it will increase in value in the future? The same question is posed with respect to non–income-producing real property and a closely held company.

Here are some additional concerns of the trust professional:

- A will usually directs the distribution of property. The will may state that tangible property goes to one beneficiary, intangible property goes to another, and real property is distributed in a particular fashion. It is important for the trust professional to be able to classify the estate owner's property.

- Classification of property—and taxation of the property—can be affected by state statutes. For example, Florida does not have a state income tax, but it does impose a tax on intangibles. A trust professional in Florida must know what property is tangible and intangible and how to determine the taxation on the intangible property.

These are tough considerations. We will look into them further in Chapters 2 through 4 when we compare investment vehicles, effective investment management, and risk with respect to a customer's needs.

Conversion of Property

The cherry trees we spoke of earlier are real property, and the cherries on the tree are real property. When the cherries are picked, they are converted into tangible personal property. If the cherries are put into a pie, the cherry pie is also tangible personal property. If the trees are chopped down and cut up for lumber to make a beautiful dining room set (on which sits the cherry pie), the trees convert from real property to tangible personal property. If the dining room set is kept for 50 years or more, it may be considered an antique, at which time a future estate planner may classify it as an intangible personal asset. **Conversion** is the change of property from one form to another. Conversion involves a physical change in the nature of the property or a change in value because of the passage of time.

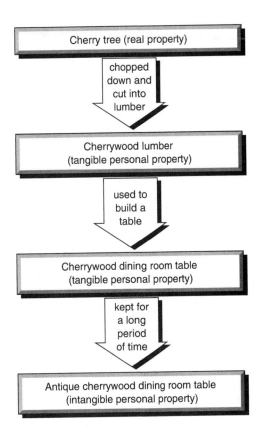

FORMS OF PROPERTY OWNERSHIP

Everything we have looked at up to this point has been owned by someone. Any type of asset previously mentioned can be held in various forms of ownership: sole, joint tenancy, tenancy by the entirety, tenancy in common, contract, or trust.

Note: As you travel through this section, keep in mind that the choice of which form of property ownership to apply to property is often based on how the owner wants to dispose of the property at death. These choices may be made ineffectual by improper or hasty planning, such as not being coordinated with the estate owner's intentions and thereby opposing the desired passage of property at death.

Sole Ownership

Property under **sole ownership** (sometimes called **separate property** ownership) is owned by only one person, without any co-owners. In sole ownership, the property is under the exclusive control of only one person. Some states refer to sole ownership as **ownership in the severalty.** Many financial planners use the term **fee simple** for real property owned by one person. When the owner dies, sole ownership property passes to others by will or by laws of intestacy (dying without a will), terms we will define more specifically in Chapter 5.

Joint Tenancy

Joint tenancy ownership is also called in some locales **joint tenancy with right of survivorship (JTWROS).** This form of ownership, mostly associated with spouses, occurs when two or more people own property that passes to the surviving owner(s), legally called **tenant(s),** at the death of an owner. This is a **statutory** right—a right dictated by law. The passing of ownership to a surviving owner(s) is automatic. There are no delays and there is no probate of the property (see Chapter 5). This form of ownership is sometimes called the *poor person's will.* A will is not needed to pass this property to someone else. Usually all that is needed for the transfer is a proof of ownership and a death certificate. A will has no dominion or control over joint tenancy ownership. Regardless of what the will says, the property passes on automatically and equally to the surviving owner(s). (A financial planning query to the trust professional: Is this the customer's intention?)

Most people associate joint tenancy ownership with a husband-and-wife relationship, and mostly with respect to their house. This form of home ownership is indeed the one most widely used between husbands and wives. When the first spouse dies, the home is passed to the other spouse without excessive fees, without probate, and possibly without estate taxes. However, any group of two or more co-owners may use this method. A more extensive analysis of taxes will show where joint tenancy ownership between nonspouses could have tax ram-

ifications. It is always best to confer with a tax planner.

Joint tenancy property is acquired by all of the owners at the same time. Joint tenancy ownership is considered to be in equal shares, even though the purchase may be made with uneven contributions: If three people own a piece of real property or another asset as joint tenants, they do not each own one-third, but *the three of them together own 100 percent.* In essence, these are not divisible one-third interests because the owners must purchase *and* sell together.

Just as joint tenancy property is purchased at the same time by all the owners, it is sold together by all the owners. One owner cannot sell the asset without the permission of the other owner(s). Nor may one of the owners transact any business with respect to the asset without the consent of the other owners. An exception to this is a joint bank account. Bank accounts (checking, savings, and CDs) can be established by joint owners (for example, wife and husband, sister and brother, or parent and child), in which withdrawals can be made only by both owners with two signatures. Seldom is this the case. The typical joint bank account conveniently permits either owner to sign checks or make deposits and withdrawals without the other owner's involvement or consent. To an extent, a nonlegal matter of trust is placed in the co-owners not to abuse the use of the jointly owned property.

Tenancy by the Entirety

In its simplest form, **tenancy by the entirety** ownership is similar to joint tenancy. However, it exists only between spouses and only in certain states. Different states apply it to different types of property (see Exhibit 1.1). Tenancy by the entirety also carries with it a right of survivorship. When a husband and wife co-own their residence, as tenancy by the entirety, this form of ownership must specifically be stated in the title listing. Absent the specific mention, it is presumed that the house is

Exhibit 1.1 Tenancy by the Entirety

States that recognize tenancy by the entirety with respect to real property (personal residence) and personal property:

Alaska	Kentucky	Oklahoma
Arkansas	Maryland	Pennsylvania
Delaware	Massachusetts	Rhode Island
District of Columbia	Missouri	Tennessee
Florida	Montana	Vermont
Hawaii	Ohio	

States that recognize tenancy by the entirety with respect to real property (personal residence) only:

Illinois	New Jersey	Oregon
Indiana	New York	Wyoming
Michigan	North Carolina	

owned in joint tenancy form. If the husband and wife divorce, the tenancy by the entirety ownership is automatically, by operation of law, converted into tenancy in common (discussed below).

A significant aspect of tenancy by the entirety ownership, in contrast to joint tenancy, is that the house cannot be forced into sale to satisfy a judgment (for example, a lawsuit) unless the judgment is against both spouses. For example, if one spouse is a medical professional and a malpractice case is brought against this spouse, the house, or **homestead,** would be protected. There is one exception to this. If the judgment involves a unit of the government (such as the IRS), the property can be sold to satisfy the tax obligation. It is also possible to protect the house in event of bankruptcy of one of the joint owners. Individual creditors cannot reach the property. Of course, if judgment is brought against *both* spouses, the scene changes.

Tenancy by the entirety and joint tenancy are initially comfortable forms of property ownership, which is why few estate planners object to their use in certain circumstances. But these are not all-purpose solutions. Joint tenancy property ownership between two owners and tenancy by the entirety ownership terminate when the first owner dies, and the transfer of ownership is not onerous. After the death of the first owner, the asset converts to sole ownership. Was this the intention? Does it pose new problems and require another type of planning? Are the tax effects the same as originally planned? Herein lies a planning task for the trust professional.

Tenancy in Common

Whereas joint tenancy is an undivided interest held by two or more people, in **tenancy in common,** interests are divided. The owners' interests need not be equal, and each tenant may deal with his share separately from the co-owners. The ownership can exist between spouses or nonspouses, and it can exist among two or more co-owners. An owner's interest upon death does not automatically pass to the surviving owner(s). If the title to property owned as tenancy in common lists Curly, Moe, and Larry as tenants in common, ownership is presumed to be one-third interests. For unequal percentages, the title must specifically state what the percentages are (for example, "Curly, Moe, and Larry, as tenants in common, 30 percent, 45 percent, 25 percent respectively"). This is important.

Upon death of a tenant in common, her interest in the property passes according to the terms of her will, or if there is no will, according to intestacy laws. The advantage of this form of ownership can be seen when a house is owned by a husband and wife who are each married for the second time. If the wife wants her share of the house to go to the children from her first marriage, she may say so in her will, and it will happen. But if she and her second husband owned the house under joint tenancy, at her death the ownership of the house would automatically pass to her husband. She could not will it to the children from her first marriage.

A joint tenancy owner cannot sell her interest without the other owners' consent. A tenancy-in-common owner can sell her interest without the other owners' consent. This contingency is usually anticipated and protected by separate arrangements, such as an agreement in which all the owners agree that if one wants to sell her interest, the offer to buy must be made to the other owner(s) first. Some planners call this the right of first refusal.

For the individual tenant, tenancy in common is similar to sole ownership. The difference is that only a portion of the asset is owned by any one co-owner. For example, four individuals may each own 25 percent of a piece of unimproved vacant land. Each owner solely owns 100 percent of his respective 25 percent interest. As with sole ownership, an individual owner's interest passes at the owner's death according to his will or intestacy.

Note: Occasionally, a title to an asset has two or more names on it with no indication as to the form of property ownership. The general rule of thumb—absent specific statute—is that the type of property determines the form of ownership. With respect to real property, the form is tenancy in common. Personal property defaults to joint tenancy.

Contract Ownership

Contract ownership has its roots in the ownership of U.S. Savings Bonds. Contract ownership is the ownership of property by one person. This form of ownership is in most respects similar to sole ownership. But whereas sole ownership property passes through a decedent's (owner's) probate estate, contract property does not pass through probate. It passes according to the property's pre-arranged beneficiary designation.

In general, contract ownership exists with respect to life insurance, employee benefit (retirement) plans, and assets that can accommodate **payable-on-death (POD)** and **transfer-on-death (TOD)** provisions, assuming there is a valid beneficiary designation. If there is no identifiable beneficiary, the asset will be subject to probate.

With respect to POD and TOD arrangements, be aware that contract ownership varies from state to state as to whether it exists, whether co-beneficiary and successor beneficiaries can be named, and what types of assets it pertains to. For example, one state may have regulations that pertain only to bank accounts. Other states may include brokerage accounts. Contract ownership does not pertain to real property, and during the owner's life the beneficiary has no rights to the property.

Trust Ownership

Ownership of property or assets by a **trust** is a distinctive form of ownership. It has its own particular characteristics. We will review just a few of them here. More extensive attention is given in Chapters 7 and 8.

A trust is a unique ownership arrangement. It can exist with and without assets in it. Just as the owner of a car cannot enjoy driving it unless there is gas in the tank, the beneficiaries of a trust cannot enjoy the trust unless there are assets in the trust. It is important to note that once assets are placed (or transferred) into the trust (this is called funding the trust), they are under dual ownership.

Earlier, we said that when three people own an asset in joint tenancy, they don't each own one-third. Together they own 100 percent. There is a commonality of ownership. A trust arrangement also has a commonality of ownership, yet it is one of a dual nature: **legal ownership** and **equitable** (or **beneficial) ownership.** Legal ownership specifically applies to an entity being the owner of public record. Equitable ownership applies to an entity being entitled to use and enjoy the property—have benefit of—within the limits established by law.

This concept of legal and equitable ownership is perhaps best explained with an example. John and Mary Doe have an extensive portfolio of stocks and bonds that they have systematically purchased over the years. All of the stocks and bonds are titled in John's name only, meaning sole ownership. For reasons that are discussed more closely in Chapter 7, John executes a trust with ABC Bank and Trust Company as trustee. According to the trust document, the bank will hold the assets, manage and invest them, collect dividends and interest, and perform several other tasks. The trust dictates that all net income be paid to John and Mary during their lives (and also to the survivor after the first spouse dies), with eventual distribution of the trust's assets to their children following the death of the surviving spouse. The wording of the trust allows John or Mary to remove principal from the trust.

The trust department, as trustee, is empowered by the trust agreement to transact investment changes and carry out the instructions John has given to the trustee. The stocks and bonds still belong to John, but John no longer "legally" owns them. The trust does. However, the trust, as legal owner, is not entitled to enjoy or use the assets or the income for its own purpose. The trust department does not receive any benefits of ownership. It does not receive income and cannot use the principal; John and Mary do. The trust department benefits from the fee John pays for its services, but it does not possess any equitable or beneficial interest in the assets. John and Mary, as beneficiaries of the trust, are the equitable (or beneficial) owners, who benefit from the assets. John and Mary are not the legal owners; they are the equitable owners of the principal and the income.

Just as an individual can be a separate, legal, property-owning entity, a trust is also a separate entity. A trust legally owns assets that are placed in it. Yet John and Mary own the assets in a beneficial way. While the assets are in a trust (as gas is in a car's tank), they are there for a purpose. Using a rough analogy, the gas is in the tank for a "legal" reason, yet the driver "benefits" from its use as he drives the car. The assets of a trust are legally there, yet the beneficiary benefits from the trust as he uses the trust.

Whereas an individual's ownership of solely owned and tenancy-in-common assets passes to others at death through a will or intestacy, trust assets do not pass through a will or intestacy because the individual does not legally own the assets. The trust does. We will revisit this concept in detail in Chapter 7.

An arrangement somewhat similar to trust and contract ownership is the Totten trust. A **Totten trust** is the name given to a bank account in a depositor's name "as trustee" for a named beneficiary (for example, "John Doe as trustee for Mary Doe"). In this example, John—as the depositor—retains ownership of the bank account and can continue to make deposits to and withdrawals from the account during his lifetime. Mary has no beneficial interest in the account during John's life, but she succeeds as the owner of the account upon John's death.

A summary of the previous sections is contained in Exhibit 1.2.

TRANSFER OF PROPERTY OWNERSHIP

We talked earlier about converting assets from real to personal, tangible to intangible. Forms of ownership can also be converted. There is a difference, though, with respect to ownership; no physical change occurs. The change that occurs is a change of how the property is owned. In most circles, this conversion is called a **transfer.**

A transfer of property ownership can occur by gift, will, intestacy, sale, trade (barter), law, trust, or contract.

Exhibit 1.2 Summary of Property Ownership

Form of Ownership	Number of Owners	Legal vs. Equitable Ownership	Owner's Right to Income	Inclusion in Decedent's Probate Estate	Type of Property That Can Be Owned
Sole (1)	1	Inseparable	100%	Yes	Personal (tangible and intangible) and real
Joint tenancy with rights of survivorship (JTWROS) (2)	2 or more	Inseparable	Split equally among tenants	No	Personal (tangible and intangible) and real
Tenancy by the entirety (3)	2	Inseparable	One-half to each spouse	No	See Exhibit 1.1
Tenancy in common (4)	2 or more	Inseparable	Split according to tenants' fractional shares	Yes	Personal (tangible and intangible) and real
Contract (5)	1	Inseparable	100%	No	Personal (tangible and intangible) and real
Revocable living trust	1	Separable	100% to grantor	No	Personal (tangible and intangible) and real

(1) Also known as fee simple (mainly with respect to real property) and ownership in the severalty.
(2) Ownership can exist between spouses and nonspouses.
(3) Notations:
    A. Not recognized in community property law states
    B. Not recognized in all common law states
    C. Ownership by spouses only
(4) Notations:
    A. Percentage of ownership is presumed equal unless indicated otherwise
    B. Ownership can exist between spouses and nonspouses
(5) Prearranged beneficiary designation:
    A. Life insurance
    B. Retirement plans
    C. POD (payable on death)/TOD (transfer on death)

Gift

When someone gives something she owns to someone else, ownership transfers from one person to another. If a sole owner retitles an asset into joint tenancy with someone else, she is transferring ownership, and she is making a gift. If the transfer were of real property, it would likely be done by a **quitclaim deed.** A quitclaim deed is a quick and simple **conveyance** (transfer of ownership) from one person to another, usually without financial consideration.

Will

Property ownership may be transferred from the owner to someone else by means of a will. A will is a legal document that expresses a person's intents regarding the distribution of her estate upon death.

Intestacy

When a person dies intestate (without a will), his property is distributed according to state intestacy statutes. Each state has laws dictating to whom a person's property (assets) will be distributed when the person dies without a will. Intestacy will be discussed in detail in Chapter 5.

Sale

A transfer of ownership occurs when someone sells an asset she owns to someone else. A sole owner of property can sell the asset to another person(s). A tenancy-in-common owner can sell her interest to another person (another tenant or not).

Trade (Barter)

A double transfer occurs here. If person A owns property A and person B owns property B, and if they swap their respective properties, a transfer occurs as assets are exchanged.

Law

By act of law, under joint tenancy ownership and tenancy by the entirety ownership, a transfer occurs from a co-owner who dies to the surviving owner(s). Transfer by law may also occur according to divorce rulings. Additionally, when a person borrows money, he may pledge an asset as collateral. If the borrower does not pay the debt, the lender can legally take ownership of the asset as satisfaction (repayment) of the loan.

Trust

Unlike the transfer of property involving the probate process (either testacy or intestacy, both discussed in Chapter 5), property can be transferred to another—during life and at death, absent probate proceedings—with the use of a living trust.

Contract

When the owner of a property dies, the property transfers—absent probate—through contractual disposition. Contract property is controlled and distributed by means of designating a beneficiary, such as is done with life insurance policies, employee benefit/retirement plans, and POD/TOD arrangements.

GATHERING FINANCIAL DATA

Everyone owns something: a house, car, bank account, or stamp collection, furniture, stocks, bonds, a vacant piece of land, or a wristwatch. The list of possible possessions is endless. Now that you understand how to classify assets and their form of ownership, the next important step is to determine how much the assets are worth. It is difficult for a trust officer to plan if he doesn't know what to plan with.

Asset-gathering (fact-finding) statements come in many forms and lengths. They range from one-pagers to monstrous, ultracomprehensive, multipage forms. Trust professionals use these forms (often called personal statements) to assist customers in listing their assets. A simple format can look like Exhibit 1.3. A comprehensive format, such as Appendix 1, provides objective (financial) as well as subjective (nonfinancial) information regarding family structure, customer aspirations, and goal setting.

Gathering comprehensive information is an integral step in helping customers to organize and construct their **estate plans**. To help you serve your customers and understand their objectives, a discussion of **estate planning** and a checklist are contained in Appendix 2.

Exhibit 1.3 Sample Personal Statement

PERSONAL STATEMENT

Assets

	Husband	Wife	Joint
Bank accounts	$ ___	$ ___	$ __5,000__ (checking)
			$ __35,000__ (CD)
Stocks & bonds	$ ___	$ __10,000__	$ __25,000__
Family home(s)	$ ___	$ ___	$ __425,000__
Other real estate	$ ___	$ __50,000__*	$ ___
Life insurance	$ __550,000__	$ __100,000__	$ ___
Pension	$ __175,000__	$ __75,000__	$ ___
Business interests	$ __50,000__ (stock options)	$ ___	$ ___
Other assets**	$ __65,000__	$ ___	$ ___
Total assets	$ __840,000__	$ __235,000__	$ __490,000__

Liabilities

	Husband	Wife	Joint
Loans	$ ___	$ ___	$ __20,000__ (home equity loan)
Mortgages	$ ___	$ ___	$ __125,000__ (family home)
Other debts	$ ___	$ ___	$ __5,000__ (credit cards)
Total liabilities	$ __0__	$ __0__	$ __150,000__

Net Worth

	Husband	Wife	Joint
(Assets minus liabilities)	$ __840,000__	$ __235,000__	$ __340,000__

* Vacation condo

** Antique cars

DOMICILE

It is important for the customer and the trust professional to know what is owned, how it is owned, and who owns it. Knowledge of a customer's objective and subjective estate planning aspirations enables the trust professional to effectively assist the customer with tax planning, asset accumulation, preservation of property, and distribution of his estate to others via gifting, wills, and trusts. Equally important to the process is knowing where the customer lives and the effect it has on property ownership planning and eventual distribution.

Where a person permanently lives is his **domicile** or, as some say, *the place of intended return*. Keep in mind that saying *residence* is not sufficient because a **residence** (a place with living accommodations) can be temporary, such as a winter home in a warm climate. Although the subject of domicile is simple and concise to most people, conflicting circumstances can make it difficult to determine permanency. Consider the following example.

Several years ago a trust department assisted a man who was born, raised, and educated in Indiana. He also married, lived, and worked there. He built a successful food company, which he sold to a British conglomerate for a hefty sum of money. That was the good news. The bad news was that the man had a cancer that would soon take his life.

Following the sale of the business, he and his wife sold their house in Indiana and bought a condominium in Florida. Shortly after they bought the Florida residence, he took up temporary residence in Canada because it was the only place that could offer certain drugs to treat his cancer. He died in a Canadian hospital. Where was he domiciled? The sale of his business and house in Indiana took him away from Indiana. The purchase of the Florida condominium was intended to be a change of residence. His stay in Canada was temporary. His recent will stated, "I consider Indiana as my state of residence." It was legally determined that he died as a resident of Indiana.

Most authorities agree that establishment of one's domicile is determined by

- Intention to reside (as expressed in a legal document, such as a will)

- Voter registration
- Location where income tax returns are filed and taxes are paid
- Establishment of bank accounts
- Driver's license
- "Certificate of Domicile," if the state issues one

Common Law Property

The subject of domicile and its effect on property ownership and disposition is further complicated by our legal system. Most of the U.S. legal system stems from English **common law,** as opposed to the ancient Roman **civil law** that exists in most non–English-speaking countries. In the United States there are two distinct forms of property ownership, depending on the state in which you live. Most states are common law states, as opposed to community property states. The concept of **community property** stems from civil law.

Common law states are sometimes called **separate property** states. This means that the form of property ownership (sole ownership, joint tenancy, tenancy by the entirety, and tenancy in common) remains separate and is controlled by the owner or owners who purchased

---

USING TRUST PRODUCTS AND SERVICES TO MEET CUSTOMER NEEDS

A trust officer recently had a meeting in the bank with a customer regarding her will and trust planning. Gertie was, as she stated, a very senior citizen. Widowed several years ago, she had no children. One of the many questions the trust officer asked her was, "Gertie, what is the value of your estate?" She guessed it was somewhere in the neighborhood of $700,000, but she wasn't positive. The trust officer explained that it was important for estate planning purposes to have a more specific idea of her estate size and asked her to take a few minutes to complete a confidential personal statement. Two weeks later, when Gertie again visited the trust officer, she proudly claimed that she spent 2 hours filling out the trust department's form. She was surprised to learn that her estate was worth more than $2 million. Gertie's estate planning took a different direction because she and her trust officer knew she was worth more. She thanked her trust officer for setting her straight. Gertie now makes more frequent visits to the trust department in order to keep her estate affairs current.

the property, regardless of their marital status. Property acquired by either spouse during marriage may stay in that spouse's name or be titled otherwise, depending on the wishes of the spouse who acquired the property. This is not true in a community property state, where ownership of property acquired during marriage *must* automatically be considered half-owned by each spouse, regardless of how the property is titled.

Community Property

The laws of several states provide that property acquired during a marriage, by either spouse, is held equally by husband and wife as community property. This does not include property owned by either spouse before the marriage or property received by either spouse by gift or inheritance during the marriage; that is separate property. When one spouse dies, his or her half of the community property, and his or her separate property, passes according to his or her will or by intestacy. The other half of the community property belongs to the surviving spouse.

The one-half ownership of community property accumulated during marriage is automatic regardless of how the property is titled. For example, a brokerage account established during the marriage (but titled only in the wife's name) is still automatically community property. Each spouse may dispose of his or her one-half ownership at death as he or she wishes.

Community property laws vary from state to state, with each state having a characteristic flavor. In reality there are ten separate bodies of community property law: Alaska, Arizona, California, Idaho, Louisiana, Nevada, New Mexico, Texas, Washington, and Wisconsin. Actually, some authors maintain there are eight "true" community property states— Alaska and Wisconsin having the peculiarities discussed below.

Community property concepts are fairly easy to understand and cope with if both spouses are born and reared, marry

and purchase assets, and die in a community property state. But, it's not always that clean-cut. People do get married in California and move to Pennsylvania, or vice-versa. Some community-property residents own property in their own state and also in non-community property states, or vice versa. Determining what is community property and what is separate property is sometimes difficult and can vary from state to state.

In general then, the following premises apply to community property (subject to alteration and interpretation and differences among various community property states' statutes).

- Community property is a form of property ownership that exists in most non-English speaking countries; it migrated to the United States primarily from Spain and France. Community property was prevalent in many more states in the past.

- Wisconsin is sometimes classified as a state that "created" a property equivalent of community property—marital property—(basically for income tax purposes) by adopting an extensive, complicated law in 1984 (effective January 1, 1986) known as the Uniform Marital Property Act (UMPA).

- Alaska has adopted "elective" community property for Alaska residents and for assets transferred to an Alaska trust. Legislation in Alaska allows for a married couple, who are both residents of Alaska, to elect to classify property as community property. In addition, nonresident spouses may transfer property to an Alaska community property trust, and it will be characterized as community property under Alaska law if at least one trustee is an individual domiciled in Alaska or is an Alaska trust company or bank.

- The community property system also applies to Puerto Rico.

- Community property only pertains to spouses.
- Community property is generally defined by what it is not. A married couple domiciled in a community property state is presumed to own all of their property as community (marital) property, regardless of titling, absent:
  - An agreement to the contrary, which is controlled by a state's requirements
  - Proof that the property was:
    - Brought into the marriage by either spouse
    - Given to either spouse
    - Inherited by either spouse
    - A spouse's separate property before the couple became domiciled in a community (marital) property state.
- Generally, each spouse owns an undivided one-half interest in each item of community property.
- The general rule is that title does not control the classification of the property; the time of acquisition and the source of funds used for an asset's acquisition determines whether the asset is community or separate property.
- General premises (subject to alteration and interpretation and differences among various community property states' statutes):
  - Any property acquired during marriage is considered owned one-half by each spouse
  - Each spouse has an absolute right to lifetime and testamentary disposition to one-half of the property (a personal residence is subject to homestead rights)
  - Property inherited individually by one spouse is not community property—it is *separate property* (called *individual property* in Wisconsin)
  - Property owned by a spouse prior to marriage remains as separate and individual property following marriage
  - Income from wages, salaries, fees, and bonuses of either or both spouses is community property
  - During marriage, spousal income on separate property is separate property in Arizona, California, New Mexico, Nevada, and Washington; it is community property in Idaho, Louisiana, Texas, and Wisconsin
  - Separate property that is commingled with community property becomes community property; because all property is presumed to be community property in community property states, the presumption is strong when separate and community property funds have been commingled; if adequate records are not kept, separate property may lose its identity due to commingling
  - Assets acquired during marriage with separate funds, or with the proceeds of sale of a separate asset, are separate property; to maintain the separate character, the assets must be clearly traceable as separate property; as a practical matter this is very difficult, although not always impossible
  - Retirement benefits are part separate property and part community property in proportion to the contributions to the plan before marriage and the contribution to the plan during marriage
  - All community property states recognize the validity of prenuptial agreements, although the rules for these agreements vary from state to state
  - Each spouse has an unrestricted right to dispose of his or her separate property
  - A gift of community property must come from both spouses

- ▲ Community property states vary as to whether community property can be converted to separate property and vice versa
- ▲ The rules of intestacy distribution of community and separate property vary from state to state

Personal Property in Community Property States

The law of the state of domicile for a husband and wife at the time an asset is purchased typically determines the nature of a married couple's personal property, both tangible and intangible.

As an example, consider John and Mary Doe, husband and wife, who are residents of California. During their marriage they purchase many assets. Regardless of whether personal property assets are purchased with John's money or Mary's (and regardless of the title of the assets), because the couple is domiciled in California the property is automatically community property, meaning each owns a one-half interest. Whoever dies first, John or Mary, may dispose of his or her one-half interest as he or she wishes. You would think that if John died first, he would will his one-half interest to Mary, but that is not mandatory.

The scenario is different if John and Mary live in Michigan. If Mary purchases personal property assets with her money and titles them in her name, they are hers. Can she will the property the way she wants when she dies? Yes! But, as we will see in more detail in Chapter 5, the surviving spouse does have some protection providing him a forced share of the deceased wife's estate. This share also applies to property acquired before the marriage.

Real Property in Community Property States

With regard to real property, the laws can get sticky. In most situations, the reach of the law ends at the state border. This means that the law of the state where the property is located prevails. The laws of the state where the real property is located characterize how the property is owned, even if the couple is domiciled in another state.

If John and Mary Doe are residents of California and also buy real property in Michigan, the laws of Michigan designate the Michigan property as common property because it is located in a common law state, regardless of the fact that the property is owned by a couple domiciled in a community property state. Then again, there are complicated situations in which the state where the property is located may choose the law of domicile. Community property states permit greater flexibility because the laws of a community property state permit couples to hold community property and separate property. By definition, a common law state does not recognize community property.

Consider how complicated situations can become by imagining the following possibilities:

- A couple domiciled in a community property state but also owning property in a common property state
- A couple domiciled in a common property state but also owning property in a community property state
- A couple moving from a community property state to a common property state (complicated further by property owned before the move that is located in different states)
- A couple moving from a common property state to a community property state (again, complicated further by property owned before the move that is located in different states)

To add to the confusion, also consider these questions:

- Is the property personal or real?
- What are the particular laws of the specific community property state? For example, some community property states, such as California, Idaho, and Texas, also recognize

another form of property known as quasi-community property.

- Do the laws of a particular common property state differ from those of other common property states? Some common law states recognize the Uniform Disposition of Community Property Rights at Death Act (UDCPRDA) and others do not.

- Depending on where the couple live and what kind of property they own, it is important to know when the property was acquired, where it is located, and how the ownership of the property has been characterized in documents. Is it mentioned in one of the spouse's wills? How is the title worded? Is there a written marital agreement? Has the property been placed in a trust?

A comprehensive introduction to these perplexing situations can be found in "Community Property: Characterization of Property With Which All Trust Officers Should Be Familiar: A Primer on the Community Property Laws and How They Affect Estate Taxes and Planning Decisions," by Roberta E. Berger (American Bankers Association's *Trust & Financial Advisor,* issue 5, 1994). Berger looks at property jurisdictions, marriage requirements, divorce, and intestate succession. Further analysis is given to income taxation and deductions, commingling, pitfalls within trust planning, and premarital and postnuptial agreements. The author also addresses the tax comparisons of community property versus joint tenancy, estate taxes, management and control, life insurance considerations, and gifting.

It is important for trust personnel in either type of state to understand what types of property exist, how property can be owned, and the importance of gathering financial data. Equally important is an understanding of the differences between separate and community property states. Trust customers domiciled in common law states may retire and permanently

move to a community property state. The trust officer must be prepared to serve customers knowledgeably regardless of where they live or move.

FORMS OF BUSINESS OWNERSHIP

Any study of estate planning for business owners must first review the various forms of business ownership. A person's business (commonly known as a **closely held business**) is an asset, but its form of ownership will affect its owner's estate planning.

Sole Proprietorship

A **sole proprietorship**—a method of conducting business without the use of a separate legal entity—is a form of business owned by one person. The easiest way of defining the business is to examine the following points:

- The assets of the business are not separate from the owner's personal assets.

- The sole proprietor owner and the sole proprietorship business are one and the same.

- The business is funded (capitalized) with the owner's personal funds.

- The business's income is the sole proprietor's income.

- The sole proprietor is liable as an individual for business indebtedness.

- The business is transferable to others by gift or sale.

- The business terminates upon the owner's demise.

Think of Mr. Clean's neighborhood dry cleaning establishment. Although the business—let's call it Zephyr Cleaners—has a business name above the door, Mr. Clean is the sole proprietorship. Only Mr. Clean owns the business. He most likely started the business with his personal assets (or a loan that he is responsible for repaying). He *is* the business. He is entitled to the business's income, and he is responsible for the business's debts. He is free to sell the business to another, and Zephyr Cleaners terminates upon his death.

Partnerships

A **partnership** is an association of two or more persons formed to carry on a trade, occupation, or profession for profit. This form of business is not incorporated, a form of business discussed in the next section. Again let's look at a listing of points that help define what a partnership is:

- A partnership can be either **general** or **limited.** The primary distinction between these two forms is one of limited liability for the limited partners.

- The general partner manages the business. A limited partner may lose his limited liability status if he participates in the management of the business.

- Partnerships are created for a specific term of time. The death or withdrawal of any partner results in the dissolution of the partnership unless provided for otherwise in the partnership agreement.

- Unlike a sole proprietorship, a partnership is in most instances regarded as a separate legal entity from the individual partners. For purposes of liability, all general partners are jointly and severally liable for all of the partnership's debts.

Capital for a partnership usually comes from the assets and credit (borrowing) limits of the individual partners. In a general partnership, each partner is individually liable for business debts. In a limited partnership, capital can be furnished from persons who wish to participate in the economic results of the business but without exposure to individual liability;

therefore, the limited partner is liable only for the amount of his contribution. Taken loosely, limited partners are sometimes referred to as "silent" partners in that they do not contribute to the management of the business—that is the responsibility of the general partners.

Limited Liability Partnership

Various states have amended their partnership statutes to allow for **limited liability partnerships** (LLP). An LLP is basically a general partnership with some limited protection for the general partners. The liability protection applies only to claims against the partnership and not to the individual actions of the partners. In every other respect LLPs function similar to a general partnership as long as the LLP registers as such and renews the registration annually.

Family Limited Partnership

More than 95 percent of all businesses in the United States are family owned. These businesses produce almost half of the gross national product and pay nearly half of all wages in the U.S. Statistics also show that less than 15 percent of family businesses stay in the family more than 60 years. There are a variety of nonfinancial reasons why this occurs, yet the main reason is because of the transfer tax system—estate taxes upon the business owner's death.

The Internal Revenue Code provides techniques to lower the tax value of an estate for transfer purposes. A fairly recent technique is the use of a **family limited partnership** (FLP). In a somewhat technical definition, an FLP limits an owner's interest in a partnership arrangement to only the capitalized value of the business's distributable cash flow. An FLP partner realizes a return from the business solely through cash distributions from the business. In this arrangement the owner's interest is usually worth less than the liquidation value of the business, whereby the owner gives up liquidation control. This "lack of control" translates into a reduction in the value of the business to the business owner.

Let's work with an example. Mom and her two daughters each own a one-third interest in vacant land valued at $1.5 million. As equal partners, each one has a $500,000 interest in the partnership. Mom and daughters decide to contribute the property to a limited partnership—a family limited partnership—in which each partner owns a 3.33 percent general partnership interest and a 30 percent limited partnership interest representing their contribution to the partnership. Since a partnership must be established for a specific term of time, these partners set a term of 40 years, unless the partners agree to end the partnership earlier. Each partner has the same pro rata rights to income, gains, and losses. With the use of their state's applicable partnership statutes, each partner takes a 65 percent discount on her interest in the partnership, leaving a 35 percent value. The discount reduces each partner's interest to $175,000 (35 percent of $500,000). The logic behind this reduction (discount) is that each partner's interest cannot hold its full value ($500,000) because each partner has limited ability to control the partnership: *that which is not controllable cannot carry full weight.*

If Mom dies 10 years later and the partnership is worth $30 million, the value of her partnership interest will be only $3.5 million (her $10 million share less the 65 percent discount, based on the lack of management rights and liquidation rights for the remaining 30 years of the partnership's life).

Corporations

A **corporation** is a business that is a separate and distinct legal entity governed by the laws of the state of its incorporation. As you study the differences between C and S corporations, note how they differ primarily with respect to taxation.

C Corporations

All corporations are taxed as C corporations unless a special election has been filed by the shareholders to be treated as an S corporation in accordance with Subchapter S of the Internal Revenue Code (discussed in the next section). In general all corporations are structured as follows:

- A corporation may have one or more owners.

- Each shareholder (stockowner) need not participate in the management of the business. Management is provided by the board of directors elected by the shareholders.

- Corporations have perpetual existence. In rare instances a corporation's life is limited to a fixed term by the articles of incorporation.

- Absent personal guarantees, the stockholders of a corporation are generally liable for the obligations of the corporation only to the extent of their capital contribution.

S Corporations

A corporation is taxed on its income in accordance with the IRS's corporate tax rules. These tax rules cause a double taxation: a corporation pays taxes on its income, and then shareholders pay taxes when the corporation distributes dividends to them. An eligible corporation can avoid this double taxation by electing to be treated as an S corporation. S corporations may pass income, losses, deductions, and credits through to the stockholders to be included on their separate tax returns.

An eligible S corporation must meet certain requirements:

- It must be a domestic corporation, that is, one organized in the United States under federal or state law.

- It must have only one class of stock. This generally means that the owners of outstanding shares have the same rights in the profits and assets of the corporation.

- There can be no more than 75 stockholders.

- The stockholders are limited to individuals, estates, and certain types of trusts. A partnership or another corporation cannot be a shareholder.

- The shareholders must be citizens or residents of the United States.

Limited Liability Company

A fairly recent development, a **limited liability company** (LLC) is basically a corporation that is taxed as a partnership for federal tax purposes. This form of business ownership combines the benefits of both a partnership and a corporation. In essence an LLC works like a partnership in which profits and losses pass through to the owners (known as members); however, like a corporation, an LLC has a level of liability protection that a partnership does not.

The main function of an LLC is to limit liability (found in a corporate structure) while providing the benefits of taxation found in a partnership. If a business possesses certain characteristics (that are beyond the scope of this book), it will qualify as an LLC. And the benefits to be gained are:

- Unlike the partners in a family limited partnership, the partners (members) in a limited liability company have limited liability; they can participate in the company's management without concern regarding loss of their liability protection.

- Unlike an S corporation, an LLC has no limit on the number of members or on what type of entity may be a member. In addition, an LLC may have membership interests (varying stock classes) with different rights to income and voting rights.

- An LLC can allocate items of income, deductions, gains and losses disproportionately according to a member's participation in the operation of the business.

- Unlike a C corporation's management, the management of an LLC is not personally liable for the obligations of the business; and the LLC avoids double taxation.

Which form of business ownership is right for the estate owner depends on varying factors, both subjective and objective.

SUMMARY

Financial products and services center on property. Knowing the types of property and how property can be owned is important to estate planners—customers and trust professionals alike.

- Property is categorized as real or personal. Real property is land and anything permanently associated with the land. Real property exists as residential, commercial, rental, agricultural, and vacant property. Personal property is all property that is not real. Personal property is either tangible or intangible. Real and personal property can be converted by physical change from one form to the other (e.g., a cherry tree is real property, the cherries growing on the tree are real property, and cherries picked from the tree are movable (impermanent) personal property).

- Property is owned in the following forms: sole, joint tenancy, tenancy by the entirety, tenancy in common, contract, and trust.

- Property ownership can transfer by gift, will, intestacy, sale, trade (barter), contract, trust, and law. Except for tenancy by the entirety, each type of property can be owned in each of the forms of property ownership, and vice versa.

- Planning a customer's estate requires obtaining detailed information from the customer. Fact-finding forms assist the planner and customer with gathering asset information.

- A person's domicile determines further how property may be owned. All states have either common law property or community property statutes, and each category dictates varying modes of property ownership. The ownership of real property and personal property in a common law state is clearly delineated. Although personal property ownership in a community property state is clear-cut, the varying laws in these states make for a complex discussion regarding real property.

- An important asset to a business owner is her business or her share of a business. Businesses are classified as sole proprietorships, partnerships, corporations, and limited liability companies.

REVIEW QUESTIONS

1. How do real property and personal property differ? List five types of tangible personal property and five types of intangible personal property.
2. How does joint tenancy ownership differ from tenancy by the entirety?
3. Using an example, explain the distinction between legal and equitable ownership of property.
4. Name five ways property may be transferred from one owner to another.
5. How is property already owned by an individual in a community property state affected by the owner's marriage? How is the ownership of property in a community property state treated when purchased during marriage?
6. List three differences between a general partnership and a limited partnership.

2

INVESTMENT VEHICLES

"Invest in inflation. It's the only thing going up."

Will Rogers (1879–1935)

In 1954 the Chevrolet division of General Motors produced three models: a two-door hardtop, a two-door convertible, and a four-door sedan. There were two engine options, the colors were limited, and extra options such as power windows, tinted glass, and a plastic holder for a coffee cup were minimal. Today, the combinations of models, options, styles, colors, and performance packages lead to a nearly infinite number of different cars available from GM, Ford, Chrysler, and all the foreign makes available. Also in 1954, it wasn't difficult to lift the hood and work on the engine. Today it's a nightmare! Gone are the days of working on your auto by yourself on a Saturday afternoon. Today we visit a mechanic to add air to our tires.

The world of investments is no different. Investment vehicles available 50 years ago are a small portion of what exists today. Yesterday's basic stick-shift, six-cylinder stock-and-bond market is today's souped-up environment of high-octane investment specialization.

LEARNING OBJECTIVES

Across the country, thousands of trust institutions are entrusted with trillions of dollars for millions of people. It is essential that trust professionals have a firm grasp of the investment basics needed to successfully manage and invest our customers' finances.

Upon completion of this chapter, you will be able to

- Identify what investments and securities are
- Define the basic concepts of stocks, the various classification of stocks, and the measurement of stock performance
- Analyze the features of bonds and the types of bonds that exist
- Compare the types of cash equivalents
- Explain the differences between common trust funds and mutual funds
- Define and use the terms that appear in bold in the text.

INVESTMENTS

Chapter 1 discussed assets: anything of value. Assets (property) are categorized as real or personal; personal property is further categorized as tangible or intangible. Stocks, as an example, are intangible assets. The stock itself is not the asset; it is something that represents something else: ownership in a company. The ownership is evidenced by an investment contract or an agreement (a document, such as a stock certificate) between an investor (an individual or institution) and an issuer (a corporation, a municipality, or the U.S. government). The generic word used for these investment contracts—and the vehicles used, such as stocks, bonds, and mutual funds—is **securities.**

Throughout this textbook, the word *securities* is used in the plural form, although one share of stock could technically be called a *security*. The word **security** normally refers to property or assets used as collateral to ensure the fulfillment of an obligation. For example, a homeowner's house is the "security" (collateral) for the homeowner's mortgage loan. This book is about securities, not security.

The word *securities* is often interchanged with the word *investment*. An **investment** is an asset acquired for the purpose of earning interest, dividends, or appreciation. Assets, securities, and property maintain their "investment" moniker even though their value may decline. For example, a stock that was worth $60 per share five years ago but today is worth $38 per share is still called an investment.

Cars can perform well, not so well, or not at all. Securities perform similarly. They may make money for the investor or lose money. Let's look at an example of investment performance.

Assume that one of your customers wants to purchase a $100,000 house. He probably does not have $100,000 in cash stuffed in a mattress for the purchase. Like most people, he saved for a down payment and will borrow the balance from a bank. In other words, he takes out a **mortgage.** If the down payment was $20,000, in essence the equity in the house at the time of purchase was $20,000. Yes, the **market value (fair market value)** is $100,000, but the bank is owed $80,000. The **equity,** or dollar ownership, is $20,000.

Let us further assume that 10 years later the market value of the house is $161,000 and that the mortgage (what is owed to the bank) is still $80,000. If the house was sold and the bank was repaid, the net proceeds are $81,000. Is this an investment, and did the investment perform well? Yes, it's a handsome investment performance! The $20,000 investment (the down payment) in the house has more than quadrupled. Equity has increased.

How do we measure how much an investment grows, how well it performs? Note that in our example of purchasing a house we are not considering many other monetary factors, such as how much money was put into the house over the years (for example, the cost incurred for a new garage, decorating, landscaping, and repairs), insurance, the payment of property taxes, and the tax-deductions based on the real estate taxes and mortgage-loan interest.

As a sage investor once said, "A $1 profit made in one year is worth more than a $1 profit made in three years." Buying a house and selling it at a profit after five years results in a greater investment return than buying and selling the house at the same amounts after ten years. But how do we calculate the investment return? One way is to compare the purchase price with the selling price. Another valid concept is to compare the beginning equity (the $20,000 down payment) with the ending equity (the $81,000 profit). Here's what we mean:

Today		10 Years from Now
$100,000	Market value	$161,000
–$80,000	Mortgage	–$80,000
$20,000	Equity	$81,000

Another way to look at the numbers is:

$161,000	Sale price
–100,000	Purchase price
$ 61,000	
+ 20,000	Beginning equity
$ 81,000	Ending equity

Exhibit 2.1 Compound Value of $1

Year	1%	2%	3%	4%	5%	6%	7%	8%	9%	10%	12%	14%	15%	16%
1	1.010	1.020	1.030	1.040	1.050	1.060	1.070	1.080	1.090	1.100	1.120	1.140	1.150	1.160
2	1.020	1.040	1.061	1.082	1.103	1.124	1.145	1.166	1.188	1.210	1.254	1.300	1.323	1.346
3	1.030	1.061	1.093	1.125	1.158	1.191	1.225	1.260	1.295	1.331	1.405	1.482	1.521	1.561
4	1.041	1.082	1.126	1.170	1.216	1.262	1.311	1.360	1.412	1.464	1.574	1.689	1.749	1.811
5	1.051	1.104	1.159	1.217	1.276	1.338	1.403	1.469	1.539	1.611	1.762	1.925	2.011	2.100
6	1.062	1.126	1.194	1.265	1.340	1.419	1.501	1.587	1.677	1.772	1.974	2.195	2.313	2.436
7	1.072	1.149	1.230	1.316	1.407	1.504	1.606	1.714	1.828	1.949	2.211	2.502	2.660	2.826
8	1.083	1.172	1.267	1.369	1.477	1.594	1.718	1.851	1.993	2.144	2.476	2.853	3.059	3.278
9	1.094	1.195	1.305	1.423	1.551	1.689	1.838	1.999	2.172	2.358	2.773	3.252	3.518	3.803
10	1.105	1.219	1.344	1.480	1.629	1.791	1.967	2.159	2.367	2.594	3.106	3.707	4.046	4.411
11	1.116	1.243	1.384	1.539	1.710	1.898	2.105	2.332	2.580	2.853	3.479	4.226	4.652	5.117
12	1.127	1.268	1.426	1.601	1.796	2.012	2.252	2.518	2.813	3.138	3.896	4.818	5.350	5.936
13	1.138	1.294	1.469	1.665	1.886	2.133	2.410	2.720	3.066	3.452	4.363	5.492	6.153	6.886
14	1.149	1.319	1.513	1.732	1.980	2.261	2.579	2.937	3.342	3.797	4.887	6.261	7.076	7.988
15	1.161	1.346	1.558	1.801	2.079	2.397	2.759	3.172	3.642	4.177	5.474	7.138	8.137	9.266
16	1.173	1.373	1.605	1.873	2.183	2.540	2.952	3.426	3.970	4.595	6.130	8.137	9.358	10.748
17	1.184	1.400	1.653	1.948	2.292	2.693	3.159	3.700	4.328	5.054	6.866	9.276	10.761	12.468
18	1.196	1.428	1.702	2.026	2.407	2.854	3.380	3.996	4.717	5.560	7.690	10.575	12.375	14.463
19	1.208	1.457	1.754	2.107	2.527	3.026	3.617	4.316	5.142	6.116	8.613	12.056	14.232	16.777
20	1.220	1.486	1.806	2.191	2.653	3.207	3.870	4.661	5.604	6.727	9.646	13.743	16.367	19.461
21	1.232	1.516	1.860	2.279	2.786	3.400	4.141	5.034	6.109	7.400	10.804	15.668	18.822	22.574
22	1.245	1.546	1.916	2.370	2.925	3.604	4.430	5.437	6.659	8.140	12.100	17.861	21.645	26.186
23	1.257	1.577	1.974	2.465	3.072	3.820	4.741	5.871	7.258	8.954	13.552	20.362	24.891	30.376
24	1.270	1.608	2.033	2.563	3.225	4.049	5.072	6.341	7.911	9.850	15.179	23.212	28.625	35.236
25	1.282	1.641	2.094	2.666	3.386	4.292	5.427	6.848	8.623	10.835	17.000	26.462	32.919	40.874
26	1.295	1.673	2.157	2.772	3.556	4.549	5.807	7.396	9.399	11.918	19.040	30.167	37.857	47.414
27	1.308	1.707	2.221	2.883	3.733	4.822	6.214	7.988	10.245	13.110	21.325	34.390	43.535	55.000
28	1.321	1.741	2.288	2.999	3.920	5.112	6.649	8.627	11.167	14.421	23.884	39.204	50.066	63.800
29	1.335	1.776	2.357	3.119	4.116	5.418	7.114	9.317	12.172	15.863	26.750	44.693	57.575	74.009
30	1.348	1.811	2.427	3.243	4.322	5.743	7.612	10.063	13.268	17.449	29.960	50.950	66.212	85.850

Compound Interest

In our example of buying a home, the initial $20,000 investment grew to $81,000. Dividing $81,000 by $20,000 gives us a factor of 4.05. Now look at Exhibit 2.1 along the 10-year line. Scan from left to right to the 4.046 factor (which is in the 15 percent column). This is close enough to the 4.05 calculation. This tells us that in 10 years a $20,000 investment grew at a compound value of 15 percent. Let's test our numbers. What would $20,000 invested at a constant compounded 15 percent rate of **return** be worth in 10 years? Cross the 15 percent column with the 10 year row. The factor is

4.046. Multiply this factor by $20,000. The answer is approximately $81,000.

Whether an investment vehicle is real estate, a savings account, or stocks and bonds, the growth of these investments over time is measured by percentages of **compound interest.**

For example, if a customer places $1,000 in a bank savings account and receives 6 percent interest, his balance at the end of 1 year will be $1,060 ($1,000 beginning balance plus $60 of interest). This is "simple" interest, and each year the account increases by the same $60. If the interest earned on the account is included as part of the savings account, it becomes compound interest—the account's balance after the second year will be $1,123.60 ($1,060 beginning balance plus $63.60 of interest). Think of it this way also:

$1,000.00	initial deposit when the savings account was established
+ 60.00	6 percent interest from the first year
+ 60.00	6 percent interest from the second year
+ 3.60	6 percent interest on the $60 of interest from the first year
$1,123.60	

Compound interest, therefore, is the payment of interest upon interest.

Present Value

In Exhibit 2.2, the same numbers appear as in Exhibit 2.1—but with a back-door approach, so to speak. If the customer's investment goal is to reach $81,000 in 10 years, and if he can get a constant 10-year compounding at 15 percent, what is needed today (**present value**) to arrive at the goal? Look where the 15-percent column intersects the 10-year row. The factor of 0.247 is then multiplied by $81,000. The answer is approximately $20,000. Or said another way, the present (today's) value of $81,000 at a 15 percent compound return for 10 years is $20,000.

Just as a rose bush needs sunlight, water, nutrients, pruning, and a bit of finger-crossing, money needs help also: time and a good rate of return.

Note that even if a $100,000 house never increases in market value, 10 years later there still will be equity in it. Because monthly payments decrease the mortgage, equity increases. If the mortgage decreases to $70,000 and the house is sold for $100,000, $30,000 of equity remains after the bank mortgage is repaid. The equity increased from $20,000 to $30,000.

From this home ownership example we see that equity represents the percentage of an asset that is owned by the investor.

Having no mortgage—no indebtedness—means having 100 percent equity. Yet the word *equity* has added meaning.

STOCKS

Let's switch gears and change your customer's asset (investment) from a house to stock in a company, say General Motors. GM is a company owned by the public, by individuals like your customers and by other companies. The evidence of ownership in GM is a **stock certificate,** a legal piece of ownership paper received from GM. If a company has 1 million shares of **stock** outstanding, and if an investor owns 100,000 shares of the stock, she owns 10 percent of the company, or a 10 percent **share.** Equity in GM, or in any other company, is measured by the number of shares an investor owns in relationship to the total number of shares issued. Therefore, percentage of equity means percentage of ownership. This is why stocks are called equities.

Now, let's review. When investors place (invest) money with a company, they are "buying into" the company or supplying the company with capital. This activity makes them owners of the company. As owners of shares they have an equitable interest—they have equity. The stock certificate is the evidence of the ownership, like the title to a car is evidence that you own the car. To discourage forgery, stock certificates, as well as the other securities certificates that we will discuss in this chapter, are printed on specially watermarked paper, and the printing on the face of the certificate is engraved with delicate etchings (microprinting). The special printing also permits transfer agents (discussed in Chapter 11) to identify a particular securities issue if the certificate has been mutilated.

When a company issues stock and investors purchase the stock, the company is said to have stock outstanding. The word *outstanding* is one of several terms relating to stocks:

- *Authorized stock.* This is the specific number of shares authorized

Exhibit 2.2 Present Value of $1

Year	1%	2%	3%	4%	5%	6%	7%	8%	9%	10%	12%	14%	15%
1	0.090	0.980	0.971	0.962	0.952	0.9430	0.935	0.926	0.917	0.909	0.893	0.877	0.870
2	0.980	0.961	0.943	0.925	0.907	0.890	0.873	0.857	0.842	0.826	0.797	0.769	0.756
3	0.971	0.942	0.915	0.889	0.864	0.840	0.816	0.794	0.772	0.751	0.712	0.675	0.658
4	0.961	0.924	0.888	0.855	0.823	0.792	0.763	0.735	0.708	0.683	0.636	0.592	0.572
5	0.951	0.906	0.863	0.822	0.784	0.747	0.713	0.681	0.650	0.621	0.567	0.519	0.497
6	0.942	0.888	0.837	0790	0.746	0.705	0.666	0.630	0.596	0.564	0.507	0.456	0.432
7	0.933	0.871	0.813	0.760	0.711	0.665	0.623	0.583	0.547	0.513	0.452	0.400	0.376
8	0.923	0.853	0.789	0.731	0.677	0.627	0.582	0.540	0.502	0.467	0.404	0.351	0.327
9	0.914	0.837	0.766	0.703	0.645	0.592	0.544	0.500	0.460	0.424	0.361	0.308	0.284
10	0.905	0.820	0.744	0.676	0.614	0.558	0.508	0.463	0.422	0.386	0.322	0.270	0.247
11	0.896	0.804	0.722	0.650	0.585	0.527	0.475	0.429	0.388	0.350	0.287	0.237	0.215
12	0.887	0.788	0.701	0.625	0.557	0.497	0.444	0.397	0.356	0.319	0.257	0.208	0.187
13	0.879	0.773	0.681	0.601	0.530	0.469	0.415	0.368	0.326	0.290	0.229	0.182	0.163
14	0.870	0.758	0.661	0.577	0.505	0.442	0.388	0.340	0.299	0.263	0.205	0.160	0.141
15	0.861	0.743	0.642	0.555	0.481	0.417	0.362	0.315	0.275	0.239	0.183	0.140	0.123
16	0.853	0.728	0.623	0.534	0.458	0.394	0.339	0.292	0.252	0.218	0.163	0.123	0.107
17	0.844	0.714	0.605	0.513	0.436	0.371	0.317	0.270	0.231	0.198	0.146	0.108	0.093
18	0.836	0.700	0.587	0.494	0.416	0.350	0.296	0.250	0.212	0.180	0.130	0.095	0.081
19	0.828	0.686	0.570	0.475	0.396	0.331	0.277	0.232	0.194	0.164	0.116	0.083	0.070
20	0.820	0.673	0.554	0.456	0.377	0.312	0.258	0.215	0.178	0.149	0.104	0.073	0.061
21	0.811	0.660	0.538	0.439	0.359	0.294	0.242	0.199	0.164	0.135	0.093	0.064	0.053
22	0.803	0.647	0.522	0.422	0.342	0.278	0.226	0.184	0.150	0.123	0.083	0.056	0.046
23	0.795	0.634	0.507	0.406	0.326	0.262	0.211	0.170	0.138	0.112	0.074	0.049	0.040
24	0.788	0.622	0.492	0.390	0.310	0.247	0.197	0.158	0.126	0.102	0.066	0.043	0.035
25	0.780	0.610	0.478	0.375	0.295	0.233	0.184	0.146	0.116	0.092	0.059	0.038	0.030
26	0.772	0.598	0.464	0.361	0.281	0.220	0.172	0.135	0.106	0.084	0.053	0.033	0.026
27	0.764	0.586	0.450	0.347	0.268	0.207	0.161	0.125	0.098	0.076	0.047	0.029	0.023
28	0.757	0.574	0.437	0.333	0.255	0.196	0.150	0.116	0.090	0.069	0.042	0.026	0.020
29	0.749	0.563	0.424	0.321	0.243	0.185	0.141	0.107	0.082	0.063	0.037	0.022	0.017
30	0.742	0.552	0.412	0.308	0.231	0.174	0.131	0.099	0.075	0.057	0.033	0.020	0.015

to be issued by a corporation's charter to operate its business.

- *Outstanding stock.* This is the number of shares that are currently owned by investors. This type of stock has voting rights and is eligible for dividends (terms that are discussed below).

- *Issued stock.* This is the portion of authorized shares that includes outstanding stock plus stock that has been reacquired (but not retired) by the corporation.

- *Treasury stock.* These are shares that have been reacquired by the corporation but have not been retired. A corporation that owns its own stock is not considered an investor; therefore, treasury stock has no voting rights and it is not eligible for dividends. Treasury stock may be re-sold again.

- *Retired stock.* This is stock that is cancelled after it has been reacquired. If the stock is cancelled (and therefore cannot be reissued), the number of authorized shares is reduced.

Perhaps an example would help clarify the definitions. HMFIC Widget Company authorized 50 million shares of stock. The company sold 30 million shares to the investing public (individual investors, other companies, mutual funds) in its first year of operation. Five years later the company sold another 10 million shares. Three years later the company reacquired 10 million shares and maintained half as treasury stock and retired the other half. Here's what the stock classifications total:

Authorized stock	45,000,000
This is the 50 million shares initially authorized minus the 5 million shares that were reacquired and retired.	
Outstanding stock	30,000,000
The company initially sold 30 million shares, then sold another 10 million shares for a total of 40 million shares, but this amount was reduced when the company reacquired 10 million shares.	
Issued stock	35,000,000
This is the 40 million shares sold minus the 10 million shares reacquired plus the 5 million shares reacquired and retained as treasury stock.	
Treasury stock	5,000,000
Yes, the company reacquired 10 million shares, but it retired 5 million shares.	
Retired stock	5,000,000
Self-explanatory.	

An investor's ownership of stock is indeed ownership of the company. The investor is a **shareholder (stockholder)** of the company. As an owner of the company the shareholder has a right to share in the company's growth and profits or its losses. Investors buy stock with the hope that their investment—the value of the stock—will increase. This increase is called **appreciation.** Of course, there is also the chance the value of the stock will decrease (**depreciation**).

A tremendous amount of literature has been devoted to why the value of a company's stock goes up and down. Simply, if a company does well, the investor wins because the value of the stock rises as the company's value goes up. Many investment professionals look at this as a supply-and-demand situation. If a company's value increases, there will be a demand by investors to purchase the stock. Because the supply of stock is finite, the price of the stock will increase to reflect the demand.

Investors also win when a company pays a **dividend,** a return of the company's profits to the owners (stockholders). As a company makes money, it pays expenses and overhead (salaries, bills, taxes, and so forth). If a corporation spends less than it makes, it has a profit. If the company is active and growing, it may retain some of the profit for future endeavors. As the expression goes, "The profits are plowed back into the company." What the company does not retain for future projects is distributed to the stockholders—the owners of the company. As a 10 percent owner of the company, an investor gets 10 percent of the dividends the board of directors declares (votes to distribute). These dividends are usually paid on a quarterly basis in cash (a cash dividend). Some companies elect to pay the dividend by issuing to the shareholders additional stock (a stock dividend) proportionate in value to what the cash dividend would have been. For example, assume that a company elects to pay a 3 percent stock dividend by issuing additional shares of stock. If an investor owns 200 shares of stock, he will own 206 shares after the stock dividend is paid:

- 200 shares of stock times 3 percent equals 6 shares
- 200 shares plus 6 shares equals 206 shares

Some companies give stockholders the option of taking the dividend in cash or stock. When opting for a stock dividend, the investor in essence is electing a **dividend reinvestment program.** Rather than taking cash, the investor takes more stock. Think of this the same way a bank depositor elects either to take interest on a savings account in cash or to reinvest the interest into the account, which, you will remember, is a form of compounding.

There always is the risk that a company will not be run effectively, markets will go bad, the economy will cause fewer people to buy cars, or management will direct the company's efforts in the wrong direction. If these things happen (and sometimes they do), the value of the company decreases (causing the stock to decrease in value) and profits can disappear (preventing the payment of dividends). This is the risk one takes in investing in stocks.

Classes of Stock

Companies such as GM build different models of cars and trucks. They also issue different classes of stock, such as common stock and preferred stock. A company's type, size, financial goals, age, products, and financial position determine the class (or type) of stock it issues.

Common Stock

Common stock is what most investors own. It is the generic (common) equity in a company. A common stockholder has the right to

- Receive a stock certificate (evidence of ownership)

- Share in corporate profits (dividends when declared)

- Have a voice in management (**voting rights** on company matters and election of officers and directors)

- Transfer stock (to sell the stock to others in the open market)

- Receive information (to receive corporate financial statements—stockholder lists, an annual report, minutes of stockholder meetings—and to inspect the corporation's records)

- Purchase additional stock (a preemptive right if issued and in proportion to the amount of stock held)

In comparison to preferred stock, the value of a company's common stock makes the greatest swings upward (appreciation) or downward (depreciation), depending on the success of the company. A common stockholder has a lot to gain and a lot to lose in relation to preferred stockholders.

Preferred Stock

All corporations must issue common stock. They may also issue preferred stock. **Preferred stock** is considered a hybrid between common stocks and bonds. In addition to the fact that both common and preferred stock are distinguished in bold letters printed on the stock certificate, the similarities and differences of preferred stock, common stock, and bonds are as follows:

- Dividends

    Whereas dividends on common stock can vary (or not be paid at all) depending on the financial condition and direction of the company, the dividend paid on preferred stock is often fixed at a percentage or dollar amount. This gives preferred stock a fixed-income characteristic, which we will talk about later in this chapter.

    Although corporations are not legally obligated to pay dividends, they may guarantee to pay dividends to owners of preferred stock. If the dividend is not guaranteed, preferred stockholders receive a dividend before common stockholders receive a dividend, hence the name *preferred*. If a preferred dividend is not paid, a common dividend is not paid.

    The dividend on preferred stock can be cumulative. *Cumulative* means that dividends declared by the company may be accumulated for a period time and paid at a stipulated date in the future. All dividends on preferred stocks must be paid (brought up to date) before common stockholders receive payments.

- Voting rights

  Most forms of preferred stock do not carry voting rights; some may possess partial or limited voting power. With regard to voting rights, a preferred stockholder does not have equity in the company. Think of preferred stockholders as having a limited ownership status.

- Call provisions

  Preferred stock may be called, or redeemed, by a corporation. As the stock certificate indicates, the company can recall (buy back) the stock after a certain date at a stipulated price. Following a **call,** the stock is either entirely canceled (becomes retired stock) or retained by the corporation (as treasury stock). We will discuss call provisions again later in this chapter with respect to bonds.

- Convertibility

  Preferred stock can be issued as convertible. *Convertible* preferred stock carries with it the right to exchange the preferred stock for common stock or bonds.

- Market value

  The market value of preferred stock can fluctuate as interest rates vary. We will discuss this concept in more detail later in this chapter with regard to bonds.

- Bankruptcy

  Businesses operate on capital received from others: money lent by banks, money lent by bondholders, and money invested by stockholders (common and preferred). If a company experiences financial failure (bankruptcy), yet retains some assets, creditors and investors are repaid their capital in the following order:

  1. Employees (wages and salaries)
  2. Internal Revenue Service (taxes)
  3. Secured debt (bank loans and bonds backed by collateral)
  4. Unsecured debt (noncollateralized loans and bonds)
  5. Preferred stockholders
  6. Common stockholders

Characteristics of Stock

Stock is further classified by the characteristics of the company offering it. Note that these classifications are not necessarily mutually exclusive. For example, a more detailed study of stocks would show examples of certain companies that are considered blue chip, yet they possess the ingredients of a growth stock: a solid financial past and a growing future. When does a stock transform itself from being speculative to growth to blue chip? Do income stocks lack in appreciation? Does a company's changing financial situation truly insulate it from market swings, therefore making it defensive? General descriptions of these classifications of stock follow.

Blue Chip Stock

Years ago, the chips used for gambling in Las Vegas were red, white, and blue. The color denoted the value. For example, red may have been worth $1, white $5, and blue $10. Blue chips were worth more. So too are **blue chip stocks.** A blue chip company is worth more than other companies because it is large, financially stable, consistently growing, constantly creating earnings, and pays dividends in good times and bad. These are all desirable investment ingredients. At one time blue chip stocks were called the "nifty 50" because of the 50 companies labeled as blue chip companies. This term is perhaps a misnomer today because several of these once-stable companies have seen financial setbacks. In addition, although more than 60 companies have boasted yearly dividend payments since the late 1800s, many of them do not necessarily meet the other characteristics of blue chip companies. For example, in the 1960s International Business Machines (IBM) was a prime blue chip issue. Some investment analysts may dispute that designation today because the entry of competitors into the computer industry has affected IBM's earnings and worth. Others defend IBM's blue-chip status because of its recent rebound.

Speculative Stock

Speculative stocks represent startup companies or ones that are on shaky financial ground. These companies may be on the edge of failure or of success. Purchasing speculative stocks is risky business! Very seldom does a speculative stock pay dividends, because its profits (if any) probably will be slim or put back into the business to help its development. If the company succeeds, the payoff to the investor can be very large. Higher risk equals higher potential reward. We will explore the subject of risk in Chapter 4.

An initial public offering (IPO) is a good example of a speculative stock. An IPO occurs when a close corporation (owned privately by a few close owners) "goes public" and sells stock to the public for the first time. The new investors are speculating on the company's future success, based on its newness. Happy are the investors who picked IPOs such as Krispy Kreme Donuts and Starbucks Coffee, but for each successful IPO there are many that fail.

Growth Stock

Growth stock is a notch above speculative stock. This stock represents young but stable, emerging, growing companies. These companies may retain most, if not all, of their earnings for development; therefore, they pay little or no dividends. Growth stocks represent an equity investment where return is expected primarily from an increase (appreciation) in the

stock's price as the company grows over time, but growth stocks are subject to wider swings in price than the general stock market.

Income Stock

In comparison to other types of stock, **income stock** pays a high dividend in relation to the stock's price and to stock of other companies. Utility companies (for example, companies that produce electricity or provide natural gas) are examples of income stock companies. The stock's price is more likely to remain stable in comparison to the stock market in general, but income stock can be heavily influenced by changes in interest rates.

Defensive Stock

Defensive stocks are securities that tend to resist general stock market declines. Stocks of consumer goods (particularly some beverage and food companies) are considered defensive. Although defensive stocks resist downturns, they generally move up more slowly than other stocks during rising markets.

Beyond the Basics

Classes and characteristics of stocks are not clear-cut. Other examples of stock classifications that can fit into one or more of the previous categories are

- Cyclical stocks (ones that fluctuate in tandem with economic cycles)

- Seasonal stocks (issues that vary in price with the seasons of the year)

- Domestic (U.S.) and nondomestic (international) stocks

- Sector stocks (energy, financial, transportation, telecommunications, healthcare, and so forth)

- Capitalization stocks (stocks of companies categorized by size, such as financial worth); the common categories are large, mid, small, and micro cap; a common formula for calculating worth is multiplying the number of shares outstanding by the current market price per share)

Stock Enhancers

Rights and warrants are facets of stock that enhance the attractiveness of stocks beyond the payment of dividends and appreciation.

Rights

We stated earlier that common shareholders have a preemptive right to additional shares of stock issued by the company. Formally called a "rights offering" or a "subscription right," offering is simply referred to as a **right** by investment professionals. Once a rights offering is approved by the shareholders at one of their meetings, the right is transmitted by means of a stock order form that indicates the number of shares the right's holder will be permitted to purchase, the price per share of the offering, and the expiration date of the offer. A shareholder has three choices when a right is offered:

1. Exercise the right (that is, purchase the additional shares offered) by completing and signing the rights offer. Trustees, agents, and other intermediaries who receive rights offerings are obligated to forward them promptly to the beneficial owners. Because rights typically may be exercised only for a brief period, this is a very time-critical process, especially to trust institutions that are providing an investment service to customers.
2. Sell the rights in the general marketplace. The sale of the rights is treated like the sale of any other stock.
3. Not exercise the right by the expiration date. A right is worthless after

the expiration date. Not exercising a right reduces a shareholder's percentage of equity ownership in the company in comparison to that of shareholders who do exercise their right.

Warrants

A warrant is another method for attracting investors and raising capital. Similar to a right, a **warrant** is also a right given to purchase shares of stock, but this right comes attached to newly issued securities—most likely preferred stock and bonds (a "bond sweetener")—when initially purchased by the investor.

Warrants permit the purchaser of the new stock to buy a set number of shares at a specific price. The warrants are attached (by means of a certificate) to the new securities at no additional direct cost to the investor. The warrant gives its holder a long-term privilege to subscribe to the corporation's common stock, and shares are specifically set aside for this purpose by the corporation. The time period during which the holder may exercise the warrant is usually fixed. Warrants lasting for three to five years from issuance are common, and some may exist up to twenty years. A few warrants, called "perpetual" warrants, are issued with no expiration date.

Warrants may be traded as independent securities. If a warrant is not exercised by its expiration date, it becomes worthless. The holder of a warrant has no voting rights and receives no dividends with respect to the warrants themselves. In this respect a warrant may be thought of as a potential investment.

Many banks act as agents for corporations in processing the exchange of warrants for stock (see Chapter 11). An agent is responsible for ensuring that the exercise of the warrant is carried out in strict conformity with the terms of the offering. Trust institutions that hold warrants on behalf of their customers also have an important responsibility. They must be sure to either sell or exercise the warrant before it expires. The trust institution must, therefore, have a good operating system that alerts personnel when warrants will expire, and the institution must be capable of determining and carrying out whatever action will most benefit the customer.

The type of stocks in customers' portfolios depends on investment objectives, time horizon, and risk tolerance. Trust professionals need a solid understanding of stocks and how they fit into a portfolio's asset allocation formula and diversification parameters (see Chapter 3).

For those looking for further information, a good introductory text to explore is *What Investing Is All About* (published by South-Western Publishing Company) by John Barnes. The author offers insight to the stock market, special terminology, investment strategies, the roles of various players in the market, how the stock market has performed, and how performance is measured.

Measuring the Stock Market

Earlier in this chapter we explored the concept of compound interest, a mathematical way to measure the growth of an investment over a period of time. Over the years several indices have evolved to measure the performance of the stock market. We will look briefly at two of these indices.

Standard & Poor's Index

The **Standard & Poor's (S&P)** index is a widely used measure of the U.S. stock market. It contains 500 stocks, representing the largest U.S. companies, and it is broadly diversified across various industry sectors. This **portfolio** of 500 stocks (also known as the S&P 500) represents approximately 75 percent of the total market value of all publicly traded U.S. stocks.

The S&P index measures the gains (appreciation), losses (depreciation), and dividend payments of this 500-stock composite. For example, if a stock is worth $100 per share on the first day of a calendar year and it is worth $110 on the last day of the year, there has been a 10 percent appreciation. If this stock also paid a $3 dividend per share (3 percent) during the year, the 10 percent appreciation and the 3 percent dividend make a 13 percent increase for this particular stock. If every stock in the S&P 500 did the exact same thing, the S&P would be "up" 13 percent for the year. Of course, all stocks don't perform the same way. Others appreciate more or less, some depreciate (go below the beginning-of-the-year value), and some pay fewer or greater dividends or none at all. (And there are times, such as 2000 and 2001, when the market as a whole is down.) At the end of the year the S&P shows an average of how this group of 500 stocks performed.

The number of stocks in the S&P index is always 500, but the list of companies represented varies throughout the year. This is called **turnover.** The changing of names makes for additional complicated calculations.

How has the stock market done in past years? Exhibit 2.3 shows the S&P's performance for each year from the beginning of 1981 through the end of 2002. Keeping the discussion of compound interest in mind, realize that the exhibit also shows the market's annual compound rate of return, ending December 31, 2002, for the entire period plus 3-, 5-, and 10-year periods. An additional way to look at the S&P's performance is to chart an initial investment over a period of years. Using the individual-year performance numbers, Exhibit 2.3 shows the compound growth of a $100,000 investment made at the beginning of 1981.

Despite the stock market's performance in 2000 and 2001, because of the S&P's overall performance in the most recent past, most individual investors and investment managers use the S&P 500 as a benchmark for comparing performance. Evidence of the S&P's performance was given in the January 28, 1997, *New York*

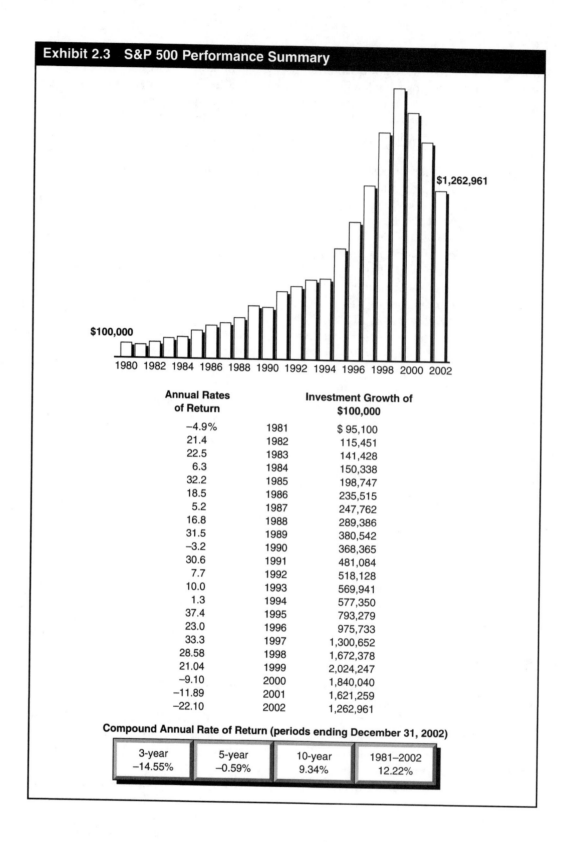

Exhibit 2.3 S&P 500 Performance Summary

Annual Rates of Return		Investment Growth of $100,000
−4.9%	1981	$ 95,100
21.4	1982	115,451
22.5	1983	141,428
6.3	1984	150,338
32.2	1985	198,747
18.5	1986	235,515
5.2	1987	247,762
16.8	1988	289,386
31.5	1989	380,542
−3.2	1990	368,365
30.6	1991	481,084
7.7	1992	518,128
10.0	1993	569,941
1.3	1994	577,350
37.4	1995	793,279
23.0	1996	975,733
33.3	1997	1,300,652
28.58	1998	1,672,378
21.04	1999	2,024,247
−9.10	2000	1,840,040
−11.89	2001	1,621,259
−22.10	2002	1,262,961

Compound Annual Rate of Return (periods ending December 31, 2002)

3-year	5-year	10-year	1981–2002
−14.55%	−0.59%	9.34%	12.22%

Times ("Wall Street on Autopilot: Investors Rush to Index Funds"). Keep in mind the period this article was published:

> Index funds are indeed one of the best ways to invest in the broad stock market, which has historically outperformed nearly all other investments. But what has caught the attention of recent investors is not just the long-run potential of index funds, but their short-term payoff. Over the last three years, index funds that track the S&P 500 performed better for their shareholders than did 93 percent of the 2,400 mutual funds that rely on money managers to pick and choose among a broad array of American stocks.

Dow Jones Industrial Average

Another stock market measurement is the Dow. When people ask, "How's the market doing?" "Where did the market close?" or "Is the market up or down?" they are often referring to the **Dow Jones Industrial Average** (DJIA). In 1884, investment pioneer Charles Dow began calculating a rough measure of stock market performance. Each day he added the prices of 12 important industrial stocks and divided by 12 to find the average. If the average rose (or fell), the market was up (or down) for the day. In 1928 the average was expanded to 30 stocks. The larger number of stocks was a more accurate representation of the stock market as a whole. In later years the companies included in the index (not necessarily industrial companies), the divisor used, consideration of stock splits and dividends, and other factors have substantially changed the nature of the average.

The original 12 stocks in the DJIA were:

American Cotton Oil
American Sugar
American Tobacco
Chicago Gas
Distilling & Cattle Feeding
General Electric
Laclede Gas

National Lead
North American
Tennessee Coal & Iron
U.S. Leather Preferred
U.S. Rubber

Currently the DJIA 30 stocks are:

Alcoa
American Express
AT&T
Boeing
Caterpillar
Citigroup
Coca Cola
DuPont
Eastman Kodak
Exxon Mobil
General Electric
General Motors
Home Depot
Honeywell
Hewlett-Packard
IBM
Intel
International Paper
J. P. Morgan
Johnson & Johnson
McDonald's
Merck
Microsoft
3M
Philip Morris
Procter & Gamble
SBC
United Technologies
Wal-Mart
Walt Disney

The industrial average (as a running number since 1928) continues to be a widely watched index, a barometer of the market. When someone says the market was up 20.35 points for the day, she is talking about the DJIA.

The following statistics indicate how fickle the stock market can be:

- The Dow's biggest one-year decline was 52.67 percent in 1931
- The Dow's biggest one-year gain was 81.66 percent in 1915

- The Dow's greatest daily net gain was 499.19 points on March 16, 2000; although it's greatest daily percentage gain was 14.87 percent on October 6, 1931
- The Dow's greatest daily net loss was 684.81 points on September 17, 2001; although it's greatest daily percentage loss was 22.61 percent on October 19, 1987
- Before the stock market crash of 1929, the DJIA was 381.17; subsequent milestones are:
  - First close above 1,000: November 14, 1972
  - First close above 2,000: January 8, 1987
  - First close above 5,000: November 21, 1995
  - First close above 10,000: March 29, 1999

Investing in stocks can be risky. There is no guarantee of growth. Although the stock market as a whole has experienced growth, there are times when money is lost. Again, as an example, Exhibit 2.3 shows how well the stock market performed as a whole from 1995 through 2002, as measured by the S&P 500. With respect to the Dow, the market climbed to a high point of 11,722.98 on January 14, 2000. Then came 2000, 2001, and 2002. On October 9, 2002, the DJIA fell to a recent low of 7,206.27.

An additional point of interest: on any given day—and in some cases during any given year—one index might move quite differently than other indices because of the types of stocks within an index. For example, the DJIA fell 7.10 percent in 2001. The S&P 500 fall almost doubled that in 2001. But over longer periods of time, the major, popular indices generally move together.

If you like investment thrill rides, the stock market is your roller coaster of choice. For the investor whose stomach cannot take the excitement, the next section will explore investment vehicles that may reduce the uncertainty of investment.

BONDS

Whereas stock represents equity (ownership) in a company, a bond does not convey ownership. A **bond** is an interest-bearing certificate of indebtedness—a loan that has to be repaid. The borrower (**debtor**) is the company. The lender (**creditor**) is the general investing public. The premise of a bond is for the company (the **obligor**) to borrow money (**principal**) from someone and to promise (be obligated) to repay the loan over, or at the end of, a stipulated period of time. During the borrowing period, the company pays **interest** (also called **income**), or the cost of borrowing, just as home buyers pay interest on a mortgage.

Because of the debtor-creditor relationship, bonds are called **debt,** whereas stocks are called equity. Yet another term for bonds is **fixed income**: the income (interest) is a fixed percentage (as with a **certificate of deposit [CD]**). As we will see later in this section, the time period of the loan is fixed (with some exceptions), and the amount invested and repaid is fixed. So when a person speaks of fixed-income investing, she is referring to investing in bonds.

Features of a Bond

As managers of our customers' investments, we trust professionals must evaluate the bonds we purchase from corporations, the government, and municipalities. And just as a mortgage is governed by a loan agreement, a bond is governed by an agreement, which should state the following terms and features:

- How much is being lent (principal)?
- When will the loan be repaid (maturity)?
- How much interest will be paid and when and how will it be paid (interest)?
- Can the borrower pay back the loan earlier than scheduled (callability)?

- What risks are associated in lending the money (safety)?
- Is the loan secure (collateral)?

Principal

Principal is the amount that is lent (invested). Bonds have a peculiar feature regarding principal. A $100,000 bond may be purchased at **par (face) value** for $100,000. A $100,000 bond can be bought at a **discount** for less than $100,000. And a bond can be purchased at a **premium** for more than $100,000. Why would an investor buy a bond for less or more than its face value? Perhaps because it is worth less or more.

Bond market values are tied closely to interest rates in general. For example, let's assume that 2 years ago XYZ Corp. issued a bond with a 7 percent interest rate. If interest rates are lower today, and if it were issuing new bonds, XYZ might offer a 5 percent interest rate. Can an investor today buy an XYZ bond that was issued 2 years ago? Yes, if he can find someone who wants to sell one. Because the current rate is 5 percent, and the 2-year-old XYZ bond is paying 7 percent, to buy the higher-interest bond, the investor would have to pay more than $100,000 for a $100,000 bond. The 2-year-old bond is worth more—it has a higher market value—because it pays more interest. The investor pays a premium for the bond. Even though the investor pays more than $100,000 for the $100,000 bond, he still gets 7 percent on $100,000 face value (not 5 percent), and he gets the par value of $100,000 when the bond matures. (We will expand on this more when we discuss yields later in this chapter.)

If today's interest rates are 9 percent, would the investor be interested in purchasing a bond that is paying only 7 percent? Perhaps. A 7 percent bond in a 9 percent interest environment would be sold at a discount. The investor gets less interest each year (7 percent versus 9 percent), but he didn't have to pay $100,000 for the bond, and he gets $100,000 when the bond matures.

Therefore, the market value of an existing bond increases or decreases as interest rates change:

- If interest rates rise (↑), the market value (what a willing buyer would pay) for an existing bond decreases (↓).
- As interest rates decrease (↓), the bond's value increases (↑).

Maturity

Every loan has to be paid back over a certain period of time (such as a 30-year mortgage). Bonds are the same. The bond certificate indicates what the **maturity** date is. This is the date by which the loan must be repaid. This is the date when XYZ will return money to the investor. There is always the risk, slight though it may be, that an issuer cannot repay the loan at maturity. This is called a default, which will be discussed later in this chapter. Maturities are classified as short, intermediate, or long. Different investors give different time frames to these classifications. A general rule places intermediate maturities in the 5- to 7-year range. Anything less is short; anything more is long.

Interest

Just as a bank pays interest to depositors for the money they lend to the bank, XYZ will pay interest to investors on the money lent to it. The interest rate is set when the bond is issued. The rate is stated on the face of the bond, and for most bonds the interest rate stays the same until maturity. Let's look at interest with respect to the bond examples below.

- *Bearer Bonds*
  Years ago, bonds were issued in **bearer bond** form, meaning that whoever was the bearer (possessor) of the bond was the owner. The owner's name was not printed on the bond certificate to indicate who the owner was. If the owner sold the bond, gave it away or lost it, it was

almost as good as cash to the person who took possession of it. A bearer bond certificate came with coupons attached to the bond certificate. The coupons indicated the date when the interest will be paid and the amount (dollar amount and interest rate). The coupons were like a sheet of postage stamps; the investor removed a coupon ("clipping coupons" was the expression) and presented it to the issuer, or more likely an agent, and in return received a cash interest payment. The interest was therefore also called the **coupon** rate. Bearer bonds have been prohibited for all new U.S. issues since 1983.

- *Registered Bonds*
  The amount of paperwork and time involved with bearer bonds and the possibility of theft led bond issuers to develop more efficient and safe ways to issue bonds. Although some old bond issues still exist in bearer form (and bearer bonds are still issued by various international issuers), today's issues are **registered bonds.** The owner's name is recorded (registered) in the issuer's books. As bonds are sold from one investor to another, XYZ Corp.—or an agent hired by the company to keep these types of records—changes its records. The interest payments for registered bonds are sent directly to the owners (usually twice a year) in the form of a check. In most instances the company will hire an agent to facilitate the interest payments. (See Chapter 11 regarding bond agency services.)

- *Partially Registered Bonds*
  A partially registered bond is one in which the owner's name and address are recorded (registered) for the purpose of receiving written notices from the issuer and the issuer's agent and for the payment of principal at maturity. Interest payments are received by

using attached interest coupons (as with bearer bonds).

- *Book Entry Bonds*
  To minimize paperwork, many issuers (primarily the U.S. government) are moving to book entry recordkeeping. This **book entry** is a paperless form of investing for new issues and for subsequent changes in securities ownership. With book entry bonds, a physical bond certificate is not issued to the investor, although proof of the investment is maintained (like making an entry into a logbook) by the issuer and its agent.

- *Zero Coupon Bonds*
  Although investing in bonds is a fixed-income form of investing, some bonds do not provide periodic interest payments. These bonds are **zero coupon bonds.** As the name implies, no coupon (interest) is paid during the life of the bond. A "zero" is purchased at a deep discount (far below par). The bond gradually increases in value, and the investor receives the full face value at maturity. For example, XYZ Corp. may sell a deep-discount, $100,000 zero coupon issue for $50,000. From the time of purchase until maturity, the investor does not receive any interest payments, but the full $100,000 is paid upon maturity. Basically, an investor's income, so to speak, comes from the bond's appreciation in value. More specifically, assume that a zero coupon $100,000 bond with a 10-year maturity is purchased for $50,000. During the 10-year period, the issuer does not make any interest payments but repays the full $100,000 at maturity. The bond increases in value each year through what is called **imputed income:** an increase in the bond's value without the payment of interest. This bond increases in value by $5,000 each year (the $50,000 growth divided by the 10 years to maturity). It could be

said that the bond's market value increases $5,000 each year. This is somewhat similar to the internal growth one sees in a house or a stock: no income is paid (except possibly dividends on the stock), but the value increases over time. Although no interest payments are made, the annual, imputed increase is taxable income, just as actual interest is. This is sometimes referred to as "phantom income."

Yield Curve

Whether a bond is a coupon-paying issue or a zero, there is a relationship between interest and the maturity length of the bond. At one time it was easy to assume, and be guaranteed, that the longer the maturity, the more the borrower (bond issuer) would pay in interest (also called **yield**). Investors need an incentive to commit their money for a long period of time. A bigger rate of return is the carrot in front of the horse.

It was once easy to construct a graph showing the relationship of maturity to yield. It was easily shown by a **yield curve** (or yield line, because the word *curve* is inaccurate in some cases). The plot of yields shown in Exhibit 2.4 sometimes is a straight line. This line is still called the yield curve.

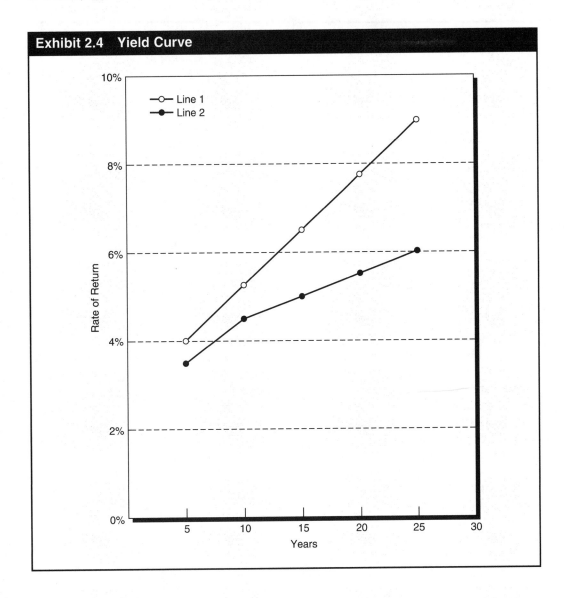

Exhibit 2.4   Yield Curve

Line 1 in the graph shows that a 5-year bond pays 4 percent, a 10-year pays 5.25 percent, a 15-year pays 6.5 percent, a 20-year pays 7.75 percent, and a 25-year pays 9 percent. The increase in yield is fairly proportionate to the number of years until maturity. Line 2 is a flatter yield curve. As the time to maturity increases, the rate of return diminishes to the point that it shows a flattening in the later years. This yield curve shows a 3.5 percent return for 5 years, 4.5 percent for 10 years, 5 percent for 15 years, 5.5 percent for 20 years, and 6 percent for 25 years.

Let's place these yields and maturities side by side.

Line 1	Years	Line 2
4.00%	5	3.50%
5.25	10	4.50
6.50	15	5.00
7.75	20	5.50
9.00	25	6.00

The difference in interest from 20 to 25 years in line 2 is only a 0.5 percent increase. Would an investor be willing to invest money for an additional 5 years to get only 0.5 percent additional yield? Probably not. With a more traditional yield curve (line 1), the investor is paid proportionately more to extend the maturity.

Most yield curves today are not like the classic line 1. In fact, these curves have sometimes inverted, meaning that the rates of return for longer maturities were less than for shorter maturities. What arose was an investment psychology that resulted in longer maturities paying disproportionately lower yields. Why did this happen? In the early 1980s, interest rates skyrocketed over a short period of time (see Exhibit 4.2). Quickly rising interest rates made investors hesitant to commit their money for longer maturities, knowing that once they committed, future bond issues would probably be higher. On the other hand, bond issuers (borrowers) weren't willing to offer longer maturities, knowing that if interest rates fell, they would be paying interest higher than the going rate. Although yield curves are not as dramatic as 20 years ago, they certainly have not come close to the traditional yield curves of yore.

Current Yield

When a $100,000 bond with an 8 percent coupon is purchased at par for $100,000, the yield is 8 percent ($8,000 per year). If a bond is bought at a discount or at a premium, the math changes.

Let's combine the premium, par, and discount concepts with interest and yield. Remember, regardless of what price a bond is purchased at, the interest rate that is stated on the bond certificate is what is received. Whether a $100,000 bond paying 8 percent is bought for $95,000 (a discount) or $110,000 (a premium), the investor still receives an $8,000 (8 percent) per year interest payment.

The $8,000 (8 percent) translates into a different yield, according to what was actually paid for the bond. This is called the **current yield.**

What is the current yield for a $100,000 bond, with an 8 percent coupon, that is bought for $95,000? The calculation is as follows:

- $95,000 is the market price paid
- 8 percent of $100,000 equals the $8,000, which is the annual income from the bond
- Current yield equals $8,000 divided by $95,000, which equals 8.42 percent

Although the investor receives $8,000, in comparison to the $95,000 paid for the bond, the current yield is 8.42 percent. If the bond was purchased at a premium, the same calculation is made. With a premium purchase, the current yield is lower than the coupon rate. Current yield expresses the true rate of return in relationship to the price paid.

Yield to Maturity

The element of time, which in this case is the time until the bond matures, must also be considered. **Yield to maturity** combines the bond's current yield, the market price (the price paid for the bond), and the maturity length of the bond. Remember, regardless of the bond's purchase price, the par value is paid when the bond matures. In the case of a bond that is bought for a discount, the investor gets back more than what she paid. Not only is she receiving the current yield each year, but also she earns more money, so to speak, by getting $100,000 back after paying only $95,000. Is the yield to maturity 8 percent, 8.42 percent, or something different? Let's calculate:

- $100,000 par value minus the $95,000 market price shows a $5,000 profit.
- If this bond matures in 5 years, $5,000 divided by 5 equals $1,000 per year.
- $1,000 divided by the $100,000 face amount equals 1 percent.
- Add this 1 percent to the 8.42 percent current yield, giving you a yield to maturity of 9.42 percent.

This is a simple way of calculating approximate yield to maturity. Algebraic equations, bond tables, and specialized calculators may be used to get a more precise calculation.

Callable Versus Noncallable

Many mortgage loan agreements contain a provision that permits the bank to call the loan, meaning that the bank can demand full payment of the loan before the end of the mortgage term. If the bank calls the loan, the borrower is required to pay the balance of the mortgage loan. Customers can do the same thing with savings account money lent to the bank; they can demand repayment (withdraw the funds) at any time.

Corporations, municipalities, and the government can issue bonds that can be called. A **callable bond** is one in which the issuer can "stop the music" anywhere along the way, give the money back to

the investor, and end the relationship. This cannot happen, however, unless it is stated in the bond certificate. Individual investors and investment managers must realize this is what they are buying. If the bond certificate states that the issuer can call the bond, it will contain a schedule of when calls can be made. The call feature may state that the corporation can do so at any time or only at specific times.

Why would an issuer do this? Assume that a 10-year bond is paying 10 percent. Five years from now interest rates on similar bonds may be 7 percent. This is expensive to the issuer, because it is paying 10 percent in a 7 percent environment. If the bond is callable, the issuer can give the money back to the bondholders and end the issue. Assuming it still needs the money, the issuer most likely would reissue a bond offering a 7 percent rate. This is referred to **refunding** or **refinancing.** If interest rates in the future are greater than 7 percent, the issuer is in good shape and, of course, would not call the issue, because it is borrowing money at 7 percent in a higher interest environment.

A callable bond may offer a higher going-in rate of return to entice investors to buy something that may be taken away from them in the future. In some instances the bond agreement may state that a premium will be paid to the investors if the bond is called. Remember, if the bond issue does not specifically state that it is callable, then it cannot be called (that is, it is a **noncallable bond**).

Safety and Quality

What guarantee is there that XYZ Corp. will continue to pay interest and return the principal upon maturity? There is no guarantee! What guarantee does a bank have that a credit card user will pay interest charges and repay the amount borrowed (charged)? Again, there is no absolute guarantee, which is why the bank, as the lender to the user of the credit card, will examine the borrower's credit history before issuing a card. So too should an investor look into XYZ's financial background, check the company's credit structure, and investigate the company's financial and nonfinancial strengths and weaknesses. How is this detective work accomplished?

In comparison to stocks, bonds are considered conservative, safe investment vehicles: money is invested, money is returned, and a fixed interest rate is paid. Yet bonds do possess investment volatility with respect to changes in interest rates. And what about the bond's individual level of safety? Is it possible for the issuer not to meet its interest payments or fail to pay the principal upon maturity? Yes, it is possible and it has happened. When the company cannot meet its interest and principal payment obligations, the bond is considered in **default.** Just as a credit card user is required to repay the amount borrowed (charged)—and any interest from a past-unpaid balance—so too is XYZ required to make interest payments and return principal upon maturity.

Ratings

How do we know a bond issuer is considered able to meet these obligations? Bond rating services do the research too complex for the average investor. The two most popular services are **Moody's Investor Service** and **Standard & Poor's.** Their research results in a **bond rating** that measures default risk (also called credit quality)—the chance that an issuer will not pay interest or repay principal. The ratings for each service are shown in Exhibit 2.5.

Let's look into the bond rating system a bit closer. Moody's system was contrived by John Moody, an investment research specialist, in 1909. The system gives investors a simple way of grading the investment quality of bonds. The top of the list (Aaa) represents high investment-quality bonds—companies with sound finances and the lowest risk. These issues are perceived to be from sound companies with the ability to pay their debts and meet their obligations. As

a rating decreases, risk increases, and the rate of interest probably will increase to attract investors to purchase a riskier bond. If an investor is willing to take the risk that an issue may default, he should get paid to take the risk. The lower C-ratings are classified as junk bonds. **Junk bonds** represent companies with a poor history of paying their debts or companies that are new and still in a high-risk position. If an investor is looking for greater than average yields, she will have to accept the risk that interest or principal may not be paid. As opposed to buying "high quality merchandise," the investor in this instance may be buying "junk." (Note: for the trust industry, ratings below Baa3 (Moody's) or BBB– (Standard & Poor's) are considered below investment grade.)

Bond ratings are not static; they can change. A strong company today may not be a strong company tomorrow. Financial woes in the future could change a company's Moody's or Standard & Poor's rating. Another aspect of successful investing is keeping a watchful eye on a customer's portfolio.

What Do the Letters Actually Mean?

Here are some examples of how the ratings are described in Moody's Bond Record:

Aaa   Bonds rated Aaa are of the highest quality. They carry the smallest degree of investment risk. Interest payments and principal are at minimum risk.

Baa   Bonds rated Baa are considered medium-grade. They are neither highly protected nor poorly secured. Interest payments and principal security appear adequate for the present. These bonds do not have superior investment characteristics and in fact have speculative characteristics as well.

Caa   Bonds rated Caa are of poor standing. These bonds may be

Exhibit 2.5   Moody's and Standard & Poor's Bond Ratings

Moody's	Standard & Poor's
Aaa	AAA
Aa1	AA+
Aa2	AA
Aa3	AA–
A1	A+
A2	A
A3	A–
Baa1	BBB+
Baa2	BBB
Baa3	BBB–
Ba1	BB+
Ba2	BB
Ba3	BB–
B1	B+
B2	B
B3	B–
Caa1	CCC+
Caa2	CCC
Caa3	CCC–
Ca1	CC+
Ca2	CC
Ca3	CC–
C1	C+
C2	C
C3	C–

in default or there may be elements of imminent danger with respect to principal or interest.

Collateral

In the previous section we asked what guarantee a bank is given that a credit card user (borrower) will make his monthly payments. On a larger scale, what guarantee does a bank have that a mortgage borrower will make his payments? A solid credit rating is the first step to show a borrower's ability to pay his loans, yet many lenders look for more than a past record. A lender may look for assurance beyond a credit history and a promise to pay. Lenders will look for a backing behind the loan, or **collateral.**

With a mortgage, the collateral is the house itself. The loan agreement assures the lender that the house will be surrendered to the lender if the borrower fails to meet the mortgage loan obligation.

What promise does XYZ Corp. or a municipality give to a bondholder (lender) if it cannot meet its obligations to make interest payments and pay back its indebtedness upon maturity of the bond? Just as a bank lender looks into credit history, an investor can look into a bond issuer's credit history by studying bond ratings and looking for collateral.

Bonds are issued as **secured** (backed by collateral) or **unsecured. Secured bonds** are backed by specific assets of the bond issuer, real estate, or a third-party guarantee, such as the issuer's bank.

When a bond is not secured with collateral, it is called a **debenture.** This type of issue is not backed by specific assets, but it is backed by the general credit of the issuer. This is similar to our discussion of credit cards. If $2,000 of merchandise is charged to a credit card, the credit card holder is taking a short-term loan from the bank that issued the card. This $2,000 loan is not collateralized—it is unsecured. The cardholder's credit history is an indication that he will pay the $2,000. Such is the case with an unsecured bond. Just as the bank takes the chance, without guarantees, that a credit card balance will be paid, so too do investors take the chance that a corporation or municipality will meet its interest payments and pay back the principal when the bond matures. A higher-rated, unsecured bond gives greater assurance that the issuer's obligations will be met.

Lending $10 to a friend, asking for this small loan to be repaid, perhaps forgiving the loan, or facing nonpayment of the loan, are simple choices, and they don't substantially affect the lender's financial picture. Investing in bonds elevates the risk and deserves careful attention. How much will be invested? What comes in return and when will it happen? What risks are assumed and what assurances are given? Also, what types of bonds should be considered? These are important decisions trust professionals must make for investment customers.

Types of Bonds

To investment professionals, hundreds of types of bonds and related fixed-income securities are available. Here we will focus on the macroclassifications of U.S. government, corporate, and municipal bonds. As the names imply, the nature of the borrower determines the name of the bond.

U.S. Government Bonds

It is sometimes difficult to understand why the U.S. government needs to borrow money. As working individuals we see a regular paycheck. Sometimes that pay-

check isn't big enough or doesn't come fast enough for us to meet our obligations, which is why we borrow money, whether it be a long-term loan as a mortgage or the short-term use of credit cards. The government doesn't see tax revenues (income) fast enough or large enough to accomplish what it wants to do, so it borrows money by issuing bonds. In fact the U.S. Department of the Treasury is the largest borrower (issuer of securities) in the world.

Government bonds (also called **Treasuries**) are issued as registered bonds, although Treasuries do not come as an actual bond certificate from the government. What is given to purchasers is a receipt showing the amount invested (which may be a discount, par, or premium purchase), the interest rate, and the maturity date. This information and the investor's name, address, and Social Security number are recorded into a computer accounting entry. This is book entry, a paperless form of investing. U.S. government bonds are categorized into three groups based on their maturities:

- Treasury bills: 4, 13, and 26 weeks
- Treasury notes: 2, 5, and 10 years
- Treasury bonds: 30 years (although the U.S. government has temporarily suspended the sale of Treasury bonds)

Currently, all government bonds are sold in $1,000 minimum denominations and are sold in $1,000 increments above the minimum.

Are government issues collateralized? No. Government securities are backed by the full credit and taxing ability of the U.S. Government. As many people say, "If the government fails in meeting its obligations, everyone will fail." Therefore, on the theory that there is virtually no risk of default, government issues are not rated as corporate or municipal issues are. Think of U.S. government securities as AAA/Aaa—the safest bonds possible.

Within the financial walls of the federal government, fixed-income securities are available from government agencies.

These agencies (arms of the government) have legal authority to borrow money to operate their programs, but their securities may or may not be guaranteed or backed by the federal government.

Government Agency Mortgage-Backed Securities

The largest purchase most people make in their lives is their home. Conventional lenders (banks, savings and loan associations, and private mortgage companies) that provide home mortgages are always concerned about the safety and integrity of their mortgage loan pool (sometimes called a book of business or a residential real estate portfolio). They are concerned what the effect on business would be if mortgage borrowers defaulted on payment or there were unfavorable changes in interest rates. Several government programs assist both parties, borrowers and lenders.

In practice, lenders pool their mortgage portfolios and either sell them to a government agency or exchange them for mortgage-backed agency securities. "Mortgage-backed" means the agency securities are secured by the principal and interest payments of the individual mortgages in the pool. These payments also provide funds for the repayment of principal and income to the individual and institutional investors who buy the agency securities. In many instances the lenders, who sold or exchanged their mortgage pools, will continue to service the loans, thus generating income for the lenders and preserving the customer relationships. An added advantage to lenders in this pooling-selling scheme is that funds provided by the government agency allow them to issue additional mortgage loans.

The three primary government agencies that provide mortgage-backed securities are "Ginnie Mae," "Fannie Mae," and "Freddie Mac."

- *Government National Mortgage Association (GNMA)*. Informally called "Ginnie Mae," GNMA was instituted in 1968 within the Department of Housing and Urban Development (HUD). GNMA sponsors the Federal Housing Administration (FHA) and Veterans Administration (VA) mortgage programs. The FHA program helps low- and moderate-income borrowers obtain loans for housing by providing insurance for lenders against borrower default. The borrower pays for the mortgage insurance by paying a fee. If the borrower defaults and the house is taken back by the lender, the agency will compensate the lender should the house sell subsequently for less than the amount of the mortgage debt. The VA program is similar, but borrowers are limited to military veterans.

- *Federal National Mortgage Association (FNMA)*. Informally called "Fannie Mae," FNMA was federally chartered in 1938 but has been privately managed since 1968. It is a stockholder-owned corporation, and, after the U.S. Treasury, it is the nation's largest borrower. FNMA administers the sell-or-exchange programs discussed above.

- *Federal Home Loan Mortgage Corporation (FHLMC)*. Informally known as "Freddie Mac," FHMLC was established in 1970. Similar in operation to the FNMA, it concentrates on mortgage loans originated by savings and loan associations. Once a government agency, it is now a private business.

These agencies of the federal government buy residential mortgages from lenders, pool them, and sell them to investors in the form of securities. The monthly principal and interest payments are made to the investors who buy participation in the pool. These monthly payments vary as some of the mortgages that back the securities are paid off or other changes—additional mortgages, defaults, and a change in interest rates—alter the composition of the pool.

Government Agency Nonmortgage-Backed Securities

The following are examples of government agencies that do not concentrate on mortgages:

- *Small Business Administration (SBA).* This agency raises money from investors to form small business investment companies that provide loans throughout the country to small businesses that would not qualify for conventional bank loans.

- *Federal Agricultural Mortgage Corporation (FAMC or "Farmer Mac").* This agency develops a secondary market in farming and agricultural loans and rural housing mortgages.

- *Student Loan Marketing Association (SLMA or "Sallie Mae").* This association is not actually a government agency. Chartered by the federal government and owed by its stockholders, SLMA purchases guaranteed loans from banks and other originators primarily for college student loans.

Corporate Bonds

Corporations borrow money by issuing **corporate bonds.** As with all bonds, an investor must weigh the issue's interest rate and maturity date, whether the bond is callable or collateralized, and the element of risk according to how the bond is rated. In general corporate bonds are categorized as secured or unsecured.

Secured Corporate Bonds

If a corporation issues bonds that are backed by a specifically pledged asset, the bonds are considered secured. Because they have a claim on an asset, the bondholders have a high level of protection should the corporation default. If the corporation were to default, the trustee of the bond issue would take possession of the pledged asset, sell it, and distribute the

proceeds to the bondholders. There are four major types of secured debt:

- *Mortgage.* The corporation pledges real estate that it owns, and the bondholders have a lien on the property. Corporations can issue bonds that are secured by first and second position loans on the same property, somewhat like a homeowner who has a first and second mortgage.

- *Equipment Trust.* The corporation pledges large capital equipment that it owns, and the bondholders have a lien on the equipment. Many transportation industry corporations issue equipment trust bonds that are secured by liens on airplanes, railroad cars, and supertankers.

- *Collateral Trust.* With this type of bond the corporation pledges securities of other companies that it owns. This is usually accomplished by a parent company that pledges the stock of a subsidiary.

- *Guaranteed.* Similar to collateral trusts, guaranteed corporate bonds are issued by subsidiaries but are guaranteed by a parent company. A good example of this would be General Motors guaranteeing the bonds issued by General Motors Acceptance Corporation (GMAC).

Unsecured Corporate Bonds

When a corporate bond is issued without collateral, it is unsecured. Payment on these securities are described as being backed by the "full faith and credit" of the issuing corporation. In general, there are three basic unsecured debt issues:

- *Debenture.* This is basically a shorter way of saying "unsecured corporate debt."

- *Subordinated Debenture.* This bond is issued without any pledged collateral, but it has a junior claim to debtors. This is similar to being in a second lien position on a mortgage bond.

- *Convertible Debenture.* Some bond offerings provide bondholders with the right to convert their bonds into common stock of the issuer. This conversion feature would be established at issuance and can only be adjusted if the issuing corporation declares a stock split or stock dividend on its common stock.

Municipal Bonds

Assume that a municipality, such as a town, is considering repaving its streets, including curb and minor sewer line repairs. The lowest bid for the work comes in at $25 million. Where does the town get the money? It can get it from real estate taxes, which will take many years. It can borrow from a bank. Or it can borrow from the public, as corporations and Uncle Sam do.

Types of Municipal Bonds

A short list of the issuers of **municipal bonds** ("munis") includes state, county and city governments, public utilities, and healthcare facilities. The basic categories of municipal debt are:

- *General Obligation (GO) Bond.* A **general obligation** bond is not collateralized, but it is backed by the full faith and credit of the issuing municipality. If the town is financially healthy and has a good tax base, the risk of default is quite low. The town will bring its taxing powers to bear to repay the debt.

- *Revenue Bond.* A **revenue bond** is secured by income generated by the borrower. For example, states borrow money for building, repairing, or expanding toll road facilities. The revenue collected at the tollbooths is used to repay the debt. This type of bond is com-

monly seen with respect to the following projects:

- ▲ Housing: low income housing, state housing, university housing (dorms)
- ▲ Utility: cable, telephone, water/sewer
- ▲ Healthcare: hospitals, health clinics, hospice facilities
- ▲ Transportation: public roadways, toll roads, public transportation systems

- *Insured Bond.* There are times when a municipality, in order to attract investors, will provide for insurance on the bond issue in order to guarantee the payment of principal and interest. Several insurance entities have been formed over the years to guarantee the nondefault of a municipal bond's interest payments and principal. This "municipal insurance" is an unconditional guarantee of the timely payment of interest and principal by a third party if for some reason payment is not made by the bond issuer. With this guarantee, a municipal bond cannot go into default. The collateral of insurance gives a municipal bond a triple-A rating regardless of how it was originally rated. Of course, there is a price to this: an insurance premium (fee). A poorly rated bond (which by virtue of its lower rating will carry a larger coupon rate) that qualifies for insurance is given the highest rating. The cost of the insurance probably will drive down the coupon rate. An investor may not gain anything financially, but he is guaranteed interest and principal payments. The three largest organizations—consortiums of several insurance companies—that provide municipal insurance are Municipal Bond Insurance Association (MBIA), Federal Guaranty Insurance Corporation (FGIC), and American Municipal Bond Assurance Corporation (AMBAC).

Taxation of Municipal Bonds

Prior to issuance of a municipal bond, the municipality will apply, so to speak, for tax-exempt status. The Internal Revenue Code provides guidance for a municipal issue to be qualified: it must generate funds for public purposes. If the issue is qualified, the income (interest) is not taxable, for the most part, to the investors.

Interest from a qualified municipal bond is exempt from federal income taxation. For this reason, municipal issues are referred to as **tax-exempt bonds.** Interest from corporate and government bonds is federally taxable. Additionally, in general, interest earned from a municipal bond is exempt from an investor's state taxation, if she buys an issue from a municipality located in the state in which she pays taxes. For example, if a resident of Colorado purchases a bond from the city of Denver, the interest is exempt from federal taxation and from Colorado taxation. If this Coloradan buys a bond from a California municipality, she will have to report the bond's interest as taxable on her state income tax return. Several states tax municipal bond interest from *any* municipality, inside or outside the state. (Note: interest from U.S. government securities is exempt from state taxation.)

Because munis are exempt from federal (and in many cases state) taxation, their yield is lower than that of taxable government and corporate issues. Why would someone invest in a municipal issue that pays a lower rate of return? The municipal bond's tax-exempt interest may be greater than a taxable bond's interest minus applicable income taxes. The difference in return between these bonds is called the **spread.** Although it is fairly easy to determine which bond gives the greater return, we must not ignore ratings, maturities, and collateral when building our customers' investment portfolios. Comparisons must be on a level basis.

CASH EQUIVALENTS

Stocks and bonds have about them an investment air that connotes duration. Investors in stocks look to value in consistent dividend payments and long-term appreciation. Bond investors expect a regular stream of interest payments and a return of principal following maturity. Yet in many instances, borrowers (issuers) and lenders (investors) need to "drive" their money (and "park" their money) for a short period of time. For them, cash equivalents—commonly referred to as **money markets**—are the investment of choice.

Cash equivalents are assets or securities that are easily and quickly converted to cash. All cash equivalent instruments possess three common characteristics: short term maturity, high investment quality, and extreme liquidity. In this section, we demonstrate these characteristics as we discuss the primary cash equivalent investment vehicles used by individual investors and trust institutions.

Money Market Funds

One of the most liquid, safe, and short forms of cash equivalents is a bank account that pays interest, such as an interest-bearing checking account or a savings account. Most people do not look at this form of account as an investment vehicle. They consider it a way of having ready access to smaller amounts of money for bill-paying purposes. Nevertheless, while funds (the balance) are sitting in the account, they are at least at work making a few dollars of interest. For the investor with a larger sum of discretionary funds that needs to be parked for a short period of time, a money market fund would be more apropos.

Money market funds are primarily mutual funds that invest in short-term debt securities (for example, Treasury bills and commercial paper). (We will discuss mutual funds and commercial paper further in this chapter.) An investor deposits his money into the fund and receives income in the form of interest. The amount of interest changes based on the types of securities used in the fund. The market value of the money invested into the fund does not change: principal is stagnant. Buying units in a money market mutual fund is similar to depositing money in a savings account. The investor puts money in, earns interest (that may vary), and withdraws his money (partially or totally) at any time.

Commercial Paper

Commercial paper is a corporate bond issued in a very large denomination (usually $100,000 minimum) with a short maturity (usually 30 to 270 days). This "paper" is generally issued at a discount and paid at par upon maturity. Commercial paper is primarily sold to institutional investors that have large funds available to invest for a short period. At times, a trust department, as an institution, will purchase commercial paper and use this investment instrument for larger accounts, or the department will split the instrument into smaller denominations for use by several smaller accounts.

Negotiable Certificates of Deposit

Most banks offer CDs (certificates of deposit). Many larger commercial banks issue negotiable CDs, commonly known as "jumbo" CDs. The minimum denomination is $100,000, but these CDs typically trade in denominations of $1 million or more. *Negotiable* usually means the maturity date and rate of return (interest rate) are negotiated (compromised) by the investor (saver) and the bank. Investors are not limited to individuals. In fact, somewhat like commercial paper, most negotiable CDs are purchased by institutional investors, and like stocks the CDs may be traded in the secondary market.

Anticipation Notes

A variation of corporate bonds is commercial paper. Variations of munis are **municipal (anticipation) notes.** These are short-term debt, usually with maturities less than one year. Because of their large minimum purchase denomination (say, $50,000), primarily institutional investors purchase these notes. Why are they called *anticipation* notes? The issuer borrows money from investors for a short period of time in anticipation of upcoming tax collections (TAN: tax anticipation note), project revenue (RAN: revenue anticipation note), and sale of a new bond issue (BAN: bond anticipation note).

Eurodollar Instruments

Eurodollar instruments are U.S. dollar-denominated securities traded on the international market. The three main types of Eurodollar instruments are Eurodollar certificates of deposit, Eurocommercial paper, and Eurobonds—all foreign equivalents of comparable U.S. instruments. Historically, Eurodollar instruments began in Europe (particularly in Europe). Today, Eurodollars represent all international securities issued in a country (other than the resident country of the principal borrower) in a currency determined by international, rather than domestic, financial considerations.

Please note that the common practice of referring to Eurodollars as "euros" should be discontinued. A new currency, the **Euro,** has been adopted by most European countries. The Euro replaces national currencies of individual countries with a unified currency and banking practices. For example, France used the franc and Italy used the lira. Today both countries use the Euro.

Eurodollars are deposits in foreign banks or in foreign branches of U.S. banks. They are denominated in U.S. dollars rather than the currency of the foreign country in which they are deposited. Eurodollar deposits may be either demand deposits (money available any time the investor demands it) or time deposits (subject to a specific maturity date). They serve as a source of funds for U.S. banks with foreign operations and as a high-quality, short-term, liquid investment for U.S. corporations. Eurodollar deposits most often offer higher yields than comparable deposits in the U.S. because they are less restricted by government regulations. (This yield may be eroded by foreign exchange rates.) Money for Eurodollar investment is made available to the banks by individual investors who participate in these investments.

Repurchase Agreements

Repurchase agreements ("repos") were invented after World War II by government securities dealers as a substitute for obtaining short-term bank loans to finance their securities inventories. Today repos are used by corporate equity underwriters, securities dealers, banks, and corporations as a way to obtain short-term loans.

Basically, under a **repurchase agreement,** a seller (for example, a dealer) sells securities to a buyer (for example, a bank) and agrees to repurchase the securities at an agreed-upon price on a future date, often one day later. This arrangement allows the seller to obtain short-term financing for its operations. On the maturity date the seller of the repo will use the cash received to repurchase the securities.

The buyer and seller agree upon the selling and repurchase price as well as the interest rate. The buyer earns interest on the repo and gains the advantage of having its loan collateralized by the securities, thereby protecting its interests from default. As is the case with Eurodollars, the money lent by the buyer is made up of funds from individual investors who participate in the investment.

Bankers Acceptances

A **bankers acceptance** is a form of money market instrument that is used to finance import and export business; it is used extensively in international trade. For example, assume an American business wishes to import a product from another country but wants to pay for the product several months later, after the business has had time to sell the product in the United States. The business could borrow money from its bank to pay for the product now, or it could use the bankers acceptance market.

If it uses the bankers acceptance market, the business has its bank prepare a **letter of credit,** a formal quasi-loan arrangement in which the bank says the business (the importer) is good for the money. The letter of credit is sent to the exporter in the country from which the goods are coming. Once the exporter ships the product, it brings the letter of credit to its bank, which, in turn, buys the letter of credit from the exporting company. The letter of credit is bought at a discount because the American bank will not make payment until some specified time in the future. The American bank, the importer's bank, guarantees payment on the **draft—bill of exchange**—hence, the name *bankers acceptance.* The draft is a negotiable instrument that is backed by three things: the American importer's pledge to pay, the product being imported, and the guarantee of the accepting bank.

INVESTING WITH OTHERS

Dave got into the good habit of saving a few dollars from each paycheck. After several years he saved $5,000. His savings account at the local bank served him quite well, but Dave needed to expand his investment horizon. He decided to put half or more of his savings in longer-term investments.

Dave thought about placing $4,000 of his savings into something more exotic than a simple savings account. Dave's problem is that he's a small investor. What can he do with $4,000? The commissions incurred to buy stocks are too high, bonds are usually bought in much larger chunks, not much real estate can be bought with a few thousand dollars, and U.S. savings bonds and certificates of deposit aren't attractive to him. An individual investor such as Dave cannot diversify much with $4,000.

Dave and his neighbor Ron were talking over the backyard fence one day, and Ron sympathized with Dave's dilemma. Ron was facing the same concerns. Dave and

Ron wondered whether they could invest more efficiently and effectively if they combined their dollars. It still wasn't enough. What if they arranged for the whole neighborhood to pool its money? What if they all invested their money together? They decided to sleep on their wild idea.

Two weeks later Dave and Ron were visiting with friends and the subject of investments came up again. One friend asked Dave and Ron whether they ever considered investing their money in a mutual fund. "I have heard of them," Dave replied, "but I don't really understand what they are." The friend explained that a mutual fund is simply a way for many individuals to invest their small amounts of money together. "Hey, a little like our crazy idea of getting the whole neighborhood to pool its money," was Ron's reply. The idea isn't crazy because this is what the mutual fund business is about—for over 60 million people.

Because of the complexity, magnitude, and size of securities issues, it is often difficult for an individual investor to purchase individual securities. The amount of money available may be too small to provide adequate asset allocation and diversification. Mutual funds and collective trust funds offer additional investment opportunities for individuals to pool their monies and reach their investment objectives.

The spectacular growth of funds investing hinges on the concept of "bringing Wall Street to Main Street." Today, individuals of all income strata have the ability to save and invest using professional money management that previously was available only to the wealthiest individuals. The rise of mutual funds has benefited investors in a number of ways. One important aspect is the diversity of holdings. Mutual funds enable investors to pool their money and spread their investments across a greater number of securities than they might be able to own as individuals. This diversification can help cushion investors from the ups and downs of the stock and bond markets. In addition, investors have the benefit of professional money managers

and analysts to evaluate companies and market conditions, a complicated effort that few individuals have the time or inclination to undertake.

Mutual Funds

Many investors think of **mutual funds** as a relatively new way of investing, but mutual funds began in 1924 when Massachusetts Financial Services, a Boston investment company, formed the Massachusetts Investors Trust mutual fund. In 1960 there were 161 mutual funds; by the turn of the century the number had grown to more than 12,000 funds totaling in excess of $2 trillion. In 1980 only 6 percent of households invested in mutual funds. Today, 50 percent of householders invest in mutual funds.

The Investment Company institute, the trade organization of the investment company industry, defines a mutual fund as follows:

A company that makes investments on behalf of individuals and institutions with similar financial goals. By pooling the financial resources of thousands of shareholders—each with a different amount to invest—investors gain access to the expertise of the country's top money managers and wide diversification of ownership in the securities market.

Investment companies are a broad class of entities that raise capital by selling the public shares in the company. This capital is then invested in securities in accordance with the specific objectives of the fund. Investment companies actively manage their portfolios, collections of securities, so as to realize a return for the benefit of shareholders. Depending on the type of securities the investment company invests in, that return could be in the form of dividends, interest, appreciation, or a combination of these things.

Mutual fund companies (as well as brokerage firms, insurance companies, and now the banking industry) provide mutual funds that pool, or combine, investors' money. An individual investment professional dedicated to the fund invests the combined funds in specific assets. What Dave and Ron want to accomplish will determine what type of fund they invest in. If Dave wants to invest in the stock market, he can place his small amount of money into a stock fund along with thousands of other small investors with the same objective. If Ron is interested in municipal bonds, there are funds that specialize in them. It doesn't take much before many people are investing in a fund worth millions of dollars.

Some of the more familiar investment company names are Fidelity, Dreyfus, Merrill Lynch, Putnam, and Vanguard. Each institution may have families of funds, with each family having a varying number of individual funds. For example, Fidelity has five separate families representing 150 different individual funds collectively managing over $200 billion. With the relaxation of securities regulations in recent years, the banking industry is now heavily involved in the mutual fund industry, and its presence has been dramatic.

A mutual fund is actually a type of investment company. Let's work our way into a more accurate definition of a mutual fund by looking at the types of investment companies:

- *Face Amount Certificate Company.* A face amount certificate company issues a certificate that is a contract between an investor and an issuer. The issuer guarantees a payment of a stated sum to the investor at a pre-determined date. The investor's investment is made either as a lump sum or in periodic installments. If the investor opts for a lump sum certificate, the investment is known as a fully paid face amount certificate. Specific assets—such as U.S. government issues, government agency mortgages, corporate debt, or preferred stock—may back the face amount certificate. Usually,

bonds back the certificate. When the bonds mature, the certificate matures. Principal and interest are guaranteed.

- *Unit Investment Trust (UIT).* A unit investment trust functions basically as a holding company for its investors. The managers of a UIT typically purchase an investment portfolio consisting of other investment company shares or of fixed income shares. Each share (unit) represents ownership of an interest in the underlying securities of the portfolio. Because UITs are not managed, once any of the securities in the portfolio are sold, become mature, or are liquidated, the proceeds must be distributed. UITs are organized without a board of directors or an investment advisor. The portfolio is not actively managed, meaning the investment returns are not reinvested and securities are not traded. A UIT may be fixed or nonfixed. A fixed UIT purchases a portfolio of bonds, and the trust terminates when the bonds mature. A nonfixed UIT purchases shares of an underlying mutual fund.

- *Management Company.* This is the type of investment company that most people are familiar with. It is commonly known as a mutual fund. Two general types of management companies exist:
  - ▲ Closed-end investment management company. A closed-end investment management company (**closed-end fund**) generally raises all of its base capital—conducts a stock offering—at one time, when the company is founded. A fixed number of shares is issued, and ownership is indicated by a stock certificate. The shares are publicly traded in the secondary market like any other corporate equity securities, and the laws of sup-

ply and demand determine their value. The bid price (the price at which an investor can sell) and the ask price (the price at which an investor can buy) for the shares are published daily in the financial sections of most major newspapers.

▲ Open-end investment management company. An open-end investment management company (**open-end fund**) constantly offers new shares (or units) and redeems shares. Unlike a closed-end fund, capital is not limited since the fund continuously accepts new money; capital increases. When funds are redeemed (sold back to the fund by investors), capital shrinks. The constant buying and selling means the fund never closes—therefore the name open-end. The price for each **unit** (or share) is called the **unit value.** The number of units owned by each investor, and the value of a unit, is based on the amount of money put into the fund and the value of the fund in relationship to the number of units.

A simple example will help. Assume that an open-end fund was funded with $1 million from 10 investors who invested $100,000 each. Assume also that the fund establishes one million units, therefore setting a value of $1 per unit. The unit value is $1. The per-unit value is commonly called the **net asset value (NAV).** Each investor in this example owns 100,000 units. If the fund increases to $1.5 million, and if no additional investors enter the fund (and the current investors do not add additional money), the unit value increases to $1.50

($1,500,000 fund value divided by one million units). Of course, a unit can decrease in value if the fund's total value decreases (depreciates). The math becomes more complicated when additional money comes into the fund from existing and new investors, when money is removed from the fund (a **redemption**), and when the value of the total fund changes. The NAV is calculated daily, and, depending on the size and interest in the fund, it is published daily in the *Wall Street Journal* and the financial section of other newspapers.

With respect to the purchase and redemption of units, an attractive feature of mutual funds is the ease and speed of depositing money into a fund and retrieving money from it. This is called **liquidity.** Liquidity is an expression of how fast an asset can be converted to cash. Withdrawing money from a savings or checking account or redeeming money from a mutual fund happens faster than converting the family station wagon into cash.

Don't confuse liquidity with gains and losses. It is easy to think that an asset is less liquid if a loss occurs in the process of converting to cash. No, this is simply a loss. Liquidity is solely a measure of how fast something can be converted to cash, regardless of whether more or less money is received for an asset compared to its purchase price.

A mutual fund buys specific securities, but an investor's money does not own the specific securities. An investor buys a number of units (a percent interest in the fund). The shares increase or decrease in value depending on the fund's overall performance and whether dividends or interest is paid, depending on the type of fund. Periodic statements from the fund and listings in the financial section of the newspaper show what units (shares) are worth.

Organization and Operation
of a Mutual Fund

All management companies (mutual funds) are organized and operated under the same rules. All mutual funds have a board of directors, an investment adviser, a securities custodian, a transfer agent, and an underwriter.

- *Board of Directors.* The shareholders of a mutual fund elect a board of directors who makes decisions and oversees investment objectives, fund strategy, portfolio funding, cash flow matters, accounting, and business administrative duties. The board does not manage the fund's portfolio with respect to investment decision making. The shareholders approve the election of the fund's board members, as well as any additions or replacements to the board. The Investment Company Act of 1940 (discussed in Chapter 12) restricts who is eligible to sit on the board. At least 40 percent of the directors must be independent (or *non-interested persons*). This means that no more than 60 percent of the board members may be interested persons: attorneys on retainer, accountants, and any other persons employed in similar capacities by the company. For example, if a fund has 10 directors, at least four of the directors cannot hold another position within the fund.

- *Investment Advisor.* The board is responsible for hiring an independent investment adviser (portfolio manager). The investment adviser may be an individual or an investment advisory company. The adviser is responsible for investing the fund's cash and securities by implementing an investment strategy according to the objectives stated in the fund's prospectus and for managing the day-to-day trading of the portfolio. The portfolio manager is bound by a written contract with the investment company.

- *Securities Custodian.* The Investment Company Act of 1940 requires each investment company to place its securities in the custody of a bank or with a stock exchange member firm. The custodian performs the important role of safekeeping the company's securities and cash, and it receives a fee for its services (which is paid from the net assets of the fund). If permitted, the custodian may deposit the securities in a depository approved by the National Association of Securities Dealers or the New York Stock Exchange. A depository makes it easier to transfer securities via book entry rather than physical delivery of the securities. The custodian is responsible for keeping the investment company's assets physically segregated from other assets; allowing withdrawal of securities only in accordance with the Securities and Exchange Commission (SEC) rules; and restricting access to the account to certain officers and employees of the investment company, authorized SEC employees, and independent public accountants who are required to verify the account's securities at least three times per year.

- *Transfer Agent.* The transfer agent (discussed in Chapter 11) is responsible for issuing and redeeming fund units, delivering customer confirmations, and remitting fund distributions. The transfer agent can be the fund's custodian or a separate provider. The fund pays the transfer agent's fee.

- *Underwriter.* The underwriter (the sponsor or distributor) markets fund shares, prepares sales literature, and receives a percentage of the sales charge paid by customers. In essence, the underwriter is the salesperson for the investment company. The underwriter of the mutual fund must be a separate and distinct entity from the mutual fund. The open-end investment company sells its shares to the underwriter at the current NAV, but only as the underwriter needs the shares to fill customer orders. The underwriter is prohibited from maintaining an inventory in open-end company shares. The underwriter is compensated by adding a sales charge to the share's NAV when sales are made to the public.

Mutual Fund Fees

Mutual fund fees (fees are called **load**) depend on the investment company and the nature of the fund. Open-end funds are categorized as **no-load funds** or **load funds.** A no-load fund is one in which no commissions or administrative expenses are paid by the investor. A load fund will incur commissions and/or administrative expenses that are paid to the fund's sales representative (underwriter) or the fund itself. Load funds come in three varieties:

1. A *front-end load fund* charges the investor a fee at the time of purchase. For example, if a front-end fund charges a 3 percent load, an investor with a $10,000 purchase will be charged $300 (3 percent of $10,000), leaving an investment of $9,700.
2. A *back-end load fund* (*read-end load fund*) charges a fee, sometimes called a "contingent deferred sales charge" or "redemption fee," when the investor makes a partial or total redemption.
3. A *level-load fund* will assess charges on an annual basis. Examples of these fees include
   ▲ Annual expense or management fees that cover the annual expenses of the fund's investment advisory staff

   ▲ 12B-1 fees (named after an SEC regulation) charged for registering the fund and for marketing and distribution services
   ▲ Reinvestment fees charged for the fund's reinvestment of bond interest or stock dividends
   ▲ Brokerage fees that pay the broker or advisor who sold the customer into the fund; this fee is commonly paid to financial planners
   ▲ Withdrawal and transfer fees charged to withdraw money from one fund and transfer it to another
   ▲ General operating fees for expenses of the fund, such as the cost of producing statements, keeping records, supporting a toll-free phone account, and maintaining a website
   ▲ Service (maintenance) fees for bookkeeping, asset custody, auditing, legal, and other expenses

Fees must be disclosed to prospective investors in the fund's prospectus. A **prospectus** is an informational document, required by law, that discloses the following details about the fund:

- Investment objective
- Date of inception
- Types of securities
- Size
- Past performance
- Redemption rights
- Management fees, sales charges, and annual expenses
- Minimum investment amounts (initially and subsequently)

If a fund's formal prospectus is not available, a quick guide to costs, investment objectives, and performance is the *Wall Street Journal's* quarterly mutual fund report, which is included in a daily issue within the first week of each calendar quarter. In addition to general investment articles, the report shows each fund's minimum initial and subsequent investment amounts, size, sales charges, annual expenses, performance, and investment objectives. (This report is an abbreviated synopsis, and it is not meant to be a substitute for a fund's formal prospectus.)

Classes of Mutual Funds

Mutual funds are categorized further by fund objectives. Each fund is designed to accomplish an investment objective. Name the investment, and a mutual fund can be found to accommodate the investment objectives. The majority of funds fall into five investment objective categories:

- In *money market funds,* investors deposit their money and receive income in the form of interest. (Recall the discussion earlier about money market cash equivalents.) The amount of interest changes based on the securities owned by the fund. The unit (market) value does not change. This type of fund invests primarily in short-term debt securities.

- *Equity funds* are investments in a fund concentrated mainly in stocks. Equity funds vary by the type of stock purchased in the fund. One fund may invest in common stock of blue-chip companies, and another may invest in speculative issues. Other equity funds concentrate on growth stocks, value stocks, income stocks, preferred stocks, small cap companies, and international equities.

- *Bond funds* invest in debt instruments, and the funds vary based on the type of bonds purchased: corporate, municipal, and government bonds. Bond funds also vary depending on the maturity ranges and bond ratings of the bonds bought in the fund.

- *Balanced funds* balance their investments among stocks, bonds, and cash. The funds' objectives determine the asset allocation and diversification.

- *Specialized funds* exist in many variations. The manager of the fund generally buys only a particular type of securities. Examples of specialized funds are stocks of a particular industry sector or geographical area, real estate, foreign investments, and commodities such as gold, wheat, or cattle.

The convenience and diversity of mutual funds have made this investment vehicle extremely popular with individual investors who because of limited funds could not otherwise participate in the securities market. The ability to spread a smaller amount of investment dollars over a wider choice of investments has given the public broader investment choices both with individual investment endeavors and within company-sponsored retirement plans such as 401(k) plans.

Bank Funds

Banks had been in the mutual fund business since its inception in the mid-1920s, but their role changed dramatically with the enactment of several securities laws in the 1930s. At that time, banks were banned from issuing and underwriting securities, including mutual funds. Fortunately, changes in the securities laws allowed banks to continue limited participation in funds' investing. The SEC permitted banks to manage funds, as long as their funds were not offered to the general investing public. In addition, bank funds could not be publicly promoted and advertised. This brought about the development of bank common trust funds; and, with the advent of current legislation, the development of bank mutual funds.

Common Trust Funds

Basically, **common trust funds** are in-house, private-label funds, so to speak. Also called **commingled funds, personal investment funds** and **collective investment funds,** these funds consist of money from many different fiduciary accounts pooled together to buy securities for the accounts managed by a bank trust organization. Usually the accounts that participate in common trust funds are smaller individual trusts, executor accounts, and guardianship accounts. Dave, Ron, and their friends cannot walk in off the street and deposit their money in common trust funds. As trust customers they can. The purpose of these funds—as with mutual funds—is to spread the risk of investing. And, the trust department benefits from being able to manage several large collective funds rather than numerous small trust accounts.

The collective funds of personal accounts and employee benefit accounts are kept separate because of the taxation involved. In many institutions, common trust funds used for employee benefit plans are labeled **pooled funds.**

A typical variety of common trust funds found in a trust department may be as follows:

- Growth equity fund
- Special equity fund (companies with smaller capitalization)
- International equity fund
- Indexed equity fund (benchmarked to the S&P 500)
- Taxable bond fund
- Intermediate taxable bond fund (shorter maturities)
- Tax-exempt bond fund
- Intermediate tax-exempt bond fund (shorter maturities)
- International bond fund
- Balanced asset allocation fund (balance of stocks and bonds)
- Short-term tax-exempt reserve fund (municipal money market funds)
- Short-term taxable reserve fund (corporate and U.S. government money market funds)

Common trust funds and mutual funds are comparable, although common trust funds may not possess the size, diversity, and number of different types of funds that an investment company has. Common trust funds operate like mutual funds, with a few differences:

- In most cases common trust funds assess a fee based solely on market value and are usually charged at the individual account level; there are no front-end or back-end loads or the numerous additional fees discussed above.

- Only certain investors—those who maintain a fiduciary relationship— may participate in trust department collective funds.

- Common trust funds are not governed by SEC regulation as mutual funds are; they are, though, subject to the regulations of the Office of the Comptroller of the Currency.

- Purchases and redemptions from a mutual fund can occur daily; many common trust funds offer purchases and sales less frequently (for example, weekly, semi-monthly, or monthly).

- Mutual funds and common trust funds are managed by an individual investment manager who chooses the securities in the fund; an added advantage of a common trust fund arrangement is that a trust department customer also has an individual portfolio manager assigned to the individual account.

Many investors look at these similarities and differences and conclude that mutual funds have an advantage over common trust funds. Bank trust departments have never denied these advantages. However, recent legislation has permitted banks to expand their investment services by using mutual funds for fiduciary accounts, agency customers, and retail banking customers who can benefit from the availability and diversification of mutual funds. This expansion into the mutual fund arena has reduced the number of trust organizations that maintain in-house common trust funds.

Bank Mutual Funds

Although banks could not legally distribute (underwrite), sponsor, organize, distribute, or control a mutual fund, individual regulatory approvals and interpretations of the laws enabled banks to engage in such activities as providing agency services (investment management, custody, transfer agent, fund accounting) to mutual funds and providing access to mutual funds for their customers. These activities and affiliations gave banking institutions a proprietary link with mutual funds.

During the past 20 years the banking industry worked diligently to alter the laws that kept banks from competing with other financial institutions and services. Some banks purchased existing mutual funds (for example, Mellon Bank purchased Dreyfus), and some entered into joint ventures to sell funds of a particular investment company (for example, NationsBank's agreement to sell Dean Witter funds exclusively).

Eventually, as a result of these activities, the Financial Services Modernization Act was signed into law in 1999. The law repealed many provisions of the Glass-Steagall Act of 1933, dismantling the walls that separate banking, insurance, and securities activities, thereby permitting banks to re-enter the mutual fund business. Banks have established new funds, converted existing common trust funds to newly established funds, and have rolled common trust fund assets into existing mutual funds. Banks' presence in the mutual fund industry has been dramatic. Bank One, as an example, created a mutual fund complex of 48 funds totaling $95 billion under one investment roof. Bank One's funds are the third largest bank-sponsored fund family and the seventeenth largest fund family overall in the mutual fund industry.

Since entering the mutual fund business, banks have provided important benefits to themselves and their customers:

- Unlike common trust funds, mutual funds are portable; the funds may be transferable to another trust account at the same or a different institution or to the customer directly, if the situation warrants.

- Although trust organizations provide complete disclosure of common trust funds to customers, mutual funds provide the added safeguard of disclosure under applicable securities laws.

- Trust institutions can eliminate some of the duplicative administrative and operational costs associated with offering common trust funds to fiduciary customers and mutual fund investment products to agency customers.

- Trust institutions and customers are provided with guidance from the Federal Reserve Board, the Office of the Comptroller of the Currency, the Internal Revenue Code, and applicable state laws.

SUMMARY

- The world of investments today is more complicated and diverse than it was yesterday. The investor of years ago used extra money to invest in a limited number of stocks and bonds. Today, the number of investment vehicles and their variations and combinations makes it difficult for the average investor to choose among the alternatives. Equity represents the percentage ownership of an asset. Equity can be measured and calculated using compound interest and present value calculations.

- Stocks are an investor's equity (ownership) in a company. Stocks are classified as common and preferred: authorized, outstanding, issued, treasury, or retired. Stocks are characterized as blue chip, speculative, growth, income, or defensive. Stock market performance is measured by various indices; the two most common are the S&P Index and the DJIA.

- Bonds are fixed-income debt securities. Bonds are distinguished by principal purchase, maturity, interest payment, callability, safety, and collateral. Bonds are issued by corporations, the U.S. government, and municipalities.

- Cash equivalents are securities that are easily and quickly converted to cash. Cash equivalent securities are money market funds, commercial paper, negotiable certificates of deposit, anticipation notes, Eurodollar instruments, repurchase agreements, and bankers acceptances.

- For the smaller investor, trust department common trust funds and mutual funds offer investment opportunities once available only to larger investors. Although collective investment funds have made investing simpler, investors still need to understand the nature of fund investing, the investment objectives of the various funds, the costs associated, and the nature of investing in funds versus individual securities.

REVIEW QUESTIONS

1. What is the difference between equity and debt? Give three examples.
2. How are stocks classified and what are some of the major characteristics of stocks?
3. How is the performance of the stock market measured?
4. What is the difference in federal and state taxation with respect to government bonds, corporate bonds, and municipal bonds?
5. Why are mutual funds attractive to small investors?

3

AGENCIES

"O world, world! Thus is the poor agent despised. O traitors and bawds, how earnestly are you set a-work, and how ill requited! Why should our endeavour be so loved, and the performance so loathed?"

William Shakespeare (1564–1616)

Each day we buy various products and services. Lunch at a local restaurant, a new pair of shoes, a refrigerator, and a second car are products. The person who cuts your hair, the one who cleans your house, and the lawyer who writes your will are performing services. Products are tangible, and they are bought *from* someone. Services may be tangible or intangible, and they are provided *by* someone. Although products and services cost money, that which is given in return differs. The purchase of a product is a buy–sell relationship. The purchase of a service denotes an agency relationship.

The word *agency* brings to mind such things as an employment agency, an insurance agency, or a talent agency. But in these pages we will not specifically discuss the place where products and services are bought; we will address a *type* of business conduct and what services are provided.

As a practical matter, an agency has elements of both a service and a place of business. Just as an insurance agency provides financial services and sells insurance products, an investment agency provides investment services and also buys and sells investment products for its customers. It's important to keep this dual nature in mind.

LEARNING OBJECTIVES

A bank trust department can function as an agency—a place that buys and sells investment products that are integral to the bank's profitability and provides investment services that are integral to its customers' financial well-being.

Upon completion of this chapter, you will be able to

- Describe an agency relationship
- Explain the forms of agencies and their features
- Profile an investment program
- Explain the attributes of a good investment management agent
- Define and use the terms that appear in bold in the text

61

AGENCY

An **agency** is an account relationship between two parties: a **principal** and an **agent.** Title to and ownership of the property, which constitutes the agency, remains with the principal. The agent acts on behalf of the principal and is charged with certain duties with respect to the property. Let's break this definition apart.

Principal

The principal is the customer, the person who hires another to do something. Loosely defined, when you employ someone to clean your house, fill a cavity, or shovel the snow from your front walk, you (the principal) hire another (the agent) to provide a service.

Agent

The agent is the one who provides the service. The agent can be an individual (the cleaning person, the dentist, the snow shoveler) or an institution such as a bank. In this chapter we will focus on the agency services provided by trust departments. As you become more familiar with these services, you will recognize that the agencies offered by trust departments can also be provided by individuals and other financial institutions. We will address the important factors that determine which agent is the better choice and discuss how bank personnel can inform customers about this choice.

Title and Ownership

In Chapter 1 we briefly discussed the trust ownership of property and how the legal title to the property transfers to the trustee and the equitable (beneficial) title remains with the beneficiary. In an agency relationship, all title and ownership—legal and equitable—remains with the principal; it does not transfer to the agent. When an agency involves a service pertaining to property, such as the management of a client's investment portfolio, the title and ownership of the portfolio's securities (assets) remain with the customer, the principal.

Charged with Certain Duties

An agent is responsible for specific duties that the principal empowers the agent to perform. In addition to the expressed, sometimes written, instructions are implied, unwritten obligations on the part of the agent. These duties and responsibilities are to

- Exercise skill in the assignment
- Adhere to the law when applicable
- Act in good faith
- Obey the principal's orders, as long as they are not illegal

Property

An agent's duties may consist solely of providing a service. In most instances, the agent's duties pertain to services with respect to property, such as stocks, bonds, and cash contained in the account. The type of agency account determines the agent's level of duties and responsibilities.

Beyond the Definition of Agency

Agreement

It is beyond the scope of this text to discuss the legal implications of and the differences between an agreement and a contract, but trust officers need to know some basic information about them. Although an agreement between a principal and an agent may be oral, it is always best (especially in the trust business) to have it in writing. This agreement is a contract. Some institutions call the contract a letter of instructions or an agency agreement. Sometimes only a fine line distinguishes an **agreement** from a **contract.** An agreement is simply a mutual understanding or arrangement between two or more individuals or institutions. When written, an agreement becomes a legally binding contract and is enforceable by law. All contracts are agreements, but agreements are not necessarily contracts. It is doubtful that the arrangement for the service provided by the cleaning person is in writing, yet it is an agreement. When the responsibilities increase and involve greater risk to property, the agreement may be defined in writing as a contract.

In the life insurance industry, for example, life insurance policies are contracts between the insurance company and the policyowner. The insurance company (as agent) and the policyowner (as principal) have certain contractual obligations to uphold. The policyowner is required not to present any falsehoods in the application for the insurance and is required to make the premium payments. The insurance company is required to uphold the insurance policy's terms and to pay a death benefit. The contractual relationship in a trust department's agency accounts is quite similar.

Let's look at the respective duties and obligations of the principal and agent by exploring some wording of one trust institution's investment management contract.

I appoint you as my agent and ask that you maintain an investment management account in the name of _____ to hold monies, stocks, bonds, and other property deposited with and accepted by you as agent, subject to the terms of this agreement. I certify under penalty of perjury that the Social Security/Tax Identification Number provided is true, correct, and complete.

I specifically authorize you to invest funds selected by you. . . . You shall collect income. . . . You will provide periodic statements. . . . You shall receive compensation for services rendered. . . . You need not send me any individual confirmations of trade unless I specifically request such. I acknowledge that you have furnished me with a statement of fees. . . . You are authorized. . . . You shall not be liable. . . . This agreement may be amended at any time as agreed by us in writing and

may be terminated in writing at any time by me or by you. . . . You shall send. . . . I reserve the right.

The words *I, me,* and *you* are key aspects of this contract. Interestingly, if you read the full four-page account agreement, the word *you* (the agent) is most prevalent. The investment agreement takes on a unilateral angle that favors the principal. This means that the agent is the one charged with most of the obligations, because it is the principal who is paying a fee for the agent's services.

Termination

Either side can call it quits. If the customer does not like the arrangement, the customer can terminate the relationship. The agent can also terminate the relationship with proper notice.

Death

Agency accounts also terminate at the death of the principal or agent. What if the agent is an institution? Can institutions die? In effect, they die when they go out of business; this would terminate the relationship. If the agent is a bank, does the agency relationship end if the bank merges with another bank or is bought by another bank? Technically, the agency relationship ends unless specific arrangements are made for the resulting or purchasing bank to continue the service. If the agent is an individual, the relationship ends upon that individual's death.

Incapacitation

The disability (incapacitation) of either the principal or the agent also terminates the relationship. This will become clearer after you understand the guardianship concepts in Chapter 6.

Joint Tenancy

What if the principal is joint in nature? What if the title (the names) on the account is *John and Mary Doe, as joint tenants?* In Chapter 1 we learned that joint tenancy assets automatically vest in the surviving tenant upon the death of the first. Does the death of John Doe terminate the relationship? One side of the coin says the agency relationship terminates now that the form of ownership converted from joint tenancy ownership to sole ownership. The other side of the coin says the agency relationship doesn't end because the surviving joint tenant did originally enter into the agreement. When in doubt, ask the surviving tenant what her wishes are. If she wants the agency relationship to continue, have a new agreement executed by the surviving tenant to reflect the new ownership.

Many institutions have solved this dilemma by providing in the written agreement language stating that the relationship will continue with the surviving tenant(s) as the principal, absent the tenant's directions otherwise.

Accounting

A checking account statement shows an opening balance, deposits, checks written, electronic funds transfers, interest earned (if it is that type of account), service charges, and a closing balance—an **accounting** of activity. The type of agency account dictates the nature of its accounting—a **statement** of activity. A simple safekeeping account may be a one-page report showing what is in the account plus additions and withdrawals. More detailed statements accompany escrow, custody, and investment management agencies because of their more detailed duties.

Depending on a customer's needs, statements may be monthly or quarterly. Statements may be present in separate formats to reflect certain levels of activity within the account, or they may be prepared in a combined form. For example, one statement format may be a capital statement—a statement of property held—which is a snapshot showing what a customer owns at a given time. Securities are listed by name and description, acquisition cost, present market value of each share or unit, an estimate of the annual income of each asset, and the rate of return or earnings of each asset. Another type of statement is a transaction statement—an activity statement—which records what has transpired in the account over the past month or quarter. The transaction statement, like a diary, shows the past period's day-by-day activities: buys, sells, dividend payments, interest income, deposits, withdrawals, fees, and commissions.

TYPES OF AGENCIES

The primary types of trust agencies are safekeeping, custody, escrow, and investment management. Although the focus in this chapter is on agency services used by individuals, we will see how agency services are used by nonpersons (retirement plans and corporations, where the principal is not an individual) in Chapters 10 and 11.

Safekeeping

A **safekeeping account** is the simplest, bare-bones agency relationship. It is built on the concept of "take it in, hold it, give it back."

Take It In

A trust department, acting as a safekeeping agent, may be asked to "receive and receipt" a customer's assets merely for the sake of holding onto them safely. The trust department may physically keep the property on its premises or arrange for its safekeeping elsewhere. Think of your personal **safe deposit box** in the vault in the basement of your bank as an example. Many trust departments maintain separate safekeeping quarters for their customers' assets. The assets might be physical stock and bond certificates, deeds to real estate, or important business and investment papers. Trust departments also provide safekeeping for original will and trust documents. You may also see jewelry, stamp and coin collections, and cash.

Hold It

This is the main activity of a safekeeping account—the core duty and responsibility. Once the agent receives the assets (either at the agent's place of business or elsewhere), the job truly begins. The agent must maintain the assets in the condition they were received. The property must be safekept from loss, mutilation, destruction, and theft. If something happens to the property, the agent must replace it or reimburse the principal for its value if it cannot be replaced.

Imagine a friend asks you to hold onto a valuable painting. Suppose you place it in what you assume is a safe place in the basement of your house. Bugs, mildew, or a leaking pipe could destroy the painting. Who would be responsible for resulting damage? You would! If you cannot return the painting in the condition it was received, you must replace it or provide monetary replacement.

However, if a natural event, such as an earthquake, caused the painting to fall off the shelf and become ruined, as agent you would not be responsible. Most natural disasters are not within an agent's control, so the agent is not responsible for destruction of the property.

Give It Back

When the principal requests the return of the property, the agent must comply. The agent's task ends when the property is returned. If only a portion of the property is requested and returned, the agent's job with respect to that portion is over, although she continues to be responsible for the property that remains in her safekeeping. Also, a safekeeping agent is responsible not only for returning the same property and in the same form, but also to the same person.

Custody

A **custody account** (also called a custodial account, securities administration, or asset/securities custody) is more aptly called a financial secretary. Now the agent is charged with additional adminis-trative duties related to the property. Not only is the agent charged with the job of security guard (safekeeper), but he also is a bookkeeper and a facilitator of purchases and sales.

What does a custodial agent not do? Make investment decisions, give advice, and take responsibility for the investment's performance. These tasks remain with the principal. Many active investors enjoy making investment decisions. What they want is relief from the paper shuffling and busywork associated with administering their portfolios.

Another way of looking at this is to compare a lieutenant to a private. The lieutenant (the principal) makes the decisions, yet he gives orders for the private (the agent) to carry them out. When the customer calls and directs the agent to carry out an order, the agent "stands at attention" and carries out the customer's direction with respect to his securities. If the customer directs the agent to sell ABC stock and buy XYZ stock, the agent is obligated to do so. However, if the customer asks the agent's opinion about the investment merit of the transaction, the agent will not comment. It is not part of the agent's duties to render investment advice.

A custody agent's duties include the following:

- Safekeeping of stocks and bonds from loss or theft
- Execution of purchases and sales according to the principal's instructions
- Issuance of itemized statements showing cash and securities transactions, including a list of current market values
- Daily **sweep** and investment of idle cash
- Collection of dividends and interest plus disbursement or reinvestment according to the principal's direction
- Collection of matured and called bonds
- Notification of securities changes such as defaults, tender offers, and

stock splits (see Chapter 11 pertaining to these terms)

- Receipt and delivery of securities according to the principal's directions
- Recordkeeping for tax purposes

The customer (principal) contracts with the bank as agent to carry out a list of duties with respect to the customer's property. Decisions of what to buy and sell remain with the principal; the administrative duties of carrying out the principal's decisions remain with the agent.

Escrow

Just as a custody agency has additional duties beyond those of a safekeeping agency, an escrow agency goes beyond custody. An **escrow account** is an agency relationship in which two or more persons (or nonpersons, such as corporations) place property (money or securities) with a third person (or institution), to be delivered in the future depending on a certain event or contingency.

The escrow account agreement dictates who the parties are, what is required of the principals, the responsibilities of the agent, and the period of time or the definite event that causes termination of the agreement. The agreement may also indicate whether the escrow agent will provide investment management of the property and, if it does, what investment vehicles the agent may use. The invest-

---

USING TRUST PRODUCTS AND SERVICES TO MEET CUSTOMER NEEDS

Marvin owned a lucrative specialty paint company. A large public corporation (one of Marvin's customers) made a $3-million bid to buy his company. Marvin asked for $3.5 million, and after a series of negotiations the potential buyer agreed to the price if Marvin would agree to something in return.

The buyer-to-be was concerned about Marvin's quality control practices over the years—specifically, that the company might have chemically polluted the plant's site. Although Marvin insisted that it had not, how else could he assure the purchaser? The buyer offered to pay Marvin $2 million in cash and set aside $1.5 million until its concerns were satisfied by environmental ground testing. The corporation said it would incur the testing cost and would not take more than 6 months to complete testing. If the results were negative, Marvin would get the $1.5 million in 6 months. If problems did surface, Marvin would get the $1.5 million minus costs (not to exceed the $1.5 million) incurred by the buyer to clean up any environmental destruction.

To allay Marvin's concerns about getting this money, he and the buyer entered into an agreement with a third party (an escrow agent) whereby the agent would hold onto the $1.5 million, taking the money out of the reach of both principals. The escrow agent would be charged with paying the total $1.5 million to Marvin at the end of 6 months or $1.5 million less costs if problems were found. The fee for the agent's services would be borne by the buying corporation, and any investment gains would go to the buyer.

The main responsibility of the escrow agent is to carry out the agreement's instructions, but not necessarily to exercise discretion. In this case, it would have been foolish for the $1.5 million to sit idle, when it could be earning interest. The escrow agent was given discretion to invest the funds, but was limited to Treasury bills of less than 6 months maturity.

ment management aspect is usually limited to bank instruments or government securities.

Many homeowners are subject to escrow arrangements with their mortgage lenders. Each month as the mortgage payment is made, a portion of the payment may include funds for the property's annual real estate taxes. The mortgage lender holds the money for the real estate taxes in an escrow account. Each year (or 6 months, depending on the locality) the mortgage lender makes the payment of the real estate taxes. The homeowner, as the principal in this relationship, agrees with the mortgage lender, as the agent, to hold the funds until the payment of the real estate taxes is due, which is the contingency part of the relationship.

Investment Management

Safekeeping provides one set of services. Custody provides the same and adds more responsibilities. Escrow takes on contingencies and possible investment management of the property in the account. Investment management goes a step further.

In today's busy world, there never seem to be enough hours to get everything done. More than ever before, we turn to others for products and services, finding that we do not have the time, the expertise, or the interest to do things ourselves.

For the person whose assets have grown, proper management of this wealth is integral to continued success. Without the knowledge, time, or interest in managing investments, we need help. The pinnacle of the agency services provided by trust departments is securities management.

Pick a term—*asset management, investment advisory, investment management* or *investment counsel, personal asset management, personal investment management service*—they all mean the same thing. An **investment management account** is an agency relationship in which the agent provides safekeeping and custody, plus the actual investment control, direction, decision making, advice, and responsibility for the property.

Before we dig deeper into the importance of investment management in trust departments, let's look at a typical trust department, as shown in Exhibits 3.1 and 3.2 to understand the magnitude of these services.

ABC Bank is a national bank located in a large metropolitan city in the Midwest.

Exhibit 3.1 ABC Bank and Trust Company Personal Trust Department Assets

Type of Account	Number of Accounts	Market Value	Percentage of Total Market Value
Revocable trust	408	$ 315,000,000	9.7%
Irrevocable trust	912	575,000,000	17.8%
IRA rollover	163	127,000,000	3.9%
Guardianship	302	293,000,000	9.1%
Estate	154	118,000,000	3.6%
Safekeeping	115	93,000,000	2.9%
Custody	377	615,000,000	19.0%
Escrow	77	115,000,000	3.6%
Investment management	679	984,000,000	30.4%
Total	3,187	$3,235,000,000	100.0%

Exhibit 3.2 ABC Bank and Trust Company Discretionary Assets Account Profile

Asset Range	Number of Accounts	Percentage of Accounts	Percentage of Assets	Total Assets
Under $500,000	1,740	66.5%	18.6%	$448,900,000
$500,000–$1 million	437	16.7%	22.0%	$530,700,000
$1–2 million	237	9.1%	21.5%	$519,200,000
$2–5 million	155	5.9%	21.2%	$511,200,000
$5–10 million	30	1.1%	7.9%	$190,100,000
Over $10 million	19	0.7%	8.8%	$211,900,000
Total	2,618	100.0%	100.0%	$2,412,000,000

ABC serves personal and commercial banking customers. It does not provide international banking services or have a credit card facility. The trust department provides corporate, employee benefit, land, and personal trust services.

Agency accounts (safekeeping, custody, escrow, and investment management) represent 39 percent of the trust department's business with respect to number of accounts, and 56 percent of total market value. What is notable is that 75 percent of the assets in this trust department is discretionary, meaning the institution is directly responsible for the management and investment of the funds; safekeeping, escrow, and custody represent nondiscretionary assets. Additionally, nearly one-third of this department's assets are investment management agency accounts. Exhibit 3.2 breaks apart the account profiles of the discretionary funds.

Consider the bottom line of Exhibit 3.1: $3.2 billion is a tremendous amount of money! Obviously ABC Bank's trust department did not attract these dollars merely by hanging a trust and investment sign out front. ABC didn't build its large discretionary base by simply opening its doors. This bank trust department built its success and numbers by recognizing the elements of a meaningful investment pro-

gram, the qualities of a sound investment manager, and the value of proactive sales endeavors.

PROFILE OF AN INVESTMENT PROGRAM

Trust professionals must be equipped to help customers define investment strategies. Effective investment strategy is built on certain key ingredients: allocation, diversification, activity, and level of control. Although the importance of each ingredient varies slightly from one individual to another (that is, from one portfolio to another), these elements are common in achieving an investor's goals. Our added task is to help customers recognize these factors and balance their significance.

Asset Allocation

Determining what percentages of a portfolio should be allocated to various investment vehicles is called **asset allocation.** Various models accomplish this; Exhibit 3.3 is one example.

Let us assume that Joan Investor inherited $700,000 from a relative. Unfamiliar with the world of investments, Joan approaches your trust department (based on a referral from her attorney) for assistance. Let us also assume that Joan's goal

Exhibit 3.3 Determination of Asset Allocation

Years to Termination		Less than 5			More than 5		
Account Size		Under $200,000	$200,000 to $500,000	Over $500,000	Under $200,000	$200,000 to $500,000	Over $500,000
Ratio of account assets to total assets	Over 2/3	A	B	C	B	C	D
	1/3 to 2/3	B	C	D	C	D	E
	Under 1/3	C	D	E	D	E	E

Fixed Income % of Portfolio

	Conservative				Moderate				Aggressive			
A	100	95	90	85	80	75	70	65	60	55	50	45
B	95	90	85	80	75	70	65	60	55	50	45	40
C	85	80	75	70	65	60	55	50	45	40	35	30
D	75	70	65	60	55	50	45	40	35	30	25	20
E	70	65	60	55	50	45	40	35	30	25	20	15

is to invest this money for her retirement, about 15 years from now. The starting point of Exhibit 3.3 is to place Joan in the "More Than 5" segment in the row labeled "Years to Termination." Although termination is defined here as the date when Joan wants to retire, it is also used generically as the time when a desired investment goal is reached. Other examples are a date for the downpayment for a house or accumulation of college funds.

The next step is to place Joan in the "Over $500,000" column. Assuming that Joan's inheritance represents over two-thirds of her total assets, we will place her in category D. To determine Joan's risk tolerance, let's do a quick analysis that places her in either a conservative, moderate, or aggressive category.

The bottom half of Exhibit 3.3 is constructed to allow for gradations. Note that each category has four levels. For exam-

ple, if Joan indicates that she can live with moderate risk, yet she leans more toward conservatism, she could be safely placed in the first or second level of the moderate shading. If she chooses to follow line D of the exhibit, Joan should consider allocating 55 percent or 50 percent of her portfolio to fixed-income (bond) investments.

However, this is not a foolproof way to determine the asset allocation of Joan's portfolio. A concerned investment manager would need to determine how the non-fixed-income portion of the portfolio should be allocated. Does simple subtraction say that a 55 percent allocation to bonds means 45 percent should be allocated to stocks? Not necessarily. Consideration must be given to what percentage of the overall portfolio should be allocated to cash instruments (such as money markets or commercial paper). Equally important in an investment manager's activity is the need to alter the percentages as years pass. For example, will the 50 to 55 percent allocation to fixed-income investments meet Joan's income objectives in her retirement years? Although the model's calculations dictate a certain allocation formula today, later needs may necessitate a further restructuring of Joan's portfolio. Her trust professionals must be ready to help her make these decisions.

Diversification

Many investors equate asset allocation with **diversification.** To a certain extent the allocation of a portfolio among stocks, bonds, and cash is a form of diversification. More specifically, diversification addresses the mix of securities within a portfolio class: How should the stock, bond, and cash portions be further broken down? An investment manager must choose between common and preferred stock and growth and income stocks, and perform sector analyses. With respect to bonds, consideration should be given to corporate versus government versus municipal issues, ratings, and maturities. Academic studies show that one of the most important determinants of a portfolio's return over time is allocation and diversification. The discussion of the relationship of risk and return in Chapter 4 (supported by Exhibits 4.3 and 4.4) shows the impact of asset allocation on a portfolio's performance. A strong investment manager is equipped to play a critical role in these tactical decisions.

Active Management

Buying stocks and bonds and holding onto them forever is not investment management. It is buying and holding. Neither is a short-term, helter-skelter buy–sell program good investment management. This is **churning,** and it only creates transaction costs (commissions) for the manager, which can seriously affect returns. Bank trust departments typically are compensated as a percentage of assets managed,

not by transaction fees. As concerned investment managers, we must monitor our customers' portfolios on an ongoing basis to determine whether we are meeting their objectives and to determine whether the direction should change because of a change in objectives. In addition, finances, family circumstances, and the economy change. It is important for an investment manager to see beyond an investor's emotional ties to certain investments or reluctance to keep her investment program consistent with objectives and risk tolerance.

Discretionary Versus Nondiscretionary

If someone turns to a professional investment manager, what level of trust should he place in the manager? In most investment circles, a **discretionary account** (also known as a full-power account) is one in which the customer places full investment responsibility and decision making in the investment manager's hands, consistent with predetermined parameters (asset allocation, diversification, and activity). A **nondiscretionary account** (also known as a shared-power account) is one in which the investment agent is not free to make portfolio changes without the principal's approval.

Depending on the agreement (or contract) between the agent and the principal, the investment manager may be permitted limited discretion within certain boundaries in a nondiscretionary account. For example, the investment manager may be allowed to freely invest interest, dividends, and matured or called bonds in short-term investment vehicles. Another form of nondiscretionary accounts is one in which the investment agent recommends several investments and lets the principal decide which route to take.

Statistically, in most investment management institutions, discretionary accounts perform slightly better than nondiscretionary accounts. If an investment manager cannot contact a nondiscretionary account customer, she may lose an investment opportunity. Nondiscretionary accounts require an investment manager to stay on top of matters for her customers—the way things should be with any effective investment manager regardless of the account's size or the manager's level of discretion.

Careful language must be used to distinguish a discretionary (full-power) investment management account from a nondiscretionary (shared-power) account. Language in the investment account contract may look like the following sample:

Discretionary

This is a discretionary account. Therefore, you will regularly review the holdings in the account and may, without prior approval, invest and reinvest the holdings in the account and determine what property is to be purchased, sold, or exchanged and what portion of the property is to be held in cash, as you determine to be in my best interest. You may perform any other actions necessary to facilitate the administration of the account.

Nondiscretionary

This is a nondiscretionary account. You will regularly review the holdings in the account and make timely recommendations to me for purchases, sales, and other transactions you deem appropriate. Although you shall not act on any such recommendations without my prior approval, you may without my prior approval purchase and sell fractional shares; exchange securities where no other option is available; accept distributions of dividends in cash or in additional shares whenever a choice is available; invest uninvested cash balances temporarily in U.S. Treasury bills, commercial paper, or money market funds you may select; and sell property held in the account to obtain funds for any payment that is due from the account, if cash is not available.

Agent or Fiduciary?

To what extent is an investment manager (an agent) responsible to a customer (a principal) beyond providing safekeeping, custody, and investment direction? Does an investment agent hold duties equivalent to a fiduciary? In other words, does an investment agent possess responsibilities beyond providing sound investment direction? To what degree can the investment manager be held liable for a breach of duties with respect to investment decisionmaking that may affect a portfolio's performance and safety?

These are difficult questions to answer, and it is beyond the scope of this text to discuss the legal and fiduciary ramifications of an investment agent that acts in a discretionary capacity. But it is important for you to keep these concerns in mind as you explore a trustee's (fiduciary's) charge to be a prudent investment manager (see Chapter 4), an executor (see Chapter 5), a guardian and powerholder (see Chapter 6), and a trustee (see Chapter 7).

Heavy discussion, debate, legal interpretation, and court rulings have addressed this subject, so much so that the Office of the Comptroller of the Currency (the OCC)—the regulator of national banks (discussed in Chapter 11) has taken a stand. The OCC states: "Fiduciary capacity means: trustee, executor, administrator, registrar of stocks and bonds, transfer agent, guardian, assignee, receiver, custodian under a Uniform Gifts to Minors Act, investment advisor if the bank receives a fee for its investment advice."

There is a trite saying: "If it looks like a duck, moves like a duck, and smells like a duck, it is most likely a duck." A discretionary investment manager looks like a fiduciary. For discretionary investment managers to behave as anything less than fiduciaries is to fail to do our jobs when customers place their *trust* and *confidence* in our capabilities.

An individual investor's bottom-line concerns should be accurate asset allocation, appropriate diversification, and a reasonable level of investment activity. When an investor realizes that her levels of expertise, available time, and interest necessitate getting assistance, how can she measure an investment manager's qualifications? A careful inquiry and honest answers will help investors choose an investment manager.

ASSESSING THE NEED FOR AN INVESTMENT MANAGER

In Chapter 1 we discussed the importance of fact-finding—learning about our customers—by using personal statements. A successful way of gaining facts is to ask questions and then listen closely to the answers. The answers help you direct customers toward appropriate products and services. This same process can be used when assessing customers' investment needs. You can assess their needs by asking the following:

- Does your portfolio have an investment strategy? Unclear asset allocation and diversification lead to ineffective results. Hyperactivity in adjusting these factors does not improve the picture.

- Are you satisfied with the results of your investment program? More and more people today face the problem of improving their investment results without really knowing how to do it. It's the rare investor whose portfolio cannot be improved.

- Is your inability to devote sufficient time to your portfolio costing you? Neglect, forgetfulness, and preoccupation are not excuses or explanations for investment losses. A portfolio's performance reflects the time devoted to it.

- Can you compete in an investment market dominated by institutions? Investing has never been easy for the individual acting alone. It is easy to become overwhelmed and confused, and difficult to keep informed.

- Do you understand what you own? Many experienced investors do not fully understand the stock and bond markets, nor do they know why certain investments are owned and how they will accomplish investment objectives.

- Would you worry less and feel more comfortable if someone else managed your investments? Time spent managing investments is time spent away from building a career; sometimes it's best to leave the driving to someone else!

- Also review the attitudinal questions posed in the last section of Appendix 1.

The trust officer's task—and opportunity—is to clearly explain the benefits of entering an investment management agency, answer customers' questions and concerns, and give reasons for using a trust department's investment services.

USING A TRUST DEPARTMENT AS AN INVESTMENT MANAGER

Like ABC Bank and Trust Company, which we looked at earlier in the chapter, the trust industry earned its stripes from years of consistent, solid investment direction. It is important to recognize and advertise that trust departments are equipped to offer their customers the keys to effective investment.

Financial Strength and Reputation

Through prosperous times as well as depressions and recessions, banks have remained solid in their performance, growth, and stability. The strength of the industry's investment prudence is a harbinger of the future success of a customer's portfolio.

Qualified Personnel and Personal Attention

Trust departments build their experience through constant education of administrative managers, portfolio managers, and support staff. This preparation allows trust departments to use their skills to satisfy customers' needs. In addition, trust departments understand the work needed to administer accounts. Administrators and portfolio managers balance account loads, enabling personnel to provide one-on-one, full-time attention to their customers. To them, customers are people, not numbers.

Research and Analysis

It is virtually impossible for one person to collect and decipher the tremendous amount of financial and investment data available, let alone decide what to use and how to use it. Trust departments employ economists, researchers, and securities analysts in order to determine what to buy and sell, what is overvalued and undervalued, and which industry groups may be expected to perform well or decline in various market conditions. Using its research, a trust department can anticipate periods of economic growth or decline and assist the direction of asset allocation, diversification, and future changes.

Investment Performance

Successful investment management is driven by objectives, not necessarily the highest returns. Trust departments help customers to understand their objectives, develop realistic investment goals, and position portfolios to achieve consistent, satisfactory, and personalized investment performance. Of course, if a customer's portfolio surpasses established investment indices and personal objectives, that's a definite plus.

Recordkeeping

Customers should become familiar with the records of their investments. Trust departments have developed user-friendly records of transactions, reports of holdings, and income and trading records. The accuracy of these statements is as important to the individual investor as production reports are to a corporate manager. Consequently, statements that provide too much information may be intimidating, even confusing to customers; on the other hand, providing too little data is insulting.

Competitive Fees

Although competitive fees will be addressed in greater detail in Chapter 12, it is important to note here that trust departments offer an extremely competitive cost structure for their investment management services when compared to nontrust financial institutions. Investors must be aware of an investment manager's fees, how they are disclosed, and the services provided. It is important to compare apples to apples. A competitor's smaller fee could easily point to hidden costs, fewer services, and lower performance.

SUMMARY

- An agency is an account relationship between two parties: a principal and an agent. Ownership of the property, which constitutes the agency, remains with the principal. The agent acts on behalf of the principal and is charged with certain duties with respect to the property.

- Each element of an agency has its specific importance and is contained in the agreement or contract that outlines the duties and responsibilities of the principal and the agent. The agreement also addresses conditions, accounting requirements, and procedures on termination.

- Agencies are categorized as safekeeping, custody, escrow, and investment management, with each of these representing an increased level and number of agent's duties. Safekeeping involves receiving, holding, and returning assets. Custody adds accounting duties but not investment responsibility. Escrow encompasses safekeeping, custody, and possible limited investment management tasks, based on the occurrence of a contingency.

Investment management is the pinnacle of agencies, in which the agent is charged with investment management advice and portfolio management.

- Successful investment portfolios are built on careful asset allocation, diversification of investments within asset classes, active management, and the level of investment discretion given to the investment manager (agent) by the investor (principal).

- The intricacies and importance of an effective investment portfolio require investors to assess whether a professional investment manager is needed and what qualifications are necessary. Trust departments offer
  - ▲ Financial strength and reputation
  - ▲ Qualified personnel
  - ▲ Personal attention
  - ▲ Research
  - ▲ Portfolio analysis
  - ▲ Investment performance
  - ▲ Recordkeeping
  - ▲ Competitive fees

REVIEW QUESTIONS

1. Explain the difference between the principal and the agent in an agency relationship.
2. What are the primary responsibilities of a safekeeping agent? Is the safekeeping agent responsible if property is lost while in safekeeping or in delivering it from the safekeeping account to the principal?
3. Aside from safekeeping responsibilities, list five duties of a custody agent.
4. Explain the differences between discretionary and nondiscretionary investment management accounts.
5. When a customer assesses the need for a professional investment manager, list five qualities that trust departments offer to satisfy a customer's objectives.

4

Investment Risk
and the Prudent Investor

"The social object of skilled investment should be to defeat the dark forces of time and ignorance which envelope our future."

John Maynard Keynes (1883–1946)

When discussing investment objectives, it is very common for the novice investor to say, "I am looking for the most return with the least amount of risk." Unfortunately, this is like asking to have the finest physique with the least amount of exercise, to be rich without paying taxes, to have your cake and eat it too. The customer who asks for big returns coupled with minimal risk does not understand the investment vehicles and the fundamentals of investing discussed in Chapters 2 and 3. Our role as trust professionals is to help our customers define their objectives and to guide them through the maze of investment risk. Whether an individual assumes the responsibility for his investments or places the responsibility in another's hands, prudence plays an integral role in maintaining a successful investment program. In this chapter we will focus primarily on risk, the role prudent investing plays in risk, and our responsibility as prudent investment managers.

LEARNING OBJECTIVES

It is important to understand the underlying concepts of how we manage the investment vehicles used to drive our customers' portfolios.

Upon completion of this chapter, you will be able to

- Describe the basic principles of investing
- Apply the concept of risk to investing
- Explain the Prudent Man Rule
- Analyze the Office of the Comptroller of the Currency's role in guiding trust industry investment policy
- List the key points of the Prudent Investor Rule
- Analyze the investment responsibilities of trust departments
- Define and use the terms that appear in bold in the text

BASIC PRINCIPLES OF INVESTING

Place $100,000 in the hands of 100 people and ask them how they would invest the money. This would elicit 100 different answers. To one person, an investment is a bank certificate of deposit. To another it's government bonds. To others it is speculation in growth stock or risky bonds. Although these investors can generally describe what they want to invest in, few can define what an investment is and what the sound principles of an investment program are.

An **investment** is the purchase of an asset (real property such as a house or intangible personal property such as stocks and bonds) for the purpose of gaining interest, dividends, or appreciation. Learning what a stock or bond is, or the merits of choosing taxable or tax-exempt securities, is a start. But the investment process goes further than putting money aside and understanding what it buys. An investor must address three sound, time-tested investment principles that successful investment professionals commonly agree make a productive investment program:

- Define objectives
- Establish a risk level
- Maintain the investment program

Define Objectives

This is the investment target. Saving a specific dollar amount for the purchase of new living room furniture, holiday gifts, or a downpayment for a house are examples. Larger goals are saving for a child's college education, the purchase of a vacation home, and adequate retirement funds.

In addition to defining the target, an investor must define a time frame: one year for the furniture, 5 years for the downpayment, 10 years until the kids start college, 25 years for retirement.

Establish a Risk Level

Dollar objectives and time objectives depend on risk. A higher investment yield will get an investor to his target faster than a lower yield. Yet higher returns come with higher risk. Risk also poses the possibility of not reaching the target within the allotted time frame. Although the stock market has shown healthy returns over long periods, is the investor willing to live with the possibility that his stocks may depreciate in value, leaving him short of his target? The market fluctuations of 2000–2002 are prime examples of the risk involved. If the investor is not willing to chance it, a lower-level risk element will alter the equation:

Dollars + Time + Risk = Target (Reward)

A variation in any one element changes one or more other elements. For example, less risk requires more dollars or more time to reach the target. An investor must determine the level of risk he or she is willing to take in order to achieve end results.

Maintain the Investment Program

Stick to your guns, unless objectives and risk tolerance substantially change. Investors who stick with a long-term investment program are more successful than investors who attempt to "time the markets," trying to gauge rising and falling interest rates and the ups and downs of the stock market.

Constantly changing investment activity often leads to lower performance. Too many times investors find themselves buying high and selling low, fearful that an investment may fall further rather than waiting for it to come back. Investment performance is also affected by commissions and transactions costs: more activity, more costs, less return.

INVESTMENT RISK

Driving 60 miles per hour in a 30-mile-per-hour zone may get you to your destination faster, but you run the risk of being stopped by a police officer, causing an accident, and putting yourself and others in harm's way. With respect to investments, risk may get you to your investment goal quicker, but you run the risk of not reaching an objective, choosing poor investments, and hurting yourself and others.

Risk is defined and measured as the chance of encountering loss or not earning an anticipated rate of return. For example, principal or income can be lost on bonds, and nonpayment of dividends or loss of value (depreciation) can occur with stocks. Types of risk are classified in Exhibit 4.1.

Risks Associated with Stocks

The amount of risk an investor is willing to take depends on the degree or amount of loss she is willing to accept. Starting with $1,000 and ending with $900 is a loss. Many people are not willing to take the chance this could happen. Others are willing to take this chance, knowing $1,000 could become $2,000. In addition, some investors are willing to live with risk if the potential loss is a smaller loss than other investors will meet. For example, during the turmoil of October 19, 1987 (the stock market's "Black Monday"), the Dow Jones Industrial Average tumbled over 500 points (a market decline of over

20 percent in one day). Some investors may have felt comfortable that their portfolio declined by only 5 percent that day.

Many investors are not willing to ride the roller coaster of investing in stocks. Therefore, investors should always keep the risk–reward tradeoff in mind when investing. Investors must be aware of the liquidity risk, inflation risk, volatility risk, and market risk associated with stocks. High winnings don't come at the poker table when the betting is low, and the rewards aren't guaranteed.

Risks Associated with Bonds

An investor may not be able to sleep at night, fearful that her investments are at risk. Such an investor may lean toward bonds (fixed-income investments) with the belief that bonds are risk-free: the interest rate is fixed and the full principal is returned at maturity. Yet Chapter 2 showed that interest and principal are at risk because of changes in prevailing interest rates, bond ratings, and potential default. These elements of risk are present in any bond investment, including U.S. government securities.

Government securities are considered risk-free because the payment of interest

Exhibit 4.1	Types of Risk
Interest rate risk	Risk that interest-bearing securities, such as bonds, will decline in value as market interest rates rise
Liquidity risk	The risk that the attractiveness of securities will fall, thereby lowering their liquidity
Exchange risk	The possibility that a loss will occur because of the appreciation or depreciation of a foreign currency in relation to the U.S. dollar
Credit risk	A risk that a bond rating will fall with a decline in the obligor's financial condition or an increase in the possibility of default
Inflation risk	The possibility that an increase in the rate of inflation will affect the relative return or appreciation of an investment
Volatility risk	A risk associated with the erratic rising and falling of a stock's price over a period of time
Market risk	The risk that a market as a whole will fall

and principal is backed (guaranteed) by the full faith and credit of the U.S. government. Yet a closer analysis shows that investing in Treasury issues does indeed entail risk. Although the following analysis focuses on T-bills, the same concept holds true for corporate and municipal bonds.

U.S. Treasury bills are U.S. government bonds having maturities of 1 year or less. Exhibit 4.2 shows the total annual returns for each individual year if a 30-day bill was bought with constant reinvestment in another 30-day bill throughout the year each time a bill matured.

Using the information from Exhibit 4.2, if in the beginning of 1981 a 30-day T-bill was purchased for $100,000 and then another 30-day bill was purchased each time a bill matured, the total return for the year would have been 14.71 percent. Income from the $100,000 bills on a total compounded basis for the year would have been $14,710. If the same investment approach was taken for 1982, income would have dropped 28 percent to $10,540. In 1992, the return dropped to $3,510! During this 12-year period (1981–1992) income decreased by 76 percent and inflation grew by 64 percent. The risk from investing in short-term (short-maturity) bonds can be declining returns. Of course, hindsight shows that if this approach was begun in 1977 and kept for the next 4 years, during which time interest rates rose, the results would be substantially different.

Investors must be aware of the interest rate risk, liquidity risk, credit risk, and inflation risk associated with bonds. As investment professionals we must apply sound investment concepts, balance risk and reward, and adhere to prudent principles when managing our customers' trusts and investment management accounts.

Relationship of Risk to Return

Decades of investment research have shown that investors care about avoiding risk as well as gaining return, and that there is a correlation between classes (types) of investment vehicles and risk. Risk/return relationships have been quantified and forecasted using probabilities and past performance.

Investment researchers have built complex graphic models that identify the highest possible expected return for a given level of risk with respect to classes of investments. Using a simple example, Exhibit 4.3 shows the relationship of expected return to the level of risk for various asset classes based on past performance numbers.

Exhibit 4.2 U.S. Treasury Bills: Annual Total Returns

Year	Return	Year	Return	Year	Return
1964	3.54%	1977	5.12%	1990	7.81%
1965	3.93	1978	7.18	1991	5.60
1966	4.76	1979	10.38	1992	3.51
1967	4.21	1980	11.24	1993	2.90
1968	5.21	1981	14.71	1994	3.90
1969	6.58	1982	10.54	1995	5.60
1970	6.53	1983	8.80	1996	5.21
1971	4.39	1984	9.85	1997	5.26
1972	3.84	1985	7.72	1998	4.86
1973	6.93	1986	6.16	1999	4.68
1974	8.00	1987	5.47	2000	5.89
1975	5.80	1988	6.35	2001	3.83
1976	5.08	1989	8.37	2002	1.65

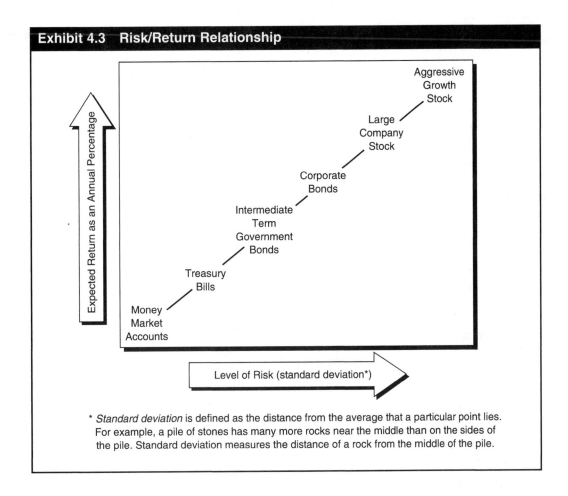

Exhibit 4.3 Risk/Return Relationship

Expected Return as an Annual Percentage

Aggressive
Growth
Stock

Large
Company
Stock

Corporate
Bonds

Intermediate
Term
Government
Bonds

Treasury
Bills

Money
Market
Accounts

Level of Risk (standard deviation*)

* *Standard deviation* is defined as the distance from the average that a particular point lies. For example, a pile of stones has many more rocks near the middle than on the sides of the pile. Standard deviation measures the distance of a rock from the middle of the pile.

Results consistent with Exhibit 4.3 are seen in Exhibit 4.4 when looking at returns in relationship to asset allocation. The results in Exhibit 4.4 are based on rates of return for the 10-year period ending December 31, 2002, using various asset allocations (portfolio mixes). The stock, bond, and cash portfolio classes consist of:

Stocks	S&P 500 Index
Bonds	5-year Treasury notes
Cash	90-day Treasury bills

PRUDENT MAN RULE

As managers of an individual's investment portfolio, we are naturally held to higher standards than customers might apply to themselves in making investment decisions. As investment management profes-

sionals, we are constantly examined under the microscope for good performance, reasonable fees for our services, and personal attention to customers. Intertwined in these responsibilities is the task of acting prudently, the definition of which has grown from historical roots.

In each of us lies the basic human need for trust: a principle of reliance and confidence in the integrity of another person or thing without fear of adverse consequences. The act of trusting another may encompass a responsibility or obligation by another. When a breach of that trust occurs, resolution may be sought for any loss that occurred.

This very thing happened in 1830 when a landmark decision was made in the Massachusetts Supreme Judicial Court in *Harvard College v. Amory*. Briefly, this case involved a group of beneficiaries of a trust who instituted a suit objecting to

Exhibit 4.4 Risk and Reward in Relation to Asset Allocation

Portfolio Mix	Smallest Gain	Average Return	Largest Gain	Average Return (1/1/1950–12/31/2002)
90% stocks No bonds 10% cash	1.0%	11.3%	18.0%	11.3%
80% stocks 10% bonds 10% cash	1.4%	10.8%	17.2%	10.8%
70% stocks 20% bonds 10% cash	1.8%	10.2%	16.5%	10.2%
60% stocks 30% bonds 10% cash	2.1%	9.7%	15.8%	9.7%
50% stocks 40% bonds 10% cash	2.5%	9.2%	15.1%	9.2%
40% stocks 50% bonds 10% cash	2.9%	8.7%	14.4%	8.7%
30% stocks 60% bonds 10% cash	3.3%	8.2%	14.0%	8.1%
20% stocks 70% bonds 10% cash	3.7%	7.6%	13.5%	7.6%
10% stocks 80% bonds 10% cash	3.1%	7.1%	13.1%	7.1%
No stocks 90% bonds 10% cash	1.4%	6.6%	12.7%	6.6%

an accounting by a trustee. The beneficiaries alleged that the trustee, by investing in corporate stock, had made improper investments. Although the trust agreement authorized the trustee to invest in safe and productive stock, including public funds, bank shares, or "other stock" at his discretion, the beneficiaries sought to have the trustee surcharged for a decline in the value of the trust from $50,000 to less than $30,000. The trustee's defense was that the stock was a permissible prudent investment. The court agreed with him.

In his decision, Justice Putnam stated:

All that can be required of a trustee to invest is that he shall conduct himself faithfully and exercise a sound discretion. He is to observe how men of prudence, discretion, and intelligence manage their own affairs, not in regard to speculation, but in regard to the permanent disposition of their funds, considering the probable income, as well as the probable safety of the capital to be invested.

This monumental court case set the stage for investment guidelines for trust departments in what became known as the **Prudent Man Rule.** Although these traditional investment beliefs give no solid guidelines or rules on what is a right or a wrong investment—what is permitted (prudent) or prohibited (imprudent)—the rule hints at the "preserve principal, then produce income" concept of investing. What is hinted more strongly is that the trustee should avoid speculation.

Before this case, many states enacted laws defining what investments were permissible for trustees. **Approved lists** (legal lists) of securities were adopted. The Prudent Man Rule represented a major shift in trust investment policy. It was a rejection of the rigid, statutory legal list concept in favor of a flexible rule granting trustees the opportunity to use their investment skills subject only to the dictates of prudence in the choice of investments. In *Harvard College v. Amory* the creator of the trust expressly approved of investments in common stocks by the trustee. Interestingly, the rationale of this case was applied in later judicial decisions in which the creator did not specifically authorize investments in corporate stock.

Although the Prudent Man Rule was a radical departure from the legal list rule, it was not universally adopted. Because the court case was an isolated situation providing general, nonlegal guidance, the legal list concept prevailed for many years with little room for individual needs. Until the 1940s, investment in common stock was often deemed unacceptable in the legal lists of most states.

OFFICE OF THE COMPTROLLER OF THE CURRENCY

In 1863, during the Civil War, Congress faced a decrease in the sale of government bonds, which was important to the North's war effort. The government's borrowing strength was weakening. To help solve this problem, Congress authorized a new class of banks—national banks—which would be permitted to issue new national bank notes (paper money) equal in value to the government bonds they might buy and hold as security. To watch over these new banks and the new paper money that was being issued, an office called the Currency Bureau was created in the Treasury Department. Under the first **Comptroller of the Currency,** Hugh McCulloch (later to become Secretary of the Treasury), the office established policies for chartering, examining, and regulating these national banks.

In December 1863 McCulloch wrote a letter to the executives of each national bank. An underlying theme of his letter was to "do nothing to foster and encourage speculation. Give facilities only to legitimate and prudent transactions."

Charged with overall supervision and examination of national banks (including trust departments), the goal of the **Office of the Comptroller of the Currency** (OCC) is to protect the general public, ensuring the safety and soundness of national banks. For example, in order for an institution to engage in the trust business, the institution must submit an application and receive a **charter**—an authority—permitting the institution to act. For national banks, the OCC is the regulatory authority. State banks are regulated and examined by state authorities (for example, The [name of state] Commissioner of Banks and Trust Companies). Both federal and state statutes set forth provisions for banks to obtain authority to act, provide guidelines for an institution's conduct in its operations, and conduct supervisions and examinations, all in the interest of the customers who place their trust in the institution.

Briefly, an application for trust powers must show that the institution has

- Adequate financial capacity
- Managerial integrity
- Experienced and qualified personnel
- Competent legal counsel

Once a charter is granted, trust institutions are examined regularly. To ensure their **compliance** with OCC guidelines, trust departments employ a **trust compliance officer.** This officer is guided by the *Comptroller's Handbook of Fiduciary Activities* (formerly titled, *Comptroller's Handbook for National Trust Examiners*). This 350-page book gives trust departments direction on OCC examinations, rules, and regulations. For example, institutions must file a statement of condition not less than four times a year; most banks do so on a monthly basis. The regulatory bodies also conduct on-sight examinations. The OCC conducts trust department inspections at least three times every 2 years, in conjunction with the examination of other areas of the bank. Failure to pass the inspection jeopardizes the institution's charter. The OCC

- Evaluates the trust department's financial condition in relation to the bank as a whole
- Provides standards of service to improve the business in the best interest of the customer
- Makes suggestions for departmental efficiency
- Ascertains whether procedures are in place to provide customer confidentiality and compliance

Three sections of the OCC handbook that are of special interest to trust departments are the sections on marketable securities, beneficiary needs, and risk management.

Marketable Securities

This section of the comptroller's handbook defines classes of securities (as discussed in Chapter 2), and also states the following:

> In making investment decisions regarding common and preferred stocks, and preferred stocks and debentures convertible into common stocks, the following factors should be considered:

- Quality and depth of management of the company

- Financial condition and position of the company in its industry
- Quality of earnings and historical growth of the company
- Assessment of future prospects of the company in terms of sales and earnings, projected price/earnings and price/dividend ratios, existing and potential competition, etc., based on comparisons with peer companies in the same industry
- Anticipated availability of raw materials to sustain future growth
- Anticipated legislation, potential governmental intervention, and labor unrest
- Trend of per capita use of the company's products
- Demonstrated ability of the company to develop new products and/or upgrade existing ones
- Marketing capabilities of the company
- Ability of the market to absorb sales of securities, i.e., whether the security is traded in a "thin" market, as is the case with many insurance and bank stocks, and municipal bonds
- Company accounting methods
- Litigation pending against the company

Most of those considerations are more easily researched for "seasoned" corporations than for new issues offered to the public.

Beneficiary Needs

Regarding the needs of a trust's beneficiaries, the handbook gives careful directions about structuring accounts. The more important considerations in determining a beneficiary's needs are

- Need for income
- Need for principal distributions
- Tax status of beneficiaries

- Loss of purchasing power
- Estimated termination date of account

Risk Management

The OCC continues to guide trust departments with appropriate investment selection with respect to

- Safety of principal
- Diversification
- Income generation
- Capital appreciation
- Marketability
- Liquidity
- Maturity of debt instruments
- Tax considerations

Despite the length of the handbook and the apparent influence of government bureaucracy, it is an extremely helpful aid to our investment services.

PRUDENT INVESTOR RULE

The science of investing has evolved and carried portfolio management and theory a long way from the horse-and-carriage days of approved lists and the Prudent Man Rule to today's modern and innovative products and techniques. The subject of investments has been studied and practiced so extensively that the 1990 Nobel prize in economic sciences was awarded to three financial economists for research in investment management and analysis. Their studies determined that investment responsibilities could no longer be governed by a set of general rules that can confine an investment manager's investment acumen.

Armed with this research and determined to carry investment activity beyond the Prudent Man Rule, in 1990 the American Law Institute presented the *Restatement Third of the Law of Trusts,* which completely restated the Prudent Man Rule. The restatement, called the **Prudent Investor Rule,** brings investment practices into the modern world. From this, in 1994 the American Bar Association approved the Uniform Prudent Investor Act, which governs investment decisions made by fiduciaries (trustees, executors, and estate guardians).

The Prudent Investor Rule is not law. The contents of the rule are not legal statutes or the words of the court, but they are a source of influence for courts to follow. Most states have enacted laws based on this model.

The American Law Institute's restatement, the American Bar Association's act, and state legislation focus on a portfolio's overall composition rather than the merits of specific assets. Investment discretion is broader than in earlier practices and legislation. These concepts are illustrated in the following analysis of the Illinois statute, which is based on the restatement. The statute is printed in indented paragraphs. Please read the statute and the commentary slowly.

Illinois Prudent Investor Rule (Effective February 5, 1992)

Sec. 5: Investments

(a) *Prudent Investor Rule.* A trustee administering a trust has a duty to invest and manage the trust assets as follows:

(1) The trustee has a duty to invest and manage trust assets as a prudent investor would considering the purposes, terms, distribution requirements, and other circumstances of the trust. This standard requires the exercise of reasonable care, skill, and caution and is to be applied to investments not in isolation, but in the context of the trust portfolio as a whole and as a part of an overall investment strategy that should incorporate risk and return objectives reasonably suitable to the trust.

The element of prudence is maintained when managing investments. What is added is that this prudence must be practiced throughout the overall investment practices of a trust ("not in isolation"). It is integral to investment success that portfolios be managed according to the circumstances and objectives of individual accounts.

(2) No specific investment or course of action is, taken alone, prudent or imprudent. The trustee may invest in every kind of property and type of investment, subject to this Section. The trustee's investment decisions and actions are to be judged in terms of the trustee's reasonable business judgment regarding the anticipated effect on the trust portfolio as a whole under the facts and circumstances prevailing at the time of the decision or action. The prudent investor rule is a test of conduct and not of resulting performance.

A portfolio cannot be judged by the performance of individual investment vehicles. Given the latitude to invest "in every kind of property and type of investment," a trustee is measured by the performance of a portfolio as a whole.

(3) The trustee has a duty to diversify the investments of the trust unless, under the circumstances, the trustee reasonably believes it is in the interests of the beneficiaries and furthers the purposes of the trust not to diversify.

Although diversification is an integral principal of investing, there are times when "it is in the interests of beneficiaries . . . not to diversify." Trustees must be given the opportunity to avoid diversification contrary to established investment norms when this action is in the beneficiaries' best interests.

(4) The trustee has a duty, within a reasonable time after the acceptance of the trusteeship, to review trust assets and to make and implement decisions concerning the retention and disposition of original pre-existing investments in order to conform to the provisions of this Section. The trustee's decision to retain or dispose of an asset may properly be influenced by the asset's special relationships or value to the purposes of the trust or to some or all of the beneficiaries, consistent with the trustee's duty of impartiality.

How an individual managed his assets during life is not necessarily the best way to do so for the trust's beneficiaries. A trustee is responsible, and must be permitted, to maintain or alter ("retention and disposition of original pre-existing investments") the trust's investment construct. An existing portfolio cannot be kept solely on the principle that it was intended to stay that way.

(5) The trustee has a duty to pursue an investment strategy that considers both the reasonable production of income and safety of capital, consistent with the trustee's duty of impartiality and the purposes of the trust. Whether investments are underproductive or overproductive of income shall be judged by the portfolio as a whole and not as to any particular asset.

Although investing in bonds generates income and provides a less risky approach to preserving principal, principal preservation is more likely to be achieved by investing in stock, where appreciation preserves principal by matching inflation. Of course, this negates income production because stock dividends are less than bond interest. The "underproductive . . . income" of a class of investments should be judged with respect to the overall objective of a portfolio and "not as to any particular asset."

(6) The circumstances that the trustee may consider in making investment decisions include, without limitation, the general economic conditions, the possible effect of inflation, the expected tax consequences of investment decisions or strategies, the role each investment or course of action plays within the overall portfolio, the expected total return (including both income yield and apprecia-

tion of capital), and the duty to incur only reasonable and appropriate costs. The trustee may but need not consider related trusts and the assets of beneficiaries when making investment decisions.

This section addresses making investment decisions based on the combination of several factors ("economic conditions . . . inflation . . . tax consequences . . . total return . . . and appropriate costs") considered together rather than individually. In addition, investment decisions may be made in relation to assets outside of the sphere of a trustee's responsibility.

(b) The provisions of this Section may be expanded, restricted, eliminated, or otherwise altered by express provisions of the trust instrument. The trustee is not liable to a beneficiary for the trustee's reasonable and good faith reliance on those express provisions.

When a trust document provides direction to investment decision making, a trustee cannot be held liable when "reasonable and good faith reliance on those express provisions" is exercised. A trustee cannot be found at fault for doing what it is told to do and acting in good faith on those instructions. Chapters 7 and 8 will examine personal trusts as sets of instructions. It is unfair to be held liable for following instructions.

(c) Nothing in this Section abrogates or restricts the power of an appropriate court in proper cases (i) to direct or permit the trustee to deviate from the terms of the trust instrument or (ii) to direct or permit the trustee to take, or to restrain the trustee from taking, any action regarding the making or retention of investments.

When it is unclear as to the investment intent of a trust, this rule does not prevent "an appropriate court" from directing a trustee "to deviate from the terms of the trust or . . . restrain[ing] the trustee from taking . . . action." There are times

when a trust's language is unclear, and a trustee needs legal guidance as to which direction to take.

(d) The following terms or comparable language in the investment powers and related provisions of a trust instrument, unless otherwise limited or modified by that instrument, shall be construed as authorizing any investment or strategy permitted under this Section: "investments permissible by law for investment of trust funds," "legal investments," "authorized investments," "using the judgment and care under the circumstances, then prevailing that men of prudence, discretion, and intelligence exercise in the management of their own affairs, not in regard to the speculation but in regard to the permanent disposition of their funds, considering the probable income as well as the probable safety of their capital," "prudent man rule," and "prudent person rule."

The Prudent Man Rule is not being scrapped by the Prudent Investor Rule. This section attempts to supplement, strengthen, and clarify a 170-year-old set of guidelines.

(e) On and after the effective date of this amendatory Act of 1991, this Section applies to all existing and future trusts, but only as to actions or inactions occurring after that effective date.

Which trusts are affected? Any trust, but only with respect to "actions or inactions occurring" after the rule is effective.

Sec. 5.1: Duty Not to Delegate

(a) The trustee has a duty not to delegate to others the performance of any acts involving the exercise of judgment and discretion, except acts constituting investment functions that a prudent investor of comparable skills might delegate under the circumstances. The trustee may delegate those investment functions to an investment agent as provided in subsection (b).

(b) For a trustee to properly delegate investment functions under subsection (a), all of the following requirements apply:

(1) The trustee must exercise reasonable care, skill, and caution in selecting the investment agent, in establishing the scope and specific terms of any delegation, and in periodically reviewing the agent's actions in order to monitor overall performance and compliance with the scope and specific terms of the delegation.

(2) The trustee must conduct an inquiry into the experience, performance history, professional licensing or registration, if any, and financial stability of the investment agent.

(3) The investment agent shall be subject to the jurisdiction of the courts of the State of Illinois.

(4) The investment agent shall be subject to the same standards that are applicable to the trustee.

(5) The investment agent shall be liable to the beneficiaries of the trust and to the designated trustee to the same extent as if the investment agent were a designated trustee in relation to the exercise or nonexercise of the investment function.

(6) The trustee shall send written notice of its intention to begin delegating investment functions under this Section to the beneficiaries eligible to receive income from the trust on the date of initial delegation at least 30 days before the delegation. This notice shall thereafter, until or unless the beneficiaries eligible to receive income from the trust at the time are notified to the contrary, authorize the trustee to delegate investment functions pursuant to this Section.

(c) If all requirements of subsection (b) are satisfied, the trustee shall not otherwise be responsible for the investment decisions or actions of the investment agent to which the investment functions are delegated.

(d) On and after the effective date of this amendatory Act of 1991, this Section applies to all existing and future trusts, but only as to actions or inactions occurring after that effective date.

In an area of investments where a trustee does not possess comfortable expertise, responsibilities can be delegated to more skilled and specialized managers when the cost of doing so is justified and the goals of the trust are furthered. A trustee's responsibilities are now invigorated by the ability (or perhaps the requirement) to turn to others when expertise is needed. This alternative must be carefully evaluated, lest the trustee be accused of "passing the buck." For example, assume that a trust contains oil and gas partnerships. If the trustee lacks the expertise to manage this sophisticated asset, it must ask:

- Should the asset be maintained, absent knowledge of how to manage it, therefore causing risk to the portfolio's performance?

- Should the asset be disposed of because of a lack of knowledge how to manage it, thereby depriving the trust the potential of income and appreciation?

- Should an outside manager be sought to assist with the management of this asset?

The Prudent Investor Rule allows trustees to delegate investment functions to another, as long as several requirements are met. The trustee must

- "Exercise . . . care" when choosing an investment agent

- Determine the investment agent's "experience . . . licensing . . . and financial stability"

- Ensure that the agent is "subject to the jurisdiction of the courts"

- Ascertain that the investment agent will be "subject to the same standards. . . applicable to the trustee"

- Determine that the investment agent will be "liable . . . to the same extent" as the trustee

- Notify the beneficiaries "of its intention to begin delegating investment functions"

Only after all these requirements are met is the trustee relieved of responsibility for an investment agent's actions. Has the trustee "passed the buck"? Yes. Is the trustee responsible for the pass? Yes.

Establishment of common trust fund. Any bank or trust company may, at and during such time as it is qualified to act as a fiduciary in this State, establish, maintain, and administer one or more common trust funds for the purposes of furnishing investments to itself as a fiduciary, or to itself and another or others as co-fiduciaries. An investment in a common trust fund does not constitute an investment in the various securities composing the common trust fund, but is an investment in the fund as an entity. A bank or trust company, in its capacity as a fiduciary or co-fiduciary, whether that fiduciary capacity arose before or is created after this Act takes effect, may invest funds that it holds for investment in that capacity in interests in one or more common trust funds, subject to the following limitations:

(1) In the case of a fiduciary other than an administrator, the investment may be made in a common trust fund if such an investment is not expressly prohibited by the instrument, judgment, or order creating the fiduciary relationship, or by an amendment thereof, and if, under the instrument, judgment, or order creating the fiduciary relationship, or an amendment thereof, the funds so held for investment might properly be invested in an investment with the overall investment characteristics of the common trust fund, considered as an entity, and if, in the case of co-fiduciaries, the bank or trust company procures the consent of its co-fiduciary or co-fiduciaries to the investment in those interests. If the instrument creating the fiduciary relationship gives to the bank or trust company the exclusive right to select investments, the consent of the co-fiduciary shall not be required. Any person acting as co-fiduciary with any such bank or trust company is hereby authorized to consent to the investment in those interests.

(2) In the case of an administrator, the investment may be made upon approval by the court.

(3) A bank or trust company in establishing, maintaining and administering one or more common trust funds for the purpose of furnishing investments to itself as fiduciary shall have a duty to invest and manage such common trust fund assets as follows:

(A) The bank or trust company has a duty to invest and manage common trust fund assets as a prudent investor would considering the purposes, terms, distribution requirements, and other circumstances of the common trust fund. This standard requires the exercise of reasonable care, skill, and caution and is to be applied to investments not in isolation, but in the context of the common trust fund portfolio as a whole and as a part of an overall investment strategy that should incorporate risk and return objectives reasonably suitable to the common trust fund.

(B) No specific investment or course of action is, taken alone, prudent or imprudent. The bank or trust company may invest in every kind of property and type of investment, subject to this Section. The bank or trust company's investment decisions and actions are to be judged in terms of the bank or trust company's reasonable business judgment regarding the anticipated effect on the common trust fund portfolio as a whole under the facts and circumstances prevailing at the time of the decision or action. The standard set forth in this paragraph (3) is a test of conduct and not of resulting performance.

(C) The circumstances that the bank or trust company may consider in making investment decisions include, without limitation, the general economic conditions, the possible effect of inflation, the role each investment or course of action plays within the overall portfolio, and the expected total return.

(4) A bank or trust company may not delegate the investment functions of a common trust fund established or operating under Section 584 of the Internal Revenue Code pursuant to Section 5.1 of the Trusts and Trustees Act except as authorized by the Bureau of the Comptroller of the Currency of the U.S. Department of the Treasury. A bank or trust company may hire one or more agents to give the trustee advice with respect to investments of a common trust fund and pay reasonable and appropriate compensation to the agent provided that the final investment decisions and the exclusive management of the common trust fund remain with the bank or trust company.

(5) On or after the effective date of this amendatory Act of 1991, this Section applies to all existing and future common trust funds, but only as to the actions or inactions occurring after that effective date.

Chapter 2 explored individual investment securities (such as stocks and bonds) and introduced the concept of fund investing (mutual funds and common trust funds). Funds consist of many individual securities. These funds are used for pooling investors' money to gain efficiency and diversification. This section of the Prudent Investor Rule gives trust departments the ability to create and maintain common trust funds and to use them as an investment vehicle irrespective of the individual securities within the fund but as an investment measured as an entity by its overall objectives. For example (and looking back at section 5(a)(2)), the merits of the fund are to be judged by its overall intent, rather than considering a particular security (invest-

ment) within the fund. In comparison to section 5(a)(5), the fund is used as an entity and should not be measured by the productiveness or unproductiveness of individual securities within the fund.

This section also clearly defines when a common trust fund can and cannot be used, whether permission to use the funds is needed from cotrustees, and what duties the trustees must maintain to manage these funds.

Sections (A) through (C) and section (4) reiterate the trustee's approach to the management of common trust funds similar to the way individual investments are addressed in the first sections, including delegation and effective dates.

This new rule now allows trustees (both corporate and individual) to rethink their approach to investments. The rule gives greater flexibility and protection to trustees. Now it is easier to design investment direction that fits a trust's independent intent and individual beneficiaries' requirements. The new rule gives trustees new opportunities, not to avoid investment risks but to manage risks that are common to any investment vehicle.

INVESTMENT RESPONSIBILITIES OF TRUST DEPARTMENTS

Somewhere between inordinate conservatism and risky speculation lies the key to successful investing. Rules have been established to protect, not impede, yet they do not make investing simple. What should be bought and sold, and when? What are the customer's needs, today and tomorrow? What risks can be taken with someone else's money? Trust departments face these decisions each day. In addition, the management of trust assets can be a long-lived responsibility having a large financial impact on the trustee's beneficiaries over many years as needs change.

Prudence vs. Performance

Amid the Prudent Man Rule, the guidelines of the OCC, and approved lists, trust departments developed a conservative, perhaps gun-shy approach to investments. Although the underlying theme and responsibility of any investment manager is the duty to preserve assets, then generate income and appreciation, trust departments wrote the eleventh commandment: *"Thou shalt preserve thy principal."* To keep this commandment, trust departments formed **Trust Investment Committees** to oversee the investment of trust assets. These committees are not directly responsible for day-to-day investment activity; they watch overall investment policy.

Perhaps committees such as these placed too much starch in the collar of investment responsibility. Consider the minutes of a trust investment committee meeting of 45 years ago in a large trust department. This committee recommended not placing more than 10 percent of trust customer assets in stocks. It appeared that nothing less than divine intervention would change their thinking. For some individual trust accounts, this is appropriate. But, a universal, across-the-board philosophy such as this is inappropriate given the diverse needs of thousands of individual trust customers.

Is there room beyond the Prudent Man Rule, the OCC's guidelines, approved lists, and trust investment committees in which investment decisions provide performance yet are not questioned? It is doubtful this will ever occur. It is comforting that the trust industry has evolved beyond speculation-frowning and prohibitive investment guidelines. Although the newer Prudent Investor Rule doesn't overtly loosen the reins and permit speculation, there now is a tendency toward a more modern and aggressive approach to investments. Trust professionals can now face each investment strategy and investment vehicle with open minds, judging it prudent or imprudent, permissible or not permissible, rather than being boxed in by rules.

Undoubtedly, prudence and trust cannot be ignored; they have their place in our practices. Yet human needs have changed and advanced since the nineteenth century. As providers of investment services we have the duty to carry our prudence and trust further. Despite our willingness, ability, and responsibility, trust departments face difficult questions and investment decisions each day for each account.

Determining Investment Objectives

Perhaps the most important work we do with customers each day is determining or modifying a clear statement of investment objectives. Ensuring that both the trust department and the customer share the same understanding of goals is a prerequisite for effective service; failure to achieve it almost guarantees dissatisfaction and unsuitable portfolio composition.

We must begin by asking, in both qualitative and quantitative terms, what our customer hopes to accomplish. Of course, every investor wants high returns with low risk. Our task is to apply the most accurate definitions possible to both of these measures of investment performance. What constraints and requirements will govern our actions? Typically, they include the following.

Risk Tolerance

What level and types of risk is the customer willing to assume? Can he tolerate significant short-term swings in the market value of assets, or is he uncomfortable with such volatility? Are investment objectives consistent with a need for growth to offset inflation? Clearly, this is a crucial decision.

Time Horizon

What time period does the customer see as relevant for her investment funds? Are there different time horizons for different needs and different components of the portfolio?

Liquidity

What are the customer's known, scheduled, or unscheduled needs for such items as tax payments, education, housing, and gifts.

USING TRUST PRODUCTS AND SERVICES
TO MEET CUSTOMER NEEDS

The university that Ken graduated from 15 years ago advertised a full-day estate-planning seminar for alumni. The program sounded interesting, but Ken thought he could not take the time from his growing business to attend. A close friend convinced him to go.

Throughout the first two speakers' presentations Ken's mind was on the office. His thoughts strayed to his wife, Kim, who was alone at the business helm for the day. When the third speaker—his friend, an attorney—told the audience that they were at the seminar to learn planning techniques for their families, not for themselves, Ken immediately thought of his daughter, who was 2 years from college, his 10-year-old son, who needed a wheelchair because of an auto accident, and the surprise additions to the family: the recently born twins.

Over the next 3 months Ken and Kim organized their estate: wills, trusts, insurance planning, and business succession plans. Kim saw the full importance of this planning 4 years later, when she met with her trust officer a month after Ken's fatal heart attack.

Kim soon learned that running a trust was different from running a business. The following were paramount in Kim's mind:

- Risk level: Ken and Kim took risks building their business. Could Kim and her trustee afford to continue taking risks with the trust assets that stood between financial success and disaster?

- Time horizons: Business goals changed from day to day. Could today's income jeopardize tomorrow's principal? How long would it be before the twins were on their own?

- Liquidity: The business's receivables were used to pay its bills. Where would the money come from for living expenses, college costs, and their son's medical needs?

- Legal constraints: Did Ken's trust place restrictions on investments and distributions?

- Taxes: Personal and trust taxation differed from business taxation. Would the sale of the business bring a new set of rules?

- Income needs: The business risk brought a good return. Could the trust assume investment risk and meet the family's needs?

- Unique circumstances: Each day Kim knew how to handle the unexpected surprises of running a business. What would the future bring?

Regulatory/Legal

Are there any legal constraints? This might refer to the provisions of the trust document or other personalized legal documents. It may also include state regulations or asset trading restrictions under the ownership or management of a business.

Taxes

What income, estate, or gift taxes are associated with the account's investments?

Income Needs

How much cash flow does the customer need or want from his assets?

Kim lost her husband and business partner. With the help of her new partner, the trust department, she built a precise definition of her goals and desires. During the administration of Ken's estate, the business was sold (and the applicable income taxes were paid), the mortgage on the house was paid off, and Ken's life insurance proceeds were collected. Methodically, the trust department allocated the net $2 million of cash in the trust as shown below.

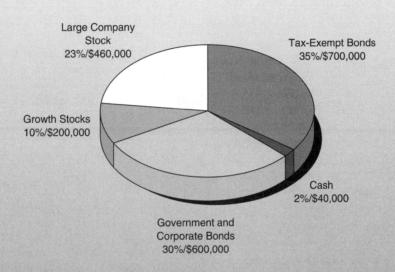

Kim's trust portfolio manager built the asset allocation (among stocks, bonds, and cash) and the diversification within the asset classes (taxable and tax-exempt bonds, large company and growth stocks) to meet Kim's objectives:

- Liquidity to meet unforeseen emergencies (cash allocation)
- Safety of principal for the generation of income to meet living expenses, college costs, and medical expenses (bond allocation)
- Protection against inflation through appreciation (stock allocation)
- Reduction of taxes (tax-exempt bonds)
- Element of risk to increase return (small-cap stocks)

Unique Considerations

Does the customer have specific preferences or aversions in composition of investments in the portfolio, such as avoidance of ethically unacceptable stocks?

For many investors, these issues have never been put into words. However, strong feelings usually arise in the process of specifically defining preferences. Moreover, objectives can change with life events and shifts in attitudes about the future.

For many years trust professionals have placed great emphasis on the word *personal*. We cannot forget this word as we manage our customers' investments. This is a business about people first, then numbers. What are our customers' circumstances? How do they vary from trust to trust? What are the requirements of the trust regarding distribution of income and principal? When will the trust end? What are the tax consequences of the trust? What financial position is each beneficiary in? Where prudent investment is absolutely tantamount to one trust or one beneficiary, such is not the case for another. Now is the time to use the decades of empirical evidence gathered by Nobel Prize–winning individuals, use the Prudent Investor Rule, march to the OCC's guidelines, and move into the twenty-first century of investing.

SUMMARY

Investing is both an art and a science. Our role as trust professionals is to apply both methodologies to our customers' investment portfolios.

- The basic principles of investing are to define objectives (in dollars and time), establish risk levels (and measure this with dollars and time), and maintain the established investment program.
- Investment risk is measured by the chance of encountering loss. Stocks and bonds face interest rate risk, liquidity risk, exchange risk, credit risk, inflation risk, volatility risk, and market risk.
- Investment guidelines for trust departments grew historically from the Prudent Man Rule, which came from an 1830 Massachusetts Supreme Judicial Court case that stated in part, "All that can be required of a trustee to invest is that he shall conduct himself faithfully and exercise a sound discretion. He is to observe how men of prudence, discretion, and intelligence manage their own affairs, not in regard to speculation, but in regard to the permanent disposition of their funds, considering the probable income, as well as the probable safety of the capital to be invested."

- The Office of the Comptroller of the Currency (OCC) provides supervision and examination of national banks and trust departments. The Comptroller's Handbook of Fiduciary Activities guides trust departments in the investment of marketable securities, beneficiary needs, and risk management.
- Modern investment practice has moved individual states to enact legislation that carries trust department investment management beyond the Prudent Man Rule. Today many trust departments are guided by the Prudent Investor Rule, which gives greater flexibility and protection to trustees.
- Trust departments must prudently yet proactively construct and manage trust portfolios. The Prudent Investor Rule expands the role and responsibility of trust department investment activity.

REVIEW QUESTIONS

1. Define what an investment is.
2. Inherent in investing is risk. Briefly define risk and list three types of risk.
3. How did the term *prudent man* find its way into the terminology of the trust business?
4. Over the years the OCC has enacted many regulations and guidelines designed to help banks deal with their customers' money. What do the OCC's guidelines direct trustees to do?
5. An important aspect of the Prudent Investor Rule is delegation. Briefly describe three requirements of a trustee when it delegates investment duties to another.

5

WILLS AND THE PROBATE PROCESS

*"Death never takes the wise man by surprise.
He is always ready to go."*

Jean de la Fontaine (1621–1695)

Preparing for the future is not an easy task; there are emotional, physical, and financial hazards along the way. Although we cannot help our customers stay healthy or build their careers, we can contribute substantially to their estate and financial planning.

There is an ultimate end to this planning: death. Are our customers prepared for it? Who spends valuable, active energy preparing for death? Part of a trust professional's responsibility extends into this area. We must help our customers plan for the inevitable.

Unfortunately, our customers will not have the opportunity to see the visible results and rewards of these preparations. Fortunately, others will. Remember, life insurance does not benefit the dead; it is bought because others continue living. Wills and trusts are not established for the customer's use beyond the grave; they are created for those who live on. Wives, husbands, and children are the loved ones who see the results of this unselfish planning.

LEARNING OBJECTIVES

There is an old superstition that to plan for death is to invite it. We hear stories about people who fear to prepare a will, thinking that the signing of such a document is an omen that the grim reaper is right around the corner. The reaper could be hovering in the wings, but the mere preparation of a will for loved ones does not invite death.

Upon completion of this chapter, you will be able to

- Explain why a person needs a will
- Contrast the differences between dying testate and dying intestate
- Describe who can establish a will, what testamentary capacity is, and how a will can be contested
- Analyze a sample will
- Define probate
- Profile the qualifications of an effective executor

- List the steps and timetable involved in the administration and settlement of an estate
- Define and use the terms that appear in bold in the text.

ESTATES

The word **estate** conjures a picture of wealth: acres of rolling land, a stable of thoroughbred horses, a driveway lined with luxury cars, and an extensive investment portfolio. This scene does apply to a few individuals, but for most people an estate is more modest; simply, it is the total ownership in property that an individual has.

Add it all up: wherever it is located, whatever it is, and however it is owned. If the property is included in Exhibit 1.3 or Appendix 1, it is part of one's estate. Regardless of how large or small an estate is, estate owners should be proud of what they have accumulated and, more important, be prepared for the day when their estate becomes someone else's.

Chapter 1 addresses how assets can be transferred from one person to another: as a sale, trade, or barter; as a gift; and as a transfer at **demise** (death) either by law (joint tenancy succession), beneficiary designation (from life insurance and employee benefit plans), or a trust. This chapter is devoted to the transfer of estate assets at death by will and by intestacy.

WILLS

A **will** (a shortened term for **last will** and **last will and testament**) is a legal document that states a person's intentions regarding the distribution of her estate at death. Technically, a will is operative only at death—*a will speaks at the time of death.* Defined simply, *a will states who gets what.*

Historically, real property and personal property were treated differently upon death. The law relating to real property originated with the common law (government) courts, and the property was distributed at death via a document called a "will." The law relating to personal property originated with ecclesiastical courts, and the property was distributed at death via a document called a "testa-ment" (perhaps from biblical terminology). The modern trend has been to eliminate the differences in the treatment of real and personal property, although historical remnants exist within the vocabulary and distribution of property in intestate situations (not disposed of by will).

Over the years, the distribution of real and personal property fell within one document: a last will and testament. This document gradually lost the words *and testament* and eventually the word *last.*

Testacy

When a person dies having made a will, he is said to have died **testate.** A competent trust professional realizes that a will answers the following questions:

- How can I make certain that those whom I want to receive my assets will actually get them?
- How can I make specific gifts, both charitable and noncharitable?
- How can I take advantage of the tax-saving options that are available to my estate?
- How can I guarantee that the right person or corporation will be there to administer and settle the affairs of my estate?
- How can I guarantee who will be the guardian of my minor children and their assets?
- How can I ensure who will care for my assets for the benefit of my spouse and children?
- Is there any way I can lower the cost and time of settling my estate?
- How can I arrange the long-term management of my assets for the benefit of my family?
- How can I guarantee that special family situations will be handled according to my wishes?

Intestacy

If a person dies without having made a will, to die **intestate,** he cannot direct the matters of his estate according to his personal wishes. Intestacy can occur when:

- A person dies without having made a will

- A decedent's will is denied probate—declared invalid—due perhaps to improper execution or a successful will challenge (contest)

- The decedent's will does not dispose of all his property (resulting in a partial intestacy) either because a bequest has failed or because the will contains no residuary clause

- The decedent's will specifies that her property should pass according to the laws of intestate succession

(The unfamiliar terms used above will be discussed later in this chapter.)

Without a will, a person

- Gives up the right to direct how property will be distributed (to whom it goes, how it goes to them, when it goes to them, and in what proportions).

- Sacrifices the opportunity to say who will administer the estate.

- Loses potential tax savings to an estate; for example, if a will provides for certain assets to go to a specific **charity,** the estate could qualify for a charitable deduction, which could reduce taxes that the estate has to pay; without a will, not only is the **charitable bequest** (gift) lost, but so is the potential tax savings.

- Gives up the right to name who will be the legal guardian of the person and guardian of the estate for minor children.

- Gives children the right to **inherit** their shares once they attain majority (which in most states is age 18), which may be earlier than desired.

Although these may not be desired ends, when an individual dies intestate, his estate is administered and distributed according to the rules and regulations set by the **decedent's** (the one who dies) state of residence. What each state is actually saying is, "Because the decedent did not make a will, we will provide one."

A somewhat farcical approach—but nonetheless serious and poignant—is the fictitious direction below, the expression of a person's intentions without a will. The impact of this piece will be seen as you work your way through each section of this chapter.

Since I do not care to spend the time and money necessary for making out my own will, I request the state of my residence and the government of the United States to do it for me. I understand that the following will happen:

1. My state will award my wife one-half of my worldly goods. My children will receive the other half.

2. The state will appoint my wife guardian of my children, but will require of her that she report regularly to the probate court and give an accounting of how, where, and why she spent the money necessary for the proper care of my children.

3. The state will also require my wife to present a performance bond to the probate court to guarantee that she spends the money for my children in the proper adult manner.

4. The state may appoint my wife— or anyone else—administrator of my estate, but will require that the administrator purchase another performance bond to guarantee that everything is done exactly according to statutes.

5. I would have liked to remember certain family members and charities to receive assets from my estate, but that won't happen.

6. I realize that there are certain legitimate avenues to lower my death taxes, but wish instead that the state and federal governments

get money that would otherwise have gone to my wife and children as a result of these savings.

7. If my wife dies before me, the state will order my relatives to decide on the guardianship of my children. If my relatives cannot agree on a suitable guardian, the probate court will do so, and will be free to nominate a social worker or anyone else as guardian of my children.

8. At age 18, my children have the right to hire an attorney to demand of their mother a complete accounting of all her financial actions with their money.

9. At age 18, my children have the right to withdraw and spend their share of the estate. They can spend these shares in any way they please, and no one will have the right to question their actions.

10. Should my wife remarry, the state guarantees that her second husband will get one half of everything she inherited from me. He is not required to spend any part of his share for the children. Furthermore, he may exclude my children from his share of my wife's estate by merely writing a will to that effect.

In witness thereof, I have read and fully understand the foregoing, agree to the consequences described, and wish to make this document public upon my death.

It is inevitable that the state's way of doing things (referred to as **statutes of distribution** or **law of descent and distribution**) will be contrary to a person's wishes. For example, if a person's intention is to leave her entire estate to her spouse (with the children receiving all assets following both deaths), this must be stated in a will. Without a will the entire estate may not go completely to the surviving spouse. A look at how state law controls the distribution of assets can be seen in the sample state intestacy law in Exhibit 5.1. Before applying this information, consultation with legal and tax professionals is recommended.

In the second column of Exhibit 5.1 is the word *escheat*. When a person dies without leaving a will and it is determined that there is no spouse, heirs, or kin, the decedent's assets **escheat** (revert) to the place she resided. This rule varies. In some jurisdictions the property escheats to the state; in others it goes to the county. In some states, this pertains to only real property, to only personal property, or to both.

In any intestacy situation, it is important to determine whether the state distinguishes between whole and half-blood kin. How are adopted children treated? Are there distinctions between within-wedlock and out-of-wedlock children? How are **posthumous** (born after the decedent's death) children and **after-born** (born after the execution of a will) children treated? Does judicial termination of marriage affect distribution? Again, probate rules regarding intestacy vary from jurisdiction to jurisdiction. It is important for the trust professional to be aware of applicable state laws.

To summarize, with intestacy a person's estate will indeed be administered and distributed upon death, but according to the rules of the decedent's state of residence at death. Without a will no one knows to whom the valuable antique collection goes, that a gift was intended for Boy Scouts of America, who will be the guardian of the 8-year-old twins, that the estate could have taken advantage of tax-saving mechanisms—or that a trust would have helped the family.

WHO CAN ESTABLISH A WILL

Anyone who has **testamentary capacity**—meaning they are of legal age and of sound mind—can establish a will. Each state determines what legal age is (18 in most states), but complications arise over the interpretation of what constitutes **sound mind.**

Although not every state has specific statutes that require a **testator** (the one who establishes a will) to be of sound mind in order to execute a valid will, testamentary capacity is a universal requirement. (Testator is a generic or unisex term. The term **testatrix,** a female testator, is seldom

Exhibit 5.1 Sample State Intestacy Distribution

How Property Is Distributed Without a Will

If the Decedent Was	The Estate Will Be Distributed
Married, with surviving child(ren) or descendents of deceased child(ren)	One-half to surviving spouse and one-half to the child(ren), divided equally*
Married, with no surviving child(ren) or descendants of child(ren)	Entirely to surviving spouse
Widow or single person with child(ren) or descendants of deceased child(ren)	Entirely to child(ren) divided equally, or to their descendants*
Widow or single person with no child(ren) or descendants of child(ren)	Entirely to parents, **siblings** (brothers and sisters), divided equally;* if only one parent survives, parent receives a double portion.

Note: If none of the beneficiaries listed survives, property passes one-half along bloodline of maternal grandparents and one-half along bloodline of paternal grandparents.

If no descendants of the respective grandparents survive, property passes along the bloodlines of maternal and paternal great-grandparents.

If no descendants of the respective great-grandparents survive, the estate passes to the next of kin; if there are no kin, property generally escheats to the county; for specific details, consult an attorney.

***Child(ren) of a deceased heir take the portion their parent would have received.**

used these days.) Testamentary capacity, too, can vary in definition from jurisdiction to jurisdiction. Many states add terms that leave room for additional interpretation. For example, an "absolute" sound mind is not a prerequisite to the execution (signing) of a valid will in many states. "Absolute" can be a subject to interpretation.

With respect to a testator's testamentary capacity, the general rules are that a testator should

- Understand the business in which he is engaged (that is, the act of making a will)

- Realize the effect of making a will

- Understand the general nature and extent of his property; most states only require that a testator have a general knowledge of the estate rather than a perfect recollection of all property

- Know the "natural objects" of his bounty or generosity; this is not limited to blood relatives

- Know and remember the people who would normally inherit the property

- Understand the manner in which the property will be distributed among the beneficiaries according to the terms of the will

- Understand the act that is being made and the outcomes of that act (a testator may not need a high degree of intelligence or education to have the mental capacity to make a will; in fact, it has been ruled that less mental capacity is required to enable a person to make a will than to make a contract)

Will Contests

The issue of testamentary capacity has led wills to be contested (challenged). A **contest of a will** is an attempt to prevent the probate of a will according to a will's provisions. Historically only 1 percent of all wills that have been submitted to probate have been contested. Most will contests are based on the grounds of **undue influence** (when one person has enough influence over the testator to prevent the testator from making a free choice) or lack of testamentary capacity. Children are the most likely candidates to bring on a contest, and more women than men initiate contests. Smaller estates are more likely to be contested than larger ones. Additional grounds for contesting a will are:

- Noncompliance with the requirements of execution (i.e., not properly signed or witnessed)

- Forgery or altered documents (after the fact)

- Mistake (signature of will is not that of the decedent)

- Fraud (i.e., misleading testator to sign the will thinking that it was another type of document)

- Duress (similar to undue influence, or forcing a testator to sign that which he does not want to sign)

- Insane delusion; this condition must be overpowering and much more than mere eccentricity

Probate laws differ with respect to the validity and contest of will variations:

- ***Holographic will***. A will that is entirely in the testator's handwriting and has no witnesses; some

states recognize this type of will only with respect to persons serving in the armed forces

- *Oral will*. A will that is spoken; in general an oral will is created during a last sickness or in contemplation of immediate death; this type of will usually pertains only to personal property, and it is seen primarily with respect to military personnel during a time of armed conflict

- *Videotaped will*. A will that is spoken and recorded on videotape

- *Foreign will*. A will prepared in another state (other than the testator's legal state of residence at the time of death) or another country

- *Foreign language will*. A will of a U.S. resident written in a language other than English

Although the statutory period varies from state to state, in most states a will contest must be filed within six months after the will is admitted to probate. If a will provides for the pourover of assets into a trust created by the testator, the contest of the will may extend to a contest of the trust, although trust contests may be limited by statute to a shorter period of time.

Only an interested party can contest a will. An interested party is a person who has an economic interest that would be adversely affected by the will's admission to probate. Probate laws differ as to whether the grounds for a contest will invalidate that part of the will that the contest addresses or the entire will. Probate statutes also differ as to the contest of a codicil; the contest may pertain only to the entire codicil, to a part of it, or to the entire will upon which the codicil is based.

Here is an example of a situation in which a will was contested on the grounds of testamentary capacity. Mrs. Smith was a widow of substantial financial means. Mrs. Smith had a will that provided that all her assets, except for her jewelry, would go to her only child, a son. Her will provided for her extensive jewelry collection to go to her daughter-in-law. Both beneficiaries were aware of Mrs. Smith's intentions. How? She told them.

Because of her son's and daughter-in-law's pending divorce, Mrs. Smith became disenchanted with her daughter-in-law, so she wanted to remove the bequest (gift) of the jewelry from her will. Mrs. Smith's attorney informed her that she could either do a new will to express her new intention, or the attorney could prepare a codicil in which Mrs. Smith acknowledged the removal of the bequest of the jewelry to her soon-to-be-estranged daughter-in-law.

Mrs. Smith was hospitalized during the time she consulted her lawyer and elected to create a codicil, which was duly prepared and executed. A few weeks later she was discharged from the hospital to her home. Two months later Mrs. Smith died.

During the administration of Mrs. Smith's will, the daughter-in-law, unaware of the codicil, approached the executor of the estate and asked how long it would be before she received the jewelry. The executor informed her that Mrs. Smith had signed a codicil that removed the bequest of the jewelry.

The daughter-in-law sued the estate (contested the codicil) on the grounds that Mrs. Smith did not have testamentary capacity when she signed the codicil. She maintained that as a patient in the hospital, Mrs. Smith was not of sound mind, and therefore the codicil should be considered null and void. Two months passed before this contest went to a court trial, complete with jury, that lasted 3 months.

The facts of the case, the outcome, and the post-trial activities are too extensive, legal, and complicated to describe here. Although the jury decided in favor of the daughter-in-law, the appellate court reversed the verdict. The plaintiff (the daughter-in-law) could have taken the case higher (to the state Supreme Court), but elected not to do so.

Trust professionals will face these situations. Customers will ask what a will is and how their estates will be affected if they do not have a will. You will be asked who can and cannot create a will and what might cause a will to be challenged at death. An understanding of these ideas, plus the following examination of a will, take the trust professional into a deeper understanding of the impact and importance of a will as a vital ingredient to our customers' estate planning.

Joint Wills

Sometimes more than one testator is involved in one or more wills. (Remember, these concepts and interpretations will vary among jurisdictions.) The distinctions are as follows:

- *Joint will.* In a joint will, two or more persons execute their will on the same piece of paper; this is seen primarily with respect to spouses.

- *Mutual will.* In a mutual will, two separate wills contain reciprocal (mirror) provisions.

- *Joint-and-mutual will.* In many states, a joint-and-mutual will is synonymous with a "contractual" will; that is, the will is determined to have been entered into pursuant to a contract that the surviving testator would not revoke the agreed-upon disposition. In general, the courts look to the terminology of the will to determine whether the existence of a contract should be inferred.

Most estate planning professionals object to joint wills, mutual wills, and joint-and-mutual wills because of the potential legal intricacies that could cause the original intentions of a testator to not occur.

SAMPLE WILL

Many, many years ago, it was common practice to have a will prepared once; and it was done in anticipation of death. The title of the document was *The Last Will and Testament of* _____. The word *last* indicated exactly that; there was an air of conclusion and termination in that word.

Early wills (and testaments) were one-page documents. In a few words the testator put in writing his wishes as to whom he wanted to give his property. Over the years, as estates have grown in size and complexity, as tax laws have flourished, and as the legal system has expanded, the one-page document of yesteryear has grown to many times that size. Improvements have been made, options have been added, and protection has been increased.

An easy way to understand the makings and purposes of a will is to look at a John Doe will. *Note:* Do not use this example as legal direction. Although many parts of the following example are taken from a sample will, they are out of context, and they should not be construed as legal assistance or direction.

Introduction

Will of John Q. Doe

I, John Q. Doe, a resident of _____, declare this to be my will, and I revoke all other wills and codicils that I have made.

Each will has an introductory paragraph that identifies who the testator is and where he resides. The statement of where John lives can help to determine domicile (a person's legal residence), yet it is of no help if John retired and permanently moved to another state.

The statement of revocation of all prior wills and codicils is sometimes thought of as superfluous language. It is thought that a new will—regardless of its language—automatically revokes previous wills and codicils associated with them. Probate statutes differ. It is possible for a testator to revoke her will without replacing it with another; she could prepare a codicil or other document that declares the revocation. Suppose that a testator executes a will and later executes another will that does not contain specific, express language revoking the earlier will. In many jurisdictions, the second will would be treated as a codicil to the first will. This is a technical legality, but it nonetheless addresses another reason for the importance of having a will properly prepared according to the statutes of where the testator is legally domiciled.

In some wills the introductory paragraph states that the testator is "of sound mind." It is presumed that the will maker has testamentary capacity, or else he could not legally execute the will.

Payment of Expenses

The expenses of my last illness, my funeral, and the administration of my estate, and taxes payable by reason of my death, shall be paid out of the principal of my residuary estate without apportionment or proration.

It was mentioned earlier in the chapter that a will directs the payment of taxes and debts. Notice that the word *debts* is not mentioned in this will. Because probate laws universally direct that debts be paid, specific mention of it is not made here.

Some states set rules that permit a personal representative (later defined and discussed) to pay only a certain amount toward funeral expenses, unless directed otherwise in a will. John Doe directs that *all* of these expenses be paid.

John's will contains a **residuary clause** in which he states that he wants all expenses (illness, funeral, administration, and taxes) to be paid from his residuary estate without **apportionment** or **proration.** *Residuary* refers to what remains after specific bequests have been made. The mention of "apportionment and proration" is sometimes called the will's tax clause. John wants his estate, not the recipients of his estate, to bear the payment of taxes. Absent this language, the recipients (beneficiaries) of the estate will bear equal responsibility for these expenses. John desires otherwise and therefore must say so in his will.

To the extent that the assets of my residuary estate are insufficient to pay the expenses of my last illness, funeral, administration of my estate and taxes payable by reason of my death, my executor may request such payment from the trustees of the trust hereinafter referred to.

What if the residuary estate does not have enough in it to pay these expenses? John's will stipulates that expenses be paid from a trust he has established. If the testator has a revocable trust, some states have recently enacted laws that entitle the personal representative of the estate to seek payment of the insufficiency from the trustee of the trust, if the assets of the residue of the testator's probate estate are insufficient to pay administration expenses and claims, regardless of mention in the will. (We will see this concept again when we look at John's trust in Chapter 8.)

Disposition of Assets

I give all of my clothing and wearing apparel to Jim Doe, my brother, if he survives me.

I give my stamp and coin collections to Joe Doe, my son, if he survives me. If he does not so survive me, I give same to Judy Doe, my daughter, if she survives me. If neither Joe Doe or Judy Doe survives me, I give same to Mary Doe, referred to as "my wife," if she survives me.

I give all of my remaining personal and household effects such as jewelry, clothing, automobiles, furniture, furnishings, silver, books and pictures, including policies of insurance thereon, to my wife, if she survives me or, if she does not survive me, such property shall be distributed to such of my children who survive me (to the exclusion of the descendants of any of them who do not so survive me), in shares of substantially equal value, to be divided as they agree, or if they fail to agree within six (6) months after my death, as my executor shall determine; except that if any child of mine is a minor at the time of such division, the guardian to the child shall represent the child in the division of the property, receipt for and hold the child's share or sell all or any part of it, and deliver the share or proceeds to the child when the child reaches majority.

Bequests

This article of John's will provides for the distribution of particular assets (property) to specific beneficiaries (individuals and charities). Several probate statutes are exacting (and hold to historical roots as seen earlier) with terms and definitions pertaining to the distribution of property at death. For example:

- **Devise.** A clause directing the disposition of real property

- **Legacy.** A clause directing the disposition of money

- **Bequest.** A clause directing the disposition of personal property (other than money)

Some wills use **bequeath** in the place of the word *give*. This is the portion of a will that says who gets what. John states that he wants his stamp and coin collections to go to his son. If his son is not living at the time of John's death, then the collections go to John's daughter. If his son *and* daughter do not survive John, he wants these items to go to his wife, Mary.

With regard to any personal and household effects, he gives them to his wife, if she survives him. If she does not survive him, then he gives them to his children who are alive at his death. What if Mary and Joe are not alive, but Joe has children? The entire property still goes to his daughter, Judy; John specifically states that he does not want these assets to go to his children's children.

Notice that John says "personal and household effects" (which are tangible personal property). This does not pertain to intangible personal property and real property, which will become part of John's residuary estate.

John gives his children the right to divide the property equally. But what if they cannot agree? John then asks his executor (personal representative) to divide the property—or to sell the property and divide the proceeds among the children—as the executor sees fit. If any of the children are minors, then the decision as to the division of the property is to be made by the child's guardian.

It appears that John has covered all the bases with respect to who gets what. But what if John sold the stamp and coin collections before his death? Then an **ademption** occurs: The bequest is considered withdrawn or extinguished. If an asset does not exist at the testator's death, it cannot be distributed according to the will's provision. Probate laws also address partial ademptions. For example, if a testator's will provides for a bequest of a large tract of land and later the testator sells a portion of the tract, an ademption applies to the portion of the property that was sold. The remaining portion would pass to the named beneficiary.

Who gets what if Mary, Joe, and Judy are not alive at John's death? Assets that are not disposed of to specific beneficiaries will be added to John's residuary estate. Again, *residuary* means what is left over. We will see later how John's will handles this contingency.

It is important that the testator clearly and specifically describe his assets and to whom they go. There should be no room for confusion. For example, let us assume for a moment that John says in his will, "I give my diamond ring to Joe Doe." From what we have seen, Joe is John's son. If John has a brother named Joe, which Joe gets the ring? Also, what if only one ring existed at the time John wrote his will, and he purchased another one after the fact? If there is confusion as to who gets what, a partial intestacy occurs.

John may ask, "Why be so specific about my stamp and coin collections? Everyone knows that I want my son to have them. When I die, I'll give everything to my wife and when she dies she will give these assets to my son. That's the way

husbands and wives do things! Besides, Mary does not have any interest in my coin and stamp collections. She knows that I want these collections to go to Joe." Picture this: John dies and his assets go to Mary. Mary remarries, and her second husband is very interested in stamp collecting. After her remarriage, Mary executes a new will, in which she bequests all of her assets to her second husband. Can she do this? Yes, she can, because she became the legal owner of everything she inherited from John. In this scenario, the second husband would receive the stamp and coin collections because Mary stated so in her will. The moral of the story: Be specific about your wishes, or an inadvertent disinheritance may occur. The **dispositive provisions** (statements of how assets are to be distributed) of John's will should state clearly what he wants.

Simultaneous Death

An important aspect of bequests in wills is the language associated with them. Look again at the language pertaining to John's stamp and coin collections. Probate laws differ as to what "survives" means. If John and Joe die simultaneously—where there is no sufficient evidence that they died otherwise than simultaneously—do the stamp and coin collections pass according to Joe's estate plan, or do they pass to Judy? Some states have specific simultaneous-death rules in effect to address this issue when a will fails to provide for simultaneous death. A technique lawyers commonly use to cover the possibility of a simultaneous death, or deaths in quick succession, is to make all bequests contingent on surviving the testator by, for example, 30 days.

Disclaimers

No one can be compelled to accept an interest in property. A person (for example, Joe, mentioned earlier) may **disclaim** (refuse to accept) any interest in whole or in part. Joe can accept the stamp collection but not the coin collection. If Joe disclaims his interest in the coin collection, most state statutes consider Joe to have pre-deceased John with respect to the coin collection only. Disclaimers also apply to lifetime gifts and interests created in a trust.

Beneficiary

The recipient of a bequest is a **beneficiary.** A beneficiary is not necessarily a person; it can be a nonperson, such as a charity, a church, or a not-for-profit organization. Beneficiaries of a will are also not necessarily relatives.

In general, people who are beneficiaries of a will are also called heirs. An **heir** is a person who may or may not be related (either by bloodline or marriage) to the decedent: Spouses are related by marriage; children are related by bloodline. John Doe can also provide a bequest in his will for Sally Jones, a neighbor, who is not related. Heirs can also be distinguished as **descendants** or **kin** (or **next of kin**). The distinguishing factor between descendant and kin is the direction of bloodline. A descendant is in direct line to the decedent, as a son or daughter is to father or mother or a grandchild is to a grandparent. Kin is of the same blood, but indirect, as in an upward (grandparent) or sideways (brother, sister, niece, or nephew) relationship, as opposed to children of a downward direction. Some writers use the word **issue**, which is a broader term for people who descended from a common ancestor. This term could include stepchildren, children by other marriages, and adopted children. Yet another term for a person, related or not, who benefits from a will is **legatee.**

Family

> As of the date of this instrument, I have two (2) children: Joe Doe, born February 29, 1993, and Judy Doe, born September 31, 1982.

If John and Mary Doe have additional children after this will is in effect, will these children be disinherited? Only with

respect to specific bequests, yet they will still share in John's estate. It is important to check with state statutes to determine how after-born and posthumous children share in a testator's estate, both testate and intestate. In addition, laws vary regarding in-wedlock and out-of-wedlock children and adopted children (whether minors or not). Also, divorce laws may affect testacy and intestacy inheritances.

Pourover or Establishment of Trust

> I give all my residuary estate, being all real and personal property, wherever situated, not otherwise effectively disposed of, to the trustees under a trust agreement dated January 1, 2002, known as the John Doe Trust, to be added to the trust property and held and distributed in accordance with the terms of this agreement.

After the bequests have been made, and after the expenses of last illness, funeral, administration, and taxes have been paid, a residuary estate remains. Assets not given to specific persons, intangible personal property, and real property are directed into John's residuary estate. John provides that these assets **pour over** into a trust that John created on January 1, 2002.

In Chapter 7, we will distinguish between living trusts (inter vivos trusts) and testamentary trusts. In this example, John has a living trust (separate from his will) into which the assets of his residuary estate will pour. In some instances people will form their trust intents (provisions) right in their will. This is a testamentary trust (from the word *testament*).

Appointment of Guardians

> If my wife does not survive me, or dies after my death without providing for the custody of a minor child of mine, I name my wife's brother, Pete Smith, and his wife, Deborah Smith, as guardians of the person and estate of any minor child of mine. In the

event that either of them fails or ceases to act as guardian, the remainder of them shall cease to act as guardian and my wife's brother, Paul Smith, and his wife, Amy Smith, shall act as successor guardians.

John is very concerned that his assets be distributed as he wishes; he also cares deeply that his minor children be properly cared for. Remember, without a will the court must appoint a **testamentary guardian,** both personal and estate, for minor children. (Refer to Chapter 6 for distinction between personal and estate guardians.) John is not concerned about the guardianship of his children if Mary survives, but what will happen if neither he nor Mary is living and Mary did not name a guardian in her will? Because their children grew up with two parents, John and Mary want a couple as guardians if John and Mary die while their children are minors. This is why John names his wife's brother, Pete, and Pete's wife together. If one cannot serve, the other is not permitted to serve alone. If they cannot fulfill their appointment, John provides for the naming of successor guardians: Paul and Amy Smith. (Note that Joe is the only one affected by this guardian article.)

As you assist customers with their will planning, you are bound to be asked for your opinion regarding who should be considered as guardian. You may be uncomfortable with this personal question and unprepared to answer because of your initial unfamiliarity with the customer and lack of knowledge about the family. You probably know very little about the children.

Your customer isn't asking you to suggest who the guardian(s) should be but what qualifications the guardian should possess. Whether Joe's guardians are Peter and Deborah or Paul and Amy, the guardians must be able to

- Instill Joe with the same principles, values, and discipline as John and Mary would

- Represent Joe fairly with regard to the division of John and Mary's estate
- Safekeep Joe's assets until he reaches the age of majority
- Interact with the trustee of John's trust that benefits his children

Joe's guardians may become his acting parents. The important chore for us is to guide our customers to choose wisely. (Chapter 6 delves deeper into the guardian's financial responsibilities.)

Executor Appointment

I appoint XYZ Bank and Trust Company (or any successor to its trust business) as executor of this will.

If the appointment of an executor of my estate is necessary or desirable in any jurisdiction in which my principal executor is unable or unwilling to act, I appoint as my executor in that jurisdiction any corporation as may be designated in an instrument signed by my principal executor, to act and to have all the powers and discretions with respect to my estate in that jurisdiction during administration.

With the number of bank buyouts and mergers that occur, John's attorney was smart to add the words "or any successor to its trust business." If XYZ Bank and Trust Company is bought or merged with ABC Bank and Trust Company, ABC bank will become John's executor. If this is not what John wants, all he needs to do is amend his will with a codicil stating whom he wants as the executor of his will.

If John owns a condominium in Florida, several hundred acres of farmland in Kansas, and interest in commercial real estate in Colorado, can his executor in Illinois administer these out-of-state assets? Does his executor *want* to administer assets that are hundreds or thousands of miles away? John's will gives his executor the freedom to appoint others to carry out its administrative duties. XYZ Bank and

Trust Company may be unfamiliar with the other states' probate statutes, or it may be less expensive for a local representative to administer the local assets because of its familiarity with the lay of the land. In this instance, XYZ Bank and Trust Company is called a **domiciliary** representative. The person or institution designated or appointed to administer property in a state other than that of the decedent's permanent home (domicile) is called an **ancillary** (supplementary) representative.

If John and Mary retire and move to Florida to live in their condominium and establish permanent residence there, is John's will that he executed in Illinois still valid? There is probably no question that the will is valid, but can XYZ Bank and Trust Company (in Illinois) still serve as executor of John's will now that he is a resident of Florida?

XYZ may not be permitted to act as John's executor. How can you determine this? The easiest way is to consult *Study 4: Rights of Nonresident Banks to Act as Fiduciaries in Various States*, published in 1994 by the American College of Trust and Estate Counsel (Los Angeles, California). This report examines the ability of a bank or trust company with fiduciary powers in its state of incorporation to serve as a fiduciary in states where it has not qualified to do business.

Each state has its own rules, and the American College of Trust and Estate Counsel's study lists what each state allows. The study addresses a nonresident bank's ability or inability to serve as administrator, ancillary administrator, executor, ancillary executor, testamentary trustee, ancillary testamentary trustee, guardian of the estate for a minor or incompetent adult, and ancillary guardian of the estate for a minor or incompetent adult. The report also addresses specific exceptions, such as state reciprocity and court approval for appointment. Familiarity with this study is recommended for all trust professionals.

Getting back to John, if he does not change his will after he establishes residency in Florida, and if XYZ Bank in Illinois may not serve as executor for a Florida resident, the Florida court will not appoint XYZ as executor and instead will appoint a personal representative. Perhaps a **temporary administrator** will be appointed until the court appoints a permanent one. This in itself should not invalidate John's will.

Earlier we stated that John's executor in Illinois—call it his principal executor—can appoint an ancillary executor in Florida. This is the case of an Illinois decedent who owned assets in Florida. If John changes his residence to Florida, his Illinois executor can neither continue serving as executor, because of Florida's rules, nor name a new executor; this is a right applicable only to John or the court following John's demise.

Seldom do our customers think about the status of their wills when they move. We must remind them of these important points, lest their estate planning intentions go awry.

Executor's Powers

> My executor shall have the following powers, and any others that may be granted by law, to be exercised in its discretion without court order:

This section of the will lists the specific powers (investment or otherwise) John gives to his executor with respect to the assets of his estate. These are the administrative provisions. To get a feel for these powers, let's list a few here:

- To retain any property of my estate
- To invest in any property, real or personal
- To sell any real or personal property of my estate and to exchange any such property for other property
- To operate, maintain, repair, rehabilitate, alter, improve or remove any improvements on real estate, to make leases, and to subdivide real estate
- To employ attorneys, auditors, and agents and to exercise all voting

and other rights with respect to stocks or other securities

- To collect, pay, contest, or abandon claims of or against my estate and to execute contracts
- To make any distribution or division of my estate in cash or in kind or both
- To borrow money for any purpose
- To retain any business interest, as shareholder and to participate in the management of any business
- In addition to the powers herein, to do all other acts in its judgment necessary or desirable for the proper administration of the estate, all of which may be executed without authorization by any court

Many of the powers listed in this section do not need to be specifically listed; each state's probate laws contain most of the powers that John directs to his executor. However, just as it does not hurt to place four nails where three will do the job, it is always a good idea to individually delineate these powers. It is wise to guide the executor carefully. If John moves to another state, he cannot assume that the new state's probate laws cover the same items as the former state. Think back to when John directed that his funeral expenses be paid from his estate. If John did not specifically mention this intent, and if the new state he moved to puts a limit on the amount of funeral expenses to be paid by an estate, his intent would not be met.

As can be seen from this discussion, an executor (unlike a trustee) is primarily a liquidator, rather than a manager. Generally, an executor must have court approval for such activities as operating a business, borrowing money, managing an investment portfolio of securities, and buying and selling property. There is a careful line to be drawn and walked with respect to what a will permits (not dictates), what the statutes and the court permit (and do not permit), and what the best interests are of the family and heirs.

Executor's Fees

A corporate executor, if acting, shall be entitled to reasonable compensation, which shall be determined by the fee schedule of the corporate executor in effect at my death.

We will discuss executor's fees in more detail in the administration and settlement section later in the chapter.

Execution (Signing)

I have signed this will on this _____ day of _____, 200____.

_____

Signature

Signatures and Security

Because of a will's legal nature and its importance to John and his heirs, John should **execute** (sign) only one original copy. Some authorities ask the testator to place his signature or initials in the border or bottom of each page of the will, except for the signature page. Sometimes an attorney will ask that each witness do the same.

What constitutes a signature? Any mark affixed by the testator, with the intent that the mark operates as the testator's signature, satisfies the signature requirement. "Pat," "Mom," "D.F.M.," the X of an illiterate person, and even the testator's fingerprint are all valid signatures. In addition, the testator's signature may be signed by another person at the testator's direction and in the testator's presence. In fact, if that person writes the testator's name and then writes his own name, the person can be counted as one of the needed attesting witnesses.

A will should be kept in a secure place: with the attorney who drafted the document, or in the vault of the bank named as executor.

Copies

Photocopies are permissible for reference purposes. If a will is kept in a safe deposit box, with an attorney or in the bank's vault, John and other parties—attorney or executor—may want to have copies for their records. Remember that upon death the original will is what counts. Only in unusual or extraordinary circumstances will the court accept a copy.

In many situations, rather than making photocopies (because today's technological advances can create photocopies that can be mistaken for originals), an attorney may prepare one or more conformed copies of a will. A **conformed copy** is a copy of a nonexecuted will on which the testator's signature, the notary public seal, witnesses' signatures and addresses, and any other handwritten features of the will are typewritten or printed. Besides indicating the will's existence, it can be used for reference purposes and it will prevent confusion about its originality.

Witnessing

We saw John Doe, in our presence, sign this instrument at its end; he then declared it to be his will and requested us to act as witnesses to it; we believed him to be of sound mind and memory and not under duress or constraint of any kind; and then we, in his presence and in the presence of each other, signed our names as attesting witnesses; all of which was done on the date of this instrument.

Name   *Address*

————————   ————————
                ————————
————————   ————————
                ————————
————————   ————————
                ————————

The last section of the will is called the **attestation clause.** This is where the will's witnesses (**attesting witnesses**) **attest** (witness) the testator's signature in the presence of each other. Each state sets rules about how many witnesses (usually two) are required, although most attorneys provide for three witnesses to sign the will. Some states require the tes-

tator's and witnesses' names to be typed below the line of their signature because not everyone's signature is legible.

Following are several issues regarding witnesses:

- *May an attorney be a witness to a will?* Yes, but bar associations recommend that the drafting attorney not serve as a witness to a will that she has prepared. The attorney's task is to legally prepare the will, not to serve as an attesting witness. A state may require that a will be notarized. Many attorneys serve as a **notary/notary public** at a will signing. In some states a notary can act as a witness.

- *May a spouse or family member witness a will?* It is unwise for anyone who will benefit from a will to be a witness. A witness should be a disinterested party whose only connection to a will is to act as a witness—someone who can say, "I saw the testator sign the will and I believe he is of sound mind."

- *May a bank employee serve as a witness?* Before we answer this question, let's ask another one. Does the bank trust department or employee have an interest in John's will when the bank serves, for a fee, as John's executor? If so, with respect to gaining fee income as John's executor, the bank does have an interest. But the employee and bank trust department are disinterested in that they do not personally benefit from the assets of John's estate. So an employee may serve as a witness. Note that as a matter of policy some institutions do not permit employees to act as witnesses.

- *Should John know who his witnesses are?* It really does not matter, as long as they are not people who benefit from the decedent's estate.

A witness's duty has been the subject of concern and debate for many years.

John's witnesses are attesting that they believe him to be of sound mind. Witnesses do not determine whether a person has mental testamentary capacity; they testify that they saw the testator sign the will and offer a belief that the document is real and that the testator is of sound mind—nothing more. Therefore, is a witness's signature binding on the witness? The courts have uniformly held that an attestation clause does not constitute sworn testimony—it does not serve as a substitute for courtroom testimony. The probate of a will does not turn upon the memory of the attesting witnesses. The witnesses are merely attesting that the signing of the will actually occurred.

A trust officer was once asked to serve as a witness to a will for an 80-year-old woman hospitalized with a broken hip. This was the first time in her life that she executed a will. The trust officer did not know the testator, but her will appointed the bank as successor executor, following the woman's son. The drafting attorney arranged for himself and the trust officer to visit his client in the hospital. The attorney left the woman's room to find two additional witnesses; he would serve as notary for the will. The trust officer, left alone in the hospital room with the soon-to-be-testator, was startled by the woman's yell as she pointed to the window of her hospital room. His back was to the window, so he asked her what she saw. "An elephant," she said. The trust officer knew this was not true because there was no way for her to see the street level from the vantage point of her seventh-floor room.

The trust officer became concerned about her mental state. When the attorney returned, the trust officer declined to serve as a witness to the will, stating his reason why. The attorney explained that the trust officer's signature was only an attestation that he saw her sign her will on that day. Still, the trust officer did not feel comfortable because the attestation clause stated, "We believe her to be of sound mind and memory." He had the right and the responsibility to decline to serve as a witness. Nor could he place his signature on a legal document attesting to someone's sound mind when he did not personally believe it. Yes, he could attest that he saw her sign her will, and that she was not under duress, but was she under constraint of any kind? Not physically, perhaps, but her mental state might have been a constraint.

CHANGING A WILL

As long as a testator is not incapacitated, a will is not an irrevocable document. It may be altered:

- A new will automatically voids a previous will and any subsequent changes that were made to the previous will.

- A will can be amended by a codicil. A codicil is a legal document that modifies one or more parts of a will. A codicil possesses and requires all the legalities and formalities of a will.

- A will can be revoked in its entirety without being replaced by a subsequent will. Very seldom is this done because this leaves a person without a will.

- Every state has probate statutes that address the amendment and revocation of a will or parts of a will by express, physical action (for example, writing on the document or intentionally destroying it by burning, tearing, or obliterating it in some fashion—with or without the intent to revoke).

- In most states, a judicial termination of marriage (divorce or annulment) following the execution of a will revokes all bequests in favor of the former spouse. The rest of the will remains valid and is interpreted as though the ex-spouse predeceased the testator.

- When a will that was last seen in the testator's possession cannot be found after the testator's death, the will is presumed to have been revoked by the intent of the testator. If the will was last seen in the possession of a third person, no presumption of revocation arises.

- Suppose that a will is accidentally destroyed or that a will cannot be located after the testator's death. Can the presumption of revocation be overcome? All states permit probate of a lost or destroyed will provided that three elements can be proved:
  1. The will was validly executed
  2. The reason why the will was not produced
  3. The contents of the will

The contents are usually proved by the testimony of at least two witnesses or by production of a carbon copy, photocopy, or conformed copy of the will. A conformed copy is a copy of the original document with the signature, seal, and other such features being typed or otherwise noted.

An important aspect of the estate planning services we provide to our customers is a regular review of their estates. (In Chapter 12 we will address the importance to our departments of serving our customer base.) A change in family status, an altered financial picture, tax law changes, or the desire to change the dispositive provisions of a will may necessitate a will modification or a new will, depending on the extent of the changes.

Post-Mortem Letter

Another supplement to—but not a substitute for—an estate plan is a post-mortem letter. In addition to preparing a will, many people write addendum letters to accompany their will. Such letters may be hand written by the testator. The letter is meant to be read and possibly go into effect following one's death. This type of letter does not carry any legal authority, yet it is often used as a testator's guidelines.

A post-mortem letter of instruction may provide:

- Guidance as to the desired disposition of personal property among relatives

- Information about the location of various items, such as safe deposit boxes or bank accounts

- Advice about which assets should be liquidated in the event funds are needed for estate administration expenses and taxes

- Any other information and guidance that the decedent wishes to give to the executor of the estate

These types of instructions are not binding upon the executor, but they can be very useful in revealing the decedent's wishes. Generally, they will be carried out unless the executor finds some compelling reason for not doing so.

A post-mortem letter may also contain burial and funeral instructions not specifically mentioned in the will. For example, the letter may state that the testator wishes to have his funeral arrangements made through a particular funeral home, to be buried in a specific cemetery, to have a military presence if the decedent was a veteran, or to be cremated. The post-mortem letter can also provide organ-donation instructions. Many times a confidential personal statement (see Appendix 1) accompanies the letter. This assists the executor in valuing the estate, locating assets, and preparing an estate inventory. The letter may also contain personal messages for certain family members.

An individual's intentions may change over the years, sometimes quite often. Rather than revise her will to state these changes, a testator could use a post-mortem letter. Changing post-mortem letters is easier, faster, and less expensive than changing a will.

Other Documents

Post-mortem letters present difficulties when they contain dispositive provisions that contradict the will. It is acceptable for it to offer "suggestions," but the post-mortem letter may or may not affect the will. For example, John might provide in his will for the division of his assets among his children according to their agreed-upon arrangement if John's spouse does not survive him. John may have made this general dispositive provision because he was ambivalent about which assets should go to whom. The post-mortem letter could offer suggestions as to which assets should go to which child; but again, only a will can offer legally binding direction.

Many states recognize "incorporation by reference," whereby a document separate (extrinsic) from the will may be incorporated/integrated into the will by reference so that it is considered part of the will. Even though the document is not physically a part of the will, it will be incorporated as part of the will if

- It was in existence when the will was executed
- It is referred to as being in existence
- It is clearly identified in the will

Until this point our discussion has focused on the predeath side of the picture: establishment of a will, consequences of having and not having a will, options open to the testator, and sample language. The day will come when the testator becomes a decedent, and the will enters the legal process called probate.

PROBATE

Unfortunately, many people think of probate as an ugly word, connoting an inordinate consumption of time, unnecessary expenses (legal and otherwise), and unwarranted court appearances, all while the family is traumatized by a loved one's death. In reality probate is a legal process that has evolved through specific laws and interpretations of the law to protect and benefit a decedent's estate. Over the past 10 to 15 years states have streamlined the probate process for executors. **Probate** is the orderly method of gathering a decedent's assets, paying debts, taxes, and administrative expenses, and distributing (transferring) assets to the estate's beneficiaries, all under the watchful eye of the **probate court,** regardless of whether a person dies testate or intestate.

Trust professionals play a very important role in educating and assuring customers that probate is not ugly, time consuming, unnecessary, expensive, and impersonal, unless the wrong executor is chosen.

Expanded Definition

Probate is a very old word. It has its roots in feudal England, although it has traveled through Latin, German, and Celtic vocabularies. Through centuries of use and interpretation, the word today has come to mean *proof*. Proof must be given to the court that a will exists, the will is valid, the will is that of the decedent, and the will is the decedent's last will. Additionally, proof must be provided, for the protection of the estate and the beneficiaries, that the estate's creditors and taxes have been paid and that the decedent's affairs have been managed according to the terms of the will and according to the precise letter of probate law.

Time Involved

The time required to probate an estate depends on the nature of the assets, the complexity of the estate's assets, the size of the estate, the terms of the will, and the expertise of the executor and the estate attorney. Although some experts in the field say probate on average will take a year, this is a rough estimate. Many estates are settled far more quickly, whereas others may take 2 to 3 years or longer. Because probate is looked on more as a process than as individual, distinct activities, there is no way to impose a time frame on the process. Much of probate involves waiting for time periods to lapse (for the IRS audit of the estate's tax return, and for appraisals, inventories, and court approvals). Add to this the family involvement and the knowledge and efficiency possessed by those settling the decedent's estate.

Personal Representative

Just as a safe, enjoyable, and successful trip depends on a careful, experienced car driver, the key to the success of probate is the driver of the estate: the **personal representative.** This is the individual or corporation (trust department) who carries out the terms of the will, deals with the family, and directs the estate through the probate process. Some states exclusively use the term *personal representative,* others use **executor** (**executrix,** the feminine variant, is seldom used). We will freely interchange the terms. When the term *personal representative* is used, this also applies to an **administrator** (the feminine form, **administratrix,** is rarely used), which is the person or corporation appointed by the court to settle an estate when a person dies intestate or the will's named executor cannot or will not act (also called an **administrator with will annexed**).

When an individual serves as an executor, she is called an individual executor. When a corporation (such as a bank trust department) serves as an executor, it is called a corporate executor. When two or more executors serve, each is called a coexecutor. When an individual and a trust department serve as coexecutors, they are called the individual coexecutor and the corporate coexecutor.

Naming an executor in the will is called a **nomination.** Naming an executor in a will does not guarantee that the person or institution will serve. As we will see later, the court must approve and **appoint** the executor named. Also, there is the possibility that the executor named may **decline** to act (a **renunciation**), may be incapable of serving, or may predecease the testator. There is also the chance that the executor is not permitted to act. Think back to John's nomination of an Illinois bank, his move to Florida, and Florida's statutes, which do not permit a foreign (out-of-state) bank to serve as a personal representative for a Florida resident. Additionally, the named executor may accept the nomination, be approved and appointed by the court,

but later **resign** or become incapable of serving. Consideration should be given to naming a "successor (secondary) executor" in the event the primary executor cannot or will not act.

If a named executor is willing to serve, very seldom will the court not approve the nomination. Reasons such as knowledge of family dissension, geographic distance between the named executor and the estate, financial ignorance, and career demands may impede the estate's administration, yet most probate statutes will find a willing person qualified if he is of legal age and of sound mind, is not adjudicated incompetent, and has not been convicted of a felony.

Executor's Qualifications

A testator should assess the qualifications of the person or institution chosen to serve as the prospective executor. When considering an executor, both the testator and executor should ask themselves a series of questions:

- Is the executor prepared, on short notice, to do everything necessary to locate and inventory every last asset belonging to the estate, leaving nothing overlooked?

- Does the executor have experience in dealing with all kinds of property, from stocks and bonds to tax shelters, business ventures, valuable collectibles, and so on?

- Would the executor be able to examine a wide assortment of securities and quickly sort the blue chips from the highly speculative issues?

- Does the executor know how to make a realistic estimate of the cash needed to pay debts, taxes, and expenses and to develop a plan for generating the necessary cash flow?

- Would the executor know where to turn for authoritative appraisals of antiques, jewelry, paintings and other hard-to-value assets?

- Does the executor possess the experience in helping financially inexperienced or elderly beneficiaries cope with difficult adjustments that result from a death in the family?

- Will the executor know the difference between probate and non-probate assets?

- If need be, could the executor negotiate the sale of a business interest or other key assets?

- Would the executor have the patience to deal objectively, impartially, and indiscriminately with disputes among heirs, family, and beneficiaries?

- Could the executor keep up with all the correspondence that is necessary to obtain tax waivers, reregister securities, settle leases, and so on?

- If someone owed the estate money, could the executor collect on behalf of the estate beneficiaries even though the task may be unpleasant?

- Is the executor prepared to keep meticulous records of all estate transactions, receipts, and disbursements?

- Could the executor investigate any questionable claims against the estate and resist those that prove unjustified?

- If questions should arise concerning the income tax returns filed in the last few years of the decedent's life, would the executor be prepared to cope with the problem?

- Is the executor familiar with the special income tax returns filed by an estate?

- Would the executor know what steps an executor can take to preserve after-tax income for the estate beneficiaries?

- Does the executor understand the various decisions and elections that executors are called on to make when federal estate tax returns are prepared?

- If the IRS challenges the valuations placed on certain assets, would the executor know how to respond?

- Could the executor pledge that the administration of the estate will not be delayed or interrupted because of personal business affairs, vacation, or illness?

- Is the executor prepared to see the job through even if it takes 2 years or more?

As can be seen, a good executor must come equipped with unquestionable ethics, financial savvy, orderly recordkeeping skills, and sensitivity to emotional and financial needs. Add to these requirements someone who truly knows what an executor's duties are, someone who will perform them efficiently and economically, someone who has the time, and most important, someone who is willing to act as executor and will continue to do so.

Individual Versus Institution

Can an individual chosen as an executor possess all of these qualities? Yes, these rare individuals do exist. Unfortunately, testators give little consideration to the qualifications needed in choosing a qualified executor.

Statistics show that most people name individuals—in most cases, their spouses—to serve as executor (personal representative) of their estates. *Yet most of these people are quick to acknowledge that their spouses know little or nothing about estate or financial matters.* In effect, these people had selected an executor without regard for the qualifications necessary to economically and expeditiously settle an estate. Interestingly, the choice of a family member is often made to avoid hurt feelings. The duties to be performed are critical, yet they must be carried out at a time when the family is hurting emotionally and under stress.

A testator who names relatives for these reasons is jeopardizing the success of his financial plans for the future. Because an executor's job is complex and exacting—a job that goes beyond merely balancing the checkbook, which many people find difficult to accomplish—there is a good possibility that the inexperienced people named will cost the estate money through inadvertent errors or unavoidable delays.

Many feel that no single person could offer all the qualifications listed. However, there is an alternative: a bank trust department. When talking to a prospective customer, the trust professional must be prepared to point out the qualifications a good executor ought to have and how trust departments meet the requirements. Exhibits 5.2 and 5.3 show the advantages and disadvantages of individual and corporate executors.

Experience

The officers and employees charged with the duty of administering estates are highly trained, experienced, and well qualified to serve. Whether the estate consists of real property, securities, special assets, or even a going business, the estate will benefit from a trust department's combined knowledge of taxation, investments, finance, accounting, and trusts.

In the settlement of even a simple estate, there are many chances for an unskilled, inexperienced, individual executor to commit costly errors. Estate assets may not be located or adequately protected. Property may be undervalued. Important investment decisions may be bungled. Improper claims against the estate may be paid. Unwise income or estate tax elections may be made. Faulty, incomplete, or tardy tax returns may be filed. Each of these common errors could be costly to the estate and

---

Exhibit 5.2 Advantages and Disadvantages of an Individual Executor

Advantages	Disadvantages
• Possible lower cost • Closer and better understanding of the testator's beliefs and objectives • Closer and more sensitive to the family	• Likely to give in to pressure • Poor judgment in hiring estate specialists (appraisers, attorneys, tax consultants) • Less impartial • Lack of professional experience and judgment • Not always available • Can die, become ill, move, resign

---

Exhibit 5.3 Advantages and Disadvantages of a Corporate Executor

Advantages	Disadvantages
• Removed from family pressure • Impartial • Knowledgeable • Seasoned, trained, and experienced • Always available • Permanent	• Perceived higher cost • Not as close as family or friends • Possible turnover of personnel

its beneficiaries. A recent examination of probate records in a large Midwestern city confirms the settlement of estates in an area where experience pays off. A survey of over 10,000 estates concluded that the costs of settling estates for which individuals served as executor averaged 13 percent higher than the costs in estates for which a corporate executor was named.

Clearly, the scope and complexity of an executor's duties are too great for anyone who lacks wide experience in settling estates. In some cases, the beneficiaries of any estate that is mishandled by an amateur executor suffer from irritating delay, inconvenience, and lack of information. Even less fortunate are the beneficiaries who have to pay the cost of their executor's inexperience in estate administration.

For example, in one recent case, a man named his two daughters from his first marriage to serve as coexecutors of his estate. The daughters, the testator's second wife, and her two sons from her previous marriage were beneficiaries. Almost immediately after the testator's death, the wife petitioned the court to remove the two daughters, due to "an unfriendly feeling that exists between my stepdaughters and myself." One of the daughters admitted that animosity indeed existed, but also stated that she had attempted to minimize it. One court ordered the executors removed. A higher court reversed the decision. Regardless of the outcome, think of the costly litigation that resulted, and the resentment that has split the family forever.

The point to remember in a scenario such as this is that controversy probably would not have arisen if the executor named had been a financial institution, with no interest in the estate but to settle it efficiently and with fairness to all, according to the decedent's wishes.

Why make beneficiaries pay for the executor's inexperience? Trust departments are in the business of managing estates. They have been educated and they are experienced. There are no unnecessary delays at the start of administration and no interruptions in the work as it proceeds.

The result is that the estate is settled as quickly and efficiently as possible.

Time Commitment

A relative, friend, or business associate who is busy with his own affairs would have to settle an estate when he could spare the time. He would not be constantly available to confer with the beneficiaries. He might leave the estate administration at a standstill while away on a business trip or on vacation. The result is that it is the beneficiaries who suffer because matters of great importance to the beneficiaries and the estate are of only secondary importance to the executor on whom so much depends. Few people can afford the time necessary for an additional job, one that may be treated as a part-time job when it should be a full-time one.

Impartiality

An executor is charged with acting in the best interests of the estate. An executor must remain impartial and cannot be accused of taking sides in any controversy that might arise. The criterion for action must always be *to map a course that will best carry out the expressed wishes of the person who made the will.* This may not be the case when an individual serves as executor, especially if the executor is a family member or is also a beneficiary. Even when such a person attempts to be strictly impartial, he or she may favor some beneficiaries at the expense of others. Bitter quarrels and dissension may develop.

Permanence

If an individual named as executor dies or becomes disabled before the testator dies (or before the job is completed), the appointment of a successor would add delay and expense to the administration of an estate. A trust department's permanence prevents this delay and expense. Unlike an individual, a bank will not move away, become incapacitated by illness, die, or be too busy with other matters to settle the estate.

ADMINISTRATION AND SETTLEMENT OF AN ESTATE

It is clear that the qualifications of an executor can be best met by trust professionals. As we discuss the duties and responsibilities of administering and settling an estate, it becomes even easier to see a trust department as the logical choice for executor. With estates, testacy versus intestacy, a sample will, and probate finished, we now turn to what the executor does. Think of the duties and responsibilities of administering and settling a customer's estate as a job description.

The administration and settlement of an estate begin with death. **Administration** of an estate is the management of the assets of a decedent's estate throughout the probate process. The settlement of an estate is the distribution of the estate's assets according to the terms of the will or the law of intestacy. Although these two functions appear to be distinct activities, they do meet each other on a common ground through the probate process. Keep this in mind as we work through the administration and settlement of John Doe's estate.

As we work through this section, we will be discussing two related issues: your activities as an employee of the bank within the trust department and the general activities of the bank as executor. In other words, technically the bank is the executor (with the trust department providing the services); you personally are not the executor.

John's funeral is over. The family took care of that and they also collected the final medical bills for the 3 weeks John spent in the hospital before his death. They talked to the hospital about John's wishes to be an organ donor (Mary almost forgot that he signed the organ donor statement on the back of his driver's license). Mary secured several **death certificates** and she found John's life insurance policies in his desk drawer (at least she thinks she found them all). She also called John's employer to tell them of John's death and she removed John's will from the family's safe deposit box (Mary always wondered what that extra key on her key ring was for). That's all she did, and for a grieving widow that was a lot. "What do I do next?" she asked John's brother, Jim.

John and Jim were always close. They always said they would do anything for each other. They were brothers! But Jim was lost for words and direction. He couldn't stop thinking about the day John signed his will and how John laughed about death. Jim witnessed his brother's will at the bank. Now Jim knows why John picked the bank as executor. The family needed the professional assistance and guidance they lacked.

Opening an Estate

In most instances, the person who possesses the original will is the one who presents it—files it, admits it—to the probate court (or the applicable court that has jurisdiction over probate matters, usually a county court). Filing a will is a relatively simple and quick task that involves submitting the original will and proof of death, completing a court form, and having a court number assigned to the decedent's estate.

If John's attorney kept the will in safekeeping, he would file the will in court. When the will names the bank as executor, it is most likely that the trust department is safekeeping the will; therefore, a representative of the trust department's probate division (estate settlement unit) would file the will in court. Regardless of who has the will, it is ultimately the executor's responsibility to locate the will and ensure it is filed with the court.

Most probate statutes direct that a will must "be offered" to probate within a specified number of years. If the will is not submitted within the stipulated period (three years in most jurisdictions), the decedent, in most instances, is deemed to have died intestate.

Estate Attorney

It is advisable for a corporate executor to employ an estate attorney who specializes in probate estate law and the probate court system. In most cases this is the attorney who wrote the will. Remember postmortem letters? John could have left instructions to use the services of a particular attorney. Or the trust department file may contain a letter from the customer directing the bank to use a particular attorney in settling the estate. Absent any specific instructions, the bank will use the attorney who drafted the will, unless this attorney is not alive or declines to act as the estate's attorney, or the bank elects otherwise.

Early in the probate process it is advisable to meet with the family and the estate attorney to introduce the family to the estate's probate administrative manager and portfolio manager. This is also an appropriate time to explain the probate process. Do not be surprised at the family's reaction. They will be confused, overwhelmed, and apprehensive. This is the time for the trust professional to manage and balance the emotions of death with the formalities of estate administration and settlement. The family must be assured that each task will be handled in their best interests and for the protection of John's assets.

Appointment of Executor

The next appearance in court entails formal approval and appointment of the bank as executor. The estate attorney prepares a formal petition that includes basic information about John: name, address, Social Security number, estimated value of John's estate (probate and nonprobate assets), names of heirs and legatees, the name of the attorney representing the estate, and the name of the executor nominated in John's will. At this time the attorney also requests that the bank as personal representative be approved and appointed by the court. After this request has been approved, the court issues a certificate stating that the will is valid, that it was John's last will, and that the bank has been appointed—

has the authority to act—as executor. Depending on locale, this certificate is called **letters testamentary, letters of office, domiciliary letters,** or **letters of authority** (see Exhibit 5.4).

This important document proves the bank's permission to act as John's executor. With it, the executor is empowered to transact business on behalf of John's estate. In some states the executor must also obtain an **affidavit** from the attesting witnesses of John's will. This assists the court in determining that this was indeed John's will.

Notification of Death

The next task is to formally notify heirs, legatees, and creditors that John died. Because neither the bank nor Mary may know specifically who John's creditors are, a **creditors notice** (also known as **notice to interested persons**) is published in the local newspaper in the jurisdiction where the estate is being probated. This notice is usually presented in one of the local legal newspapers if one is available. This notice gives creditors the opportunity to present **claims** against John's estate for John's debts. The notice is published, usually for 3 consecutive weeks. Creditors are given a specific statutory period of time to present their claims; the time period varies from state to state. For example, the time period may be 6 months from the time of the first notice or 3 months if the notice is given directly to the creditor. The family may express concern about airing John's affairs in the open. You will have to explain that probate is a matter of public record—it's the law.

As executor you will also need to notify heirs and legatees of John's demise with a **notice to heirs and legatees.** This informs them of John's demise, the potential extent of their inheritance, and who the executor and estate attorney are.

Level of Administration

At this time it is usually determined by the court what degree of probate administration is warranted. Depending on the

Exhibit 5.4 Letters of Office

Letters of Office
Estate of John Q. Doe
Form #ABC–123

In the Circuit Court of Jones County, Alaska
County Department, Probate Division

Estate of John Q. Doe, deceased

No.   02Q1234
Docket 007
Page   001

XYZ Bank and Trust Company of Bear Lake, Alaska, has been appointed Independent Executor of the estate of John Q. Doe, deceased, who died February 28, 2002, and is authorized to take possession of and collect the estate of the decedent and to do all acts required by law.

Witness, April 15, 2002

_____
Mary Smith
Clerk of Court

Certificate

I certify that this is a copy of the letters of office now in force in this estate.

Witness, May 10, 2002

_____
//signature//
Clerk of Court

size and nature of the estate and the expertise of the executor, different jurisdictions provide various levels of **estate administration:**

- **Supervised administration.** This level of administration occurs when the court determines that the executor is not familiar with the workings of settling an estate. Most of the executor's actions are reported to and approved by the court. Courts rarely assign this level of administration when a bank serves as executor because of the trust department's familiarity with probate matters. In most circumstances, this level of probate occurs only when requested by

interested parties and when the executor is an individual; this can prolong the probate process.

- **Independent administration, independent executorship,** or **unsupervised administration.** Except for the opening and closing court documents, most actions are reported only to the heirs and legatees. Some states call this nonintervention power. It is less formal than supervised administration and is approved when the court is familiar with the appointed executor and is aware of its credentials.

- **Summary administration** or **small estate affidavit.** This applies to smaller estates. Although $50,000 is a common maximum value, this will vary from state to state. This is usually not available for real estate holdings in the estate.

In addition to notifying creditors, heirs, and legatees, the executor also notifies other interested parties of John's estate, including

- The postmaster
- Charge card companies and other known creditors
- Dividend-paying agents and bond registrars
- Auto, homeowner, and casualty insurance companies
- Utility (gas, electric, phone, and water) companies
- Business partners
- Social Security office
- Veterans Administration
- Employers and employee benefit plan administrators
- Life insurance companies

Notification to these parties assists the executor in determining debts and expenses, inventory of estate assets, budget planning, fees, tax liabilities, and asset valuation.

Collection and Inventory of Assets

Each state has a prescribed period of time (for example, 60 days) for the executor to collect and prepare an inventory of the estate's assets. The executor may wish to use the IRS Form 706 (Federal Estate Tax Return) as a guideline. Probate courts and bar associations also provide inventory guidelines. Perhaps John's records contained a confidential personal statement, which can help.

Beyond Collecting and Listing

A thorough search must be made of the decedent's safe deposit boxes, personal home records (all residences, if more than one), and perhaps his office. It is the executor's responsibility to physically **marshal** (collect), take custody, and safekeep John's assets. The **inventory** of John's assets is not merely a list of what John owned. It also includes an accounting and valuation of each asset and a determination of which assets pass through probate and which do not.

Collection and inventory also require

- Collecting employee benefits
- Filing claims with the Veterans' Administration and Social Security Administration
- Carrying out corporate and partnership duties
- Arranging for appraisal of valuable personal property (artwork, collectibles, antiques) and real estate
- Making claims and collecting life insurance proceeds (both individual policies and those through John's employer)
- Collecting accounts receivable and anything owed to the decedent
- Acting as landlord and collecting rents with respect to income-producing real estate
- Purchasing, continuing, or increasing property and liability insurance

Asset Safety

When John was alive he was responsible for the safety of his assets. Now the job belongs to the trust department, as his executor. The executor is now responsible for the security and insurance of *all* assets, and the executor can be held liable for loss, destruction, and theft. For example, the executor is responsible for safekeeping the valuable French impressionist painting that hung in John's office; for seeing that John's condominium in Vail, Colorado, is insured against loss; for assessing John's stock and bond portfolio as to adequacy of investment grade, production of income, and minimization of risk; and for administering John's business.

Administering a Closely Held Business

One of the more difficult tasks of an executor is finding answers to the difficult questions that arise when an estate consists of a closely held business.

- Is the management that is in place able to continue the operation of the business?
- Will the business produce sufficient income to provide for the family?
- Can the business afford to employ family members?
- Should the business be sold?

A general probate rule is that an executor must liquidate a business as quickly as is reasonable or continue to run the business at the executor's personal risk. The executor does obtain some relief if the decedent's will provided the executor with the power to continue the business or if state laws or the court permit such. Nonetheless, it is the executor's personal obligation to run the business and be responsible for it. This task cannot be delegated.

The executor must assess whether the decedent had set plans to provide for the continuation of his business. Are there key employees who can hang out a *business as usual* sign? Did John have a buy–sell agreement or stock redemption agreement in place to ensure the sale of his business to a partner, key employee, or competitor? Absent specific plans, the executor is faced with a difficult decision, one that never seems to have the right answers.

For example, if the executor chooses to keep the decedent's business active for the sake of the family's financial welfare, and the business decreases in value or income production falls, the family will not be pleased and may hold the executor financially liable regardless of the will's language ("to retain any business interest . . . to participate in the management of any business") permitting continuation of the business. If the business is sold for an attractive price to an interested buyer, the family may criticize the executor for selling at too low a price, the business may appreciate in the future, or the production of income from the business might be greater than the amount generated by a more liquid investment portfolio.

These are important decisions to make. Remember, John placed utmost confidence in your bank when he named it as executor. So too does John's family place their trust and confidence in the bank.

Developing a Budget: Paying Claims and Debts

The activity of probating an estate is by no means completely mechanical. Don't forget the personal, family side of matters: patience, compassion, personal and financial advice to family members, guidance, and an understanding shoulder for grieving family members to lean on. John died, but there is a family that needs to continue living. What are Mary's financial needs? What about the children?

Budgets

John's death caused a major roadblock: Income has stopped! Although the executor is responsible for paying taxes, claims, debts, and expenses of administration, the family needs to meet living expenses: groceries, tuition, mortgage, and the endless miscellaneous bills. For these reasons a **budget** must be set, and income must be generated from the estate for the family.

Nearly all states provide for an allowance (a budget) to support the family during the period the decedent's estate is in probate administration. This allowance is often referred to as a **spouse's allowance** (or **widow's award**) if a spouse survives the decedent. If there is no surviving spouse but there are surviving children, the allowance is called a **family allowance** (or **child's award**). The award is available whether the decedent died testate or intestate, and in most instances it takes precedence over all creditors' claims except for funeral expenses and expenses of administration. The executor petitions the court for the allowance (which in most states is limited to a specific dollar amount, such as $10,000), and the budget will contain the amount of cash needed to settle the following:

- Debts
- Cost of final illness (medical bills)
- Income taxes and estate taxes
- Attorney's and accountant's fees
- Bequests
- Executor fees
- Appraisal costs
- Insurance premiums

The executor must consider the liquidity of the estate to meet these expenses and determine whether estate assets (and which ones) must be sold to raise the necessary cash.

In addition to providing for the family allowance, most states have passed statutes (homestead laws) that protect the family residence or farm from creditors' claims. These statutes usually exempt a certain amount of land from the claims of the decedent's creditors. The amount of land exempted depends on whether the residence is urban or rural. These laws often include a provision that the surviving spouse or minor/dependent children are entitled to occupy the homestead as a residence for as long as they so choose despite the disposition of the residence in the decedent's will.

Claims

A good executor must ascertain which claims against the estate have priority, which ones are substantiated (and defend against those that are not), which can be maintained during administration rather than being immediately paid, and which ones can be assumed by the beneficiaries, such as mortgages.

Executor Fees

How much can an executor charge for its services? This depends on the size and complexity of the estate, the amount of work and time needed, and the results and benefits to the beneficiaries.

How does an executor calculate its **fee?** Many states regulate an executor's fees by statute—either by a schedule according to the size of the estate or a set hourly rate—regardless of whether the executor is an individual or a corporation. Some states set guidelines (based on the concept of *what is reasonable*). Others judge the fee after the fact, depending on the time put into the estate administration.

Regardless of the state's approach, the court monitors the executor's involvement and activity. The beneficiaries must agree to the fees before the court will approve the executor's fee and permit the executor to be paid from the estate's assets.

Insolvency

John probably planned financially for his death. However, some estates are insolvent. **Insolvency** occurs when claims, taxes, and expenses exceed the value of the estate. Statutes exist for determining the order and priority of paying claims, expenses, taxes, and support of the family. (In general, debts due to the United States must be paid first.) Similarly, there are circumstances when, after the payment of an estate's claims, debts, and expenses, the remaining assets are insufficient to fully meet the will's dispositive provisions. For example, what if a testator's will states that ABC charity is to receive a bequest of $1,000 and XYZ charity is to receive a bequest of $2,000, yet the estate has only $600 remaining? The bequests will abate. **Abatement** means the bequests will be reduced proportionately. Because ABC's bequest is 50 percent of XYZ's, ABC will receive $200 and XYZ will receive $400, unless the testator's will specified otherwise how the bequests would be made in this event. This is a simple example, not a legal interpretation. Again, check your local statutes.

Widow's Rights

A mind can play funny tricks, especially when strained by the emotions of a loved one's death. Mary hasn't slept well since John died. That's understandable. Mary abruptly awoke at 3 a.m. from a dream that John's will left her nothing—she was disinherited. Family members will approach you with many questions. Don't be surprised with concerns like this one.

Can a spouse be disinherited? Assuming that there is no **nuptial agreement** (further distinguished as an **antenuptial** or **prenuptial agreement**) to the contrary and assets are subject to probate, a spouse cannot be disinherited completely. Laws are in place to prevent this. If a will attempts to disinherit a spouse, the surviving spouse can **renounce** the decedent's will, thereby allowing a statutory share. Depending on the jurisdiction and context, the various terms used for this action are **election against the will, forced heirship, taking against the estate, renouncing the will, right of election, widow's election.** The right to an elective share is not automatic. The surviving spouse must file notice within a specified period (usually six months) after the will is admitted to probate.

Children's Rights

Can a testator disinherit children? In essence, yes, assuming the intention is clearly stated so that the disinherited children cannot argue that the disinheritance was unintentional or a mistake. Of course, children can argue (contest) that the testator did not have the testamentary capacity to disinherit or that undue influence was exercised to make the testator disinherit the children. In some states parents are required to provide postdeath support for their children. The children cannot be disinherited completely regardless of the situation. As always, check local statutes.

It is important to be aware of these concepts. If the testator's will did direct actions such as these, the executor must be prepared to defend the testator's wishes and explain the beneficiaries' rights. This must be handled delicately.

Intentional Disinheritance

An additional consideration with regard to disinheritance is an *in terrorem* clause. An **in terrorem** clause (also known as a no-contest clause) provides that a beneficiary who contests the will forfeits his interest under the will. In most states, a no-contest clause is enforceable and the beneficiary forfeits his legacy unless he had probable cause for bringing the contest. Let's look at an example. George dies leaving a will that bequeaths $25,000 to his son Ron, and the rest of his sizeable estate to his friend Jane. The will contains a no-contest clause that reads: "Should any beneficiary named herein contest this will or any of its provisions, he shall forfeit all interests given to him by my will." Ron contests the will on the grounds of undue influence and lack of testamentary capacity. Ron loses the will contest, and George's will is admitted to probate. In most states, Ron forfeits the $25,000 bequest.

Intentional Death

A person who intentionally and unjustifiably causes the death of another forfeits any property, benefit, or other interest that passes by reason of that death. The property, benefit, or other interest passes as if the person causing the death predeceased the decedent.

Taxes and Estate Valuation

Earlier in the chapter we discussed an estate: everything owned, wherever it is located, no matter in what form it exists, and however it is owned. These words connote the present tense during one's life. John's estate still exists after his death, which is where the past tense enters the picture. Although it is easy to say that his estate is zero because he is no longer alive (how can a deceased person own anything?), that is not actually the case.

Ascertaining the Decedent's Estate

John built an estate during his life. His estate has a value the second before he dies, at the time of his death, and afterward. John's assets do not become someone else's until they are transferred. At his death John's assets pass (transfer) to others by way of law (joint tenancy and tenancy by the entirety), by beneficiary designation (life insurance and retirement plans), by trust, and by the terms of his will. Until the assets are transferred, they are still considered John's, although now they are called the decedent's estate.

Tax Identification

While John was alive, for tax purposes he was identified by a **tax identification number** (TIN), which was his Social Security account number. Although John was a separate tax entity, he may have reported and paid taxes (federal, state, city, and so forth) on a joint return basis with Mary. Upon John's death, a new tax entity exists—John's estate—which also is a taxable entity. Following John's demise, the personal representative must obtain another TIN—an **employer identification number** (EIN)—for John's estate. The EIN is used by the personal representative as the tax identifying number for John's estate income tax return(s) and John's estate tax return, if need be. How many income tax returns will be submitted depends on how long it takes to settle John's estate.

During John's life, the income he earned from January 1 to December 31 (his tax year) was reported on applicable federal, state, and local income tax returns by April 15 of the following tax year. Depending on John's income, deductions and credits available to him, and the amount of taxes withheld by John's employer during the tax year, John's income tax return(s) indicate whether he owes additional taxes, doesn't owe anything, or receives a refund. Of course, regardless of the tax consequences, a tax return still must be submitted to the IRS. If John died on October 20 of the year, he still earned income from January 1 until the date of his death. A tax return is still required. Because John cannot file his return, his executor is now responsible.

Executor's Tax Responsibilities

As John's personal representative, the trust department wears the additional hats of accountant, bookkeeper, and taxpayer responsible for

- Filing final income tax returns and paying from the estate's assets any income taxes applicable to John's income before his death.

- Filing and paying income taxes that are applicable to John's estate from the date of death until the closing of the estate. Until John's estate is distributed to others, the assets of the estate may still generate income. During John's life he was responsible for reporting income and paying taxes. The income now belongs to John's estate, and therefore is reportable and payable by the estate. For example, John may have owned a stock portfolio that during his life generated $10,000 in dividends. While alive, John reported these dividends on his tax return as income and paid taxes on this income. Although these stocks may be distributed to Mary (or pourover into John's trust) following the probate of John's estate, John's estate owns the stock before distribution. Therefore, John's estate (again, as a separate tax entity) must submit an income tax return and pay income taxes. This is the executor's responsibility.

- Depending on the size of John's estate and how it is distributed, there may be federal estate taxes and state estate taxes. These taxes require special, separate tax returns. The completion and submission of the tax returns, and payment of relevant taxes, are the executor's obligation.

A comprehensive listing—and explanation—of the various tax forms that are applicable to a decedent's estate (and are the responsibility of the executor) are found in IRS Publication 559 ("Survivors, Executors, and Administrators").

The executor is subject to a penalty for failure to file a tax return when due unless the failure is due to reasonable cause. Relying on an agent (for example, an attorney or accountant) is not reasonable cause for late filing. It is the personal representative's duty to file the returns for the decedent and estate when due.

Advanced estate and financial planning courses dig deeper into the tax consequences of an estate and the various tax-saving mechanisms that are available. Suffice it to say here that an executor is not required to submit a Federal Estate Tax return (IRS Form 706), and the decedent's estate will not be subject to any federal estate taxes unless the estate's value is in excess of a stipulated amount called the *applicable exclusion amount.* Under current law, this amount is $1,000,000 for decedents dying in 2003, and it is scheduled to increase in increments to $3,500,000 in 2009. The current law repeals all estate taxes in 2010. Although an estate may exceed the applicable exclusion amount, taxes may not be due depending on the deductions and credits available to the estate and how the estate is distributed. Despite the fact that an estate may exceed the applicable exclusion amount and that estate taxes may not be applicable, an IRS Form 706 is still required. Complying with this requirement is a heavy responsibility for the executor.

Valuation of the Estate

In conjunction with the estate's inventory and calculation of tax liabilities, an integral part of an executor's tasks is the **valuation** of the estate. A personal representative can elect a **valuation date** for an estate as of the date of death or as of an **alternate valuation date.** The alternate date is 6 months after a decedent's death. The executor has a choice depending on the nature of the estate, general financial conditions (such as a material decline in the value of the estate's assets), and tax planning consid-

erations. The entire estate must be valued on either date. The alternate date can be chosen only if the estate's value at the time results in lower federal estate taxes.

One of the major delays an executor encounters in settling an estate is the filing and acceptance of the estate tax return (Form 706). Because of the care a personal representative must give to inventorying and valuing an estate and because of the time required to give creditors the opportunity to make claims against the estate, it will be several months before a personal representative is in a position to submit the federal and state estate tax returns. For these reasons the IRS, and most state departments of revenue, give an executor 9 months from the date of death in which to submit the estate tax return(s) and to pay any applicable taxes. Once the IRS receives the return, it must audit and approve the tax returns before the estate can be officially closed. In many cases this may take as long as a year. By law, the IRS is permitted up to 36 months to audit the return. The IRS may also challenge the return, questioning the executor's appraisals and valuation of estate assets.

Accounting to the Court

The executor is continuously responsible for **accounting** (reporting) its activities to the court: opening the estate, submitting an inventory, developing a budget, seeking tax approval, distributing assets, and closing the estate. Additionally, the executor must regularly submit an accounting of all receipts and disbursements to the court and to the estate's beneficiaries throughout the probate period. The beneficiaries have a specific period of time to approve the accounting, including the executor's and attorney's fees. If no objections are received, the executor begins to distribute the estate. If the probate process was a supervised administration, the executor prepares and submits a **final report and petition for distribution** (this title differs from state to state) to the court. If the court is satisfied, it approves the accounting and directs the final stage of probate.

Depending on the nature of the estate, the beneficiaries' needs, and funds available to the estate, an executor may be able to make partial distributions before the final closing of the estate. A cautious executor maintains assets in the decedent's estate to cover additional administrative costs, claims, and taxes. The executor is personally liable for additional costs if there are insufficient funds in the estate with which to meet them. Once all final tax returns and payments have been made and audited and approved by all taxing bodies, the executor can then move into the final process of closing the estate.

Closing the Estate

The last activity of the probate process is the **estate settlement:** the final reporting of activities to the court and to the beneficiaries and the distribution of the estate's assets.

Following the payment of claims, taxes, and administrative costs, the court issues an **order of distribution** that permits the executor to distribute the estate's assets according to the dispositive provisions of the will. Specific bequests are made and the residual estate is distributed. (Note that if an asset is to be given to a minor, the executor is responsible for identifying the minor's guardian and distributing the asset to the minor's guardian.)

There are times when distribution of the estate will be made according to the decision of the beneficiaries: *". . . such property shall be distributed to such of my children who survive me . . . in shares of substantially equal value, to be divided as they agree."* The key to this distribution is the words, "in shares of substantially equal value." John's children may choose not to take equal shares of assets, but they will share the estate in equal value. This distribution may have to be approved by the court. At times the beneficiaries may need to sign a document agreeing to a non-pro-rata distribution and listing the specific assets to be dis-

tributed. This agreement in most instances will constitute a receipt of the assets and an **indemnification** agreement holding the personal representative harmless from any liability that may arise from the distribution. Bear in mind that a distribution scheme such as this may cause an income tax liability to the beneficiaries. (Advanced probate studies address this in greater detail.)

In many instances a personal representative may make **distribution in kind. Kind** is an actual asset: a specific piece of real property, a stock, type of tangible personal property. John's will stated, "as my executor shall determine." If John's children cannot agree on how to distribute the estate, the executor is responsible for determining how the estate will be shared among the children. If the will and the state's applicable probate laws permit, the executor may be permitted to sell all the assets (the kind) and distribute the proceeds equally among the children.

What happens if an asset cannot be divided equally? For example, how can 1,000 shares of stock be distributed equally among three beneficiaries? A total of 333 shares per beneficiary is equal, but the last share cannot be split into thirds. The executor's distribution schedule indicates how this will be handled, as long as the distribution of the estate is done equally in value, not necessarily equal in kind. Perhaps the 1,000 shares of stock will be **split** so that one child receives 500 shares of the stock and the second and third receive 250 shares each. This is fair as long as the remaining assets of the estate are distributed to all three beneficiaries so that each child's total inheritance is of equal value. If an estate's assets are divided disproportionately, the beneficiaries must provide the executor with a written approval of the distribution schedule.

Sometimes a personal representative may set aside a reasonable amount of assets, in good faith, for the payment of unascertained or contingent liabilities and expenses. Local probate statute may permit the closing (termination) of the estate despite the fact that not all of the estate's assets have been distributed. Until such time that the assets are totally distributed, the estate is not considered closed for federal income tax purposes. After total distribution of the estate, all tax matters are considered those of the person(s) succeeding to (becoming entitled to) the property of the estate.

Is the executor's mission accomplished? Unfortunately, no. The executor is responsible for retitling the assets into the names of the applicable beneficiaries, physically delivering the assets to the beneficiaries, and obtaining receipts for the assets.

In addition to—and in conjunction with—the activities discussed in this chapter, the executor is responsible for:

- Funding trusts
- Defending contests
- Distributing charitable bequests
- Determining and proving ademptions
- Assisting with the appointment of personal and estate guardians for minors
- Ascertaining, modifying, and adjusting any contracts and leases associated with the decedent's assets
- Determining the disposition of an asset that an heir elects to disclaim
- Providing notice of power of appointment (this is discussed further in Chapter 8)
- Defending possible tax audits

Once the distribution of the estate is complete, a final accounting of the receipts is presented showing the proper distribution of assets. At this time a petition is made to the court that the estate be closed. The court does a final review of the executor's activities to determine that everything has been accomplished correctly. If the court is satisfied, a court order is prepared that discharges the executor, and the estate is closed.

SUMMARY

- Wills are not omens of death; they are an effective means of preparing an estate for death. Without proper planning a person's estate cannot be distributed according to her wishes.

- A will is a legal document that states a person's intentions regarding the distribution of assets at death. A testator's intentions include the naming of a guardian for minors, the payment of debts, taxes and administration expenses, nomination of an executor, and the establishment of a trust. Dying with a will is called dying testate; dying without a will is intestacy, in which an estate's distribution is dictated and guided by probate law.

- A will can be established by anyone of legal age and of testamentary capacity. Although a will may be perceived as valid, it can be contested (challenged) based on lack of testamentary capacity, undue influence on the testator, forgery, and fraud.

- Wills can be changed by creation of a new will, codicil, or revocation. Wills can be supplemented by postmortem letters, which further assist the executor in administering and settling the testator's estate.

- Probate is the orderly court-guided process of gathering a decedent's assets, paying debts, taxes, and administrative expenses, and distributing the estate's assets according to law in the event of intestacy or according to a will's direction. The key to successful probate lies in the hands of an effective executor (personal representative). Although an individual can serve as an executor, there are several distinct advantages to choosing a trust department for the task. Trust departments lend experience, time, training, impartiality, permanence, and cost-efficiency.

- The probate of a will involves administration (management) and settlement (distribution) of an estate. The steps in administering and settling an estate are opening the estate, collecting and inventorying assets, developing budgets and paying claims and debts, paying taxes and valuing the estate, accounting to the court, and distributing assets.

REVIEW QUESTIONS

1. Explain the difference between dying testate and dying intestate. Give some examples of why it is preferable to avoid intestacy.
2. List at least three factors that are considered in determining whether a person had testamentary capacity when creating a will.
3. Identify some of the major expenses typically connected with the settlement of an estate.
4. Effective administration of a decedent's estate depends on a reliable, knowledgeable executor. Give some examples of the advantages of using a corporate executor (bank trust department) as an executor.
5. Briefly describe the step-by-step process of administering and settling an estate.

6

GUARDIANSHIPS AND ADVANCE DIRECTIVES

"The chief misery of the decline of the faculties, and a main cause of the irritability that often goes with it, is evidently the isolation, the lack of customary appreciation and influence, which only the rarest tact and thoughtfulness on the part of others can alleviate."

Charles Horton Cooley (1864–1929)

Little Johnny was talented. He also had a bit of luck, a handsome appearance, and a knack for "being in the right place at the right time"—ingredients that landed him a lucrative contract to do commercials for a national fast-food chain. From the commercials he moved to a weekly television sitcom and two major movies, earning an astronomical income by the age of 13.

Seriously hurt in an auto accident when she was eight years old, Nancy will be a quadriplegic the rest of her life. In the ensuing lawsuit, the jury found the other driver at fault and awarded Nancy over $3 million for future care, replacement of lost potential earnings, and suffering.

Across town was Mr. Sullivan. Everyone knew "old man Sully." He and his wife had owned a small delicatessen from what seemed the beginning of time. Mrs. Sullivan died 5 years ago. Mr. Sullivan's children closed the store last spring because Sully couldn't handle it anymore; his Alzheimer's disease had become too much for everyone.

Johnny's fortune as a minor and Nancy's and Sully's misfortune leave minors and adults alike unable to manage their affairs personally and financially. These people have special needs and will need extra guidance and protection.

LEARNING OBJECTIVES

Our cast of characters underscores the message that life comes with few guarantees. Circumstances are complex, unanticipated, and emotional. As trust professionals we can ensure that Johnny, Nancy, and Sully will have their assets protected when they cannot manage their own affairs. While exploring guardianships and advance directives, we will touch on very detailed and specific aspects of fiduciary and probate laws, which differ substantially from state to state. This text does not interpret the law but introduces its complexity and importance.

Upon completion of this chapter, you will be able to

- Define incapacitation
- Distinguish the types of guardians and guardianships
- List the duties of an estate guardian
- Describe the newer forms of guardianships
- Compare healthcare and property directives
- Define and use the terms that appear in bold in the text

INCAPACITATION

Nancy and Sully are incapacitated. So is Johnny, within the definitions of this chapter. **Incapacitation** is the inability of adults or minors to look after their physical care or the inability to manage their financial affairs. Incapacitation is either physical (**disability**), caused, for example, by a stroke, senility, an accident, or a disabling illness; or legal (**incompetence**), such as being a minor, an adult with a mental illness, addicted to drugs or alcohol, or confined. When someone is incapacitated, the law requires that the court appoint a **guardian** to care for the person or to protect his estate.

GUARDIANSHIP

Two different guardianship arrangements exist: personal and estate.

Personal Guardian

A personal guardian is the person responsible for the physical care of an individual. Think of parental care given to a child: support, care, comfort, health, education, and the hundreds of other tasks associated with general upbringing and well-being. In the case of a disabled adult, this would also include deciding where the disabled person will reside and arranging for his or her physical care. This is the **guardian of the person.**

Estate Guardian

An estate guardian, or **guardian of the estate,** is a person or institution respon-sible for the financial affairs of an individual. This chapter is devoted primarily to this arrangement because this is the type of guardianship trust departments can provide.

Every state has guardianship statutes (usually contained in the state's probate laws). These statutes are very serious and specific in their intent. For example, a court will not appoint a guardian for a person just because the person makes what others consider frivolous decisions. For example, a representative state statute states that "guardianship shall be utilized only as is necessary to promote the well-being of the disabled person, to protect him from neglect, exploitation, or abuse, and to encourage development of his maximum self-reliance and independence. Guardianship shall be ordered only to the extent necessitated by the individual's actual mental, physical and adaptive limitations."

The statute addresses Johnny and Nancy as minors who are legally incapable of managing their financial affairs. It may apply to Nancy after she reaches majority if her disability renders her unable to manage her assets, and it protects Sully's incapacitation.

Although an individual can serve as both personal guardian and estate guardian, in cases involving substantial assets, the courts most often do not consider individuals for the tasks of estate guardian. Johnny's and Nancy's **natural guardians** (their parents) and Sully's children are probably quite capable to serve as guardian of the person. Yet their lack of time because of jobs, travel, and family size, and their lack of expertise with investment management, the law, and the administrative tasks associated with an estate guardian's responsibilities make them unprepared to serve as guardian of the estate.

The courts will turn to professionals: trust departments. As the trust professional, you can provide effective management of Johnny's, Nancy's, and Sully's assets; provide guidance to Nancy's parents with regard to assessing and meeting the expenses of her medical care; and provide direction to Sully's children about his continued healthcare.

Whom the Guardian Protects

Johnny, Nancy, and Sully need physical and financial protection and assistance. They are the "protected persons," or as the courts say, the **wards.** A ward can be a minor without a disability (Johnny), a minor with a disability (Nancy), or an incapacitated adult (Sully).

Minors

Each state defines at what age children become legal adults. Most states have chosen either 18 or 21. Before children reach that age, they are **minors** and unable legally to handle their own finances. Once children reach the age of **emancipation,** they are no longer minors; they are of **majority.** Legally, once a person reaches the age of majority—becomes an adult—he or she can vote, join the Marines, consume alcohol in certain states, and manage finances. Until then, if a minor earns, inherits, or is awarded money (not in trust), a guardian of the minor's estate must be appointed to manage the assets of his or her estate.

Adults

In some states a guardianship is called a conservatorship. Some jurisdictions use the word *guardian* for minors and **conservator** (or **tutor**) for adults. Others distinguish minors from adults, as in *guardian for a minor* or *guardian for a disabled adult.*

Types of Guardianships

Before the military's Selective Service System (the Draft Board) ended in the early 1970s, men were drafted into the Armed Forces involuntarily. Their entry into the military was not by choice; it was the law. Today, young people are not drafted; they enlist voluntarily. The sharply defined differences between choosing to enlist and having the decision mandated by law are also found in voluntary and involuntary guardianships.

Voluntary Guardianship

An individual may request the appointment of a guardian to manage his or her affairs, although it takes a brave and self-knowing person to request such an arrangement. In such a scenario, an individual may **petition** (ask) the court to appoint a person or an institution to be his guardian. The person may suspect he is becoming senile, he may fear his alcoholism is getting the best of him, or he may be scared that his mental disorder will cause him to harm himself and injure others. Other exterior factors may prompt such requests: During the Vietnam War a military advisor, before his departure, asked his local court to appoint a bank trust department as guardian of his assets during his dangerous assignment. The court granted it.

Just as an individual may ask for a guardian arrangement voluntarily, he may ask for restoration, which discontinues the guardianship. If adequate proof is given to the court that the guardianship is no longer warranted, it will be discontinued.

Voluntary guardianship does not exist in certain states, and it is not common even in states where statutes permit it because other alternatives provide this kind of protection without involving the courts. A personal trust arrangement (discussed in Chapters 7 and 8) or a power of attorney, which we will look at shortly, can accomplish the same end with greater breadth and flexibility.

Involuntary Guardianship

In most circumstances involving involuntary guardianships, the protected person is not the one asking for the guardian arrangement. In most states anyone can petition the court to appoint a guardian (or coguardians) for someone else. Most often it is the person's nearest relatives who are seeking the appointment of a guardian. The petitioner nominates (names or proposes) a guardian. Petitioners can ask to be appointed guardian of the estate. They also can nominate XYZ Bank and Trust Company, another individual, a public agency, or a not-for-profit organization.

In some jurisdictions (counties or states) the petitioner is called an interested person. In other jurisdictions the interested person is a legal entity such as an attorney or court judge. Check your local rules and definitions before becoming an estate guardian.

GUARDIANSHIP PROCESS

The duties of an estate guardian are plentiful, onerous, and laden with precise responsibilities. The letter of the law, as the guiding light, defines the serious trust placed in a guardian as it provides guidance and financial security. A guardian of the estate is a fiduciary charged with the challenging and demanding responsibilities of administration, investment management, legal adherence, tax planning, and custody. Few individuals can adequately manage these full-time responsibilities. Fortunately, trust departments come equipped to meet each requirement in serving the ward and the ward's family.

Petitioning

Once the court has been petitioned, the ward and all interested people are notified of the guardianship court hearing, which is held to determine whether the guardianship is indeed necessary and whether anyone objects to the request for the guardianship or the requested guardian. If incapacitation is an issue, it is often necessary to obtain a report from a physician about the nature of the disability and the need for guardianship. The hearing also addresses whether the ward needs a guardian of the person, guardian of the estate, or both. If it is determined that a guardian is needed, the court appoints the necessary guardian(s) and issues **letters of guardianship** (also known as **letters of office**), which are the evidence of the court's appointment and the guardian's authority to act. In the case of a disabled adult, this step also includes the legal **adjudication** (declaration) of the ward's incapacitation.

Trust departments take a somewhat passive role in this process. Trust departments do not serve in the role as petitioner, but when nominated as guardian of the estate, a representative of the trust department (most likely a probate officer) is present in court to formally accept the nomination and appointment.

Bonding

Law dictates that the guardian of the estate be financially sound and responsible and ensure the safety of the ward's assets. The guardian must guarantee that the estate will be reimbursed if the guardian mishandles the estate's assets. The guardian is required to post a bond (secure or collateralize the estate assets). The bond can be money or assets actually placed aside, such as an escrow account. Usually, however, the guardian purchases a **surety bond**—an insurance policy equal to a multiple of the estate's value (dependent on the jurisdiction's rules)—from an insurance company. The guardian who puts up the money for the bond or the insurance company that provides the surety bond is called the **surety.**

Trust departments, because of their insurance coverage, are not required in most circumstances to provide this bond. As the courts say, the bond is waived. If the court requires a bond of a nonbank guardian or of a trust department because of inadequate insurance coverage, proof must be given that the bond has been purchased before the court's approval (appointment) of the guardian.

Bear in mind that not every state has exactly the same rules. For example, states differ as to which court handles guardianships. For example, in New York the court responsible for this activity is the **Surrogate Court.** In other states it may be a **Probate Court, Prefect's Court, Ordinary Court, Orphan's Court,** or **Chancery Court.**

Duties of the Guardian of the Estate

Once the trust department is appointed as guardian of the estate and the bonding requirements have been met, your tasks begin immediately after the court hearing. Under the court's strict supervision, the guardian is charged with responsibilities for the ward and to the court, as shown in Exhibit 6.1.

The variation in statutes from jurisdiction to jurisdiction makes it difficult to comprehensively list what an estate guardian may do (without court supervision) and may not do (but, perhaps may do with court supervision). As you will see in the later section on advance directives, a power of attorney for property in most instances may permit a powerholder (agent) more freedom of action than an estate guardian. For example, jurisdictions generally allow a powerholder—with permission—to make gifts on behalf of the powergiver (principal). Such may not be true with a guardian arrangement. There are circumstances when the court has agreed to a guardian's request (petition) to make gifts (either directly to a donee or into a trust for the benefit of the donee) from the ward's estate. Statutes and court decisions vary.

In some circumstances a petitioner may request appointment as guardian, but he will seek several specialists to provide the necessary services listed above. This is called unbundling. The guardian hires separate agents for

- Budget planning
- Asset valuation
- Tax preparation
- Asset custody
- Traditional investment management
- Management of special assets
- Medical need evaluation
- Education need assessment
- Court filing
- Collection and disbursement of funds

The cost of these individual services is greater than if they were handled by a single agent. Although trust departments cannot directly provide each service (i.e., insurance, education, medical care), they are experienced at guiding the ward and family in each area. Trust departments provide an economical, bundled service that meets each situation in a cohesive way. Several providers may financially and philosophically step on each other's feet and cause duplicative costs, in addition to the guardian's bond, that exceed a trust department's guardianship fee.

The court exercises ongoing, strict supervision for the benefit of the protected person. As the fiduciary who serves as guardian, you must be familiar with the tasks required. Experience is essential to handling the complexities of a guardianship. Leaving the tasks to a guardian who does not have the time, inclination, energy, and knowledge is dangerous. The law leaves little room for the ignorant guardian. And although guardianships impose myriad tasks and responsibilities and are typically not short-lived, they will come to an end.

Termination of Guardianship

A guardian's job is far from enviable, often unrewarding, and constantly onerous. As guardian, a trust department must

Exhibit 6.1   Duties of an Estate Guardian

For the Ward	To the Court
• Identify and marshal (collect) and safeguard the assets of the ward's estate. This entails custody, valuation, and full inventory of all assets.	• Report and file an inventory of estate assets with the court within a stipulated period of time (for example, 60 days) following the guardian's appointment.
• Meet with the ward's personal guardian, family, and financial and legal advisors (accountant and attorney, for example) to develop a sense of initial and long-term expenses and to develop a budget.	• File the ward's budget for court approval; preapproval enables payment of routine, ongoing expenses, such as living accommodations and monthly medical expenses.
• Construct an investment plan to provide for the ward's needs with consideration of the tax consequences and the need to make assets productive and profitable.	• Seek and receive court approval for the proposed investment program. Historically, guardianship investments were mandated restrictively, but some courts recently have relaxed the limitations within the prudence of investment activity.
• Manage special, out-of-the ordinary assets such as commercial or income-producing real estate, a closely held business, collections, and partnerships.	• Obtain court approval to manage special assets; strict court supervision is required when these asset classes are involved.
• Ascertain the need for nonbudgetary disbursements such as one-time expenditures for the purchase of handicapped- accessible transportation; modification, repair, or renovation of the ward's residence; and adaptive devices for communication (phone, computer, etc.).	• Appear in court when necessary to gain approval for the purchase of these items and services.
• Determine the need for specialized physicians, medical supplies, therapists, nursing services, and home healthcare providers.	• Arrange for court approval to buy these items *before the actual purchase.*
• Obtain health insurance benefits (if available), special-need consultants, transportation vendors, and special education needs.	• Appear in court to gain approval for these expenditures.
• Prepare an accounting of receipts and disbursements, inventory, and list of assets and investments and their values.	• Provide the court with an account of the guardian's activities (usually on an annual basis).
• Prepare and file local, state, and federal income tax returns; this includes estimating income and making appropriate quarterly and annual tax payments, if necessary; investment direction is driven by what is tax deductible to the ward's estate and the applicable income tax bracket.	• Submit tax returns to the court for review.
• Collect income from all sources, such as monthly annuity, pension, insurance, and Social Security payments.	• Report income collection to the court via the annual accounting procedure.

exercise utmost care, answer to court supervision, and balance the sometimes conflicting needs of the ward with a family's desires. But what appears to be a never-ending list of chores will someday come to a close, through attainment of majority, improved health, or death.

Attainment of Majority

In circumstances involving a guardian for a minor, once the ward attains her state's age of majority, the guardianship ends unless someone can show why the ward should continue under the supervision of a guardian. This abrupt role change from minor to adult, responsible for managing sometimes considerable assets, is a major concern for parents and guardians. Imagine Nancy getting her $3 million when she attains majority. She may not be prepared to manage the money sensibly, yet there is nothing to prevent her from squandering it. As trust professionals, we must direct customers such as Nancy toward sound investment management and personal trust planning.

Resolution of Disability

If an adult's physical or legal incapacitation ends (for example, recovery from a

---

USING TRUST PRODUCTS AND SERVICES TO MEET CUSTOMER NEEDS

Bob was a well-paid ironworker. His wife, Beth, had a long career as a high school math teacher. They paid their bills, owned a big house, and put their four kids through college. They managed to save money. Bob owned a healthy life insurance portfolio, and he faithfully contributed to his company's 401(k) retirement plan; but that was the extent of their estate and financial planning. The last time Bob and Beth talked to an attorney was when they bought their house 18 years earlier.

Bob always felt indestructible, on and off the job. But when he fell off a ladder while painting the top eave of his house, any idea of being indestructible ended. So did life as he and Beth knew it. Bob spent the rest of his days in a hospital. The trauma to his head rendered him incapable of remembering his kids' names, let alone managing his financial affairs.

At an attorney's suggestion, Beth brought a lawsuit on Bob's behalf against the manufacturer of the ladder. The ladder was found defective and the manufacturer was at fault. A substantial amount of money was awarded to Bob.

On the advice of the attorney who represented Bob in the personal injury lawsuit, a trust department was appointed guardian of Bob's estate. At Bob's death, the family turned to that trust department again to act as administrator for Bob's estate because he did not have a will. When his estate was distributed to the various family members, they looked once more to the trust department for investment and estate planning help.

Still, despite the trust department's help, without the will and without prior planning, a substantial, unnecessary amount of money went to legal fees, guardianship costs, estate settlement, and eventually estate taxes. Bob couldn't foresee his fall, but he could have put into place a few additional estate planning tools, such as a healthcare directive, a power of attorney for property, and a personal trust, all of which would have made his disability and incapacitation a bit easier for him and Beth financially.

debilitating stroke, rehabilitation from substance abuse, or release from prison), the guardianship may end. The court must be furnished with proof that a guardian arrangement is no longer necessary. The guardian then turns the assets over to the former ward.

Think back to our earlier discussion about voluntary and involuntary guardianships. Let us assume that someone was placed under guardianship on an involuntary basis because of a stroke. After months of recovery and therapy, the ward is back on his or her feet. At that time, the ward or an interested person can petition the court to have the guardianship removed; in such a case the protected person can be the interested person.

Death

When a ward dies, the guardianship ends and the assets of the estate are turned over to the deceased ward's executor if the protected person had a will. If the protected person died intestate, the assets are turned over to the administrator of the decedent's estate. This may also occur when the ward was a minor who could not legally have a will.

NEW GUARDIANSHIP HYBRIDS

Very seldom does the ward choose his guardian. Because of minority status or physical or mental inability to participate in the decision-making process, the nomination and appointment of the ward's guardian are placed in the hands of the ward's family or interested persons and the court. But times and laws change. Opportunities now exist for people to provide for the future appointment of a guardian for their dependents and to choose whom their personal guardian will be.

Recently a few states (California, Florida, Illinois, and New York) enacted legislation to create new procedures allowing for greater flexibility in providing guardianship protection for minors and disabled adults. Even in those states, provisions differ widely. In addition, many authorities think these approaches should not be thought of as guardianships at all, perhaps because of their lack of court supervision and involvement and their resemblance to the advance directives, which we will discuss later in this chapter.

Let's look at the background behind these new concepts from a trust professional's perspective. In Chapter 5 we discussed how a will can be used to nominate a guardian, coguardians, and successor guardian(s) of the person and of the estate for minor children upon the testator's death. This is a testamentary guardian. However, this act covers only the need for a guardian for a child after a parent dies. An equally important concern is the need for a guardian for the child if the parent is incapacitated.

Standby Guardian

The easiest way to introduce this arrangement is with an example. Denise Woods is a single mother with a 10-year-old son. If Denise were to become terminally ill, her son would probably need a guardian. In some states Denise can provide for the appointment of her son's guardian in the event she becomes incapacitated. Denise can petition the court to appoint a standby guardian.

A standby guardian procedure allows Denise to petition the court today, while she is healthy, to appoint the person she wants as guardian for her son. One advantage of the procedure is that it allows Denise to handle this matter while she is well, ensuring that all will go smoothly later when she is too ill to manage her affairs. Another advantage is that she, not someone else, chooses the guardian. This is especially important if there is a potential family dispute; disagreements can be settled while Denise is alive and well enough to testify about her views. In addition, a standby guardian is usually authorized to act immediately upon Denise's disability without possible court-appointed delays. In some jurisdictions the standby guardian is not limited to a defined period of time; the guardian also can act as guardian of the person as well as guardian of the estate.

Short-Term Guardian

What if Denise is diagnosed with the AIDS virus, suffers from occasional bouts of clinical depression, or frequently travels out of the country? Several states have created a short-term guardian procedure to provide a way, *without* going to court, to provide for temporary, private care of Denise's son. She can execute a document that appoints a guardian of the person (only) for her son, for a period of up to a certain number of days (for example, 60) without court supervision. In some instances this arrangement, if challenged, can be limited or terminated by the court. In addition, some jurisdictions allow for a short-term guardianship to be amended, renewed, and revoked.

Temporary Guardian

Another variation on guardianships is a temporary guardian. This is a special kind of guardianship used only when an individual—minor or adult—faces an acute emergency and a guardian has not yet been appointed. A petition is filed for temporary guardianship. If the petitioner can show that there is an emergency (for example, the hospital must amputate a gangrenous leg or the person will die), then a temporary guardian is appointed without delay. Again, the guardian is limited to handling only the specific emergencies, and this arrangement is good only for a specific number of days.

Our role as trust professionals extends to these new guardianship arrangements. Not only must we be familiar with these forms of guardianship, but we must be prepared to serve in these capacities.

ADVANCE DIRECTIVES

To this point our discussion has focused on directives (directions) that individuals can make and trust departments can provide for the care of *others:* the appointment of a guardian for one's children in a will, the court appointment of a guardian for others, and the new legislation for the appointment of a guardian for others in the event of future contingencies that would necessitate a guardian. A vital estate planning tool and technique for our customers are directives that will assist in the care of *oneself.* Our familiarity with these techniques allows us to provide effective estate planning and recognize what our role is when these directives come into play.

If a person is capable of communicating to others and he can think clearly, he can direct his medical care and manage his financial affairs. But if he is incapacitated and unable to manage his personal affairs and unable to communicate his wishes, a guardianship may be warranted. There are alternatives—personal arrangements—that can be put in place today to direct who will manage his care (health and property) tomorrow if incapacitation strikes.

One arrangement for property is the personal trust, discussed in Chapters 7 and 8. Others are the previously discussed hybrid guardianships. Another is the power of attorney. Powers of attorney (commonly referred to in the shortened form "power(s)") are called advance directives because they are put in place in advance of a need.

Before we cover property powers, we will discuss directives pertaining to health. Although a trust professional is not a party to a healthcare directive, and although it is not a financial estate-planning device, a healthcare directive may be part of a customer's life-and-death planning. When assisting a customer, it is helpful to understand the concept and purpose of a healthcare directive as it fits into her overall planning.

Healthcare Directives

Medical providers, by virtue of their nature, education, and ethics, are com-pelled to provide medical care and sustain life. Denying that care can be questioned, even in cases in which family members decide medical providers should not prolong an inevitable death.

Many people today take advantage of the legal right to spell out their personal desires, while they are competent, for their medical care and choose who will be responsible for making decisions for them if they are not capable of doing so in the future. Such desires are called advance healthcare directives. They are written directions telling others what should happen and who will be responsible for their wishes.

Living Will

A **living will** (which is neither a will nor about living) is a written document directed to healthcare providers (physicians, hospitals, convalescent homes, and so forth.). It is referred to as a *right-to-die* directive (or as some jurisdictions call it, a "declaration of a desire for a natural death"). A living will is an individual's declaration directing health care providers to omit or terminate medical care in the event of a terminal condition. A terminal condition has these qualities:

- It is irreversible
- It is incurable
- Death is imminent
- The application of death-delaying procedures serves only to prolong the dying process
- The individual becomes personally unable to direct his healthcare

A living will directs healthcare givers on whether to use life-sustaining or death-delaying procedures, depending on the individual's request. This directive can also define when treatment should stop, under what conditions treatment should cease, and who can make these decisions. Most states provide in their statutes a measure of assurance that such directions can be carried out without adverse consequences to the healthcare providers involved. These statutes are also careful to express that living wills are not condoning, authorizing, or approving mercy killing or suicide, despite the fact that they are highly personal and often viewed in light of religious and philosophical beliefs.

Keep in mind again that a living will is prepared in advance of an illness or injury, when a person is legally capable of making these decisions. This directive applies only to terminal conditions, and it pertains only to life-support issues. Therefore, generally, living wills state that the individual's life should not be prolonged by extraordinary means or by artificial nutrition if his condition is determined to be terminal and incurable or is diagnosed as a persistent vegetative state.

Do-Not-Resuscitate Order

A "do not resuscitate" (DNR) order—or "no code" order—is a physician's order (directed by a patient) that tells nursing and hospital staff not to resuscitate (revive) the patient if he suffers a cardiopulmonary arrest (heart attack). Medical practice and the policies of most patient-care facilities require that cardiopulmonary resuscitation (CPR) be started unless there is an order to the contrary in the patient's chart (record). Remember that statutes vary from jurisdiction to jurisdiction as to whether DNRs are recognized and to what extent they are carried out.

Healthcare Power of Attorney

A **power of attorney for healthcare** is a document that permits a person (called a principal) to delegate to another person (called an agent)—other than the principal's physician or healthcare provider—the power to make any healthcare decisions the principal (powergiver) could make. The scope of the power given to the agent (powerholder) may be as broad or narrow as the principal wishes. (Note: the foregoing terms are in general use from state to state; however, the following paragraphs are not necessarily consistent in all states. Please consult your local statutes.)

In general, states recognize the right of an individual to control all aspects of his or her personal care and medical treatment, including the right to decline medical treatment or to direct that it be withdrawn, even if death ensues. The right of the individual to decide about personal care overrides the obligation of the physician and other healthcare providers to render care or to preserve life. However, if the individual becomes disabled, her or his right to control treatment may be denied unless the individual can delegate the decision-making power to a trusted agent and be sure that the agent's power to make personal and healthcare decisions will be as effective as if made by the principal.

To this end states recognize the right of delegation for healthcare decision making. (We will visit this "delegation" aspect again when we discuss power of attorney for property.) States recognize that powers concerning life and death—and issues involving healthcare decisions—are more sensitive than property matters. Rules and forms have therefore been established to guide healthcare providers and ensure validity and efficacy. The rules and forms are designed to relieve healthcare providers, who rely in good faith on the actions and decisions of the agent, from fear of civil or criminal liability to the principal, the state, or any other person.

Although an individual can use a standard, statutory (legislative-provided) form, law does not mandate that such a form be used. A powergiver can choose other forms (perhaps drafted by the principal's attorney), and these forms will be effective if they materially comply with the requirements set forth in law.

A power of attorney for healthcare transcends the specific purposes of a living will and a DNR order. Note the breadth of a healthcare power by reading the opening paragraph of a representative state's power of attorney for healthcare statutory form:

> The purpose of this power of attorney is to give the person you designate (your "agent") broad powers to make

health care decisions for you, including power to require, consent to, or withdraw any type of personal care or medical treatment for any physical or mental condition and to admit you to or discharge you from any hospital, home, or other institution. This form does not impose a duty on your agent to exercise granted powers; but when powers are exercised, your agent will have to use due care to act for your benefit and in accordance with this form and keep a record of receipts, disbursements, and significant actions taken as agent. A court can take away the powers of your agent if it finds the agent is not acting properly. You may name successor agents under this form but not co-agents, and no health care provider may be named. Unless you expressly limit the duration of this power in the manner provided below, until you revoke this power or a court acting on your behalf terminates it, your agent may exercise the powers given here throughout your lifetime, even after you become disabled.

As you may sense, the subject of healthcare directives can easily be a specialized field of law. This book is not intended to provide legal advice; therefore, anyone contemplating the use of a healthcare directive should consult with a knowledgeable professional. With this said, let's look at some additional topics pertaining to a healthcare power of attorney. A healthcare power can

- Dictate withholding or removing life-sustaining treatment; the powergiver can state his desires to prolong—or not prolong—life

- State when life-sustaining treatment goes into effect and when it will terminate

- Provide for anatomical gifting, disposition of remains, and autopsy

- Adjust healthcare instructions to be consistent with the principal's religious beliefs

- Allow the agent to access the powergiver's medical records

- Name the powerholder as guardian of the person

In Absence of Direction

Despite the opportunity to create a healthcare directive, there are people who do not choose to create one. If a person without a healthcare directive becomes terminally ill, permanently unconsciousness, or incurably or irreversibly ill—and is incapable of making decisions—someone else (who might not be the person the principal would have chosen) will have to make healthcare decisions. Such a turn of events could place burdens (emotional distress, for example) on family and physician.

To help mitigate the lack of planning, many states have enacted statutes to provide a surrogate who would make life-sustaining healthcare decisions. When a patient is incapable of making decisions, the healthcare provider first must make a reasonable inquiry as to the availability and authority of a healthcare power of attorney. If no healthcare agent has been authorized or the agent is unavailable, the healthcare provider must make a reasonable inquiry as to the availability of possible surrogates. The surrogate decision makers, as identified by the attending physician, are then authorized to make healthcare decisions.

A surrogate decision maker must be an adult individual or individuals who

- Have the capacity to make decisions

- Are available (within reason)

- Are willing to make medical-treatment decisions on behalf of a patient who lacks the capacity to make decisions, and

- Are identified by the attending physician as the person or persons who are to make those decisions in accordance with the provisions of the statutes

Surrogates are not selected when a patient has an operative and unrevoked living will or power of attorney for healthcare. Remember that the laws relating to the existence and the functions of surrogate decision makers vary from state to state.

Medical treatment decisions, including whether to forego life-sustaining treatment on behalf of the patient, may be made without court order or judicial involvement by the following in order of priority:

1. The patient's guardian of the person
2. The patient's spouse
3. Any adult son or daughter of the patient
4. Either parent of the patient
5. Any adult brother or sister of the patient
6. Any adult grandchild of the patient
7. A close friend of the patient
8. The patient's guardian of the estate

Where there are multiple surrogate decision makers at the same priority level (such as two or more children), the surrogates must make reasonable efforts to reach a consensus in their decision on behalf of the patient.

Yes, this is a lot of discussion pertaining to a subject that trust institutions do not act upon, and it does not pertain to financial matters—the core of our products and services. Nonetheless, knowledge of these directives is an indispensable aid to us as we assist our customers. We cannot advise customers about such issues, but by being aware of the issues, we can explain why it is important for them to consider getting legal advice on healthcare matters.

Power of Attorney for Property

The strict yet necessary rules and restrictions associated with asset management in an estate guardianship, the public court's involvement, and the attendant lack of privacy may lead people to choose alternatives to a guardianship arrangement. We will discuss one variety, a living trust, in Chapters 7 and 8. The other alternative to a guardianship is the power of attorney for property. Both options alleviate the need for a guardian of the estate if they are planned ahead of time.

A **power of attorney for property** (generally referred to as a **power of attorney**) is a legal document, many times only two pages long, permitting someone else to handle an individual's financial affairs whether he or she is or is not capable of doing so. The person who is doing the designating is called the powergiver, or the principal. The person (or persons) given the power is the **attorney in fact,** or the agent. (Think back to the principal and agent discussion in Chapter 3.) Unlike an **attorney at law,** who is legally qualified and authorized to represent another in legal proceedings, an attorney in fact is authorized to transact business for another outside of court. Coagents and successor agents (in the event the named agent refuses to act or cannot act because of disability or death) may be permitted depending on the state's rules. A power of attorney can be any of the following:

- **General power of attorney.** This type of power is effective upon execution (signing). It can be all-encompassing or specific (limited), and it terminates if the principal becomes incapacitated.

- **Durable power of attorney.** This type of power may be general or specific. It is effective upon execution and does not terminate upon the principal's incapacitation.

- **Springing (or standby) power of attorney.** This power becomes effective only when a future contingency arises, such as incapacitation. It can be general or specific.

- **Specific (or limited) power of attorney.** This type of power can be general, durable, or springing. It limits the agent to specific (special) tasks. Frequently, these powers are institution-specific documents pertaining only to the account(s) at the institution.

In states where the Uniform Probate Code is used, a durable power of attorney is defined as follows:

A durable power of attorney is a power of attorney by which a principal designates another his attorney in fact in writing and the writing contains the words "This power of attorney shall not be affected by subsequent disability or incapacity of the principal, or lapse of time," or "This power of attorney shall become effective upon the disability or incapacity of the principal," or similar words showing the intent of the principal that the authority conferred shall be exercisable notwithstanding the principal's subsequent disability or incapacity, and, unless it states a time of termination, notwithstanding the lapse of time since the execution of the instrument.

All powers terminate upon the power-giver's death; all powers are amendable; and all powers are revocable.

What an Agent Can Do

In essence, a power of attorney is a strong legal permission that one person gives to another. Individual A gives individual B the authority to deal with A's property to the same extent that A can manage his or her own property, consistent with the power's direction as defined in the power of attorney's document.

Notice that we say *individual*. Trust departments and trust professionals do not serve as the agent, the attorney in fact. But our role as estate planners extends to B when he or she exercises his or her power for A. Just as we provide products and services to A, we can provide the same for B with respect to A's assets.

An agent can act in regard to transactions pertaining to

- Real estate
- Social Security, employment, and military benefits
- Financial institutions
- Tax matters
- Stocks and bonds
- Claims and litigation
- Tangible personal property

- Business operations
- Safe deposit boxes
- Insurance and annuities
- Retirement plans
- Borrowing
- Estate planning

A may have chosen B because she trusts him. When B acts on behalf of A, he too will need our products and services.

Although the list above appears to be cut-and-dried, a state's power of attorney statutes will define each category in detail. To give you an example of how detailed these definitions are, we have included one state's treatment of real estate and financial institution transactions in its power of attorney form:

REAL ESTATE TRANSACTIONS. The agent is authorized to: buy, sell, exchange, rent and lease real estate (which term includes, without limitation, real estate subject to a land trust and all beneficial interests in and powers of direction under any land trust); collect all rent, sale proceeds and earnings from real estate; convey, assign and accept title to real estate; grant easements, create conditions and release rights of homestead with respect to real estate; create land trusts and exercise all powers under land trusts; hold, possess, maintain, repair, improve, subdivide, manage, operate and insure real estate; pay, contest, protest and compromise real estate taxes and assessment; and, in general, exercise all powers with respect to real estate which the principal could if present and under no disability.

FINANCIAL INSTITUTION TRANSACTIONS. The agent is authorized to: open, close, continue and control all accounts and deposits in any type of financial institution (which term includes, without limitation, banks, trust companies, savings and building and loan associations, credit unions and brokerage firms); deposit in and withdraw from and write checks on any financial institution account or deposit; and, in general, exercise all powers with respect to financial institution transactions which the principal could if present and under no disability.

Additional Powers and Limitations

Beyond the short list above, a power may provide many specific directions, depending on state statutes. For example,

- Some statutes permit the principal to name a guardian of person or a guardian of estate, or both, if a court decides that one should be appointed. The court will appoint the person(s) nominated if it finds that such appointment will serve the principal's best interest and welfare.

- A power of attorney gives the agent broad powers to handle property, which may include powers to pledge the property, sell it, or otherwise dispose of any real or personal property without advance notice or approval by the principal.

- The power may authorize that the agent be entitled to reasonable compensation for services rendered.

- When a power is exercised, the agent must use care to act exclusively for the benefit of the principal and in accordance with the document. A court can rescind the powers of the agent if it finds the agent is not acting properly. Unless expressly limited, the duration of the power lasts until revoked by court action.

- A power may be amended or revoked at any time and in any manner. Absent any restriction, amendment, or revocation, a power of attorney becomes effective at the time it is signed and continues until death unless the effective date and duration are specified or limited within the document.

- In designating a power, the powergiver may include any specific limitations he or she feels are appropriate, such as a prohibition on the sale of particular securities, tangible personal or real property, or special rules regarding the agent's ability to borrow money.

- In addition, a power can include permission to make gifts, exercise powers of appointment, name or change beneficiaries or joint tenants, or create, amend, and revoke any trust specifically mentioned within the document.

- The power may give the powerholder (agent) the authority to employ other persons as necessary to enable the agent to properly exercise the powers granted.

- The agent may be permitted to exercise any powers the principal permits with respect to all possible types of property and interests in property as long as it is consistent with state law.

The last bullet point is interesting and important. *Read the following words carefully:* In general, if state statute does not permit something, a power cannot permit it. (The statute and power cannot contradict each other.) In many states, even if the statute permits something and the powergiver wishes the powerholder to be able to do it, the task must be specifically stated in the power. (The statute and power must be consistent.) If it is not stated in the power, it is not permitted (despite the statute permitting it).

A trust officer recently met with two sisters who were looking for advice regarding their mother's assets. Mom was aging and becoming more forgetful. Because of the sisters' respective careers, family commitments, and lack of financial knowledge, they were finding it difficult to assist their mother. How could the trust department help?

The trust officer explained the uses of a personal trust. The sisters felt comfortable recommending a trust to their mother. An attorney was recommended who drafted a living trust naming the bank as trustee based on information gathered from the sisters during a meeting with them and from two telephone conversations with their mother. The attorney could detect the mother's mental deterioration from his third conversation with her, during which he arranged a time and place to meet her for execution of the trust and a new will. The sisters, attorney, and trust officer planned to meet in the attorney's office the day after the trust was to be signed.

During the meeting at the attorney's office, he explained to the sisters that their mother refused to sign the trust. She did not recall talking to her daughters or the attorney about the trust.

The sisters could have considered having their mother adjudicated incompetent and petitioned the court to name the bank as guardian of the estate. The cost, the lack of privacy, and the strict investment rules associated with a guardianship did not set well with the sisters. They also wanted to know how this action would affect the power of attorney their mother signed a year ago.

The trust officer and attorney smiled and asked the sisters to provide them with a copy for review. From one sister's briefcase came the original power: a statutory, durable, general power of attorney naming the sisters as co-powerholders. The power gave the sisters the ability to establish a trust for the benefit of their mother and the ability to fund the trust. The attorney quickly altered the trust draft, changing the grantor from mother to the sisters as cograntors.

Statutory Forms

A power may be individually designed by an attorney; generally, however, statutory forms prescribed by state law are used. Remember that laws governing powers vary from state to state. For example, some states do not provide for healthcare decisions in a durable power. Instead, they may have laws for a power of attor-

ney for property (used for any financial or business matters) and a power of attorney for healthcare, which provides for healthcare decisions such as consenting to or withdrawing treatment.

Trust professionals must be familiar with the types of powers they encounter with their customers. The power can affect what we can and cannot offer. For example, if a customer who is not a resident of your state executed a power in his former state of residence, does it apply to his new residence? Additionally, if the agent of a power is seeking your assistance, does the power give her the ability to use your products and services?

Execution of Powers

When a power is established in conjunction with a will and a trust, trust professionals must remember that powers should be executed with the same formalities as a will. For example, both the principal (the one giving the power) and the agent (the one receiving the power) must be competent at the time the power is given, and they must be of legal age in their state. The same care given to choosing the executor of a will should be applied to choosing a power's agent. The document should be witnessed and notarized, and it should be complete in its content and intent. A poorly drafted power may be challenged and limited, just like a will. Also, it is a good idea to review and restate the power periodically. A concerned trust planner can direct his customer down the proper path in using this estate planning tool.

Issues Relating to Legal Liabilities and Responsibilities

Does a powerholder under a power of attorney assume the same legal responsibilities and legal duties that a trustee assumes? The law in this area differs in many states and isn't always clear. It is safe to assume that the powerholder assumes at least some of the potential liabilities and duties, as does any fiduciary. This possibly includes claims that the powerholder made imprudent investments, failed to protect the best interests of the power-giver, or was negligent with respect to recording significant actions pertaining to the powerholder's actions. May the powergiver or any interested person seek legal restitution against the powerholder? Perhaps. A person who is being considered as a powerholder should be fully informed of his or her potential liabilities and duties.

Guardianships and Powers

Probate statutes vary from jurisdiction to jurisdiction. The powers permitted an estate guardian may restrict the ability to implement estate-planning tasks. In those states that recognize it, the Uniform Probate Code (UPC) gives the court and court-appointed fiduciaries (that is, guardians) for an incompetent individual all the powers over the individual's estate and affairs that the individual could exercise if present and not under a disability, except the power to make a will. Such powers specifically include the power to

- Make gifts
- Convey or release contingent interests in marital property and survivorship interests in jointly held property
- Create revocable or irrevocable trusts that may extend beyond the individual's disability or life
- Exercise options to purchase securities or other property
- Elect options or change beneficiaries under insurance and annuity policies and to surrender the policies for their cash value
- Exercise any right of election in the estate of the individual's deceased spouse
- Disclaim any interest otherwise receivable by the incapacitated person under a will, by intestate succession or by *inter vivos* (between living persons) transfer

The UPC also states that these powers may be exercised only if the court (after notice and hearing) is satisfied that an action is in the best interests of the ward.

Because of the above issues, effective estate planning for an incapacitated individual is facilitated by a durable power of attorney. But agents are not always satisfied with durable power of attorney. Many third parties (banks, stock transfer agents, insurance companies, and the IRS) are often hesitant to accept a power unless it is created using one of *their* forms. A financial institution sometimes requires

- A separate power for each account
- A power that is less than six months old
- A guarantee by the agent to hold the institution harmless regarding the power's authenticity
- An indemnification in the event any liability is incurred as a result of reliance on the power

Additional Thoughts

- Just as a will can be contested (challenged), so too can a power of attorney, especially if it is poorly drafted.
- Laws change and individuals change; it is important to review and restate a power periodically.
- Perhaps specialized powerholders should be chosen for different tasks (powers). Some people are suited to run a business, invest common and special assets, and provide tax and estate planning, and others are not. Choose the right person for each responsibility.

SUMMARY

- Incapacitation is the inability of an adult or a minor to look after his or her physical care or financial affairs because of a physical or mental disability or legal incompetence.

Incapacitation may necessitate a guardian.

- Two different guardianship arrangements exist. A personal guardian is responsible for a person's physical care. An estate guardian is responsible for a person's financial affairs. Guardianships are applicable to minors and adults. Guardianships are either voluntary (requested by an individual for himself) or involuntary (requested by another).

- The guardianship process involves posting a bond, petitioning the appropriate court, and performing an extensive list of guardianship duties, such as collecting assets, budgeting, developing an investment program, filing tax returns, and accounting to the court. Guardianships terminate upon attainment of majority, resolution of disability, or death.

- In several states newly created guardianship arrangements exist that allow individuals to name today who will be their guardian or their children's guardian in the future. These guardianships are standby guardian, short-term guardian, and temporary guardian.

- Advance directives consist of healthcare directives and powers of attorney for property. A power of attorney is a written document permitting another to manage the powergiver's financial affairs and healthcare directions, whether or not the powergiver is incapacitated. Powers of attorney for property are general, durable, springing, or specific. Powers can be individually designed, or statutory forms can be used. Powers should be carefully planned, legally prepared, and formally executed.

REVIEW QUESTIONS

1. Define *incapacitation*. What types of incapacitation exist?
2. What two guardian arrangements exist and how do they differ?
3. List at least five general duties of an estate guardian.
4. What events cause termination of a guardianship?
5. What is a power of attorney for property? List the four types.

7

PERSONAL TRUSTS: THE GROUNDWORK

"Put not your trust in money, but put your money in trust."

Oliver Wendell Holmes, Sr. (1809–1894)

Pat toiled long and hard to build a very handsome estate. Some say he paid for it dearly: 80-hour work weeks, two divorces, a former partner (his brother) who no longer talks to him, and triple bypass surgery last year. Pat doesn't regret the bad times. He was willing to trade them for a $20-million estate consisting of a very healthy pension package, an enviable income and investment portfolio, the biggest house in town (plus one in the mountains and one on the beach), several antique automobiles, and a valuable, debt-free, money-making computer company.

From talking with the members of his estate planning team, Pat knows he could pass his entire estate on to his third wife, free of any estate taxes. This provision is contained in tax laws. But Pat doesn't want things to happen that way. He wants his wife to inherit half of his estate, and the other half will go to his children from his first marriage. This arrangement will create a heavy tax liability (see Exhibit 7.1 later in this chapter). An additional problem Pat recognizes is that his wife and children may be incapable of managing and preserving the assets they inherit.

Pat is an estate owner—an estate planner—who has set his goals loosely. His next step is to explore the uses of a trust for his family's welfare. The type of trust that would assist his planning, the reasons for a trust, and the best candidates to serve as trustees are the concepts presented in this chapter. (Chapter 8 will continue the discussion by addressing sample provisions Pat may consider in his trust.)

In contrast to other chapters, where concepts and terms are easily and succinctly defined, this chapter and the next offer a multipage definition of a personal trust. Because of the breadth of personal trusts, their variety and complexity, two chapters are devoted to one of estate planning's most versatile tools and techniques. Each page should be approached carefully and treated as a step-by-step guide.

LEARNING OBJECTIVES

Chapter 5 introduced the concept of planning for death. Planning does not end with the end of one's life because the family must continue living and benefiting, or pay the price of poor planning. Estate planning as an ongoing, dynamic process—a life-and-death proposition—can be bolstered by trust planning.

Upon completion of this chapter, you will be able to

- Distinguish types of trusts
- Define a personal trust
- Compare testamentary and living trusts
- List the reasons for having a trust
- Describe the characteristics of a good trustee
- Define and use the terms that appear in bold in the text

TYPES OF TRUSTS

Trusts will be described in several ways in this chapter: by definition, by description, and by examples. Trusts in general are classified according to the method of their creation. (Note: it is beyond the scope of this book to dwell on the legality of these types.)

Express Trust

Express trusts arise when a property owner purposefully expresses his intention to create a trust relationship with respect to the property. An express trust is manifested by words, writing, or conduct, and it is either "private" (for the benefit of certain ascertainable persons) or "charitable" (for the benefit of an indefinite class of persons or the public in general). Our discussions focus on express trusts.

Resulting Trust

Resulting trusts arise from the presumed intention of the owner of the property. A resulting trust, whether implied by a matter of law or imposed by courts, involves a reversion of interest when property is not completely disposed of due to the presumed intent of the grantor. This could happen when an unintended gift is made or a sale is made without consideration (that is, without a purchase price). In other words, the transfer of property from "A" to "B" is given to be a trust rela-tionship (where "B" holds property for "A"). This type of transfer is not a gift.

Constructive Trust

A constructive trust is created by a court (regardless of the intent of the parties) to benefit a party that has been wrongfully deprived of its rights. For example, in a constructive trust, a court declares that because of fraud, duress, breach of fiduciary duty, or some other inappropriate behavior, one party who has title to property is deemed to hold that property on behalf of the party who suffered from the wrongful or inappropriate behavior. Constructive trusts do not depend on the intention of the parties involved; they constitute a useful equitable remedy in cases involving fraud and unjust enrichment. Constructive trusts are developed primarily by an action of a court as a means of granting relief—a remedy—in cases where a person obtains legal title to property that rightfully belongs to another. The purpose of a constructive trust is to prevent unjust enrichment by the person who has obtained title through fraud, undue influence, or breach of fiduciary duty.

(The unfamiliar terms, such as *grantor* and *fiduciary,* in the discussion above will be addressed shortly.)

PERSONAL TRUST

In Chapter 5, a will was defined as a legal document that expresses a person's intentions of how his or her estate will be administered and settled upon death. A personal trust steps beyond the who-gets-what direction of a will to the when, how, and why.

Definitions, Legal and Otherwise

A **personal trust** (or simply a *trust*) is a short story, a set of instructions, a financial road map, an estate blueprint, a list of duties. A trust is a legal document that provides direction about who will benefit from the estate, what they will receive, how it will be received, and when it will be received. A trust can provide benefits and flexibility that are restricted only by the bounds of the creator's imagination. As long as the trust does not say anything immoral or illegal or contrary to certain public policies, the sky is the limit with respect to what a trust can accomplish and how an estate owner can direct his or her estate.

Austin Wakeman Scott, late Dane Professor of Law Emeritus of Harvard University and the foremost authority on trusts, defined a trust as

> A fiduciary relationship with respect to property, subjecting the person by whom the title to property is held to equitable duties to deal with the property for the benefit of another person, which rises as a result of a manifestation of an intention to create it.

Admittedly, Scott's definition is unwieldy. A longer but less technical description is as follows:

> A trust is an arrangement (a relationship or a contract) whereby an individual (known as the grantor) transfers ownership (legal title) of property (known as corpus) to an individual or institution (known as the trustee) to hold, manage, and invest for the benefit of the individual or others (known as the beneficiary). The document (known as the trust agreement) contains specific instructions as to how assets are to be managed during life or afterward.

Understanding the definition is made easier by looking at the five parts:

- **Grantor:** the person who creates (establishes) the trust. A grantor is also called a **creator, settlor,** and **trustor.**

- **Trustee:** an individual or **trust institution** empowered to carry out the terms of the trust agreement; the trustee serves as the trust's fiduciary. (We will delve further into *fiduciary* shortly.)

- **Beneficiary:** one or more people or charities who benefit from the trust.

- **Corpus:** the assets **transferred,** by legal title, to the trust. Corpus is also called **res, principal,** and **trust estate.** (We will discuss *legal title* shortly.)

- **Trust agreement:** also known as the **trust instrument,** this is the formal written document that sets forth the terms of the trust.

A trust's ingredients parallel those of the makings of a will:

	Trust	Will
The creator	Grantor	Testator
The driver	Trustee	Executor
Who benefits	Beneficiary	Beneficiary/ heir
The property	Corpus	Probate estate
The document	Trust agreement	Last will

The distinguishing element of a trust is how it transcends a will's terminal administration and settlement of an estate at death. In this way, a trust can benefit a person during life and others following death. A trust provides for the management of assets beyond a will's act of distribution. A trust extends beyond who gets what to include when and how.

At this point you may be thinking, "I think I understand what is being said, but it's not completely clear. Someone sets up a trust for the benefit of someone else; assets are placed in this trust, and a trustee is picked to manage the assets for the beneficiary according to the terms of a long legal document. I'm a bit fuzzy about what a fiduciary is. And what does transferring assets—changing legal title—mean?"

Fiduciary

There are times and reasons for asking others to do things for us because we don't want to, we don't have the time, we don't have the expertise, or we are incapable. We do this constantly in our lives when we look to others for their products and services: a plumber, the kid who shovels snow from our sidewalk, dentists, and countless others, professional and nonprofessional. With respect to our assets and estates, we also may not have the time, desire, expertise, or capability to care for matters for ourselves and our families. Whom do we turn to? Someone we can trust to hold, manage, and invest our assets for us and our families. As selfish as estate planning can be, the decision to turn to another is extremely important. It is on this premise that the trust industry grows.

Let's work with an example. Everyone understands the importance of a good sitter for their children. Enjoyment of an evening away from home hinges heavily on the comfort parents have in the person who watches their home and children while they are away. Would they go out if they could not trust the sitter? Before Mr. and Mrs. Gregory leave the house, they probably review a set of instructions with the sitter: phone numbers of where they will be, emergency names and numbers, neighbors' names and numbers, directions regarding bedtimes, what not to watch on television, medicines, where things are located in the house, operation of locks and appliances, safety precautions, and so on. The sitter cannot be second-guessed. Whereas the parents place trust in the sitter, the sitter must be reliable, strong, and fair. Neither should expect or provide less.

Interestingly, many people spend more time developing and reviewing their sitter's instructions than their own estate planning. They've told others how to care for their kids for 4 or 5 hours, but they haven't developed a plan for their estate in the event their evening results in disaster. Mr. and Mrs. Gregory have taken special care in choosing and instructing their children's sitter. Yet who will take care of the family if they are killed or incapacitated?

What we have been describing by analogy is a **fiduciary:** a person or institution Mr. and Mrs. Gregory can entrust to manage family affairs and assets for them and others, today and tomorrow. A trustee as a fiduciary holds one of the highest stations in life, as expressed by an anonymous writer who once said, "There is no duty known to the law greater than the duty which a trustee owes to a beneficiary of a trust."

We are not describing a simple task. Think about it this way: How many people would trust another to drive their car? Would that number be smaller if they were passengers? Would it be even smaller if their families were the passengers? Trust is not a simple five-letter word. Beyond the car, who can be trusted without any hesitation to manage assets? This is what trusts and fiduciaries are about.

To allow someone else (a fiduciary) to care for their assets and family affairs, the Gregorys must give the trustee the power. The trust agreement—the financial roadmap—gives direction to the trustee (fiduciary), but not the power.

Legal Title

The only person or entity who can manage and direct assets is the one who legally owns the property. If A owns an asset, B cannot deal with it. But there are two exceptions: a power of attorney (discussed in Chapter 6) and trust ownership. Both a power of attorney and trust ownership allow B to deal with A's assets.

In trust ownership, A is not giving away her assets to B as the trustee; she is merely transferring ownership of her assets so that B can legally manage A's property according to A's instructions, contained in the trust agreement. This is a core ingredient of a trust relationship.

In Scott's works pertaining to trust, he states,

- "It is possible for one person to have the legal title of property and for another to compel him to exercise his legal rights for the other's benefit." When A gives B the legal ownership of A's property, A walks away from "legally" owning the property, yet simultaneously retains an interest in the property as a "beneficial" owner.

- "You give the beneficiary an interest in the property and give him protection in the enjoyment of that interest. Beneath is the trustee who holds the legal title; above him is the beneficiary who has the equitable ownership." A dual form of ownership exists.

Beyond the Definitions

Scott's legal definitions of trust and the dual ownership of assets within a trust are far from clear. If they were, the chapter would end, and so would the learning experience.

Unfortunately, many people stop at this point, convinced that trusts are complicated legal instruments developed for the rich, who can afford attorneys to interpret the legalese. As a customer once stated, "Understanding a trust is like a blind person searching in a dark room for a black cat that isn't there." Others perceive a trust as a formal arrangement invented by banks in which a stodgy trust officer doles out nickels and dimes to widows and orphans.

It is your obligation as a trust professional to educate the public about trust planning. There can never be anything negative about helping people with their finances and aspirations for their families, but people tend to fear what they do not understand.

A trust is not a magical string of words and paragraphs that solves all financial woes. However, it is one of estate planning's strongest tools, as Joan found in the introduction to this textbook. Joan, as a widow, had no one to depend on. She learned it was easy to inherit assets, but inheritances do not come packaged with the ability, time, desire, experience, or emotional stability to manage them. Our task as trust professionals is to be there for customers like Joan when they say, "I trust you can help me."

TYPES OF PERSONAL TRUSTS

Regardless of the appearance, language, and title of any trust, there are only two types of trusts: testamentary and living. Any trust you encounter will be one type or the other.

Testamentary Trust

A **testamentary trust** (also called a **trust under will,** or T/U/W) is part of a will. It is not a separate document like a living trust, which will be explored shortly. A testamentary trust is not effective during life; it is a set of instructions that goes into action only after a person's death. Because the trust language is contained in a will, and because a will pertains to activity following death, a testamentary trust lies dormant. Everything this trust is meant to do happens only after the creator's death, never before. A testamentary trust can be revoked (canceled) and amended (modified) before death because it is part of a will, which is by its nature revocable and amendable (unless, of course, the testator is incapacitated and cannot legally change his or her will because of lack of testamentary capacity). Revoking or changing the terms of the trust is accomplished with a codicil to the will that contains the trust provisions. Because the only one who can change a trust is the trust's creator, once the testamentary trust's creator dies, the trust becomes irrevocable and cannot be altered or terminated by anyone else.

Later in the chapter we will discuss how trust assets are isolated from probate upon incapacitation and death. This pertains to living trusts, which are created and are effective during one's life. This advantage (avoiding probate) does not exist for a testamentary trust. Although a testamentary trust is created during life, it is not effective until death. Therefore, assets cannot be placed by the trust's creator (or anyone else, for that matter) during the creator's life into a trust that does not become effective until after death. Therefore, the assets must first go through probate.

Living Trust

A **living trust** (also called an **inter vivos trust,** a Latin term that means *during life* or *among the living*) is a document separate from a will. It becomes effective once it is signed. At times called a **trust under agreement** (T/U/A), a living trust goes into effect during one's life and continues after death. An interest in property that has not yet come into legal existence cannot be held in a trust (e.g., a son's hope of inheriting his father's property). A living trust can be revocable or irrevocable. At death or incapacitation a living trust becomes irrevocable. A living trust can be funded with assets today and tomorrow and in several ways that will be explored in this and the next chapter. Many trust experts refer to "funding a trust" as an actual delivery, meaning an act that places the trust property out of the grantor's control (unless the grantor is to serve as trustee, which is discussed below with respect to self-declaration of trusts).

Revocable Trust

A **revocable** living trust can be terminated (canceled) by **revocation** or changed (modified) by an **amendment.** Some authorities use *revocation* to describe only a total cancellation of a trust; others use the word for a total cancellation and a partial cancellation or deletion of parts of a trust.

An amendment, like a codicil to a will, is an addition to a trust's language or a deletion or modification to parts of a trust.

Irrevocable Trust

An **irrevocable trust** cannot be revoked and cannot have its dispositive provisions altered (amended). **Dispositive provisions** are the terms of a trust that direct the distribution of the trust's corpus. A trust can be irrevocable from its inception, and all trusts become irrevocable upon the grantor's incapacitation or death. Trusts can be irrevocable for a stipulated period of time or irrevocable with respect to certain provisions, both depending on the grantor's intentions. Irrevocable trusts are used primarily for tax planning purposes. (Because this text is not intended to address taxation issues, we will not delve into the intricacy of mixing trusts and taxes.)

Although an irrevocable trust travels a *path of no return,* minor aspects of an irrevocable trust can be altered without destroying the irrevocable intent of the trust. For example, there are occasions when a grantor or the beneficiaries can change trustees without changing the irrevocable integrity of the trust.

A trust agreement must state whether it is revocable or irrevocable. If a trust does not say whether it is revocable or irrevocable (in other words, if the document is silent), then it is understood to be irrevocable.

Although most estate planning involving irrevocable trusts is approached from a tax perspective, there are meaningful nontax reasons for making a trust fully, partially, or temporarily irrevocable.

Life Insurance Trust

A **life insurance trust** is a living trust in that it is in place and active now, yet does not make its full impact until death. Many estates consist of substantial amounts of life insurance, purchased both personally and through employee benefit programs. Trusts have been developed that are meant to catch the life insurance proceeds at death via beneficiary designation. Although created during the grantor's life, a life insurance trust does not become fully active until the insurance proceeds are collected.

Life insurance trusts grew in popularity in the '50s, '60s, and '70s as postwar estates grew because of rising incomes, increased retirement benefits, asset accumulation, and the purchase of larger sums of life insurance. Purchasers wanted to protect their families if they died too young or died before their estate had grown sufficiently. Although the trust can receive assets from the pourover of the grantor's will, and possibly retirement plan proceeds, the major part of the trust's corpus consists of life insurance benefits.

Many planners think of these trusts as hybrids between testamentary and living trusts. They act like a testamentary trust in that they do not truly go into action until after death, when the trust is funded. Yet they are living trusts in that a trust document is created now, separate from a will, and the trust can be funded before death. In its simplest form, David creates a living trust in which ABC Bank and Trust Company is named as trustee now. David is the beneficiary of the trust during his life, and his family benefits after his death. David then **funds** the trust by naming the trust as the beneficiary of the life insurance death proceeds. (Keep in mind that David remains the owner of the insurance, so he, not the trustee, is responsible for the policies.)

There is some controversy over whether the naming of the trust as the beneficiary of life insurance is truly a funding exercise. Yes, the trust will be funded at death and yes, this trust is a living trust created during the grantor's life, but the contingency of receiving death benefits does not make the life insurance an asset owned by the trust. If an insurance policy is one that possesses cash equity (cash value and dividends), which can be reached by the grantor at any time, the equity of the policy is not an asset of the trust because the trust does not own the policy. David does. With this in mind, disagreement surfaces as to whether a life insurance trust is a living trust because, in essence, nothing happens until the grantor's death. The trust waits in a prepared mode, as does a testamentary trust. Some planners label this arrangement a *standby* trust.

David knows he can fund his life insurance trust with additional assets (real property, an investment portfolio, bank accounts, or a business), but he is hesitant to do so. David may ask, "Why do I need to place my assets into a trust of which ABC Bank and Trust Company is named as the trustee? I am perfectly capable of managing my assets. I don't need to pay a fee to the bank to manage what I can do myself. What I am concerned about is using the bank later when I die." David is correct, to a point. Additional thoughts occur to him: "What if I become incapacitated? What if I don't die, but I become incapable of managing my financial affairs? What if I get to the point in my life when I don't want to manage my financial affairs? What about privacy, confidentiality, and peace of mind? What do I do then?" David is thinking ahead, but he has a dilemma: He needs a trust to manage his assets and keep them from probate in the event of incapacitation or death, but he doesn't need to pay a trustee to do so while he is capable of managing his own affairs. Realizing this, the prepared trust professional will offer the following solution.

Self-Declaration of Trust

Over the years, a living trust called a **self-declaration of trust** (or a *self-dec* trust) evolved. Beverly, as the trust's grantor, declares herself (and perhaps her family) as the trust's beneficiaries. She funds the trust with her assets (including naming the trust as the beneficiary of her life insurance policies, perhaps retirement plans, and a pourover of assets from her will). She also declares herself to be the trustee.

USING TRUST PRODUCTS AND SERVICES
TO MEET CUSTOMER NEEDS

A trust administrator met a young man several years ago who was 3 weeks away from his eighteenth birthday. Joined by his aunt, he came to visit the trust department unannounced and unscheduled.

Hector's aunt was his guardian. Hector's mother and father died in an auto accident when he was 12 years old. The person who was driving the truck that hit his parents' car was sued and found at fault. Hector received a wrongful death settlement of $500,000. Hector's aunt was appointed his personal guardian, and a financial institution was appointed guardian of his estate. When Hector became 18, the money (close to $750,000) would be turned over to him.

Fearful that he might spend the money foolishly, and that others might learn of his wealth, Hector approached the trust department to discuss how they could help. Hector had heard about trusts in a high school economics class, and he wanted to learn more. Two months ago Hector's aunt received in her checking account statement a stuffer advertising the bank's trust services. As a result, she suggested that they talk with the trust department of her bank.

Hector had recently been accepted to a prestigious East Coast university. Fortunately, the money was there for tuition, travel, room and board, expenses, a car, and a lot more. Unfortunately, the money was also there to be squandered, to tempt others, and to be inappropriately invested. For a soon-to-be 18-year-old, Hector had keen insight. During the meeting with the trust administrator, he expressed the concern that this money was his financial fortune; it also could easily burn a hole in his pocket.

Hector had asked his aunt for help, but she kindly declined. "Hector, I don't know anything about investing money. Also, I can't keep your money away from you." For these reasons, they felt a trustee could help.

An extensive meeting showed Hector and his aunt the merits of using a trust: confidentiality, professional investment management, and distribution of money for tuition, and an estimated budget. Yet despite all the good things Hector recognized in a trust, the thought that he could take his money out of the trust at any time bothered him. Had the trust administrator solved all his needs?

Of the attorneys suggested to Hector, the one he chose to construct the trust agreement recommended that he make his trust irrevocable until Hector finished his college education (and perhaps postgraduate work). The trust's money would be there for tuition, living expenses, and so on, but the trust would direct the bank as trustee not to distribute money to Hector when he asked for it, if the trustee felt that his request was not warranted according to the instructions given in the trust agreement.

Today, Hector is married and has three children. He recently finished his master's degree in chemical engineering, and he bought a large house in the suburbs. His trust still exists and will be there for his family.

Let's examine this type of living trust by looking at the five elements of a trust.

- *Grantor.* As in any other trust, Beverly is the creator of the trust. Assuming she makes her trust revocable, she can revoke parts or all of the trust and amend it during any period in which she is not incapacitated. She can add, withdraw, and use the trust's assets according to the trust's provisions.

- *Beneficiary.* During her life, Beverly benefits from her assets through investment appreciation, income generation, and the ability to change assets and use them as she desires. This ability does not change just because her assets are in a trust. Beverly and her family can continue to benefit from the trust's assets as before.

  Regarding beneficiaries, they do not have to be identified at the time the trust is created, but they must be "susceptible" of identification by the time their interests are to come into enjoyment. An unborn beneficiary may be described in the trust agreement, and the trust will be valid, even for the unborn child's interest. So, for example, "A" can convey to "B" in trust for "B's" life, with the remainder to "B's" children. The beneficiaries are definite (susceptible) even though "B" did not have children at the time the trust was formed. It is sufficient that "B's" children would be susceptible of identification at the time their interests were to come into enjoyment, meaning at "B's" death.

- *Trust agreement.* The trust document can contain language that allows Beverly, as the grantor, to revoke and amend, and it can permit her to add and withdraw assets. In essence, the trust can allow Beverly to deal with and benefit from the assets as she pleases, as the grantor in full control and as the beneficiary.

- *Trustee.* In a self-dec trust, Beverly is the initial trustee; as a person she is an **individual trustee.** A key element of a self-dec trust is that the trust can give her, as the trustee, the power to manage, invest, and dispose of the trust's assets to the same extent as if Beverly owned the assets outright in her individual name. Beverly achieves the benefits of a trust (discussed in the next section) without a reduction in the control and enjoyment of her property. If Beverly becomes incapacitated and is unable to continue as trustee, if she no longer wishes to manage her trust assets, and, of course, when she dies, the trust can provide for an automatic **successor** trustee. This can be another individual or a **corporate trustee.** The bank will step in when Beverly no longer can do the job of managing her assets.

- *Corpus.* Beverly transfers her assets from herself-as-owner to herself-as-trustee. This transfer takes the assets from Beverly-owned to trust-owned. Life insurance proceeds, retirement plan proceeds, pourover of assets from her will, and the addition of property from any source (spousal assets and power of appointment property, which will be discussed in the next chapter) will add to the trust's estate.

A self-dec trust gives Beverly opportunities beyond a testamentary trust and a life insurance trust, both of which involve primarily postmortem planning. A self-dec trust permits Beverly to wear all three hats simultaneously: grantor, beneficiary, and trustee. The trust document is written with Beverly and her family in mind during her life (in good times and bad) and for the benefit of her family following Beverly's demise.

In looking at a self-dec trust's flexibility and planning opportunities, there are subtle additional benefits to Beverly.

- A self-dec trust does not involve any fees while Beverly is serving as trustee. Beverly is not asking another to provide her with trust services. She is doing so herself.

- Although many states prohibit nonresident individuals and out-of-state corporations from acting as executor in a resident's will, they usually do not impose such restrictions on successor trustees (individual or corporate). Thus, Beverly may be able to name as successor trustee a person or bank that could not have acted as executor of her estate in a particular state. This will be important to the continuity of Beverly's estate planning if she moves to another state.

- Because self-dec trusts are recognized and valid in most states (many states call these one-party trusts), generally no separate tax identification number is required as long as Beverly continues to act as trustee or as a cotrustee. The trust and its assets will carry Beverly's Social Security number, so the trust will not need to file a separate tax return. All items of income are reported on Beverly's personal income tax return.

- A self-dec trust helps alleviate the need for ancillary probate (discussed in Chapter 5). If Beverly owns property in a state other than where she is domiciled, the other state may require that a probate estate be opened there for those assets, in addition to the probate estate in her state of legal residence. Assets owned (titled) in trust are not subject to probate—in either state.

At this stage a potential trust customer might think, "This sounds okay, but do I really need a trust at all? My dad lived to 87, never sick a day in his life; he and mom owned everything in joint tenancy. Why do I need a trust?" Assuming the potential customer understands what a trust is and the types that exist, the trust professional's next task is to motivate him by outlining the reasons and advantages for having a trust and placing it with the bank's trust department.

REASONS FOR HAVING A TRUST

To be successful, all large undertakings are planned. Objective parts of a plan are blueprints, guidelines, action plans, lists of ingredients or supplies, sets of instructions, and schedules. Subjective elements are philosophy, purpose, mission statements, intent, and reason. Whether building a skyscraper, planning a business endeavor, or constructing an estate plan, each step of the plan depends on the others. The parts blend into the whole as the planning and construction unfold.

Without a plan and reasons for making one, it is easy to balk at any endeavor, trust planning included. Armed with an understanding of what a trust is and the types that exist, the trust professional must educate customers. Only we can convey why a trust should be established. The success of our profession hinges on motivating the customer, weighing the alternatives (including nontrust competitors that offer trust services), and showing him whom to turn to for help.

Investment Management

A common reason for using a trust is the investment management it provides for our customers and their families during life, in the event of incapacitation, and following death. Although investment management can be found temporarily throughout the financial service industry (brokers, investment counselors, insurance companies, and mutual funds, for example), a trust is an all-encompassing estate planning tool that persists through various life cycles. Investment management is uninterrupted regardless of whether the customer doesn't have the time, desire, or ability to manage his or her assets. A soundly planned trust can enable a trustee to share these duties with a customer or completely step into the customer's shoes.

With the world of investments becoming more complex, skilled, specialized assistance is a must. But to whom do our customers turn?

The smart choice is someone who can provide expertise to conserve a hard-earned estate and understand present and future investment objectives. The trust professional comes qualified with the expertise and knowledge in finances and investments to provide prudent direction. Unlike investment providers who concentrate on one time-phase or a particular investment scheme, trust departments come equipped to provide professional investment management across the board: construction of a growing base of stocks and bonds, investment of life insurance and retirement funds, real estate transactions, and management and disposition of a business, through varying economic conditions and with consistent results, personalized service, and competitive fees.

Protection from Incapacitation

Unfortunately, people can suffer from an illness or accident that renders them temporarily or permanently incapable of managing personal and financial affairs. (This is incapacitation, which was discussed in detail in Chapter 6.) If an individual does not provide direction as to the management of his or her affairs, states have laws that direct how his or her assets will be managed. But people do have the option of having their estate managed by their own rules, not the rules of others.

Many people rely mistakenly on joint tenancy ownership of property to protect and distribute their assets. Joint tenancy provides a clean, simple distribution of an asset (such as home ownership) upon death to a surviving tenant absent probate proceedings. The shortcomings arise when a joint tenant owner becomes incapacitated. Joint tenancy property, like solely owned or tenancy in common property, does not avoid the need for court supervision in the event of incapacity. Because joint tenancy property is purchased, managed, and disposed of by all of the joint tenants, the incapacitation of one owner renders the other tenants incapable of directing the management, transfer, or sale of the property.

Because a trust legally owns what is in it, trust assets are not subject to statutes that control a person's assets in the event of incapacitation. Trust assets fall under the grantor's set of instructions, not the public (probate) instructions dictated by law. With a trust the grantor is afforded the opportunity to keep assets confidential and to give direction to the trustee about how he or she wants these assets managed and to whom they go.

Isolation from Probate upon Death

Chapter 5 addressed the considerations that must be given to constructing a will. Also addressed were the time and cost associated with probate of a decedent's estate. Minimizing the cost and time involved with a probate proceeding is an integral advantage to trust planning.

Property in a living trust does not become part of a person's probate estate upon death, simply because the property is not owned by the decedent; it is owned by the trust. Thus, the restrictions associated with probate proceedings are simplified, expenses and publicity are minimized, and time delays are avoided. Probate runs contrary to these goals.

Incapacitation and death are traumatic. They are uninvited, unexpected, and laden with financial snags. A trust won't remove the trauma, but it will lessen family strain by simplifying matters, reducing costs, and keeping the estate running efficiently and without interruption.

Unlike probate, trusts

- Give privacy to the assets (unlike a will, which is a matter of public record)

- Offer a quicker distribution of estate assets

- Do not expose the estate to multiple ancillary probates when assets are located in states other than the decedent's residence

Taxes

During life we all face state, federal, and perhaps local income taxes, capital gains taxes, sales taxes, and many more classifications. Death does not take taxes away. Depending on an estate's size and how it is structured and distributed, death may bring federal estate taxes and perhaps state estate and inheritance taxes.

As mentioned earlier, this text purposely skirts the issue of taxes. It would take several chapters, if not several books, to address taxation at death. In the larger, more complex world of taxation, techniques are addressed that provide ways of reducing and possibly eliminating taxes according to established tax laws. Trusts are one of these techniques.

The reduction of taxes is an important financial planning objective during life and at death. Although a trust cannot eliminate all taxes at death, a properly constructed trust plan (revocable or irrevocable) can reduce the large slice federal estate taxes take from an estate at death. Exhibit 7.1 shows the impact of federal estate taxes even on modest-sized estates.

Consolidation of Estate Assets

Experienced estate planners (attorneys, trust officers, accountants, and insurance underwriters) and family beneficiaries tell repeated stories of common planning nuisances: disorganization, disheveled records, and a potpourri of assets and their ownership. As people accumulate their estates, it is easy to lose track of personal and employee benefit holdings, types of ownership, and eventual dispositive schemes. Our role as trust professionals is to bring organization to our customers' estates and, in so doing, direct them to the benefits of using a trust as an estate planning solution.

- *Life insurance* (personally purchased and employer provided). Who are the beneficiaries? If it is a spouse, are secondary or contingent beneficiaries named? Are they children? Are the children minors? Can they handle the death proceeds sensibly? Should the proceeds be paid in a lump sum?

  Benefit to customer. A trust into which various fragmented insurance death benefits are paid. From here distribution of an estate can be directed according to the grantor's personal wishes and the family's needs and financial temperament.

- *Retirement plans.* Over many working years, these plans can grow to considerable size. Are family members prepared to handle the proceeds before or after retirement?

  Benefit to customer. Depending on the family's needs and tax planning circumstances, a trust is a logical, organized **depositary** for retirement plan benefits. A trust provides for continued management and investment of funds. (As an aside, a depository is a place where something valuable is placed, such as a vault.)

- *A will.* A sound starting point. But where do assets go from there? Are outright bequests of estate assets to family members a sound decision?

  Benefit to customer. A pourover of estate assets to a trust to provide controlled, planned estate distribution according to family needs. A trust can also make bequests. A trust can direct immediate distribution, at death, of trust assets. A trust can serve as a "will substitute." Actually, it is more correct to say that a trust serves as a will enhancer, adjunct, or complement.

- *Solely owned assets.* What happens to them in the event of incapacitation? Why subject them to probate at death?

Exhibit 7.1 Unified Transfer Tax Rate Schedule

A Taxable amount over	B Taxable amount not over	C Tax on amount in column A	D Rate of tax on excess of amount in column A
0	10,000	0	18
10,000	20,000	1,800	20
20,000	40,000	3,800	22
40,000	60,000	8,200	24
60,000	80,000	13,000	26
80,000	100,000	18,200	28
100,000	150,000	23,800	30
150,000	250,000	38,800	32
250,000	500,000	70,800	34
500,000	750,000	155,800	37
750,000	1,000,000	248,300	39
1,000,000	1,250,000	345,800	41
1,250,000	1,500,000	448,300	43
1,500,000	2,000,000	555,800	45
2,000,000	——	780,800	49

The Economic Growth and Tax Relief Reconciliation Act of 2001 changes the maximum estate tax bracket shown in column D to:

48% in 2004	46% in 2006
47% in 2005	45% in 2007–2009

The decrease in estate tax rates for the upper brackets is shown below.

A Taxable amount over	B Taxable amount not over	C Tax on amount in column A	D Rate of tax on excess of amount in column A
2004			
1,500,000	2,000,000	555,800	45
2,000,000	——	780,800	48
2005			
1,500,000	2,000,000	555,800	45
2,000,000	——	780,800	47
2006			
1,500,000	2,000,000	555,800	45
2,000,000	——	780,800	46
2007–2009			
1,500,000	——	555,800	45

- Estate taxes are repealed in 2010.
- In 2011 estate tax rates will return to the 2001 level:

2,000,000	2,500,000	780,800	49
2,500,000	3,000,000	1,025,800	53
3,000,000	10,000,000	1,290,800	55
10,000,000	17,184,800	5,140,800	60
17,184,000	——	9,451,200	55

Benefit to customer. Placing them in trust avoids probate.

- *Joint tenancy assets.* Is the subsequent ownership what was intended? Under ideal circumstances, this is a viable planning technique for the first owner who dies.

  Benefit to customer.: A trust can provide for the surviving joint tenant to place assets into the decedent's trust. In advanced estate planning courses, consideration is given to placing specific assets or specific amounts of assets into individual ownership by spouses and by using trusts for each spouse.

On the surface it is easy to characterize trust agreements as putting all your eggs in one basket. Admittedly, the consolidation of assets into and planning with a living trust, before and after death, appears one-dimensional for the creator and family. Yet a trust offers an unlimited, multifaceted set of estate planning instructions bounded only by the trust planner's imagination.

Contestability

Although contests of a will are rare, they can interrupt and misdirect a planner's intentions. Each state has statutes governing the contest of a will, yet very few states legally address the contest of trusts because of their unique ownership arrangement. Some states put a time limit on when a trust can be contested, often limited to the amount of time allowed for creditors to make claims against an estate through a will. This is not to say that a trust cannot be contested, but doing so is difficult.

Family Protection

We learned a little about Pat's estate at the beginning of the chapter. We also heard Pat indirectly ask for help and direction when he admitted that his wife and children may be incapable of managing and preserving the assets they inherit. This is a common concern that the trust professional will hear often and must be prepared to address.

Although death brings an end to Pat's ability to protect his family from physical dangers, provide income, and run his business, he still can provide financial protection and direction, as long as proper plans have been made.

Trust planners who listen closely will hear customers say,

- "My wife is the most intelligent person I know, but financially she is naive."

- "If I gave my son a thousand dollars, he would spend it in less than a week and he would have a difficult time accounting for it."

- "Life is unfair. Dad's stroke took away a strong man, someone we depended on to guide the family business."

- "Although I am divorced, I love my kids. How can I fairly provide for them and my new husband?"

- "Our family was always close, until Dad and Johnny had their falling-out. Can Dad still help Johnny's kids with college tuition?"

- "My daughter has the biggest heart I know. She helps stray animals, works in homeless shelters, and gives to others who don't have. I'm afraid to leave any money to her for fear she may be a soft touch."

A trust is a very effective way to preserve and dispose of an estate and provide financial protection to assets and family, the customer's way:

- For the spouse whose financial knowledge is limited, a trust directs affairs.

- For the son whose spending will deplete resources, a trust protects the estate from being squandered.

- For the incapacitated business-owner, a trust provides continuity and covers special needs.

- For the divorced person who wishes to help new and old families, a trust provides fair treatment.

- For the estranged family member, a trust can provide for other generations. A trust is not limited—yet it can limit—to whom benefits are paid.

- For the generous child who is open to fast talkers, a trust protects assets from the unscrupulous.

Additional Considerations

Many of life's situations warrant the inclusion of a trust in an estate plan. Aside from the more obvious uses of trusts to provide financial protection and management for family—and absent the use of a trust to minimize estate taxation—trusts may be appropriate to provide protection for other beneficiaries or to attain other objectives in any one or more of the following scenarios.

- Where a beneficiary has a mental or physical challenge, such as a developmental or learning disability

- When a beneficiary is prone to substance abuse

- For the protection and care of pedigree pets (for example, a thoroughbred show horse)

- To control gifts to charitable beneficiaries by limiting the timing and amounts payable or by permitting the trustee to select appropriate charitable beneficiaries

- To provide for elderly parents or other relatives

- To provide for domestic partners, employees, business partners, or friends

- To encourage certain behavior or achievement by incorporating incentives that will foster self-sufficiency and discourage actions that may be considered socially unacceptable

These examples are certainly not inclusive. The concerned trust professional should always explore a customer's particular situation to determine whether a trust might be beneficial.

Trust professionals should make it their responsibility to assist customers in determining what a trust should say, what should be in it, and who should benefit from it. Based on sound financial fact-finding, trust professionals can assist customers in determining needs and family objectives, such as avoiding probate, saving taxes, providing privacy and peace of mind, and protecting assets and family. Tantamount to the construct of a trust is the driver—the trustee—on whose shoulders rest the success of the creator's plans.

SELECTING A TRUSTEE

In Chapter 8 we will look at the careful planning John Doe and his attorney took in constructing John's trust. We will examine several additional estate-planning suggestions and see how trust professionals can guide customers through the maze of a seemingly complicated legal document. But foremost to John's planning is the trustee.

Attorneys, physicians, and nurses are formally educated, examined, and licensed. Plumbers, barbers, and carpenters are trained and licensed. Interestingly, no formal education, training, or licensing is required for individual trustees.

Just as plumbing and carpentry reflect the skill of the plumber and carpenter, a trust is only as effective as the trustee. When making critical trust planning decisions, the trustee can make or break the grantor's intentions. The right trustee can effectively provide the following services.

- Tax planning
- Investment decision making
- Legal interpretations
- Asset custody and protection
- Dealing with the emotions, needs, and idiosyncrasies of the beneficiaries
- Distribution of income or principal (discretionary and nondiscretionary)
- Financial responsibility

- Business acumen
- Transaction recordkeeping
- Statements of account and tax reports
- Preparation of tax returns
- Payment of bills and expenses and seeing to the beneficiaries' financial needs
- Dealing with special assets such as real estate, a partnership, and a closely held business

Trustee Qualifications

Potential trust customers must be aware of the grave responsibility placed on a trustee who is asked to fill the void of a departed grantor and to manage a family's finances for many years to come. Trust such as this depends on experience, training, and competence.

In a 1928 New York Supreme Court case (*Meinhardt v. Salmon*), Justice Cardozo wrote,

> A trustee is held to something stricter than the morals of the marketplace. Not honesty alone, but the punctilio of an honor the most sensitive is then the standard of behavior. As to this there has developed a tradition that is unbending and inveterate.

A trustee's tasks are serious, dynamic, solemn, extremely personal, and often lengthy. Once a trustee accepts the appointment, the trustee is legally liable for carrying out the trust's instructions; abuse is a felony. No duty known to the law is greater than the duty a trustee owes to the beneficiary of a trust, and trustees have a legal obligation to serve the trust's beneficiaries prudently, according to the trust's instructions, and with utmost care. *How* a trustee carries out the instructions is more important than *what* the trustee is instructed to do. Therefore, the choice of the trustee is extremely important.

Choosing a trustee is a personal call, and we must recognize that bank trust departments are not the only ones available. Without our putting off potential clients with a "hard sell" approach, we need to help prospective customers realize that no formal education, specialized training, or licensing is required for an individual to be a trustee. There is danger in choosing a trustee who is uneducated, untrained, unlicensed, unexamined, and unprepared. How often do we assess our strengths, boast our qualifications, and show the public that we possess the necessary traits? It is up to us trust professionals to explain our credentials and how they may benefit people in need of advice on trusts.

Characteristics of the Right Trustee

Choosing the right trustee is not difficult if the customer is prepared with a true understanding of her personal objectives and what it takes to meet them. Although individuals may be capable of performing the tasks of a trustee for, say, a family member, rarely can one or even two individuals possess the breadth and depth of experience available in a bank trust department.

Let's examine what we must offer in order to help our customers solve their problems.

Accountability

Trust statements and recordkeeping must be frequent and understandable. Statements must include a concise list of assets, including initial cost and present market value. Transaction lists should be timely, clear, and chronological. A statement isn't worth the paper it is printed on if it cannot be understood. A grantor may understand where his assets stand today, but his family may not later.

Financial Planning Acumen

Assisting a customer with financial planning does not stop with the assets listed on an account statement. It is important to balance and coordinate inside (trust) and outside (personal) assets. Problems can emerge when tax planning and budgeting do not consider the whole financial picture. As concerned trustees, we are responsible for helping our customers organize all their assets, not just those in the trust.

Using Trust Products and Services to Meet Customer Needs

Several years ago while on a trans-Atlantic flight, Mike was seated next to a woman who was traveling with three friends. They appeared to be financially well-off. They also seemed to be very happy and very healthy. Their actions and conversation brought merriment to all around them.

Shortly after the seatbelt sign turned off, Mike and Myrtle struck up a conversation. Myrtle spoke about her fellow M's: Mary Ann, Melissa, and Mollie. Equally interesting were their husbands: Paul, Peter, and Perry. "And your husband's name?" Mike asked. Her smile disappeared. "Hank died 3 years ago. He was 59. He was handsome, athletic, and humorous; everyone loved him, but not with the passion I held for him. Hank and I were married 34 years. His heart attack came unexpectedly 2 days after our anniversary. This trip was the one he and I had planned."

"As sad as I will always be that Hank is no longer with me, he will always remain so close to me—a partner who stood by me and cared for me during our many years of marriage, a partner who stands near me and cares for me today. I don't think I could continue smiling, living, or traveling, or have paid for the girls' college education, if it wasn't for Hank's planning, as much as I strongly objected to it each time an insurance premium arrived in our mailbox and each time we visited our attorney and the bank."

Myrtle talked loosely and in fragments about Hank's business, something about a complicated pension plan, and Sandy, whom she meets at the bank twice per year. "I've never been much for understanding money, although I do know how to spend it when I get it. Sandy in the trust department helps me with Hank's planning. I don't know what I would do without her."

"I never saw Hank's insurance money, I never wrote a check for the girls' college costs, and I never saw his stocks. I never got involved when Hank's business was sold. The mortgage on the house is paid each month, and the bills from this trip will go to Sandy. To be perfectly honest, I don't understand any of this, except for one thing: Hank is taking care of things."

"Hank's attorney set up, what do you call it, a trust—something else I didn't like or understand. Long legal papers put chills up my spine. I would tell Hank, 'Why do you think about that stuff; you're just inviting death.' The bank takes care of things. Thank goodness for that. If it was left to me, I'm sure I would mess it up, spend the money foolishly, and do something wrong."

"It's terrible to be alone. Mar, Mel, and Moll are great friends, great company, but my bed is empty. And as strange as it sounds, I think I love Hank more today than yesterday. He was there for me yesterday, and he's here today because of his past planning for the future. I tell Sandy that she is in the greatest business in the world. She helps people tomorrow by helping them today."

Compassion

Beneficiaries are often emotionally distraught at the death or disability of a loved one, usually the grantor of the trust. Trustees are called on to hold a beneficiary's hand, listen to problems, and offer an understanding shoulder. Managing a trust involves more than managing money; it involves helping beneficiaries cope with their emotions and improve their family stability. Implicit in a trust's set of instructions is the trustee's role as a concerned planner. A heavy burden is placed on a trustee; it must be welcomed.

Cooperation

At times the trust department will be asked to serve along with one or more individual trustees. The grantor may have chosen the individual trustee because of her familiarity with family idiosyncrasies and selected the corporate trustee for investment research and management, legal support, technology, and permanence. The presence of an individual trustee cannot be used as an excuse not to become familiar with the beneficiaries and their needs. Two or more trustees may complement each other, but several trustees who don't communicate with each other may step on each other's feet.

Communication Skills

A monthly statement is never sufficient. A concerned trustee makes the time to talk with all parties involved—family members, attorney and accountant, and concerned advisors—and keep them informed of investment performance and the logic behind investment changes. Active communication also keeps the trustee aware of changes in family needs.

Reliability

The beneficiary must be able to rely on her trust representative. We can never give beneficiaries any doubt as to our patience, empathy, and devotion. Our customers take special care in choosing us; never let them or the beneficiaries down. A trustee's fee must buy more than a statement, the purchase of a few stocks and bonds, and a monthly disbursement check.

Permanence

Bank trust departments don't die, become ill, or take vacations. Personnel do. Each trust professional in the department must be prepared to serve any customer at any time. This preparation comes from continued training and education and awareness of tax law changes.

Organizational Skills

Never get caught in the unkempt desk syndrome (too much to do, too little time to do it). Beneficiaries come first, so you must be constantly geared to do the job. Good carpenters work with good tools.

Regulatory Supervision

Assure your customers that for their welfare the trust industry is continually supervised, audited, and examined both internally by the bank itself and externally by regulatory agencies (such as the OCC). Our adherence to the law assures beneficiaries they will never have the wool pulled over their eyes.

Investment Expertise

The trust industry's investment strength and track record is essential to the success of the trust and the satisfaction of the beneficiaries. We cannot measure our services solely by healthy investment performance. We must balance investment prudence with investment risk and tighten or loosen the reins of a trust portfolio depending on economic conditions, stock and bond returns, and family circumstances. A true trust professional understands sound investment practices and family psychology. A stellar investment return can be offset by poor attention to beneficiaries, and vice versa.

Fairness

Just as children constantly test their parents, beneficiaries test their trustees. As trustee you must have the strength to say no when needed. As trustee you must understand your beneficiaries' needs and emotions yet be able to be unemotional when responding to frivolous demands. You will be placed in the position of playing referee, uninfluenced by outside forces and the pulls of the beneficiaries; you will need to be impartial, unbiased, and non-self-serving as you satisfy the varying needs of all beneficiaries.

Educated

Education for trust personnel is a necessity, not a luxury. Today's trust professional is trained in aspects of law, investments, and taxation. These professionals are proficient in computer skills, sales and marketing skills, and interpersonal relationship building. It is common today for trust personnel to reach beyond their institution's internal education and development programs by striving toward professional certification, such as the ABA's Certified Trust and Financial Advisor (CTFA) designation.

Objectivity, Competence, and Loyalty

Trust professionals must judge what will suit each customer's circumstances. Our customers must believe we are the trustees with whom they want their families to deal.

SUMMARY

- Trusts are categorized as express, resulting, and constructive. This chapter focused on express trusts.

- A personal trust is a trust established by an individual for the benefit of individuals. Beyond a will's who-gets-what dispositive direction, a trust provides a set of instructions for the ongoing management of assets for others. A trust consists of a grantor, trustee, beneficiary, corpus, and agreement. An integral aspect of a trust is the fiduciary relationship built between the trust's creator—and beneficiaries—and the trustee. A trust's legal ownership of assets allows the trustee to act on behalf of the trust's creator for the benefit of the trust's beneficiaries. The purposes of a trust are multifaceted. Properly constructed and properly guided, a trust can meet most estate planning objectives.

- Personal trusts are either testamentary or living. A testamentary trust is formed in a will and comes into effect only after death. A living trust is effective before, and continues after, death. Living trusts can be revocable or irrevocable. Living trusts vary based on their purpose. Two common living trust arrangements are the life insurance trust and self-declaration of trust.

- There are advantages to having a trust. A trust can provide for investment management, protect an estate from an owner's incapacitation, and minimize the costs and delays associated with probate at death. Additionally, a trust can minimize taxes, consolidate estate assets, reduce the element of contestability associated with a will, and offer protection to family.

- The prime element of a trust is the trust's driver: the trustee. As important as the instructions of a trust agreement are, only the right trustee can effectively carry out the instructions. It is imperative that trust professionals recognize the characteristics of an effective trustee and provide accountability, financial planning, compassion, service, communication, reliability, organization, investment acumen, objectivity, competence, and loyalty.

REVIEW QUESTIONS

1. Define a personal trust.
2. What are the five ingredients of a trust? Briefly describe each one.
3. What are the two types of trusts? Briefly describe them.
4. List five reasons for establishing a trust.
5. List five services a trustee provides.

8

THE PERSONAL TRUST DOCUMENT

"Generosity lies less in giving much than in giving at the right moment."

Jean De La Bruyere (1645–1696)

We first examined the structure of trusts by looking at the definitions of its elements (Chapter 7). These elements included the types of trusts, the reasons for having a trust, and the process of selecting trustees. In this chapter we look at trust language—a set of instructions—by explaining samples of it. The sample language gives a fuller explanation of what a trust is, what it can do, who can benefit from it, and how they benefit from it.

Read the sample trust language slowly. It *does* make sense. Remember not to use these words as legal advice and direction when speaking to your customers. Nor should you use this book as a planning device for personal use or for customers. A trust is a legal document that should be prepared only by competent legal counsel. Although several trusts may appear to have certain provisions in common, each trust is individually designed to meet specific needs, tax considerations, and family objectives. What John Doe's trust says is meant to help you understand the workings of a trust, not the making of one. Remember, when assisting customers, a trust professional's responsibilities do not include making recommendations of what a customer should do. Our task is to provide suggestions of how to do it.

LEARNING OBJECTIVES

Upon completion of this chapter, you will be able to

- Describe the parts of a personal trust document
- Profile a trustee's responsibilities to the beneficiaries with respect to discretionary decision making and investments
- Distinguish per stirpes from per capita distribution of assets and the various powers of appointment
- Explain the rule against perpetuities
- Define the purpose of state trust statutes
- Define and use the terms that appear in bold in the text

JOHN Q. DOE'S REVOCABLE TRUST

The development of John's trust involves three important players: John, a trust officer, and an attorney. Several planning aspects are accomplished individually, and many others are combined. John must carefully define his objectives and intentions: who will benefit from his trust, how, and when (the trust's dispositive provisions). As his trust officer, you are instrumental in helping John define his objectives and understand what type of trust to use, the trust's dispositive provisions, and why your bank should be his trustee now or later. An attorney is responsible for drafting the trust agreement. Competent legal counsel can succinctly spell out John's intentions and clearly direct the trustee down a well-defined path in John's trust document.

Most trust departments have a legal staff (trust attorneys) who can assist outside counsel and who will review trust documents to ensure that they are properly written. Are the documents inclusive? Do they clearly express John's intentions? Are they legally sound? Although a trust department's attorneys are highly trained, educated, and experienced in trusts, trust counsel should not draw up John's trust. The writing of a trust is tantamount to the practice of law, and trust departments are not in the business of practicing law.

Opening Words

I, John Q. Doe, as grantor, transfer to John Q. Doe, as trustee, the property described in the attached schedule. That property and any other property that may be received by the trustee shall be held and disposed of upon the following trusts.

Grantor

John is the grantor, or the creator, of this trust. It is possible for a trust to be created by more than one person, in which case the creators are cograntors. Although trusts with more than one grantor are seldom seen, in most circumstances the cograntors are husband and wife.

Trustee

As Chapter 7 showed, when John declares himself the trustee, he establishes a self-dec trust. John could have stated that he and his wife, Mary, will be cotrustees and that the survivor would act as sole trustee. Appointment of the successor trustee(s) following John's death, incapacitation, and resignation is accomplished later in the document.

Corpus

Because of the dynamic nature of estates (assets bought, assets sold, changes and modifications of life insurance plans and employee benefit plans), the schedule of assets (the corpus) will probably not be complete. It would be close to impossible to update this schedule constantly to accurately reflect one's estate at all times. However, it is important that assets be properly retitled to reflect that they are, or will become, an asset of the trust.

Assets that have formal **titles** and **deeds** (for example, real property and automobiles) may be retitled easily into the name of a trust. What about those assets that do not come with ownership papers, such as expensive tangible personal property like antique pianos, artwork, and coin and stamp collections? Many estate-planning professionals concur that mention of an asset in the trust or an accurate listing of an asset in the trust's schedule is tantamount to re-titling the asset into the trust. Therefore, the trust would be considered funded with these assets, and these assets would not be part of the owner's probate estate.

"Property and any other property that may be received" pertains to additions to the trust from whatever source:

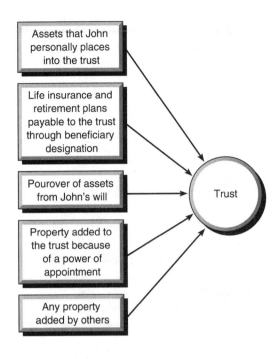

Boxes connecting to Trust:
- Assets that John personally places into the trust
- Life insurance and retirement plans payable to the trust through beneficiary designation
- Pourover of assets from John's will
- Property added to the trust because of a power of appointment
- Any property added by others

Trust

Why is it important to properly designate funds, including life insurance, to a trust? Let's look at an example. John's employer provided life insurance coverage for all employees equal to five times annual income. The cost (premium) was shared 50/50 by John and his employer. John named his wife, Mary, as the beneficiary. As is often the case, several years later John's employer enhanced the employee benefit package, and in so doing replaced the life insurance benefit with one from another company. All employees were notified to submit updated beneficiary designation cards. If an employee did not complete a new beneficiary form within a stipulated period of time, the new company would use the prior beneficiary designation. John failed to submit a new form.

A few years later, when John executed his self-dec trust, he still did not change the beneficiary of his employer-provided insurance to his trust. After John's death, Mary completed the necessary paperwork for the payment of the life insurance proceeds, but she did not pay attention to the beneficiary designation.

Several weeks later Mary was surprised to receive a registered letter from the insurance company containing a substantial check payable to her. But before Mary deposited the check into her savings account, she called her attorney to ask why the insurance money was paid directly to her rather than to John's trust. The simple answer is that John did not change the beneficiary designation of the insurance plan at work from Mary to the trust. Did John overlook an important aspect of his estate planning? John's trust was intended to manage his assets for Mary and the kids, insurance included, but this policy didn't make it into the trust.

May Mary add this insurance check to John's trust so that the bank can manage it along with John's other assets? Yes. And once they are added to the trust, the insurance proceeds will be managed and disposed in accordance with the terms of the trust. Other assets from other sources can be added to John's trust because the language of the trust provides for this.

Changing the Trust

I reserve the power, by signed instruments delivered to the trustee during my life, to revoke this agreement in whole or in part and to amend it from time to time. This power is personal to me and shall not be exercised by others, including any legal representative.

Revocable

John's trust is revocable and amendable. It can be canceled or changed. The only person with the power to cancel or change it is John.

Authorities sometimes distinguish between the words *revocation* and *amendment*. Some experts use *revocation* to refer to the total cancellation of a trust and *amendment* to refer to changing only a part of the trust. Others refer to revocation with respect to total cancellation of the trust and with respect to partial cancellation or revocation of parts of the trust. Either definition is acceptable. This is a revocable trust: John reserves the right to cancel the trust, cancel parts of the trust, and amend (change) the entire trust or parts of it.

In Chapter 5 we saw that the execution of a new will automatically cancels all prior wills and codicils. Such is not the case with trusts. Creation of another trust without formally revoking in totality the old trust does not cancel all prior trusts and amendments; it merely results in two trusts.

Assume that many years ago John created a life insurance trust that was later amended to a self-dec trust and that the self-dec trust had been subsequently amended several times to reflect changes in the nature and size of his estate, changes in family (newborn children, older ones going off on their own, divorce, death, and so on), and changes in John's intentions of how trust assets should be managed and distributed. John's original trust and its many amendments now represent a considerable stack of paperwork. Contemplating a few more changes to his trust, John now thinks that perhaps he should revoke the trust and start anew with a less cumbersome document.

Restatement

To reduce the existing paperwork, additional documentation is required: a revocation. John's will probably has a pourover provision that specifically mentions his original trust created in 1973. If the 1973 trust is revoked and replaced with a 2002 trust, John's will must be rewritten or amended with a codicil because his will currently refers to the 1973 trust, which will no longer exist if it is revoked. Also, the beneficiary designations of John's life insurance policies (both individual and employer coverage) and pension and profit sharing plans may specifically mention his 1973 trust. Each policy and employee benefit plan must be changed to reflect the 2002 trust.

The solution to minimizing the paperwork is to restate the original trust. A restatement is a trust amendment, but its purpose is to amend totally all that has been written before. After John signs the 2002 restatement of his 1973 trust and all of its subsequent amendments, is the trust called the John Doe Trust of 2002 or 1973? The trust is still a 1973 trust that has been totally reworked. There is no need to change beneficiary designations, retitle assets, or modify will provisions.

Whereas a revocation totally cancels a trust, a restatement amends a trust and all its subsequent amendments. A restatement serves as a rewriting of the trust, but it leaves the original trust date intact. A restatement is a viable suggestion to keep in mind when counseling trust customers regarding the review of their estate plan. As in the writing of a trust, the creator's intentions must be carefully evaluated, and the document must be prepared by an attorney.

The language "any legal representative" pertains to others who are empowered by John to manage his financial affairs. Think back to the discussion of powers of attorney for property in Chapter 6. Many states allow a powergiver, such as John, to permit a powerholder to transact estate planning matters on behalf of the powergiver, to include creating, funding, and amending a trust. The language in John's trust document negates a powerholder's ability to amend his trust. It doesn't stop the powerholder from funding John's trust.

Family

> Mary Z. Doe is my wife. I have three children, now living: Curly Doe, born March 11, 19XX; Moe Doe, born April 10, 19XX; Larry Doe, born November 26, 19XX

All John is doing here is identifying his family at the time the trust is executed. It would be advisable for John to amend his trust later if the status of his children or marriage changes, including births and deaths. If John and Mary have additional children, but they are not mentioned in any subsequent amendments, this oversight does not preclude (disinherit) the after-born children, except for specific bequests made in the trust.

What if John and Mary divorce? Remember, this book is not a legal interpretation and we don't want to get ensnared in the nuances of various states' divorce laws, but it is generally ruled that divorce is equal to death of the beneficiary spouse for the purpose of trusts. Therefore, the trust and subsequent amendments executed before divorce will be administered and interpreted as if the grantor's former spouse had died upon the effective date of the divorce.

In many states a more inclusive term for divorce is *judicial termination of marriage*. This includes, but is not limited to, divorce, dissolution, annulment, or declaration of invalidity of marriage. Unless the trust document or judgment of judicial termination of marriage of the trust's grantor provides otherwise, the termination revokes every revocable provision of the grantor's trust and subsequent amendments relating to the grantor's former spouse, providing that the trust and its amendments were executed before the judicial termination of marriage. Subsequently, the trust and its amendments will be administered and interpreted as if the grantor's former spouse had died upon the judicial termination of marriage. Consequences may be different if John refers to Mary Doe (without qualifying her as his spouse) or if John refers "to his spouse" (without attaching a name).

Dispositive Provisions During John's Life

During my life the trustee shall pay all the net income of the trust to me or for my benefit or as I otherwise direct in writing, and the trustee shall pay any part of the principal of the trust to me as I direct in writing. However, during any period in which I am in the opinion of the trustee incapable of managing my own affairs, the trustee may in its discretion pay to my wife and me, or use for our benefit, so much or all of the income and principal of the trust as the trustee determines to be required or desirable for our support, welfare, and best interests.

John feels he is capable of managing his own financial affairs. Yet he knows the importance of having his assets titled in a trust for avoidance of probate (at death and due to incapacitation) and for privacy and confidentiality. Therefore, John established a self-dec trust through which he personally manages his assets as his own trustee.

John-as-beneficiary tells John-as-trustee that he is entitled to all the income and principal of the trust. John is the initial or **primary beneficiary.** (Later in the trust, secondary or contingent beneficiaries and remaindermen are stipulated.) It is assumed that Mary will also benefit from the trust because of her marriage to John. John clearly states that his trust will benefit Mary and him if he becomes incapacitated,

It is also important to note the word *shall*. In trusts the word *shall* means *must*. Note that John used the word *may* in the event he is incapacitated. This is an item of protection. If John developed a mental problem and his trust stated that the trustee shall make distributions of principal and income, there would be nothing to stop John from squandering the trust's assets through inappropriate decision making and spending. John is asking his trustee (most likely the successor trustee) to make sound, discretionary decisions with respect to distributing money from the trust to him or for his benefit and protecting the assets from John's impropriety and improvidence.

What if John is a charitable person? He may be giving money to his favorite charities on a regular basis and also giving assets to family members. In order to continue these practices, John can direct his successor trustee in writing ("as I otherwise direct in writing") to make these charitable and family gifts.

The words *support, welfare,* and *best interests* will be addressed later in the chapter.

Insurance

I retain during my life all rights under insurance policies payable to the trustee, including the right to change the beneficiaries, and to assign any policies to any lender as security for any loan. The rights of the assignee of any policy shall be superior to the rights of the trustee. During my life the trustee shall have no responsibility with respect to any policies for the payment of premium or otherwise.

In Chapter 7 we spoke about irrevocable trusts and how this type of trust is used primarily for tax purposes. It is inevitable that at some point your advanced estate and financial planning endeavors will introduce irrevocable life insurance trusts (ILITs). These are very precise documents used for very specific tax purposes. One aspect of this type of trust is that life insurance on John's life is owned by the trust, not by John. This is not the case here, which is why John's trust specifically states that John's insurance is owned by him, not by his trust, and that John is solely responsible for every aspect of his insurance coverage, such as, payment of premiums and designation of beneficiaries.

If John (as a debtor) borrowed money from a bank (as a creditor) and used a life insurance policy as collateral against the loan, even though the life insurance policy's beneficiary designation is John's trust, the bank has a right to the cash value of the policy (in the event of non-payment of the terms of the loan) or to the death benefit of the policy (in the event John dies before the loan is paid in full). "The rights of the assignee [the bank to which the policy is assigned as collateral] of any policy shall be superior to the rights of the trustee" means that the full death benefit, or part of it, will be used to satisfy repayment to the bank before

being paid to the trust as the designated beneficiary.

Coordination of Will and Trust

After my death, if the assets of my probate estate are insufficient to provide for the following payments, the trustee shall pay my funeral expenses, reasonable expenses of administration of my estate, and any death taxes payable by reason of my death. All such payments shall be charged generally against the principal of the trust and shall be made without apportionment or proration.

Imagine John's funding his trust to the extent that very few assets are in his probate estate. Although his entire estate—that which goes through his will, joint tenancy property, and trust assets—may not be insolvent, it is possible that his probate estate has insufficient assets to meet the expenses of debts, administration, and taxes. If there are insufficient assets in John's probate estate, John's trust is directed to meet these expenses.

This section of John's trust directs the trustee to pay these expenses. In Chapter 5 John's will stated, "to the extent that the assets of my residuary estate are insufficient to pay the expenses of my last illness, funeral, administration of my estate and taxes payable by reason of my death, my executor may request such payment from the trustees of the trust hereinafter referred to." John smartly coordinated his estate planning documents.

Some states have statutes covering this aspect of expenses. For example, Florida recently enacted a law that provides that upon the death of the settlor of a revocable trust, the trustee must file a notice of trust setting forth certain information with the court of the settlor's county of domicile and the court having jurisdiction of the settlor's estate. This filing of notice is required to ensure compliance with another statute that provides that if the residue of the settlor's probate estate is insufficient to pay administration expenses and claims, the personal representative of the settlor's estate is entitled to seek payment of the insufficiency from the trustee of the settlor's revocable trust.

In the next section we will see that John's trust splits into two trusts following his death. John directs that the payment of expenses and so on be made from his trust's principal before the split without prorating ("without apportionment or proration") the expenses among the two trusts.

Following John's Death

> After my death the trustee shall hold and dispose of the trust property as follows:
>
> If my wife survives me, the trustee shall as of the date of my death allocate a fraction to a separate trust, the "Marital Trust," and the balance to a separate trust, the "Residuary Trust."
>
> If my wife does not survive me, the trustee shall as of the date of my death allocate the trust property to a separate trust, the "Residuary Trust."

John planned for his wife's surviving him or not surviving him. If Mary survives John, his trust provides for a formation of two **trust accounts:** a marital trust (commonly referred to in trust vernacular as Trust A) and a residuary trust (commonly called Trust B). Trust B is sometimes called the children's trust or family trust. If Mary does not survive John (meaning she predeceased him), only the residuary trust is formed. Depending on John's intentions and circumstances, he could form additional trusts (C, D, and so forth).

Our discussion here omits the very specific language about the various formulas used for allocating percentages (fractions) to the marital and residuary trusts. An advanced estate planning course would discusses this, in conjunction with the tax reasons for doing so, in more detail.

Let's briefly review John's trust agreement to this point:

- John created a trust of which he is the trustee.

- John's trust will consist of what he placed in it before incapacitation or death, what came into the trust by way of pourover from his will, what life insurance and employee benefit plans pay to the trust by way of beneficiary designations, and what other property, such as assets added by Mary and property over which John had a power of appointment, he may have directed into his trust.

- John has a right to amend or revoke his trust before death as long as he is not incapacitated.

- John is married to Mary and he has three children: Curly, Moe, and Larry.

- Before death and incapacitation John has the right to all principal and income of his trust.

- If John is incapacitated, the trustee may expend principal and income to him and Mary or for their benefit.

- While alive John has all rights, ownership, and control over his life insurance.

- John's trust will be a source of funds for funeral expenses, estate administration expenses, and taxes if the assets of his probate estate are insufficient.

- Following John's death, his trust will split into two trusts if Mary survives him, one trust if Mary does not survive him.

What is beginning to develop in John's trust is an "if this then that, if not this then that" pattern. With his trustee's and attorney's help, John designed the trust to meet various contingencies of life, death, and taxes. As we move further through John's trust, more of this contingency planning (if Mary survives John or not) will be seen as well as why it is important to carefully plan and word a trust.

Common Disaster

> For the purpose of this instrument, my wife shall be considered to have survived me if the order of our deaths cannot be determined.

With respect to advanced tax planning, it is ideal for John's death to occur first. If John and Mary die in a **common disaster** (such as together in an auto or plane accident)—a **simultaneous death**—the common disaster clause of John's trust dictates that Mary is considered to have died second.

Dispositive Provisions Following John's Death

John's trust will continue for his family after his death. Here is where the trust goes beyond the who-gets-what to the how-and-when. These are the **dispositive provisions,** the terms that state how and when John's A and B trusts will be disposed (distributed). This is a very important section of a trust. Many customers will ask for your guidance and suggestions with this planning. Here is where you must be familiar with the grantor's intentions and family situation as well as the finer aspects of trust planning.

> The trustee shall pay all the net income of Trust A to my wife in convenient installments.
>
> The trustee may, in its discretion, pay to my wife, or use for her benefit, so much or all of the principal of Trust A as the trustee from time to time determines to be required for her support, medical care, education, and best interests to enable my wife to maintain the same standard of living maintained by her during my lifetime.

Fees

Later in the trust John specifically addresses the subject of fees. It is appropriate here to mention that when fees are charged against income (as opposed to principal), net income is equal to the trust's gross income minus fees. If fees are not charged against income, net income is the gross income.

Shall Versus Must

Note the word *shall* in the first section and the word *may* in the second section.

- *Shall = must*
- *May = discretionary*

John's intent is that income be paid. Mary may refuse to take the income. Nonetheless, the income is still taxable to her based on the **constructive receipt** principal. Regardless of whether the money is taken, it is taxable by virtue of the fact that it can be taken. If not taken, the income is added back to principal.

Discretionary Versus Nondiscretionary

John states that payment of the trust's principal will be discretionary—that is, decided by the trustee. John is placing a very important responsibility on the trustee's shoulders: the discretionary decisions of when and why principal will be distributed.

Here lies the meat of placing trust in someone else. This can be a scary decision for John, as well as for the trustee. John is asking another person to make decisions for his family. With this responsibility it is natural for a trustee to feel apprehensive about stepping into John's shoes. A trustee's actions and decisions are guided by law and by the trust document; therefore, a trustee looks for carefully defined language and direction in the trust. A trustee has nothing else to depend on. Herein lies the trustee's power to act or not act on the family's behalf as John would have acted and desired.

A carefully constructed trust will guide the trustee with *ascertainable standards*—ones that reasonably assist a trustee in measuring a beneficiary's needs; nevertheless, careful examination is required to properly interpret *support, medical care, education, best interests,* and *standard of living.* Where certain beneficiary needs and circumstances seem quite objective, many others force a trustee to make subjective decisions that vary from trust to trust and from family to family.

- *Support.* This term (and also the term *maintain*) generally includes distributions for a beneficiary's normal living expenses, such as housing expenses, clothing, and food. These terms may also include support of the beneficiary's dependents, payment of life insurance premiums, and possibly payments of the beneficiary's debts.

- *Medical care.* This includes routine healthcare and medication as well as surgery, nursing care, and hospitalization. This could also encompass expenditures for mental health such as psychoanalysis or psychiatric care.

- *Education.* This term includes tuition, room and board, books, expenses of traveling to and from school, and perhaps tutors. This term normally includes college education but may not include graduate or professional education unless specifically authorized by the document. The term *college education* has been held to also include paying for a beneficiary's high school expenses because a high school education is normally a prerequisite to a college education.

- *Best interests.* This term (and also the term *comfort*) is broader than support and maintenance. It includes a wide range of purposes that a trustee believes will be in the beneficiary's interests. This term gives the trustee, and the beneficiary as well, a broad standard to encompass the beneficiary's enjoyment, satisfaction, and peace of mind. For example, broader language may permit a trustee to purchase an automobile for a beneficiary's daughter to enable her to

visit the beneficiary where it was shown that such visits eased the mind of the beneficiary.

- *Standard of living.* This term could pose problems for the corpus of the trust. If the beneficiary is accustomed to an annual overseas vacation and a new, expensive sports car every two years, it would be difficult for the trustee to deny distributing principal, when requested by the beneficiary, to keep the beneficiary maintained at the same lifestyle. Herein lies the danger to the corpus: It may dwindle quickly.

Standards such as *comfort, welfare,* and *happiness*—mentioned by themselves—are difficult to interpret and ascertain. They do not provide "certainty."

According to most statutes, if the trust instrument does not contain any standards or allows distributions in the trustee's sole discretion, generally a trustee is considered to have exercised reasonable judgment when discretionary distributions are made in good faith, when it is in fact done honestly, whether it be done negligently or not. Nonetheless, the trustee must walk a careful line and make sound, prudent decisions for John's family, consistent with John's intentions as outlined in his trust. Trustees must think and act with the needs of the beneficiary in mind. Although the trust's language may set standards and guidelines, each beneficiary is not a typical beneficiary. A trustee cannot categorize beneficiaries or compare one to another.

Depending on the terms of Trust A, the trust may later benefit another beneficiary or group of beneficiaries, such as Curly, Moe, and Larry, following Mary's demise. A **contingent** or **secondary beneficiary** may not have a financial interest in the trust today, but may eventually. If a contingent or secondary beneficiary is not entitled to principal or income today, its interest is seeing the trust grow in value.

Distribution of principal and income is at odds with growth. The trustee is faced with the dilemma of producing income and distributing principal to the primary beneficiary and preserving principal for the **remaindermen,** which is another word for an ultimate beneficiary. Does the trustee balance the interests of both beneficiary classes or favor one beneficiary over another? Getting to know the beneficiaries and their needs and analyzing the intent of the trust should assist the trustee in solving the dilemma. In most cases a trustee considers the principal beneficiary first. Perhaps additional language would help the trustee in determining whom to benefit or favor. A trust can use additional language ("my primary concern is for the support, welfare, and best interests of my wife," for example) to help clarify intent.

Some trusts direct the trustee to consider other assets and sources of income of the beneficiary when deciding on the discretionary distribution of principal. It's up to the grantor. Perhaps Mary is a highly paid professional with assets of her own. Perhaps Mary won't need the principal and income of Trust A. Perhaps John would rather see the trust's value grow for Curly, Moe, and Larry.

Trust B and the Sprinkle Clause

> The trustee may, in its discretion, pay such amounts from the net income and principal of Trust B as the trustee may deem necessary for the support, medical care, education, and best interests of any one or more persons living from time to time of the group consisting of my wife and children. Any income not thus paid shall be added to principal. The trustee may make unequal payments of income or principal and do so to the exclusion of one or more of the aforesaid group. Such payments shall not be considered advancements. I desire that the trustee give primary consideration to the support of my wife.

Some beneficiaries have greater needs than others. Curly may have a physical dis-

ability that necessitates more income or principal. Moe may be attending an expensive Ivy League school, and Larry may be at a less expensive trade school. John's trust permits his trustee the flexibility to distribute income and principal ("in unequal payments") as needed. In a garden, more water is sprinkled where it is more needed. This is a trust's **sprinkle clause** (or **spray clause**).

"Such payments shall not be considered advancements" says that in the future, when it comes time to divide Trust B among the remaindermen, John wants equal division of the remaining trust assets to be made among the beneficiaries regardless of the amounts of principal and income previously made to them. If prior payments were considered advancements, the amount expended for Moe to attend an Ivy League school would have to be deducted from his ultimate distribution.

Five-and-Five Power

There are specific tax reasons for creating Trust A and Trust B and for the wording of the distribution of principal and income of each trust. Absent a minor treatise on tax planning, one of John's estate planning objectives is to reduce federal estate taxes at his death and at Mary's subsequent death. He also wants flexibility and latitude in his trust to provide for Mary's and his children's financial support, well-being, and independence. Some trusts supplement the ability for Mary to gain additional principal from Trust B, without jeopardizing John's tax planning, by using the **five-and-five power.**

> The trustee shall pay to my wife commencing 1 year after my death such portion of the principal of Trust B as she from time to time requests in writing, not exceeding in any calendar year the greater of $5,000 or 5 percent of the value of the principal of Trust B as of the end of the preceding calendar year.

Upon Mary's Death

John's trust contains a provision to direct what happens with the assets of Trust A when Mary dies. John can state specifically what will become of Trust A or he can leave that decision up to Mary. If he gives Mary the say-so, he gives her a **power of appointment**—the power to appoint—to say what will become of the assets of Trust A.

General Power of Appointment

John can give Mary a **general power of appointment** in which she can direct distribution of Trust A's assets to whomever she wants. If she happened to remarry and wants the trust's assets to go to her second husband, so be it. She can appoint the assets to her children, to charity, to her relatives, equally or unequally, however and to whomever she desires, in trust or outright.

Limited (or Special) Power of Appointment

A **limited** (or **special**) **power of appointment** gives Mary the ability to appoint the assets to whomever she wants within a limited group.

> Upon the death of my wife after my death the trustee shall distribute any accrued or undistributed income of Trust A to the estate of my wife and shall distribute the principal of Trust A to such person or persons among my descendants and their spouses, in trust or otherwise, and at such time or times as my wife appoints and directs by will, specifically referring to this power of appointment.

John can mix the powers depending on circumstances. John can give Mary a general power of appointment if no children survive Mary. If children do survive Mary, then she can be given a limited or special power of appointment, or none at all. In addition, the grantor can give powers of appointment to any beneficiary. Powers are not reserved specifically for spouses.

Before we leave our discussion of powers of appointment, look closely at the words "as my wife appoints and directs by will, specifically referring to this

power of appointment." In John's trust he directs that Mary's power of appointment must be exercised (stated) in her will, and the power will be effective upon her—the powerholder's—demise. Powers of appointment do not have to be exercised in a will. Most statutes recognize that a power can be exercised elsewhere (upon the powerholder's decision), unless there is specific language stating where and when it will be exercised.

Lapsation

A power of appointment can **lapse,** meaning it is not exercised. If the holder of the power (in this example, Mary) dies intestate, if the power is not mentioned in Mary's will (meaning she didn't exercise her right), or if the trustee is not notified within a reasonable period of time, the power lapses. John's trust could say,

> In determining whether and to what extent a power of appointment has been exercised by will, the trustee may rely on any instrument admitted to probate in any jurisdiction as the will of the holder of the power. The trustee may act as if the holder of the power died intestate if the trustee has no notice of a will within 3 months after the holder's death.

John's trust may address what happens if Mary does not exercise her power or it lapses:

> To the extent my wife does not effectively exercise her power, upon her death the trustee shall distribute the principal of Trust A to Trust B to be held and distributed as if it had been an original part of Trust B.

Trust B Upon Mary's Death

> Upon the death of the survivor of me and my wife, the trustee shall divide Trust B into separate trusts, equal in value, one for each then living child of mine and one for the then living descendants of each deceased child of mine, per stirpes.

According to the language above, if Curly, Moe, and Larry are all alive upon Mary's death, Trust B will split into three equal trusts, one each for Curly, Moe, and Larry. Pay close attention to this section. If a child does not survive Mary and does not have any surviving children, then Trust B is divided into separate equal trusts among the remaining living children of John and Mary. For example, if Curly does not survive Mary and if Curly has no surviving children, then Trust B is split into two equal trusts, one for Moe and one for Larry. If Curly did not survive Mary but he had children who survive him, a per stirpes distribution occurs.

Per Stirpes

Per stirpes is a Latin phrase literally translated as "by the branch" or "by representation." The phrase is commonly used as legal shorthand to describe a division of property among descendants of a designated person (in this case, John). One share goes to each of John's living children. One share also goes to the living descendants of a deceased child of John. The division of a share for descendants of a deceased person continues at lower generation levels until each share is allocated to a living person. To have a share allocated to a child, he must be alive on the date fixed for distribution or division (in this example, upon Mary's death after John's death).

To see how per stirpes works in more complicated trust divisions, consider the following situation: John and Mary have three children: Curly, Moe, and Larry. John states that after both he and Mary are deceased, Trust B will split into equal parts, one for each then living child (meaning all children who survive both John and Mary) and one for the then living descendants of a deceased child of John and Mary, per stirpes. Let us assume that at the death of the survivor of John and Mary, Curly is deceased (and he is survived by one child, Zappa), Moe is deceased (and he is survived by two children, Cheech and Chong), and Larry

survived (and he has no children). Schematically, look at the family this way:

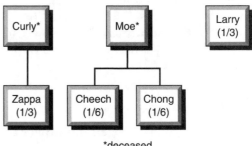

*deceased

Now, read the words again: "one for each then living child of mine" (Larry is the only living child) and "one for the then living descendants of each deceased child of mine, per stirpes" (Curly and Moe are deceased, but they are survived by children). If Curly and Moe were alive, they each would have received a one-third share. Because they did not survive, their share goes to their descendants. Therefore, Zappa gets Curly's one-third share, and Cheech and Chong get Moe's one-third share (one-sixth apiece). Think of Curly, Moe, and Larry as "branches" splitting from the trunk (John and Mary); likewise, Zappa is a branch from Curly, and Cheech and Chong are branches from Moe.

Here are three additional concepts to grasp regarding per stirpes distribution:

- What if a beneficiary (sometimes also referred to as a "taker"), who is a child of the grantor, is deceased, but the child was married and his surviving spouse is pregnant? Common law recognizes the unborn child as *a life in being,* meaning that the deceased child's share will be passed down as long as it is determined that the unborn child is of the deceased beneficiary. In other words, the unborn child must be of the deceased person biologically. (You may want to read this again.)

- There are occasions when the distribution language says "separate trusts, equal in value, one for each then-living child of mine and one for the then-living descendants, collectively, of each deceased child of mine." In the schematic above, Cheech and Chong would not have distinct one-sixth shares. They would together (collectively) benefit from a one-third share. This arrangement is sometimes called a "one-pot trust." Cheech and Chong would not necessarily benefit from the trust equally, as we saw in the previous section pertaining to the sprinkle (spray) clause.

- Some state statutes (probate mostly) provide different per stirpes distribution schemes. For example, in the previous example, if Curly, Moe, and Larry are all deceased, Zappa would receive 50 percent and Cheech and Chong would each receive 25 percent. Another per stirpes distribution scheme would be one-third each to Zappa, Cheech, and Chong.

Per Capita

Per capita is an alternative to per stirpes. **Per capita** means *head count*. Under this arrangement, each beneficiary alive at the time of distribution receives one share. Thus, in the schematic example above, Larry, Zappa, Cheech, and Chong would each receive a one-fourth share of Trust B. They are the number of persons (the head count) alive at the time of distribution. Very seldom is per capita used when there is more than one generation surviving. Most grantors want to favor their children more than grandchildren or great-grandchildren. In our example, John's only surviving son would get only one-fourth, yet the three grandchildren would each get one-fourth.

Distribution of Trust B, per stirpes or per capita, is not limited to descendants. John could also include spouses of descendants. Of course, John could also provide distribution in any fashion and to anyone he desires.

Disposition of Trust B

The trustees may, in their discretion, pay to any such child of mine, or use for his or her benefit, so much of the net income and principal of his or her trust as the trustees from time to time determine to be required or desirable for his or her support, welfare, education, and best interests. Any income not thus paid shall be added to principal.

The trustees shall pay all the net income of a child's trust to the child in convenient installments, at least as often as quarter-annually upon the child's attaining age 21.

Upon such child attaining age 25 the trustees shall distribute to him or her such portions or all of the principal of his or her trust as he or she from time to time requests by signed instruments delivered to the trustees during his or her life, not exceeding in the aggregate, however, one-third in value before he or she shall have reached age 30, nor two-thirds in value before he or she shall have reached age 35.

The language in the first paragraph is already familiar. As trustee you have discretionary control of the distribution of principal and income. This is a responsibility not to be taken lightly. Remember, John is placing serious trust and responsibility on your shoulders as trustee of his assets for the benefit of his family. You are stepping into John's financial shoes. The decision making regarding the discretionary distribution of principal and income to the children is many times more difficult than the decisions made on behalf of Mary. Whereas Mary's principal and income needs are probably clear-cut (mortgage payments, transportation needs, budgetary living expenses), the children's needs beyond tuition and school expenses may be subjective and questionable: purchase of a car, money for downpayment on the purchase of a first house, funds to begin a business. Best interests will differ widely between

Mary and the children. A trust professional must be careful when considering requests from beneficiaries.

The second paragraph introduces a new concept. To give his children a taste of his estate and place them in a position of frugally using principal they may get in the future, John wants the income of each child's trust paid to them once they reach age 21.

The third paragraph outlines the eventual distribution of principal. Again, customers will seek your advice regarding the schedule of distributions. Notice that principal distributions will be made only if a child requests it. If a child doesn't request it, the principal remains untouched and continues to be managed by the trustee. The trust language is carefully worded to say that when a child reaches age 25, he is entitled to one-third of the trust's principal; when a child reaches age 30, he is entitled to another third (or two-thirds if he never took the first third); and at age 35, the child is entitled to the last remaining third (or all remaining principal if he did not take any prior distributions).

John may have established this schedule of distributions because he felt that his children would gain more maturity and a better sense of financial management as they age. Therefore, John would rather have his estate be placed in his children's hands when they are more mature.

If a child does not request a distribution when he or she is entitled to it (such as one-third at age 25), the principal remains in the trust to be managed and invested by the trustee. John gives his children the opportunity to take distributions at various ages, and John also gives them the opportunity to continue using the trustee's services. Curly, Moe, and Larry may not take the distributions they are entitled to for the same reasons John intended using a trustee: financial and investment management, privacy and confidentiality, and avoidance of probate.

Let us assume that Curly does not request a distribution at age 25 or 30. The trust states that Curly is entitled to mandatory income, and distribution of principal is discretionary. But this is now a moot issue because Curly can request up to two-thirds of the principal at his discretion. If Curly is age 30 or over, but not yet 35, the remaining one-third is still under the discretion of the trustee.

What happens to any remaining corpus of Curly's, Moe's, and Larry's trusts upon their deaths? You can help John with this contingency during the planning phase of his trust by offering several suggestions:

- Distribution to grandchildren
- Reallocation of corpus to surviving children
- Distribution to charity
- Payment to a child's spouse
- Distribution according to a power of appointment given to each child

These possibilities can be uniform among the children, different depending on family circumstances, or any combination. Distribution upon a child's death may be outright, or the corpus may be held further in trust.

Bomb Clause

There is a possibility that there will come a day when John, Mary, and all descendants are deceased. If this trust or any subsequently formed trusts are in existence at that time, the **bomb clause** comes into play. As morbid as it may sound, this clause found its way into trust terminology many years ago following the bombing death of all the beneficiaries of a trust during a family gathering. Although the grantor had surviving family relatives, they were not named in the trust as eventual (contingent) beneficiaries. The trustee was not directed to whom to distribute corpus. Today, trust planning prepares for this contingency. John may wish to distribute corpus to charity, spouses (nonbloodline) of descendants, or kin. John may need your help sorting out his plans.

Considering Other Sources of Income

Another area in which a trust professional can help is analyzing the financial position of John's beneficiaries. John has empowered his trustee to make discretionary decisions regarding the payment of principal or income dependent upon certain standards and guidelines. What if a beneficiary is capable of meeting her financial needs from her personal income and resources? John does not want to deny principal or income to his beneficiaries, yet he certainly does not want assets to go to a beneficiary who is financially self-sufficient. Meeting a flexible balance is tough.

In addition to explaining the trust's ascertainable standards regarding discretionary distributions, you might suggest that John's trust permit the trustee to take a beneficiary's other sources of income and assets into consideration. John's trust could contain discretionary language such as "In determining whether and to what extent to make discretionary payments of income or principal to, or for the benefit of, any beneficiary, the trustee may, but shall not be required to, take into account any other property or sources of income or support of the beneficiary known to the trustee." This coupled with the sprinkle clause gives John the assurance, and gives the trustee the leeway, to determine the proper and logical distribution of income and principal to those who truly need it.

For the Benefit Of

Many times we have seen the words "to or for the benefit of." At times a trustee will make a payment of income or principal directly to a beneficiary. At other times the payment will not, or should not, go directly to the beneficiary but will go somewhere for the beneficiary's benefit.

For example, let's assume that a beneficiary of John's trust is 21 years old and is attending college. We saw earlier that John directs the trustee to make mandatory payments of income to a beneficiary who attains age 21. This payment of income will be made directly to the beneficiary by way of check or direct deposit into the beneficiary's bank account. Assume the trustee receives a request for a distribution of $20,000 from the trust for the payment of tuition and room and board. Assume that the trustee researches the validity of the request and agrees to the distribution. At this point the trustee should make the payment (distribution) directly to the school for the benefit of the beneficiary; there is no absolute guarantee that the distribution will go to the school if payment is made to the beneficiary. This may sound as if the trustee does not trust the beneficiary, but the trustee is responsible for safeguarding John's trust estate and ensuring that payouts accord with his wishes.

Spendthrift Clause

> No interest under this instrument shall be transferable or assignable by any beneficiary or be subject during such beneficiary's life to the claims of such beneficiary's creditors or to any claims for alimony or for the support of such beneficiary's spouse.

The **spendthrift clause** protects John's trust property from a beneficiary's improvidence and financial impropriety. A trustee's duty is to spend the assets in a thrifty way. This clause protects trust assets from a beneficiary's creditors and alimony claims. John established this trust to benefit his family members, not their mistakes. Note that spendthrift clauses are not recognized or effective in some states.

Kickout Clause

> If at any time the trustee determines that the value of any trust under this instrument is $100,000 or less, the trustee may in its discretion distribute that trust to the beneficiary or beneficiaries.

Because of the distribution of income and principal over the years and the fractionalization of trusts through deaths and powers of appointment, your trust department may find itself in the position of maintaining several small trusts. Numerous small trusts can become inefficient to administer, and fees may become disproportionate to the principal and the income generated. This **kickout clause** (also called a *small trust termination clause*) gives the trustee the discretion to terminate any trust and distribute the proceeds to the beneficiary if the value of the trust falls below a stipulated amount. Although a trust may be at or below the kickout amount, the trust can direct that a trustee still maintain the trust if the trustee feels a beneficiary is incapable of properly managing affairs.

Rule Against Perpetuities

This next section is the most confusing part of a trust.

> Notwithstanding anything to the contrary, the trusts under this instrument shall terminate not later than 21 years after the death of the last survivor of my wife and my descendants (and the spouses of my descendants) living on the date of my death, at the end of which period the trustee shall distribute each remaining portion of the trust property to the beneficiary or beneficiaries, at that time.

There is no way for John to know how long his trust will need to last. Different beneficiaries will have different needs, and these needs will change over the years. Some beneficiaries will die and others will come into play. Distributions may be made and discretionarily held back. Yet there is a difference between how long a trust should last and how long it can last. Most states have enacted statutes that do not permit a trust to last forever. This is the **rule against perpetuities.**

There are exceptions and variations to the rule against perpetuities. Some states have entirely abolished this rule. Some states allow a grantor to elect not to include this rule in her trust. Other states impose a time limit (for example, 100 or 150 years) at which time all trusts resulting from John's document must terminate.

Additionally, an exception applies to charitable trusts, which are exempted since they are recognized as existing for the best interests—for the benefit—of the

---

USING TRUST PRODUCTS AND SERVICES TO MEET CUSTOMER NEEDS

Several years ago a grandmother established a trust for the benefit of her grandson, who was 26 years old at the time of his grandmother's demise. XYZ Bank was named as sole trustee. The document provided for the mandatory payment of income and discretionary payment of principal. The trust's kickout amount was $250,000, but in the discretion of the trustee.

Five years later, after payments of income and various payments of principal, the value of the trust fell to $240,000. The beneficiary was familiar with the document and questioned the bank as to when the trust would be distributed to him now that it was below the kickout amount. In the bank's discretion the kickout was not activated; the bank decided to maintain the trust rather than distribute the full amount to the beneficiary.

The beneficiary had a history of substance abuse. Not only had he been arrested several times for possession and use, but he also spent two long sessions in a rehabilitation center (of which the cost was paid by the trust). It was the trustee's obligation to protect the assets of grandmother's trust. The bank felt it was not in the beneficiary's best interest to receive the trust corpus for fear that the money may be used foolishly and perhaps illegally.

public. Charitable purposes include the relief of poverty, the advancement of religion and education, the promotion of health, and the accomplishment of governmental purposes (for example, parks, museums, or playgrounds). A purpose that limits the benefits of the trust to a particular class of the public (say, Chicago orphans) may be charitable, but the class may not be defined so narrowly that it designates only a few individuals upon whom the grantor wishes to confer private benefits. A trust for the dissemination of ideas may be charitable even though the ultimate purpose may be to accomplish a change in present law (for example, a trust that promotes the abolition of discrimination against women, tariffs, or capital punishment).

There are occasions when a trust is referred to as being "mixed." This occurs when the beneficiaries are both charitable and noncharitable. The rules for charitable trusts do not apply in this instance. Two separate trusts will be found if there is some indication as to how much of the corpus is intended to be applied towards charitable purposes, or how long the grantor intended the corpus to be applied towards charitable purposes.

"Lives in being plus twenty-one at the time the trust becomes irrevocable" is another way of stating this rule. In other words, John's trust becomes irrevocable upon his death. At that time, a figurative picture is taken of all living beneficiaries. If at the time of John's death he is survived by Mary, Curly (and his child, Zappa), Moe (and his children, Cheech and Chong), and Larry, John's trust (and any trusts formed thereunder) must terminate no later than 21 years after the death of the last survivor of these family members.

Determine which beneficiaries are alive at the time of John's death. One of these beneficiaries will outlive the rest. Suppose that the youngest is Cheech, who is 2 years old at John's death, and that he outlives all the others. Actuarially, that is a safe assumption. Upon Cheech's death, any and all existing trusts must terminate within 21 years. If Cheech lives to be 80 years old, the trust can potentially stay in effect for 99 years (78 years until Cheech's death plus 21 years).

Fees

Any trustee shall be entitled to reasonable compensation for services in administering and distributing the trust property, and to reimbursement for expenses. The trustee's regular compensation shall be charged half against income and half against principal, except that the trustee shall have full discretion at any time to charge a larger portion or all against income.

This language permits your trust department to collect a fee. But what is meant by *reasonable compensation?* In most instances this means the bank trust department's published fee schedule at any particular time.

You may encounter trusts that dictate the amount of fees you can charge. The trust agreement may state, "Any trustee shall be entitled to compensation not to exceed one-half of one-percent of a trust's principal value." Your trust department may find this fee inadequate in order to provide the high level of professional services that you offer. You are faced with a decision: Explain why the fee is inadequate, and the grantor may recognize the oversight and change the language; or you may have to decline to act. A **declination** is refusing to accept the nomination as trustee.

In some states, statutes set guidelines as to how much a trustee can charge, within a range of dollars or percentages.

Adoption

Many states have statutes in effect that direct trusts to treat adopted children and natural children equally, unless the grantor specifically states otherwise.

Exculpatory Language

It is not unreasonable for a trustee to look for protection from being second-guessed when making investment and discretionary decisions. Trustees are constantly under the microscope regarding the decisions they make.

It is likely that a trust will contain **exculpatory language:** words that give a trustee room to exercise judgment and hold it blameless. This does not mean that trustees should be given wide-open permission to act, but in reality not every decision will be found acceptable by every beneficiary. As a trustee, you should make certain that this language is included: "The trustee shall incur no liability for any payment, distribution, or investment made in good faith and without actual notice or knowledge of a changed condition or status affecting any person's interest in the trust." Trustees who are careless should be held accountable, but if they acted in good faith, they should not be held accountable.

Trustee Powers

How people invest for themselves and their families during their lives is not necessarily how they want someone to invest for their families after they are gone. Although John may have taken risks with his investments, he probably would not want his trustee to do the same.

With John gone, your trust department as the successor trustee may find itself with myriad assets: real property, tangible personal property, intangible personal property, and liquid and illiquid assets. Do you maintain these **trust investments** or sell them? What should be purchased next? A trustee must be given the powers to manage such assets. If John's trust contains an expensive stamp collection, a condominium in Florida, and a closely held business, what power is the trustee given to maintain these assets or sell them?

With the help of a trust professional, John can design his estate plan to be flexible, with as few limitations to investment authority as possible. This is not to say the trustee desires free rein to go investment-wild. But it is important to give the trustee the leeway to deal with the myriad assets that may find their way into the trust. Restrictions on the trustee may work against the best interests of the beneficiaries. John should give his trustee the same flexibility he had to effectively manage, invest, and administer the assets he worked so hard to build:

> The trustee shall have the following powers, and any others that may be granted by law, to be exercised as the trustee in its discretion determines to be in the best interests of the beneficiaries.

Trust professionals may see trusts in which investment decisions are placed in the hands of someone other than the corporate trustee. This is commonly called a **directed trust.** Investment responsibility may belong to an individual trustee or to a nontrustee. As was previously stated, when our trust departments are not given investment discretion, the trust agreement *must* contain exculpatory language that holds us blameless for the decision-maker's potential investment shortcomings and mistakes.

Many estate planning attorneys suggest a variation to a directed trust: a trust advisor. The advisor may be an individual or a committee that is responsible for various aspects—or assets—of the trust. The thought is that a named trustee may not have a certain type of management expertise (for example, experience dealing with special assets such as oil and gas interests or a closely held business). Perhaps the grantor's choice is simply to place responsibility in someone's hands other than the trustee's. This is commonly seen when a bulk of the trust's assets is a multi-generational closely held business. The grantor may appoint a family member and/or a business associate as the trust advisor(s).

It is important that the trust document clearly delineate the advisor's and trustee's duties and responsibilities:

- Does the advisor maintain a fiduciary role?

- Is the named trustee held harmless from the advisor's decisions?
- Does the advisor hold authority, or is the advisor's role to do nothing more than settle disputes among cotrustees?

Boilerplate Language

Most trusts contain boilerplate, certain language common to every trust. Boilerplate language is important to **trust administration,** or management of trust assets. Most boilerplate language is found in the section that outlines the powers given to the trustee. Sample language could look like this:

The trustee shall have the following powers:

- to retain any property received from any source and to invest and reinvest the trust in any other property; to make or retain any investment without regard to any lack of diversification or marketability, risk or nonproductivity and without being limited by any statute or rule of law concerning investments by the trustee;
- to sell any trust property, for cash or on credit; to exchange any trust property for other property;
- to operate, maintain, repair, rehabilitate, alter, or improve real estate and to make contracts relating to real estate;
- to borrow money for any purpose, either from the banking department of the trustee or from others and to mortgage or pledge any trust property;
- to employ attorneys, investment counselors, and other agents, with or without discretionary powers, and to rely on their advice;
- to receive additional property from any source and add it to the trust estate;
- to make any distribution or division of the trust property in cash or in kind or both;

- to collect the net proceeds of any employee benefit plan, individual retirement account, deferred compensation plan, or life insurance policy;
- to transfer the assets of any trust to another **situs** (a physical place); to appoint and to remove an individual or another corporation as special trustee for any assets as to which no trustee is able or willing to act; and
- to have all other rights and powers and perform all other acts that the trustee considers desirable for the proper administration of any trust.

Resignation of Trustee

I may resign as trustee by giving written notice to the successor trustee. Any other trustee may resign by giving written notice to the beneficiaries.

If I die, resign, or am unable to act as trustee, ABC Bank and Trust Company and my wife shall become trustees in my place. If my wife dies, resigns, or refuses or is at any time unable to act, the corporate trustee shall have all the powers and discretion of the trustees without the appointment of a successor individual trustee.

In Chapter 5 we spoke about the testator nominating an executor. To serve, the executor must be approved and appointed by the court. Such is not the case with a trustee. Court appointment is not necessary for either a **trust company** (a corporation that manages trust accounts) or an individual to serve. Just as in the naming of an executor, a named trustee or successor trustee may decline. Even if the trustee accepts the position, he may resign at any time.

If any corporate trustee at any time resigns or is unable or refuses to act, a successor trustee shall be appointed by an instrument delivered to it and signed by a majority in number of the beneficiaries. Each successor to any corporate trustee shall be another corporation authorized under the laws of the United States or of any state to administer trusts and shall have a capital and surplus of not less that $xx million.

While John is alive and capable of doing so, he may name who will act as trustee during his life and following death and incapacitation. If John resigns as trustee, he still may appoint who the trustee(s) will be—even himself again—currently and in the future, as long as he is not incapacitated, which would render him legally incapable of doing so. These actions are accomplished by amending the trust.

After John's death or incapacitation, ABC Bank and Mary will serve as cotrustees. John gives his beneficiaries the ability to appoint a successor corporate trustee (a national or state bank) if ABC Bank resigns, is unable to act, or refuses (declines) to act. The appointed successor corporate trustee must be authorized to conduct trust business and be large enough to provide adequate services to the trust. John could also name a specific corporate trustee to act following ABC Bank, and John could give his beneficiaries the right to fire a trustee by saying, "After my death, the majority of my wife and the adult beneficiaries may, by giving written notice to each trustee acting at the time the notice is given, remove any corporate trustee."

Disputes Among Cotrustees

Mary and ABC Bank are cotrustees. *Co* comes from the word *cooperation*—Mary and ABC Bank working cooperatively together. But sometimes trustees cannot agree on all matters, such as investment decisions and discretionary decisions pertaining to distribution of income and principal. Absent specific language in the trust agreement, if one trustee says yes and the other says no, the outcome is a stalemate. In helping John plan his trust, you may wish to suggest adding language in the trust document that resolves potential disagreements.

Seldom do disputes occur. When they do occur, they usually happen when cotrustees with diverse backgrounds differ about how the trust should be administered. For example, a bank trust department recently encountered a self-dec trust in which the grantor named her two sons and husband to serve as cotrustees following her incapacitation, but not following her death. The trust agreement named her two daughters, her accountant, and her attorney to act as cotrustees with the bank following her demise. Following the grantor's death, but before the bank's formal acceptance as trustee, the trust department met with the cotrustees and the husband and two sons, who could no longer serve as trustees. The former trustees were present at the meeting as beneficiaries. From the onset there were disagreements among the daughters and the accountant as to investment decisions. One daughter and the attorney disagreed about the discretionary distribution of principal to the grantor's husband and sons. The trust did not contain language that would resolve disputes. The bank decided not to accept its appointment as trustee, lest it be caught in never-ending rounds of dispute.

With your assistance, John should consider the possibility that Mary and the bank could disagree. With respect to investment decisions, John could leave the final say to either Mary or the bank (the better alternative), with additional exculpatory language relieving the dissenting trustee from liability. With respect to making discretionary decisions pertaining to distribution of income or principal, John could say,

> No trustee shall participate in the exercise of any discretion with respect to the distribution of income or principal in which he or she, or any person he or she is obligated to support, has any beneficial interest, and the discretion shall be exercised only by the remaining trustee.

Suspension of a Trustee

The individual trustee may at any time by a signed instrument delivered to the corporate trustee delegate to it any or all powers under this instrument either for a specified period of time or until the delegation is revoked by a similar instrument.

Let's assume that Mary has a health problem—surgery and a long recuperation period—that keeps her from adequately attending to her responsibilities as a trustee. Still, she does not want to give up her position. This language enables Mary to suspend her duties temporarily.

Incapacitation

Trusts become irrevocable following a grantor's death or incapacitation. A decedent cannot amend a trust, and an incapacitated grantor cannot amend a trust.

If John became incapacitated (therefore making his trust irrevocable) and his incapacitation later was resolved, does his trust become revocable again? Yes, as long as the statement of incapacitation is removed, similar to the way it was instituted.

The same premise applies to incapacitation of a trustee. John's trust could determine incapacitation by saying,

Any individual acting in a fiduciary capacity or any person required to be able to act shall be considered unable to act if adjudicated incompetent or if a doctor familiar with his or her physical or mental condition certifies in writing that such individual is unable to give prompt and intelligent consideration to business matters.

Successor Banks

Banks are bought. Banks merge. Banks exit the trust business. Where does this put John's trust if his bank trustee finds itself in one of these situations?

If any corporate trustee designated to act or at any time acting hereunder is merged with or transfers substantially all of its assets to another corporation, or is in any other manner reorganized or reincorporated, the resulting or transferee corporation shall become the corporate trustee in place of its corporate predecessor.

Of course, there always is the possibility that the beneficiaries do not want the resulting corporation as trustee. John can name (by amendment) a different corporate trustee during his life while he is not incapacitated. With proper language in the trust document, John can give his beneficiaries the right to name a corporate trustee of their choice following John's incapacitation or death.

Execution

This instrument is signed on this _____day of_____, 200_.

_____
Grantor

_____
Trustee

The grantor's signature signifies the actual creation of the trust; the trustee's signature signifies acceptance of the position.

States differ in whether a trust must be witnessed and notarized and how old one must be to execute a trust. Always check your local statutes.

Testamentary Capacity

Many states have recently added statutes that provide that testamentary aspects of a trust or an amendment are invalid unless the trust or amendment is executed with the same formalities required for the execution of a will. The term *testamentary aspects* means the provisions of the trust or amendment that dispose of the trust property on the death of a settlor, other than to the settlor's estate. These statutes apply to both revocable trust agreements (where the grantor is not the initial trustee) and self-dec trusts.

Proof of Existence

Trusts are private, yet people other than beneficiaries may need proof of their existence. John's concern is proving that the trust exists without showing the whole trust, thereby giving up confidentiality. Some states allow an **affidavit of trust** (or an **abstract of trust**), a document that briefly outlines the trust's key provisions (see Exhibit 8.1). This document proves to others that the trust exists. At other times, the title page, signature page, and the pages that are applicable to the situation or that must be seen by concerned parties constitute sufficient proof.

When funding a self-dec trust, a brokerage firm, insurance company, bank, or

---

Exhibit 8.1   Affidavit of Trust

This affidavit of the John Q. Doe Declaration of Trust dated November 10, 2002, is made by John Q. Doe, the grantor of the trust. This affidavit is subject to the terms, conditions, and provisions of the said trust, which is revocable during the lifetime of the grantor.

John Q. Doe as the grantor and as trustee under the trust, and the successor trustees named therein and serving in that capacity, from time to time shall have the power and authority to bind the trust in any and all transactions. Such powers shall include, but not be limited to (i) collecting receipts and income, (ii) paying disbursements and obligations, (iii) retaining, securing, and disposing of assets, (iv) writing checks and making withdrawals and transfers from accounts, including bank accounts, (v) purchasing, selling, and pledging securities, real estate, and all other property, (vi) lending, leasing or borrowing to, from, or on behalf of the trust, including personal dealings between the trustees and the trust, (vii) voting, in person or by proxy, any corporate securities or shares or otherwise exercising stock rights and powers, (viii) electing options or otherwise exercising discretion with respect to insurance contracts, employment benefit plans, individual retirement plans, including the mode of distribution or proceeds, (ix) employing and designating power to agents, attorneys, accountants, and investment advisors, and (x) exercising any power conferred to the trustees pursuant to the terms of the trust agreement. Any third party dealing with the trust may rely upon this singular authority without any further evidence.

The undersigned does hereby certify that, as of the date of the execution hereof, he is the trustee acting under the terms of the trust, that the trust remains in full force and effect and has not been revoked, and he is acting within the authority as set forth in the trust. Any person or entity acting in reliance upon this affidavit may so rely upon it without the necessity of securing the original or a copy of the original trust instrument and may continue to rely upon this affidavit until written notice to the contrary is received by such person or entity acting upon such reliance hereunder.

This affidavit is executed this tenth day of November 2003.

_____
(signature)
John Q. Doe, Trustee

real estate title company may ask for proof of the trust's existence before retitling an account into the name of a trust. Institutions may also need a copy of the principal's trust (or parts of it) to ensure that the trustee is permitted to hire agents; the principal would not want to be a party to an unauthorized activity.

TRUSTS AND TRUSTEES ACT

In Chapter 5 we saw that wills and probate estates are guided by state probate laws with regard to the administration and settlement of estates, testate or intestate. These probate laws also provide direction when there is doubt or confusion regarding the wording of a will. Trustees face similar predicaments when faced with a dilemma, a crossroads, or a decision that cannot be helped by the trust document's language.

States have enacted trust laws, known by varying names (The Trusts and Trustees Act, for example), to assist trustees in interpreting ambiguous language or responding to a situation that has no prescribed answer. If a trust lacks specific language (if it is silent), unless otherwise indicated, these statutes provide direction for a trustee's action. In the review of John Doe's trust, several of these concerns were addressed.

A trust professional's careful planning should help resolve future interpretations. In situations in which outside planning was minimal, the Trusts and Trustees Act assists trustees. For example,

- If a trust does not specifically state that assets may be added by others, statutes may allow additions to be made.

- If a trust does not address a trustee's compensation, the statutes may.

- The statutes may include subparts that direct how fees will be charged (for example, half against income and half against principal) when the trust agreement is silent.

- When a trust lacks specific language about how a trustee may manage specific assets, the statutes probably will address a trustee's investment latitude. (Remember the Prudent Investor Rule from Chapter 4.)

- These statutes may also address judicial termination of marriage issues, appointment of successor trustee when no direction is given, and the treatment of adopted beneficiaries.

Of course, despite the assistance the statutes provide to trustees, they cannot override the aspects of John's trust that are clearly contrary to them, unless the trust stipulates actions that are immoral, illegal, or contrary to public policy or that violate the rule against perpetuities. John's intentions in his trust are limited only by his creativity. Absent this, the law awaits as an assistance.

SUMMARY

- Trusts are binding legal documents filled with extensive direction on the grantor's part and heavy responsibilities on the trustee's part. Trusts should be prepared by competent legal counsel. Generic words taken from a book will not suffice.

- The opening section of a trust identifies the grantor, trustee, and corpus. If the trust is revocable, there is language that addresses revocations, amendments, and restatements. Trusts identify family, dispositive provisions during the grantor's life, the grantor's responsibility over his or her life insurance, and coordination of the grantor's will and trust pertaining to payment of probate expenses and taxes.

- Following the grantor's death, separate trusts (family, residuary, and so forth) may be formed. The trust gives direction if a common disaster (simultaneous death) occurs.

- Trusts contain extensive provisions for the distribution of principal and income for the beneficiaries. Principal or income may be discretionary or nondiscretionary. Discretionary payments are decided upon by the trustee and are based on needs for support, medical care, education, best interests, and standard of living.

- A trust may provide for a sprinkle clause (uneven payments to beneficiaries), a five-and-five power, and powers of appointment (a beneficiary's right to direct distribution of corpus upon the beneficiary's death). Eventual distribution following the grantor's and spouse's death may be per stirpes (by the branch) or per capita (by head count). If the grantor, spouse, and all descendants are deceased, a bomb clause directs the distribution of assets.

- When considering payments of principal or income from the trust, a trustee may or may not be directed to consider a beneficiary's other sources of income. A trust may contain a kickout clause (termination of the trust when it falls below a certain value) and a spendthrift clause (protection of the trust's assets from a beneficiary's creditors and alimony requests). Trusts may not be permitted to last forever, or in perpetuity. Trusts address fees, treatment of adopted beneficiaries, and exculpatory language (protection from errors).

- A trust's boilerplate language addresses the trustee's investment powers, ability to resign, appointment of successor trustees, varying cotrustee responsibilities, definition of incapacitation, and the requirements for execution, witnesses, and notarization.

- When a trust's language is ambiguous or direction is absent, trustees can rely on state statutes that assist in interpreting a grantor's intent with respect to trust additions, fees, investment management, termination of marriage, and treatment of adopted beneficiaries.

REVIEW QUESTIONS

1. When trustees are empowered to provide discretionary payments of trust principal or income to beneficiaries, what must a trustee take into consideration?
2. Can a grantor authorize someone else to decide to whom the trust's corpus will go?
3. What is the rule against perpetuities?
4. Can a grantor stipulate in her trust a limit on what the trustee can charge in fees? What effect would this have on the trust?
5. Why is it generally in the grantor's and beneficiaries' best interests to impose few limitations on the trustee's powers to manage investment property?

9

LAND TRUST

"Land is the only thing in the world that amounts to anything, for 'tis the only thing in this world that lasts. . . . 'Tis the only thing worth working for, worth fighting for—worth dying for."

Margaret Mitchell (1900–1949)

Ownership of land and any interests in property on land have always been the most visible, physical evidence of wealth. The ownership of real property carries a quality of permanence. Acres upon acres of land or a 10-story commercial office building cannot be easily concealed, misplaced, or destroyed.

As we saw in Chapters 7 and 8, intangible property can be placed easily in a personal trust, thereby offering privacy to the owner. Land trusts offer a similar advantage with regard to real property.

LEARNING OBJECTIVES

Land trusts are an additional tool for trust professionals to use when assisting customers with their estate planning.

Upon completion of this chapter, you will be able to

- Trace the origins of land trusts
- Describe how a land trust differs from a personal trust
- List the advantages of a land trust to customers and trust departments
- Define and use the terms that appear in bold in the text

A BRIEF REVIEW OF PROPERTY AND TRUSTS

In Chapter 1 and again in Chapter 7 we explored how various types of property can be owned in various forms. For example, intangible property can be owned in sole ownership form and by tenants in common, and real property can be owned by joint tenants and also by a trust. Property (of whatever form) owned by a trust is managed by the trustee, and owned in dual ownership: legal ownership by the trustee, equitable ownership by the beneficiary. If the trust owns real property (for example, a personal residence or a piece of commercial property), absent specific direction in the trust document the trustee is responsible for each aspect of the property, such as maintenance, insurance, payment of taxes and indebtedness, and the dozens of other tasks owners of real property face.

ORIGINS OF LAND TRUSTS

In past centuries, a person's wealth was measured more by his ownership of land (real property) than by intangible personal property. From the land came additional wealth: crops, cattle, and rents and taxes levied on tenants who occupied the land or worked on it. When speaking of a parcel of real property, it was common to associate it with the owner. In fact, the land was often named after the owner. Common examples that we are familiar with today are Houston (land owned by Sam Houston), New York (once owned by the Duke of York), and Sioux City (land once owned by the Native American Sioux tribe).

Governments have always attempted to exercise authority over wealth. In feudal England, if a property owner's conduct was found unacceptable to the government (because of nonpayment of taxes, failure to serve in the military, contrarian expression of political views, or treason), the ruling authorities punished the owner; a questionable landowner could be forced to forfeit his land to the government. This was public policy and a way of teaching others a lesson.

Feudal England also had the law of **primogeniture:** the right of the eldest son (not necessarily the first-born son, because that son might die before his father's death) to inherit his father's property. It was impossible for a father to leave his estate to children other than his eldest son.

Landowners searched for means to get around the laws of primogeniture and to avoid the pitfall of attachment of their land because of the government's whims. One such device was to place the ownership of property with a trusted friend with the understanding that the friend would handle the land as directed.

The five ingredients of a trust, discussed in Chapter 7, were present even then. The landowner (as the grantor) would place his property (the corpus) in a trust arrangement, subject to various terms as delineated in the agreement (the trust document). A trusted friend (the trustee) would carry out the terms of the agreement for the benefit of the grantor and family as beneficiary.

Not surprisingly, the government intervened. In 1536 King Henry VIII passed a law (the **Statute of Uses**) that challenged such trust arrangements by attempting to get the property away from the confidentiality of a trust and to get the property back on the public tax rolls. The courts later ruled that the trusts created were indeed valid, and the king's laws were not applicable to their use.

The ownership of land, the early formation of England's common laws pertaining to land, and the subsequent precepts of a trust have found their way into the common laws of the United States. The arrangement by which one person holds property for the use of another has become a familiar part of our trust practices.

LAND TRUSTS TODAY

The sixteenth-century English practice of placing land in trust has survived to present day. From that practice evolved the trust concepts discussed in Chapters 7 and 8. A **land trust**—a legal device under which a trustee holds title to real estate for the use and benefit of others—differs from personal trusts in several ways. For example, land trusts may contain only land, not other types of property that personal trusts may hold.

Land in this context can mean all forms of real property: improved and unimproved vacant land, commercial buildings, personal residences (single-dwelling, free-standing houses and condominiums), and the other examples of real property discussed in Chapter 1. A land trust, unlike a personal trust, is confined to holding only real property located in the same state as the trustee. In other words, if PDQ Trust and Savings Bank in South Bend, Indiana, is trustee of a land trust, that trust may contain only property located (that has situs) in Indiana, although the grantor of the trust may be domiciled outside of Indiana.

Additionally, land trusts currently exist only in eight states: Arizona, Florida, Hawaii, Illinois (the first state in which land trusts appeared and spread widely), Indiana, North Dakota, Texas, and Virginia. There is nothing to prevent land trusts from existing elsewhere. The other states do not recognize land trusts solely because they have not enacted laws for them.

Five Ingredients of a Land Trust

The five ingredients of personal trusts (trustee, grantor, beneficiary, corpus, and trust agreement) also exist, with some differences, for land trusts. Exhibit 9.1 charts the similarities and differences.

Trustee

The trustee of a personal trust can be an individual or a corporation (a trust department). The same holds true for a land trust.

Grantor

Both persons and nonpersons (corporations and partnerships) can own personal and real property. Both entities can own property in any ownership form (sole, joint tenancy, and so forth). The creator of a land trust may be a person, a corporation, or a partnership. However, the creator of a personal trust can be only a person.

Beneficiary

Chapters 7 and 8 introduced the entities that can benefit from a personal trust: individuals and charities. In a land trust, the beneficiaries can be the same entities as the grantors. The beneficial interest in the trust, owned by the beneficiary, is intangible personal property and not legally an interest in real estate. The beneficiary retains the full responsibility of management and control of the property. The trustee may do nothing except as directed in writing by the beneficiary or as ordered by the courts in a legal proceeding or by statutes of law.

Corpus

Exhibit 1.2 showed how the various types of assets could be owned in the various forms of ownership. Based on this concept, a personal trust can own both real and personal property. A land trust is limited to holding real property.

Trust Agreement

Because of the unique estate planning nature of personal trusts, the written trust is individually prepared by a grantor's attorney. The trust document carefully directs the trustee in the manner of investment management, payments of principal and income to beneficiaries, and the eventual disposition of the trust's corpus. Land trusts are also written agreements, but because of the standard nature of the corpus, the defined life of the trust, and the limited choice of the eventual disposition of the corpus, land trusts do not vary in their direction and use and therefore are prototype documents within a given trust department.

Exhibit 9.1 Personal Trust versus Land Trust

	Personal Trust	Land Trust
Trustee	Individual(s) Corporation	Individual(s) Corporation
Grantor	Individual(s)	Individual(s) Partnership Corporation
Beneficiary	Individual(s) Charity	Individual(s) Partnership Corporation
Corpus	Real property	Real property Tangible personal property Intangible personal property
Trust agreement	Written contract Individually drafted	Written contract Trust prototype document
Legal ownership (legal title)	Trustee	Trustee
Equitable ownership (equitable title)	Beneficiary	Trustee
Form of property	Personal property or real property	Intangible personal property
Trustee's Duties	Hold property title Administration and investment management Deal with property according to terms of trust agreement or powers given in trust law, absent trust direction	Hold property title Deal with property only upon beneficiary's direction Convey or sell property upon trust termination

Ownership of Land Trusts

A land trust is a unique trust relationship. It has many of the attributes and advantages of a personal trust, yet it purposely lacks several trustee duties and ownership traits.

A land trust is a common law trust used to hold title to real estate. Most often, the trust is used for business purposes, rather than for estate planning, and is often used as a substitute for a corporation or a partnership. Although the trustee has title to the property, under the trust agreement the beneficial owners (or beneficiaries) of the trust exercise management and control, and the trustee agrees to follow instructions. *The trustee's role is passive.* This differs from a personal trust, in which the trustee has management and control of the trust, whereas the beneficiaries have a passive role.

Legal Title and Equitable Title

Over the years, a confusing crossroads of property ownership in land trusts has led to considerable debate. But before we proceed, let's look at what is meant by *title*. In a land trust, both **legal** and **equitable title** (legal and equitable ownership, as discussed in Chapter 7) are vested in the trustee, and the beneficiary has no interest in either. The beneficiary has an interest in the trust's corpus (which is the real property).

Title is the legal right to ownership of property, and it is the document proving the ownership. The title can be a bill of sale, a receipt, or a deed. In the world of real property (**real estate**) transactions, a **deed** is the written instrument showing the transfer of ownership of real property from one owner to another. The written transfer of ownership is also called an **assignment;** this may be done for cash consideration, as a gift, or to satisfy a debt.

Form of Property

The corpus of a personal trust can be personal property or real property. Although an individual may transfer property from sole ownership to a trust, the form of the property remains unconverted. What was real when it was solely owned is still real after it is placed in a personal trust. When an individual transfers solely owned real property to a land trust, the property takes on an intangible personal property right because title of ownership, the document proving the ownership, is classified as intangible personal property.

Stock and bonds—the paper that proves ownership and indebtedness—are examples of intangible personal property. Because the title ownership of real property in a land trust vests in the trustee, and because title ownership is intangible personal property like stocks and bonds, the real property in a land trust assumes an intangible personal property right. This may be a concern to those domiciled in locales (such as Florida) where there is an intangibles tax.

Who really "owns" the property? First answer: the trustee, with respect to the property's legal and equitable title. Second answer: the beneficiary, because she has control. This can be confusing. Court cases over the years have concluded that *ownership* has no fixed meaning under all circumstances with respect to land. In a land trust, the beneficiary does not possess the title ownership of the land, but

does possess control ownership. The U.S. Supreme Court went so far as to rule that ownership does not necessarily involve title, but control. When weighing a trustee with interest in the property's title against a beneficiary with pure control over the property, the beneficiary wins out as the pure owner of the trust's assets (corpus). Yes, the legal and equitable title vests in the trustee, but the trustee cannot exercise any control over the property other than what the beneficiary directs the trustee to do. And with this control goes the responsibility. The beneficiary is therefore the owner.

Think of it this way: Assume that a person bought a limousine for cash and hired another person to drive business travelers to and from the airport for a fee. Let's call this business venture LimboLimoLtd. When the limo was purchased, the dealer asked the buyer how he wanted the title (the ownership papers) to read. He answered: LimboLimoLtd. Now, who owns the limousine? The buyer or LimboLimoLtd? On paper LimboLimoLtd does. But from a control-of-asset perspective (and because it was the buyer's cash that paid for the limo), the buyer is the true owner. Who benefits from the operation of the limo? The passengers do in a sense because they are provided a service for a fee, and the driver does because he gets paid, but the true benefit is to the buyer because he profits from the money paid by the passengers.

In a land trust, the trustee has no duties or powers other than to deal with the property as directed by the beneficiary. The property is held by a trustee for the benefit of another person (the limo is driven by the driver for the benefit of the buyer).

Trustee's Duties

Chapter 8 discussed the extensive duties and responsibilities of the trustee of a personal trust: administrative and investment management, holding legal title to the corpus, and dealing with the property according to the trust agreement or the powers given by trust law. A land trust trustee has three simple duties: hold title to the property, convey it to the beneficiary or sell it upon the trust's termination, and deal with the property only according to the beneficiary's direction.

Hold Title

The trustee not only holds title to the initial corpus placed in the trust, but also accepts title or removes title to parcels of real estate added to or removed from the trust.

Convey to the Beneficiary

By law, land trusts are created to end in 20 years. Upon termination of the trust the trustee must convey the corpus to the beneficiary or sell it, depending on the beneficiary's direction. The trust is permitted to last longer, by way of amendment, than the originally prescribed 20 years as long as the trust does not violate the rule against perpetuities (see Chapter 8).

Deal with the Corpus upon Beneficiary Direction

The trustee's only additional specified duties are to deal with the property at the direction of the beneficiary or another named authorized person (discussed later in the section on centralized management). In essence the trustee's duties are defined more concisely by what the trustee is not responsible for.

Responsibilities of the Beneficiary

In a land trust, the management, control, development, and operation of the property (called a power of direction), as well as rights to rents, profits, and proceeds of a sale, are vested in the beneficiary. The beneficiary retains complete control. The beneficiary is responsible for repairs, maintenance, insurance, financing (if applicable), and leasing. The beneficiary can sell the property, add additional property, or terminate the trust.

But with the power goes the responsibility. The beneficiary's position is analogous to the limousine owner's. Like the owner of the limo, the buyer has control over it and is responsible for it in every way. He can sell it and buy another one. He is responsible for its insurance and upkeep (oil changes and tune-ups). He can terminate the business. He can also hire an agent (perhaps a driver) to do these things for him. The owner has the power to direct the driver or others to do these things, yet he is the only one with the total responsibility. Therefore, the trustee is not required to inquire into the propriety of any direction received from the beneficiary or authorized person.

Take care not to misinterpret the word *agent* in the previous paragraph. (It may help to review the principal-agent relationship discussed in Chapter 3.) A land trust agreement restricts a trustee from dealing with the property except for duties that are directed by the beneficiary. We might easily assume that the trustee who is performing the duties is acting as an agent for the beneficiary, but we would be wrong. In trust law, a power of direction creates a fiduciary rather than an agency relationship.

Rights and Liability

A land trustee has no right of management or control of the property; these rights belong to the beneficiary. Therefore, law limits the personal liability of the trustee.

To see the confusion that might result from a government or agency failing to understand the finer points of trust rights and responsibilities, consider the plight of ABC Bank.

Several years ago ABC Bank, as trustee of an apartment building in a land trust, received a notice from the city regarding building code violations. In accordance with law, the beneficiary's name was disclosed to the city serving the notice, and the notice was passed on to the beneficiary. The beneficiary ignored the building's violations. The city sued the trustee.

A court ruled that the bank trustee was responsible for the building and was ordered to vacate and board up the building. The bank refused to take action based on trust doctrine, which places all responsibilities on the beneficiary's shoulders. Again, no action was taken and the city began to impose hefty monetary fines on the trustee. The fines were not paid. Upon appeal, a housing court judge recognized the bank trustee's position and lack of control. The suit was dropped, fines were removed, and the bank was absolved. Although the interest in the title of the property vests in the trustee, control and responsibilities vest in the beneficiary; therefore, the beneficiary was held liable for the infractions.

In this example, we see that the trustee is responsible for communicating all inquiries, notices (such as tax bills), and other information to the trust beneficiary. The trustee also cannot voluntarily disclose the identity of the trust beneficiary unless compelled by law. The trustee can sue and respond to litigation under proper circumstances and direction if indemnified by the beneficiary, and the beneficiary must indemnify the trustee for any expenses. (We will visit the subject of liability again in the section on centralized management.)

Summary of Land Trust Features

A land trust is basically a simple way to manage real estate.

- The title is held by the trustee, and rights of ownership and direction are retained by the beneficiary.

- The trust agreement defines the trustee's responsibilities and duties and each party's rights and obligations.

- The trust is created easily and quickly, and it can be established at the time the real estate is purchased or at any time thereafter.

- The trust can contain one or numerous and varying parcels of real property, but *only* property within the state where the trustee is located.

- A land trust can be amended or revoked.

- It cannot last for more than 20 years; however, the 20-year limit can be extended by amendment, as long as the relationship does not violate the rule against perpetuities.

- A trustee can be changed by the beneficiary, and a trustee can resign.

ADVANTAGES OF A LAND TRUST

Understanding what a land trust is and knowing how it differs from a personal trust are important when we assist customers with their trust planning. An in-depth knowledge of the uses of a land trust and how it benefits our customers and our trust departments will prove invaluable as the planning process develops.

Advantages to the Customer

Land trusts are another important segment of estate and financial planning for customers who live in, may move to, or own property in states that recognize this type of trust. In dealing with these customers, trust professionals cannot ignore the advantages of a land trust.

Privacy of Ownership

Despite the fact that the title is held by the trustee, the trust agreement is not recorded, and the names of the beneficiaries remain confidential, it is nonetheless a myth that land trusts provide immunity from creditors and that they are covert arrangements that skirt the law.

Trustees cannot voluntarily disclose a beneficiary's identity. Confidentiality is maintained unless law dictates that names be disclosed. Under certain statutes, building code violations, suspected arson investigations, personal injury or property damage suits arising out of negligent maintenance, and health and safety violations require a trustee to reveal an owner's name, and valid court orders require disclosure.

However, unlike in nontrust ownership, beneficiary names are not generally available as a matter of public record. The difference a land trust can make in protecting customer privacy is demonstrated by the experience of Val Rogers.

Val recently received an unsolicited, direct-mail piece from an insurance broker offering to sell life insurance coverage to provide for payment of her remaining mortgage indebtedness in the event of her death. She guessed that a direct-mailer wouldn't waste time mailing to just anyone without knowing that they had a mortgage. So Val questioned how they got her name, address, and mortgage information. (They also knew what the mortgage balance was.)

Val called her bank and asked whether it was giving out names and addresses of mortgage customers. It didn't and didn't have to. Because her name, address, and mortgage information are a matter of public record (such as tax rolls), anyone could get this information.

Would this have happened if her house were in a land trust? No. Public records would only have shown the name of the trustee. Val's privacy would have been protected.

Simple Transfer of Ownership

An important aspect of the trust professional's relationship with customers is advising them about the specific benefits land trusts can offer in terms of streamlined real estate management. Homeowners who have bought or sold a piece of real estate know how cumbersome and lengthy the paperwork is. Beneficial interest in a land trust removes these chores and is accomplished by a simple instrument (that is, by an assignment), leaving the paperwork to the trustee.

Centralized Management

Imagine a large piece of real estate owned by eight co-owners as tenants in common. The different needs, desires, and goals of eight individuals can create havoc with the management of the property. The eight owners, as cograntors, can substantially reduce management and administrative tasks by simply conveying the property into a land trust and selecting one individual (the authorized person) or one beneficiary to provide direction to the trustee.

The authorized person mentioned in the previous paragraph is also referred to as the "holder of a power of direction." How much power does a holder have? Can the holder be held liable for breach of responsibilities? Is the holder a fiduciary? Illinois, as an example, has addressed these issues.

Recent Illinois legislation significantly affects the rights and duties of the beneficiaries to an Illinois land trust. Illinois law states that the holder of a power of direction in an Illinois land trust owes a fiduciary duty to all of the trust's beneficiaries. Holders of the power of direction should be advised of the higher standard of care involved in a fiduciary duty. The holder should understand the nature of this standard and the additional responsibilities that arise in a fiduciary relationship.

Holders of a power of direction should consider amending existing land trust agreements to clarify the relationship between all parties. The amendment can provide that the holder does not owe a fiduciary duty to the beneficiaries and that the power of direction is held in less than all the beneficiaries in order to reduce excessive management.

The law does not appear to place any additional duties upon the trustee. Trustees should nonetheless notify beneficiaries of the change in the law.

Alteration of Beneficial Interests

If Ralph and Betty Crawford own their home in joint tenancy, when the first spouse dies, his or her interest will automatically vest (transfer) to the surviving spouse without the involvement of probate. However, if the surviving spouse wills the house (now owned in sole ownership by the surviving spouse) to their children upon death, probate is inevitable. The problem of probate may also arise in the event of incapacitation.

In such situations, a land trust is a vehicle for your customers to use. Because a land trust is indeed a trust, and trust assets avoid probate, a land trust can contain contingent beneficiary language that provides for successive transfer of the assets absent probate. The trust can state that the use and enjoyment of the property can be passed on to successor takers (spouse, children, grandchildren) without giving future beneficiaries an immediate interest. Dad can pass to Mom, Mom to children, children to grandchildren. Rather than owning their home in joint-tenancy, Ralph and Betty could transfer (convey or deed) the house out of joint tenancy into a land trust created by Ralph or Ralph-and-Betty. Here is a sample of what the beneficiary language could look like:

> Ralph Crawford solely during his lifetime and upon his death, all right, title, and interest in and under this trust agreement, including any and all powers vested in him during his lifetime, shall pass to his wife, Betty Crawford, or in the event of her death before the death of said Ralph Crawford, to his daughter, Alice Crawford, provided that Ralph Crawford, during his lifetime, shall have the unqualified right to revoke or terminate this trust agreement and to assign or change the beneficial interest hereof in any manner whatsoever, including the right to cause the trust property to be conveyed to others, by means of sale, mortgage, lease, or other disposition, and receive the proceeds therefrom.

Similar arrangements can be accomplished with tenancy-in-common property. Curly, Moe, Larry, and Shemp own a shopping mall. Curly owns 25 percent, Moe owns 20 percent, Larry owns 15 percent, and Shemp owns 40 percent. When any of them dies, his ownership share will pass through probate according to the terms of his will (or intestate succession absent a will). These four individuals could establish a land trust, convey the property into the trust, and provide beneficiary language. By doing that, they would avoid probate and also simplify the ownership. In addition, they would provide protection and control of their percentage interest in the event of incapacitation.

Protection of Multiple Owners

If the mall that Curly, Moe, Larry, and Shemp own is not in trust, an action against one individual might affect the others. For example, a divorce judgment against Curly could place a lien against the property. (In contrast, judgment against Curly does not automatically result in a lien on the trust real property.)

In many instances, one of several co-owners of real property has an absolute right, through what is called a **partition** suit, to compel an actual division of the real estate or force its sale. Courts hold that real property in a land trust cannot be so partitioned because a beneficiary's interest in the trust is one of intangible personal property, not real property.

Land Development

Land trusts also offer customers respite from the details of land development paperwork. Henry's grandfather died 30 years ago, shortly after Henry graduated from college. Grandpa willed his 200-acre farm to Henry, who didn't continue the farming operation and left the land vacant, unimproved, and inoperative. Today, Henry plans to divide the land into 100 two-acre plots and to build an expensive house on each lot. As the houses are built and bought, ownership title will transfer to 100 individual purchasers. What a lot of activity and paperwork! By comparison, a land trust can provide that as lots are sold and developed, the trustee will execute the paperwork to transfer title of each lot to each individual buyer. Numerous parcels may be conveyed (transferred) into a single land trust and then conveyed individually as parcels are sold.

Fractional Interests

What if Grandpa willed the farm 25 percent to Henry, 25 percent to Henry's sister, 30 percent to Henry's dad, and 20 percent to a cousin? A land trust provides an easy vehicle for creating and transferring fractional interests to each beneficiary, as opposed to the complicated title paperwork associated with tenants owning their shares with each as sole owner, or in the percentage ownership of one continuous piece of property as tenants in common. Furthermore, if Henry sells his interest to his cousin, transfer of ownership is accomplished without formal requirements.

Avoidance of Probate

The trust agreement may provide for the transfer of a beneficiary's interest upon death. Because the property (corpus) is indeed in trust, land trusts bypass probate and preserve privacy.

Avoidance of Ancillary Probate

Consider the value of a land trust as it applies to a more complicated scenario facing your customer. Grandpa was a resident of Iowa. When he died, his will was probated in Iowa. Regardless of the fact that his farm was in Illinois, it too had to be probated, but on an ancillary basis. *Ancillary*, in this instance, means Grandpa's Iowa property was probated in Iowa under Iowa probate laws, and the Illinois property was probated in Illinois under Illinois probate rules. Grandpa could have avoided the time and expense to his overall estate by establishing a land trust with an Illinois trust company as trustee of his Illinois property. Trust assets are not probatable assets.

Advantages to the Bank

In Cook County, Illinois' most populous and real-estate-dense county, four out of five parcels (personally and commercially owned) are estimated to be held or to have been held at one time by land trusts. The many advantages to customers account for this widespread use of land trusts. These advantages also translate into income and profitability to land trust departments.

Income and Profitability

One particular bank in Cook County serves 47,000 land trusts containing just over 250,000 parcels of real estate. With fees on

---

MANAGING TRUST DEPARTMENTS IN A COMPETITIVE ENVIRONMENT

Years ago, time permitted us to make three shopping stops: for beef at the butcher shop, for green beans at the fruit-and-vegetable store, and for aspirin at the pharmacy. Today people opt for the megastore, where specialized aisles fulfill virtually every consumer need. In the same way, customers would rather move from floor to floor of their bank building than drive from institution to institution for personal and commercial banking needs, employee benefit planning, land trust and personal trust products, and investment management. If XYZ Bank cannot offer customers what they need, the customers will probably go elsewhere.

By selling many goods under one roof, the food store chains take business away from smaller one-product shops. In today's competitive environment, XYZ Bank must offer more than "green beans." If not, wealthy customers who feel land is the only thing in the world that amounts to anything will cease doing business with XYZ Bank and move to the competitor down the street.

the value of the properties ranging from $100 to over $7,000 each, this bank generates an annual fee revenue of over $8 million—an important source of income.

Land trust business is profitable for trust departments because of volume, uniform administration and operating procedures, abbreviated recordkeeping, absence of the physical custody of assets, and minimal accounting and statements. There are no income tax reporting requirements and only minimal government filing or reporting requirements.

Cross-Selling

Land trust services also expand a bank's customer base, attracting prospective customers to the bank's other trust services (personal, employee benefit, corporate) and personal and commercial banking relationships. Land trust facilities provide existing banking and trust customers with another important service expected of a full-service bank. Additionally, mortgage lending departments can provide a source of high-net-worth individuals, real estate management companies, real estate developers, and brokers for cross-referral purposes, a practice commonly known as cross-selling.

In states where land trust statutes exist, it is surprising that trust departments of many larger banks do not offer land trust services. Perhaps the standardization of land trust procedures works better in a smaller institution, where minimal personnel are available and needed to service a large customer base. Nonetheless, trust departments of any size that do not offer a wide range of products and services may lose a competitive edge.

SUMMARY

- Land trusts originated in feudal English common law. The law of primogeniture and the Statute of Uses laid the groundwork for the arrangement by which one person holds property for the use of another: a trust.

- Land trusts, which exist in only eight states, are a legal device under which a trustee holds title to real estate for the use and benefit of others. The trust's beneficiary holds an intangible personal property right in the real property and retains full responsibility for the management and control of the property. The trustee's duties are limited by the beneficiary's power of direction.

- Although land trusts have the same ingredients as personal trusts, they differ from personal trusts in the following ways:
  - The grantor and beneficiary can be an individual, partnership, or corporation.
  - They can hold only real property.
  - The trust agreement is usually a prototype document.
  - The trustee holds equitable ownership.
  - The form of property is one of intangible personal property.
  - The trust has a predetermined termination date, which can be extended by amendment.

- Land trusts offer the following advantages to the trust customer:
  - Privacy of ownership
  - Simple transfer of ownership
  - Centralized management of property
  - Collateral use
  - Ease of altering beneficial interests
  - Protection of multiple owners
  - Land development
  - Fractional interests
  - Avoidance of local and ancillary probate

- Land trust business offers advantages to trust departments: income, profits, and the benefits of cross-selling bank products and services through the land trust department's base of attorney contacts, commercial banking customers, and mortgage holders. To this we can add the ability to meet the competition by offering multifaceted, one-stop shopping to our customers.

REVIEW QUESTIONS

1. Personal trusts are found everywhere. Which states recognize land trusts and why do the other states not recognize them?

2. List at least five differences between land trusts and personal trusts.

3. What is the difference between a land trust and a personal trust with respect to how long they can last?

4. Give at least five examples of how a land trust benefits a trust customer.

10

EMPLOYEE BENEFIT TRUST AND AGENCY SERVICES

"When a man retires and time is no longer a matter of urgent importance, his colleagues generally present him with a clock."

R. C. Sherriff (1896–1975)

According to a 1996 Social Security Administration bulletin, 52 percent of Americans over age 60 and 41 percent of those over age 50 do not have a pension plan. A 1996 Merrill Lynch survey of 800 preretirees and baby-boomers confirmed that. That report concluded that less than half of those surveyed are saving anything for retirement, yet many are expecting to retire early and don't think Social Security will be a significant source of income for them. This is a paradox. With inflation, rising taxes, and an unpredictable economy, the reality is that most Americans will not be financially independent at retirement.

Financial advisors agree that in order to maintain an adequate standard of living after retirement, at least 60 to 70 percent of final preretirement income—adjusted for inflation—is needed. America's inflation rate has ranged during the last three decades from a high of 13.3 percent in 1979 to a low of 1.4 percent in 1998. Assuming that inflation in the coming years will continue at the past 30-year average of 3.1 percent, a person making $80,000 today would require an income of $126,465 fifteen years from now to maintain the same standard of living. These same advisors suggest it is possible to achieve financial retirement objectives by adhering to the key rules of starting early, saving regularly, and using tax-deferred investments. With the third rule, employers and the services of trust departments come into play.

LEARNING OBJECTIVES

Employee benefits come in various shapes, forms, and amounts. Beyond the standard benefits of employment—an income, paid vacation days, and a medical plan—an employer may offer a dental program, paid sick days, life and disability insurance coverage, and child care and legal assistance programs, to name only a few. These **employee**

benefit plans, costing employers 37.5 percent of company payrolls (according to a 2001 U.S. Chamber of Commerce study, an average cost of $16,617 over wages per employee), are commonly called **fringe benefits.** The largest and most expensive of these benefits is the retirement plan, the centerpiece of a corporate employee benefit package.

Upon completion of this chapter, you will be able to

- Identify employee benefit programs
- Describe the types of corporate retirement plans
- Define an individual retirement account
- List the requirements for a retirement plan to be qualified
- Distinguish the differences between qualified and nonqualified plans
- Profile the entities involved in establishing and administering a retirement plan
- Define and use the terms that appear in bold in the text

EMPLOYEE BENEFIT PROGRAMS

Employee benefit programs are benefits that an employer offers to employees over and above salary. Employee benefit programs are often called fringe benefit or welfare benefit plans and pension plans.

- *Employee Benefit Welfare Program.* Any one or several plans established by an employer or employee organization for the purpose of providing the following services for plan participants or their beneficiaries: health insurance, sick leave, vacation, short- and long-term disability pay, training, and any other fringe benefits exclusive of retirement plans.

- *Employee Benefit Pension Program.* Any one or several plans, funds, or programs that are established or maintained by an employer that provide retirement income to employees or result in a deferral of income by employees for use in retirement.

Beyond the benefits already mentioned, an extensive array of welfare programs has evolved over the years. Employers can offer:

- Legal services
- Stock options
- Auto insurance
- Physical exams

- Dental insurance
- Sick days
- Severance pay
- Employee assistance program
- Bonus/incentive compensation
- Dependent care
- Life insurance
- Travel and entertainment
- Moving expenses
- Adoption assistance
- Service awards
- Tuition reimbursement
- Long-term care insurance
- Vision care
- Personal property insurance
- Parking and commuting reimbursement

Employers are not bound by law to provide employee benefit programs, and when employers do provide benefits, they are not bound to pay for them. Further, when they offer benefits, companies must determine whether to pay for the benefit(s)or to share the expenses with its employees and in what percentages. Companies must also decide whether to provide the benefits before tax, after tax, or a combination.

RETIREMENT PLAN HISTORY

Preserving wealth for retirement is an integral aspect of estate and financial planning. With today's increased life expectancies, retirement years are longer, yet they can be financially challenging for the unprepared.

Social Plans

Recognizing the need for retirement planning, society has addressed the perplexities of retirement with government programs for providing economic security and welfare plans that help to defray the loss or deficiency of income due to sickness, unemployment, and old age.

The first formal social security program was established in Germany in the 1880s. Great Britain's program began in 1911. Unlike the United States, whose program was established under the Social Security Act of 1935, most countries provide complete funding of the program without employee contributions. Social Security is a basic program, not an answer-all. Sometimes called the OASDHI (old age, survivor, disability, health insurance), the program is funded by employer and employee contributions.

The following facts provide a quick summary of the Social Security retirement program. For 2003:

- Employees are taxed (contribute) 6.2 percent (up to $87,000 of wages) for non-medical benefits.

- Employees are taxed (contribute) 1.45 percent (no limit on wages) for Medicare.

- Employers match (contribute) an amount equal to the two previous amounts.

- Social Security retirement benefits may be taxable depending on one's income level.

- Social Security retirement payments are reduced $1 for every $2 of income earned over $11,520 for recipients age 62 to 65.

Employer Plans

Formal corporate retirement plans have existed for more than a century. But only in the past 40 to 50 years have they seen substantial growth. Yesterday's less urban society viewed life and retirement in a different perspective. Most people felt they would "die with their boots on." If a worker did retire (which most of the time was not voluntary), families were close enough that the oldsters lived with the youngsters.

In the early 1950s, in an attempt to revitalize the economy, the government imposed wage and price freezes. Employers had difficulty recognizing valuable, veteran employees with pay raises. But the competitor across town could woo the key employee away by offering a larger salary. When an essential employee said he was leaving for another job, there wasn't much the employer could do to entice him to stay, other than a promise to pay more tomorrow.

Telling employees they will get more money, but not today, was an empty way of thanking them for a job well done. What the employer could do was promise to pay them later, when their working years ended. This is called a retirement plan. Here was a way to reward employees for their long years of faithful work. Retirement plans became a main attraction. Given the choice of working for ABC Corporation for $17 per hour or XYZ Company for $16 per hour plus a retirement plan, key employees were more likely to stay at XYZ. Retirement plans therefore became a way of not only retaining and rewarding employees, but also attracting them. The value of this employee benefit fueled its own growth, which today is estimated to be a $6+ trillion industry.

As we introduce the various types of retirement plans and the laws that govern them, keep the five-ingredient concept of trusts in mind. The terms and concepts will be used frequently and explored again at the chapter's end, when establishment of retirement plans is discussed.

In Chapter 7 we stated that a personal trust is created by an individual for individuals. An employee benefit trust is created by a corporation for individuals. Other than this simple distinction and the different set of laws that governs employee benefit retirement plans, the trust concept differs further in terminology:

	Personal Trust	Employee Benefit Trust
Grantor	Individual	Corporation (the **sponsor**)
Trustee	Individual or corporation	Individual or corporation
Corpus	Personal or real property	Annual **contributions,** which are determined by formula
Beneficiary	Individuals or charity	Employees (**participants**)
Trust agreement	Personalized document	Individually prepared or prototype document

CORPORATE RETIREMENT PLANS

Although employees do not see the financial benefits of retirement plans until later years, the money that is contributed by an employer is nonetheless a form of compensation: **deferred compensation.** What began years ago as a simple plan to set money aside for employees' retirement years has today become a complex environment of laws, reporting systems, investment direction, and choice of plans in the largest known pool of money. This chapter addresses the basic retirement plan structures employers use today. Our knowledge of how these plans work makes our tasks as professional planners easier when we provide guidance on choice of plan, construction of the plan, fiduciary responsibility, and investment management for our customers.

Despite the magnitude of money contributed to retirement plans by employers, these dollars alone will not make for a financially comfortable retirement. As we will see in this chapter, it is imperative that employees also contribute toward their retirement funds in addition to saving outside of formal retirement plans.

According to a recent study ("Promises to Keep: How Leaders and the Public Respond to Saving and Retirement" from the Public Agenda Foundation and Employee Benefit Research Institute) the way we save—or don't save—for retirement is governed by personality. Four distinct patterns influence how individuals approach financial planning.

- *Planners* are in control of their finances and are twice as likely as others to own three or more retirement investments and put money into them regularly. They are disciplined, less conservative in their investment strategies, and usually respond to incentives to increase savings. Planners are confident that they're doing everything possible to accumulate a retirement nest egg.

- *Strugglers* want to save for retirement but believe they don't earn enough money. Unpredictable expenses prevent them from making regular contributions to a plan. Anxious for greater financial discipline, they generally prefer investments that keep cash out of reach and don't need their attention.

- *Deniers* view retirement as far off and believe financing will take care of itself. Saving for a house or for college seems more important. Most won't give up extras. They are apt to contend that they may not live long enough to enjoy retirement. Conventional savings strategies don't work. Deniers avoid instruments that feature automatic salary deductions or put savings out of reach.

- *Impulsives* are motivated by immediate gratification and tend to buy things they don't need. Part of the don't-worry-be-happy group, the more money they earn, the more they spend. They are reluctant to choose savings options to help them overcome these traits. Fewer than half want investments that can be deducted automatically from their salaries and only 30 percent favor investments that are difficult to access.

Many individuals are not planning ahead effectively. As financial professionals, we can suggest strategies to help our customers better prepare for their future.

Defined Contribution Plans

In contrast to defined benefit plans (discussed later), which predetermine retirement benefits and not contributions, a **defined contribution plan** predetermines the contributions to the plan and not the future benefits. The basic defined contribution plans are money purchase, profit sharing, 401(k), 403(b), and employee stock ownership plans (ESOPs).

Money Purchase Plans

In this type of defined contribution plan, the employer chooses a fixed (defined, predetermined) contribution to be made into the plan each year on behalf of each employee (participant). This plan allows the employer to control how much it will contribute toward employees' retirement. For example, the employer may pick a percentage of compensation (say, 10 percent of each employee's annual income). If the employer's total salary expenditure this year for all employees is $1,500,000, a $150,000 contribution will be made to the retirement plan. If an individual employee's salary is $30,000, then $3,000 will be contributed to the plan for that employee. In this type of plan, the amount of contributions is easily known each year. Eventual retirement benefits depend on the amount of contributions made (which are determined by the employer's contribution formula, employee compensation, and number of employed years), plan expenses, and investment performance.

Profit Sharing Plans

Although retirement plans are instituted by employers to attract employees, foster allegiance, and provide a reward for years of employment, early plans were not very generous. With the growth of company profits, employers instituted the profit sharing plan as a retirement supplement to pension plans. **Profit sharing plans** are designed to reward employees for the contribution they make to a company's profit. At the root of this plan is the incentive for employees to work smarter and harder, with the result being higher profits to the company, which in turn are shared with the employees.

In a profit sharing plan an employer is not under any strict commitment with regard to the contributions to the plan. An employer can retain the right to decide annually whether to make contributions. It is doubtful that a company with a healthy profit would not make a contribution to its profit sharing plan unless there is a compelling reason to maintain the profits for other company purposes. Interestingly, an employer can choose to make a profit sharing contribution even if the company doesn't make a profit.

The contributions to the plan can be determined by a definite formula (such as 10 percent of the company's profits, before taxes) or by a discretionary method (for example, the company's board of directors determines the amount of contribution to be made each year). Regardless of the formula or method used, contributions are allocated among the individual participants. As in all defined contribution plans, the contribution formula is defined—the benefits are not.

Benefits are paid to the employees from the plan upon the occurrence of certain events (attainment of a certain age, death, layoff, disability, employment termination) or annually (or any other discretionary basis) as a cash bonus.

401(k) Plans

Expanded lifestyles, earlier retirement ages, varying investment results, and the impact of inflation cause basic Social Security and employer-funded retirement plans to fall short of a retiree's financial needs at retirement.

Employers recognized this problem but were hesitant to bolster retirement plan benefits because of the heavy cost.

The government, also aware of this problem, enacted legislation that allows employees to share in and add to the building of their retirement funds on a tax-preferred basis. One such way is the 401(k) plan, named after the section of the Internal Revenue Code that governs this type of plan.

401(k) plans are the most popular and fastest growing retirement plans. According to the most recent statistics from the Employee Benefits Security Administration, more than 300,000 U.S. companies have established 401(k) plans. These plans benefit more than 30 million workers, and their assets exceed $1 trillion.

A 401(k) plan, also called a *salary reduction plan,* is a defined contribution plan, established by employers, into which employees (and perhaps employers) make contributions. The employee's contribution to the plan is subtracted (withheld) from her annual income, thus reducing reportable income and, consequently, income taxes. The contributions and earnings of the plan grow tax-deferred until benefits are taken from the plan, usually at retirement, when the benefits are taxed.

Understanding how employee and employer contributions work will help you when assisting a corporate customer and its employees to construct a 401(k) plan.

Employee Contributions

In essence, in an employee contribution plan, employees take (or share) the responsibility for their retirement future. An employee elects to defer receipt of a portion of his annual compensation. The plan's formula will structure the deferral as a percentage of salary. This is another element of defined contribution. Under current law, the maximum amount that an employee can defer is 15 percent of income, subject to a maximum amount of

$12,000 for 2003
$13,000 for 2004
$14,000 for 2005
$15,000 for 2006

Maximum dollar contributions in 2007 and subsequent years will be indexed for inflation in $500 increments.

Let's work with an example. Suppose a company's plan allows an employee to defer any amount, up to 8 percent of salary. If annual salary (compensation) from the employer is $40,000, the employee can defer (set aside into the plan) a maximum of $3,200. The employee's W-2 for the year will report taxable income of $36,800 ($40,000 minus $3,200). Thus, the employee's income taxes for the year will be less because taxes are calculated on an income of $36,800, not $40,000. The $3,200 is placed in an individual plan account, and contributions and earnings grow tax-deferred.

A 401(k) plan also can allow the employee to make additional voluntary after-tax (nondeductible) contributions beyond the limits stated above. The voluntary contributions are not a reduction from salary for tax purposes. Think of the added contributions as regular additions to a bank savings account. The difference, though, is that the earnings on the voluntary contributions also grow tax-deferred. The IRS places an annual limit ($40,000 in 2002—indexed for inflation in $1,000 increments in subsequent years) on all contributions to a 401(k) plan. This includes the employee's salary-reduction amount, voluntary employee contributions, and employer contributions.

Other advantages of 401(k) programs include the following:

- Employees are immediately 100 percent vested in their contributions. (We will discuss vesting later in this chapter.)
- Participants can start or stop contributions and change the contribution percentage during the course of the year, subject to plan specifics.
- When an employee leaves his company, he can roll the account into an IRA (discussed later in this chapter) or perhaps to a new company's 401(k) plan.

Employer Contributions

Law does not require an employer to make contributions to a 401(k) plan, but an employer may elect to do so by matching the employees' contributions, to a certain degree. For example, the employer may make contributions on a 1-for-2 basis, meaning the employer will contribute $1 into the plan for every $2 the employee contributes. Using this formula with the previous example, the total contribution to the plan would be $4,800: the employee's $3,200 plus the employer's 1-for-2 contribution of $1,600.

Variations on employer contributions include the following:

- Employer stock as opposed to cash
- Discretionary contributions
  - An equal contribution (in cash or other securities) per employee regardless of age, number of years of employment, position, and compensation
  - A lump-sum amount payable to the plan and then divided among employees proportionate to their compensation
  - An equal percentage proportionate to employee compensation

If an employer elects to contribute to the plan—in a way other than a specified matching formula—contributions must be made on behalf of all employees regardless of whether an employee does or does not contribute to the plan.

Plan Investments

Most 401(k) plans are designed as individual account plans. This arrangement allows each participant to direct the investment of her funds, most commonly among investment funds preselected by the plan sponsor. Future benefits are based on contributions (employer and employee), income, gains and losses, and plan expenses. Each participant, in essence, has an individual account—a mini-plan, so to speak—within the overall employer-provided plan.

Although the individual participants in a 401(k) plan exercise investment direction over their respective accounts, this does not make the participant (employee) a fiduciary of her plan assets. But the participant cannot hold the plan's trustee accountable for fiduciary responsibilities with respect to individual investment decisions and eventual performance, unless the trustee does not carry out the participant's instructions, such as asset allocation.

Asset Allocation

A 401(k) in which a participant directs the investments places a burden on the participant. "How should I direct the investments? How should I allocate my funds to provide adequate retirement funds?" Inherent in these questions is the consideration of asset allocation (see Chapter 3) and risk tolerance (see Chapter 4).

When planning investment choices, a participant must consider his number of years until retirement, inflation rates, and risk–return relationships (see Exhibits 4.3 and 4.4) of various asset classes. The participant must also consider other assets, income and investments (for example, equity in real property), other retirement plans and IRA assets, and savings.

Younger participants may wish to allocate a larger percentage of their funds to growth investments (stock, for example). Older participants may wish to allocate a larger percentage to fixed-income investments that provide capital preservation. A participant in the 40 to 55 age range may want to allocate his investments as follows:

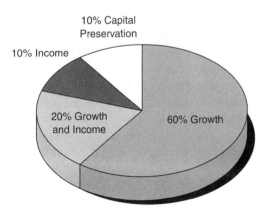

Trust professionals can be instrumental in helping plan participants review their financial situations, define their risk tolerance, and construct asset allocation over the years.

To Save or Not to Save

Saving money is difficult. Retirement plans, such as 401(k) plans, give employees an opportunity to save for retirement. Although the contributions reduce take-home pay, they are easily deducted from the paycheck. What an employee doesn't get today brings more tomorrow. An added advantage to a 401(k) plan is that contributions are subtracted from current taxable income and the growth of contributions and earnings is tax-deferred. Let's work with an example.

Let's suppose that at age 30 Jenny established a savings program to set aside $3,000 per year. She anticipates doing this for the next 30 years. Assume that the interest she receives on her savings is a constant 6 percent. Three thousand dollars per year with a compound interest of 6 percent for 30 years would give her approximately $237,000 at age 60 (see Exhibit 2.1). But what about taxes?

Although Jenny set aside $90,000 of principal ($3,000 per year for 30 years), the $147,000 of interest ($237,000 minus $90,000) is taxable income, which she must report and pay income taxes on each year. Assuming Jenny is in the 31 percent federal tax bracket (we'll ignore state and local taxation in this example), after the payment of income taxes each year her net interest is approximately $101,000 ($147,000 times 69 percent).

If Jenny placed her $3,000 each year in a 401(k) plan, the 6 percent interest grows tax deferred (that is, it is not currently taxed). When Jenny begins to take distributions from the plan at age 60, the distributions will be taxable, but she will probably be in a lower tax bracket. Jenny is saving for retirement on a tax-deferred basis, and she will probably pay less tax in the future. Let's look at these calculations side by side.

Savings Program		401(k) Plan
$ 3,000 (1)	Amount saved each year	$ 3,000 (1)
90,000 (2)	Amount saved in 30 years	90,000 (2)
147,000 (3)	Interest earned	147,000 (3)
45,600 (4)	Taxes paid	0 (4)
101,400 (5)	Net interest earned	147,000 (5)
191,400 (6)	Net balance in 30 years (2 + 5)	237,000 (6)

The $3,000 Jenny contributes to her 401(k) plan is deducted from her gross pay. Therefore, her W-2 form reflects a lower taxable income, which reduces her income taxes for the year. Three thousand dollars less taxable income means $930 ($3,000 times 31 percent tax bracket) less in income taxes. In essence, Jenny's take-home pay is only $2,070 less ($3,000 minus $930). In other words, Jenny's $90,000 of contributions cost her only $62,100 ($2,070 times 30 years). This makes the $237,000 at age 60 more impressive because it cost less to get there.

403(b) Plans

Prior to recent legislation (most notably the Economic Growth and Tax Relief Reconciliation Act of 2001), 403(b) plans possessed a few similarities and many differences in comparison to 401(k) plans. Today these two plans differ primarily only with respect to the participants.

A **403(b) plan** is a defined contribution plan available to educators, healthcare workers, and employees of religious institutions and nonprofit organizations. 403(b) plans are also known as tax-sheltered annuity (TSA) and tax-deferred annuity (TDA) plans. At one time these plans could only invest in **annuity** contracts. Except for religious institutions, 403(b) plans are governed by ERISA (discussed shortly).

Employee Stock Ownership Plans (ESOP)

A fairly recent development in retirement planning is the **employee stock ownership plan (ESOP)**. In most instances ESOPs are used as a supplement to an employer's basic retirement plans. Whereas all retirement plans invest in a variety of investment vehicles—either in individual securities or through a funds approach—ESOPs are unique in that the plan's investments are concentrated entirely or mostly in securities of the employer.

An ESOP not only provides a source of retirement funds; it also gives the employees an opportunity to own the company they work for. Similar to a profit sharing plan, an ESOP serves as a medium for placing the strength and growth of the company in the employees' hands. ESOP plans give employees the opportunity to control the fate of their company and eventual retirement funds. Because sufficient retirement dollars hinge on investment performance, employees are motivated to contribute directly to their company's effectiveness and efficiency, which therefore increases the company's worth, which therefore adds to increased retirement funds. On the other side of the coin, there is an investment risk in having all your eggs in one basket. Investment professionals constantly emphasize the importance of investment asset allocation and diversification. ESOPS stare into the face of this concept. One wrong turn by the company (such as the recent Enron collapse) can easily turn an ESOP plan into a nightmare.

Defined Benefit Plans

Defined contribution plans have a lackluster popularity because of their uncertainty about amounts available at retirement. Only assumptions can be made about contribution levels, number of years of employment, compensation, and investment performance. Employees prefer to know what their retirement benefits will be in order to avoid retirement plan shortfalls. Employer-sponsored retirement plans migrated from defined contribution to defined benefit plans, then moved later again to defined contribution plans based on the expense and administrative overload requirements of defined benefit plans.

A **defined benefit plan** (also referred to by many as a *target plan*) does not define the contributions; it defines (targets, predetermines) up front what the employee's retirement benefit will be when she retires. These plans are funded entirely by the employer, and the responsibility for the payment of benefits and all risks associated with the monies invested to fund the benefit rest with the employer. The calculations made to determine the annual contributions required to meet the retirement benefit are aided by actuarial services. (See the discussion of an actuary later in this chapter.)

The benefits payable upon retirement are usually made in the form of an annuity distribution. The ultimate defined retirement benefits are determined by the benefit formula chosen by the employer. Examples of the common benefit formulas (in order of descending common usage) are

- *Unit benefit.* A retirement benefit equal to a certain percent (say, 2) of final pay times the number of years an employee is in the plan

- *Flat benefit.* A retirement benefit of 50 percent of compensation regardless of the number of years the participant was in the plan; compensation may be computed using a "career average" formula (compensation averaged over an employee's entire career with the employer) or a "final average' formula (such as the average compensation for the employee's three to five years of compensation immediately prior to retirement)

- *Fixed benefit.* A benefit of a set amount (say, $300 per month, a *floor*) at retirement for all participants regardless of final pay and years of service

- *Cash balance.* A fairly new benefit formula that is being criticized because of the potential erosion of plan benefits at retirement based on the calculation; this formula provides a participant with a hypothetical amount that increases or decreases annually as a result of a participant's compensation and a guaranteed interest credit stated in the plan

Again, the onus of hitting the target rests with the plan, which is designed to continually (actuarially) adjust its sights—adjust to employee turnover, morbidity and mortality experience, and investment performance—to meet the defined benefit. In most plans, adjustments are made to the contributions each year.

Retirement planning can be confusing and complicated to employer and employee alike. Exhibit 10.1 lists references that will help a trust professional assist customers.

INDIVIDUAL RETIREMENT PLANS

So far we have explored various retirement plans that are provided by employers. We also emphasized the importance of this planning to employers and employees alike. But not all businesses provide retirement plans for their employees. Despite the magnitude of retirement plans, law has never dictated that an employer must provide a retirement plan for employees, other than the employer contributions to the Social Security system. Therefore, in 1974 the Employee Retirement Income Security Act (ERISA), which we will discuss in more detail later in the chapter, created an opportunity for working Americans who do not participate in an employer-sponsored retirement plan to establish their own personal individual retirement plan: the **individual retirement account (IRA).** IRA rules have changed dramatically since 1974, so much so that today anyone—including employees covered by an employer plan—can establish an IRA.

Contributory IRA

A **contributory IRA** is an individual retirement account—a personal retire-

ment plan—into which *eligible* individuals *may* make annual *tax-deductible* contributions with the benefit of tax deferral on the investment earnings of the contributions. Whether an individual is "eligible," whether he "may" make a contribution, and whether the contribution is "tax deductible" depends upon a complex set of rules. The reader should consult IRS Publications 575, 590, and 970 for an in-depth analysis of IRAs.

Several types of IRAs currently exist:

- Traditional IRA
- Spousal IRA
- Roth IRA
- Education IRA
- SIMPLE (Savings Incentive Match Plan for Employees) IRA
- SEP (Simplified Employee Pension) IRA

An individual's employment status, income level, and tax objectives will determine which one or more of these IRAs are applicable or desirable. It is beyond the scope of this section to discuss the particulars of existing IRAs, especially in light of pending legislation that may change the scope of IRA eligibility, deduction, and contribution limits.

In general, with respect to a traditional IRA, an individual is limited to a maximum contribution of the lesser of $3,000 or 100 percent of earned income. The Economic Growth and Tax Relief Reconciliation Act of 2001 raised the individual limit to $4,000 for 2005–2007 and $5,000 for 2008. After 2008, IRA contribution limits will be indexed for inflation each year in $500 increments. From here the rules get complicated and vary according to the participant's circumstances:

- Is the IRA participant single or married?
- Does either spouse participate (actively) in an employer-maintained retirement plan?
- Does a married couple file a joint tax return or separate returns?
- What year is it?

Exhibit 10.1   Retirement Plan Reference Guides

- "Savings Fitness: A Guide to Your Money and Your Financial Future"
  This is a guide developed by the U.S. Department of Labor (DOL) and the Certified Financial Planner Board of Standards. The booklet addresses key financial planning issues, including assessing financial situations, establishing goals, creating a savings habit, building investments, using appropriate retirement savings plans, and keeping track of progress toward savings goals. The 20-page booklet can be downloaded from the DOL's web site at www.dol.gov or obtained by calling 1-800-998-7542.

- "IRA & QRP Compliance Update"
  This monthly newsletter from the Pension Management Company of Malvern, PA., provides technical guidance and current regulatory updates pertaining to IRAs (individual retirement accounts) and QRPs (qualified retirement plans).

- "What You Should Know About the Pension Law"
  U.S. Department of Labor booklet.

- "Guide to IRAs, SEPs, and Keoghs"
  Research Institute of America publication.

- "Tools and Techniques of Retirement Planning"
  A comprehensive study of retirement plans published by the National Underwriter Company, Erlanger, KY.

- IRS Publication 590
  This publication covers most of the basic rules for IRAs. It devotes a complete chapter to each type of IRA and includes an alphabetical index, applicable IRS forms, contribution and deduction worksheets, and quick-reference charts. The publication also includes the majority of the life expectancy tables to be used to calculate required minimum distribution amounts. Although this publication is no substitute for advice from a competent tax professional, many financial organizations find that answers to many of the questions posed by IRA owners and beneficiaries can be found in this publication.

- IRS Publication 575
  This publication will help individuals determine the tax on QRP distributions. It also shows how to report QRP distributions, and it discusses the rules for rollovers from QRPs to IRAs. Although it is designed for taxpayers who receive a distribution from a qualified retirement plan or an annuity, this publication is very helpful to tax professionals, tax preparers, and plan administrators.

- IRS Publication 970
  This IRS publication will be especially helpful to taxpayers who have expenses for higher education. It discusses the education tax credits available through the Hope Credit and the Lifetime Learning Credit. It also includes a chapter on IRAs, including the Education IRA rules and the exception to the IRS 10 percent early distribution penalty for higher education expenses. The publication also discusses education savings bonds, state tuition programs, student loans, and employer-provided educational assistance.

IRS publications may be obtained from the IRS without charge. IRS forms and publications can be ordered by calling 1-800-TAX-FORM (829-3676). IRS forms and publications can also be downloaded from the IRS web site located at www.irs.ustreas.gov.

The answers to these questions determine if an individual can obtain a full or partial tax deduction—or none at all—on his or her federal income tax return. Exhibit 10.2 is a partial presentation based on the 2001 rules. These numbers may change in subsequent years.

Rollover IRA

Upon retirement (or upon preretirement separation from employment), employees face several decisions. Should plan benefits be delayed into the future (not everyone who retires needs to take an immediate distribution from his retirement plans)? Which distribution option should be cho-

sen? Should benefits be taken in monthly installments? Should the plan benefits be taken as a **lump sum distribution** (if the plan permits)? Trust departments that act as trustees or investment managers of plan assets should provide direction to their corporate and individual customers regarding these issues. Depending on the solution, trust departments have an opportunity to further assist their customers with rollover IRA products and services, investment management of these funds, and tax guidance.

It is not uncommon for trust departments to see $1-million lump sum distributions. Employees who build large retirement nest eggs will need investment

Exhibit 10.2	IRA Deduction Rules			
Federal Income Tax Filing Status	Year	Full Deduction (if MAGI* is at or below)	Partial Deduction (if MAGI is more than/less than)	No Deduction (if MAGI is at or above)
Single (not an active participant)	Any year	No limit	N/A	N/A
Single (active participant)	2003	$40,000	$40,000/$50,000	$50,000
Married, filing jointly (neither is active)	Any year	No limit	N/A	N/A
Married, filing jointly (active)	2003	$60,000	$60,000/$70,000	$70,000
Married, filing jointly (not active, but spouse is)	Any year	$150,000	$150,000/$160,000	$160,000
Married, filing separately (not active)	Any year	No limit	N/A	N/A
Married, filing separately (active)	Any year	N/A	$0/$10,000	$10,000

* MAGI is modified adjusted gross income. Refer to the IRS rules to determine how to calculate this amount.

expertise to manage these funds properly, just as they were managed while in the qualified plan. The opportunity for rollover business will increase as retirement benefits grow and the baby boom generation reaches retirement age. Trust departments must increase marketing efforts to position themselves to attract these customers.

In its simplest form, a **rollover IRA** is a specialized IRA designed to accept lump-sum distributions from qualified plans. A rollover IRA therefore has no contribution limit. The funds placed in this IRA continue to grow tax-deferred and are subject to the same withdrawal rules as contributory IRAs.

QUALIFIED RETIREMENT PLANS

In the discussion of employer-sponsored plans and individual retirement plans, the word *qualified* was used. Retirement plans can be qualified or nonqualified. A **qualified plan** is one that meets the requirements of the Internal Revenue Code and any supporting laws. The qualification of an employer-sponsored plan allows the employer to deduct its contributions to the plan, thereby reducing corporate income taxes. This is an important benefit to the employer.

Employee Retirement Income Security Act of 1974

Despite retirement plan growth since World War II, there was minimal government regulation and intervention to protect workers' rights. More than 50 million workers were at risk of losing benefits upon job separation, plan termination, inadequate funding, and improper investment management. In 1974 the **Employee Retirement Income Security Act (ERISA)** was enacted. ERISA set forth requirements that provide rights, protections, safeguards, and guarantees for participants and their beneficiaries. ERISA has since been modified, further defined, and supplemented by the following legislation:

- Multi-employer Pension Plan Amendments Act of 1980
- Economic Recovery Tax Act of 1981
- Tax Equity and Fiscal Responsibility Act of 1982
- Retirement Equity Act of 1984
- Tax Reform Act of 1986
- Single Employer Pension Plan Amendments Act of 1986
- Unemployment Compensation Amendments Act of 1992
- Family and Medical Leave Act of 1993
- Pension Annuitants Protection Act of 1994
- Small Business Job Protection Act of 1996
- Taxpayer Relief Act of 1997
- Economic Growth and Tax Relief Reconciliation Act of 2001

These laws set standards that dictate retirement plan protection and the requirements for a retirement plan to be qualified.

Qualification Requirements

For an employer to qualify for the tax deduction of its contributions to an employee benefit plan, the plan must meet the rules of ERISA. ERISA does not define who can serve as trustee. But the following discussion of ERISA shows why employers turn to the experience and knowledge of trust departments.

Plan Exclusiveness

A retirement plan must be established exclusively for the benefit of employees. A plan cannot include nonemployees (such as the owner's spouse and children). The assets of the plan cannot be used for any purpose other than providing benefits for employees, such as borrowing to expand company facilities. When a company uses a corporate trustee (trust department), it can be assured the trustee is familiar with this aspect of the law and that the plan will not violate this exclusiveness provision.

Formal Construction

A plan must be formally adopted by an employer and governed by a plan document. The plan must be qualified from the onset and subsequently through its life by adhering to ERISA standards. In other words, the plan must maintain "form" and "operation." The plan must be adopted no later than the last day of the employer's tax year for which the initial deduction is sought.

Nondiscrimination

Retirement plans cannot discriminate in favor of highly compensated employees (such as officers, directors, board members, and shareholders), who are at times in a position to control the plan. The plan must be structured to treat everyone fairly. **Discrimination** occurs when contributions or benefits are lopsided in favor of a particular group. Although a plan that fixes its contributions as a percentage of salary will see higher contributions made to higher-paid employees than to lower-paid employees, the plan remains qualified if the contributions do not exceed amounts established by law (see next section).

An employer can exclude (discriminate against) certain employees based on age, employee classification, and hours worked. An employer may

- Require employees to be 21 years old before contributions are made on their behalf; an employer does not have to contribute to a plan for employees under the age of 18; if a company elects to begin coverage of employees over 18 years of age, employees must be 100 percent vested when they enter the plan (vesting is discussed shortly)
- Require employees to complete up to 2 years of employment before they are eligible to participate in the plan; if more than one year of service is required for eligibility, employees must be 100 percent vested when they enter the plan

- Exclude union employees if retirement benefits have been the subject of good-faith bargaining
- Exclude employees who are nonresident aliens with no U.S. taxable income from the employer
- Exclude part-time (defined as less than 1,000 hours per year) employees, seasonal workers, and leased employees

An experienced trustee will carefully monitor these discrimination factors.

Contribution Limits

For a plan to remain qualified it must maintain contribution and benefit limits. Trust departments are familiar with the complicated details and dollar amounts pertaining to plan contributions and the exceptions and additional rules applicable to employers that maintain more than one retirement plan.

The applicable limits are as follows:

- *Annual compensation limits.* For 2002, the maximum amount that can be taken into account is $200,000; thereafter, compensation is indexed with inflation in $5,000 increments.
- *Annual contribution limits.* For 2002, the maximum amount is the lesser of $40,000 (indexed for inflation thereafter in $1,000 increments) or 100 percent for all contributions (tax-deductible and non-tax-deductible employee and employer contributions).
- *Limit on payable benefit.* For 2002, either $160,000 (and thereafter indexed for inflation in $5,000 increments) or 100 percent of a participant's average compensation is the limit; this limit is reduced if benefits begin before the participant is age 62 and is increased if benefits begin after age 65.

These limits are also applicable on a combined basis when an employer maintains more than one qualified plan.

Let's look at how the bullet points above interface. If a plan sets a contribution rate of 25 percent of an employee's salary, the plan is not necessarily discriminatory, even though higher-paid employees will have higher dollar contributions than lower-paid employees, as long as no more than $200,000 of compensation is used. If an employee's compensation is $300,000, only $200,000 may be used when calculating the 25 percent contribution—first bullet point. But wait, we're not done. Twenty-five percent of $200,000 is $50,000; the second bullet point limits the contribution to $40,000.

Active Funding

Once a retirement plan is established, it must be funded on an active basis. Contributions according to the plan's formula must be made each year (except for profit sharing plans). They cannot be put off until later years. Interestingly, law permits an employer to borrow money in order to meet the active contribution requirement.

Plan Disclosure

A disclosure that describes the plan must be in writing and communicated to employees in an easily understandable way (plain language). Employers are required to provide their employees with a **summary plan description** (SPD) at regular intervals—and whenever a participant requests one. The SPD must include information about the sponsoring employer and the fiduciaries, the requirements for eligibility, how benefits accrue, the vesting formula, and how to make a claim for benefits. In addition, the SPD must include an explanation of a participant's rights under the program. Many employers provide this information via confidential access through a corporate Intranet.

Other required disclosures include:

- *Summary Annual Report.* A brief summary of the plan's financial information presented in the sponsor's annual filing to the IRS

- *Individual Participant Benefit Statement.* A statement of a participant's contributions to the plan, earnings, account balance, and vested percentage

- *A summary of any amendments to the plan.*

Plan Permanence

Although retirement plans can be terminated, for reasons that are beyond the scope of this text, a plan must be designed and maintained as permanent in nature, meaning no set termination date can be established when the plan is installed (initiated).

Investment Prudence

Law dictates that the trustee of the retirement plan take a prudent approach to the investment of the plan's funds. The plan's trustee is required to exercise utmost fiduciary responsibility, exclusively for the plan's participants. (Refer to Chapter 4 for a discussion of prudent investing.) The investment management experience of trust departments is the level of expertise needed to meet this requirement.

Vesting

Benefits for employees must be nonforfeitable at some point. This nonforfeitable interest is called **vesting.** *Vested* means that a plan participant has a legal right at retirement, and possibly earlier, to receive benefits that have accrued. This guarantees that employees will get a portion or all of the employer's contributions and earnings. Pension law sets three formulas, and retirement plans must adhere to one of them:

- *Immediate vesting.* One-hundred percent immediate vesting. (This formula is required if the employer imposes more than a one-year-of-service eligibility requirement.)

- *Cliff vesting.*

Years of employment	Percentage of vesting	
	2001	Effective 2002 (for matching contributions*)
1	0	0
2	0	0
3	0	100
4	0	
5	100	

- *Step or graduated vesting.*

Years of employment	Percentage of vesting	
	2001	Effective 2002 (for matching contributions*)
1	0	0
2	0	20
3	20	40
4	40	60
5	60	80
6	80	100
7	100	

* "Matching contributions" pertains to the contributions that an employer matches, as in a 401(k) plan. This does not apply to the earnings.

An employer may alter the cliff and step vesting formulas as long as the result is more liberal than the prescribed law.

Using a simple example, assume Jerry has a salary of $50,000 and his employer is making a contribution of 20 percent ($10,000) of his income into a retirement plan. For the ease of calculations, let's say that Jerry's income remains at $50,000, contributions are made for 4 years, and earnings on the contributions are $10,000. After 4 years of employment, Jerry's employer contributed $40,000 ($10,000 times 4 years). Including the earnings, the plan consists of $50,000 for his benefit. If Jerry left his employer for a new job after these four years of service, he would not be entitled to any of the benefits under the cliff vesting formula. According to the step formula, Jerry would be entitled (vested) to 40 percent ($20,000). Whether he gets his

vested amount at the time of separation or later depends on the terms of the plan.

Regardless of which vesting formula is used, if a plan permits voluntary employee contributions, the employee contributions are not subject to the plan's vesting formula. Therefore, employee contributions are always 100 percent vested from the first day. A plan cannot require an employee to make contributions.

What happens to the money that is not vested? The employer will either use the unvested money to reduce future contributions to the overall plan or reallocate the money to other participants' accounts, depending on the type and terms of the retirement plan. If an employee who is partially or fully vested dies before retirement, law requires guaranteed spousal survivorship benefits.

Trust departments are familiar with the recordkeeping needed to ensure accurate vesting amounts (for employer and employee contributions), payment of benefits to employees and surviving spouses according to the plan's provisions, and reallocation of nonvested amounts.

Establishment of Retirement Age

Retirement plans must contain provisions for normal (usually age 65) retirement age and benefit calculations for early and late retirement. Retirement plans generally cannot mandate a retirement age.

Calculation of Benefits at Retirement

Different kinds of plans calculate benefits differently at retirement. For example, a plan may establish a normal retirement age of 65, at which time 100 percent of retirement benefits are available. If an employee retires earlier than age 65, the plan may prescribe a reduced benefit, such as a two-percentage-point reduction for each year before normal retirement age (65). For example, if an employee retires at age 60, he may receive 90 percent of the predetermined full-retirement amount. This is the general approach for defined benefit plans. Defined contribution and profit sharing plans usually pay the portion that has accumulated up to the age at which the employee retires. For retirement after the plan's normal retirement age, benefits may be increased or fixed, depending on the type of plan and the plan's provisions.

Regardless of the type of plan and regardless of whether an employee retires early, at normal age, or later—at full or reduced benefits depending on age of retirement or vesting percentages—the employee is not required to begin receiving benefits at the time of retirement; they may be delayed.

Constructive Receipt

Contributions and earnings are not taxable income to the employee until benefits are received. Remember, benefits are tax deferred, not tax free. The deferral is until the time an employee begins to receive benefits (actual receipt), not when benefits are available to be received (constructive receipt).

Assume that John is age 65 and fully vested, and he decides to retire. Assume also that John's retirement plan provides for a lump sum distribution of $300,000 or a payout of $3,000 per month. John may not need the retirement benefits when he retires. He can delay payment (lump sum or monthly) until a later date.

Income tax regulations state that once taxable money is available to a person, it is taxable at that time regardless of whether it is taken. This is the **constructive receipt** principle. Pension law for qualified plans states that an employee is *not* in constructive receipt of retirement plan benefits until the benefits are actually paid. Therefore, if John retires at age 65 and he is eligible for the payment of benefits upon retirement, he will not be taxed on the benefits just by virtue of his ability to receive benefits. John is taxed when he receives benefits, not when he *can* receive benefits.

Plan Integration

Many employers provide more than one retirement plan. For example, an employer may have a defined benefit plan (solely funded with employer contributions) and a 401(k) plan (funded with both employer and employee contributions). Some employers believe that Social Security is a supplemental retirement plan sponsored by the employer, because the employer contributes to it on behalf of the employees.

Pension law allows employers, within certain parameters, to integrate the benefits of retirement plans with Social Security benefits. Again, the complexity of retirement law prohibits a detailed discussion in this short space. But the following example of plan integration shows how a plan's benefits may be reduced by a percentage of Social Security benefits received. Working with numbers, assume that Pat Smith's defined benefit pension plan provides for a payment of 70 percent of her final-year-of-employment income, minus 50 percent of her Social Security benefits. If Pat's final income was $50,000 and her Social Security retirement benefits were $16,000, the retirement benefits from her employer's plan would be $27,000 (70 percent of $50,000 [$35,000] minus 50 percent of $16,000 [$8,000]). Of course, Pat would still receive $16,000 from Social Security.

Trust departments will be asked for guidance in determining a plan's retirement age, calculating reduced benefits for retirement earlier than the established retirement age, and the mathematical recordkeeping involved with the integration of several plans. Interestingly, you will be asked often to explain the constructive receipt principle and provide guidance with respect to management of benefits once they are taken from the plan.

Insurance Coverage

An additional requirement for certain qualified retirement plans is participation in the **Pension Benefit Guaranty Corporation (PBGC).** The PBGC, a government-owned corporation, administers an insurance program that guarantees the payment of basic retirement benefits to participants of defined benefit plans. The employer pays an annual insurance premium to

PBGC; in return, the PBGC protects retirement benefits if a plan is terminated and has insufficient funds to pay employee-accrued benefits. Insufficient funds can result from inadequate funding, mismanagement, and misuse of plan assets, all of which are more likely to be prevented if the retirement plan uses a trust department as trustee.

The PBGC guarantees basic benefits, or vested monthly pension benefits that provide income when an employee retires. The amount received depends on several things: how long the employee worked, the provisions of the pension plan, funding by the employer before the plan's termination, and the employee's age. The maximum benefit the PBGC can pay is set by law. For plans terminating in 2003,

If a participant retired at	Maximum guarantee
Age 65	$43,977.24 per year ($3,664.77 per month)
Age 62	$34,742.04 per year ($2,895.17 per month)
Age 60	$28,585.20 per year ($2,382.10 per month)
Age 55	$19,789.80 per year ($1,649.15 per month)

Benefits received from the PBGC may be less than the plan's prescribed benefit, but without the PBGC, retirees might receive nothing at all.

Additional Requirements

The Internal Revenue Code also requires that for a plan to be qualified it must

- Begin paying benefits no later than a required beginning date: April 1 of the year following the year a participant attains age $70^1/_2$

- Provide requirements for protecting plan assets in the event of a plan merger

- Designate what kind of plan it is (money purchase, profit sharing, and so forth)

- Allow for a direct rollover option if a lump-sum distribution is permitted

NONQUALIFIED RETIREMENT PLANS

Despite the magnitude of pension law, nonqualified plans do exist. Retirement laws dictate the maximum amount of compensation that may be considered for calculating contributions and the maximum dollar amount that may be contributed to various plans. Retirement plans cannot discriminate in favor of highly compensated employees, so how does an employer attract, retain, and reward the higher-paid executive? One answer is to pay her more, but this goes only so far in satisfying the executive who is already highly paid. Additional income is eroded by increased income tax rates.

More compensation today is not truly what many executives are looking for, because income is already sufficient. Larger retirement benefits are the key. But the employer may not be able to provide increased pension benefits to the key employee because of the limits the law places on how much can be contributed to a qualified plan.

One way to supplement the key employee's income is with the use of a **nonqualified retirement plan,** which can discriminate in favor of certain employees. Also called a **supplemental employee retirement plan (SERP),** a nonqualified retirement (deferred compensation) plan gives an employer the opportunity to set aside funds today, to be paid later, for select employees. In essence, the employer enters an agreement with the employees of its choice and promises to pay them increased benefits in the future for work they do now. The contributions (active or deferred until retirement) and the discrimination of covering only select employees renders the plan nonqualified; therefore, the contributions are not tax-deductible to the employer.

In what is sometimes called a golden handcuff, the employer, knowing it cannot obtain tax benefits, promises to supplement the key employee's retirement income, but in exchange the employee must work for a given number of years or until a certain age in order to benefit. (These arrangements can be based on varying contingencies, depending on the employer's and employee's needs.) Both parties to the agreement have something to gain and something to lose. If the employee remains "handcuffed" to her employment agreement, the reward is "golden."

A nonqualified retirement plan, sometimes also called a salary continuation plan, is therefore defined by what it is not. It is not an IRS-qualified plan subject to eligibility, participation, and nondiscrimination provisions as set forth in ERISA and the Internal Revenue Code. Nonqualified plans are devoid of government involvement. Law does not mandate who is eligible, at what point they are able to participate, and to what degree they benefit. A nonqualified plan does not require IRS compliance and approval, reporting, or tax returns. This is truly a discriminatory benefit.

Although the employer contributions are not tax-deductible to the employer, a properly structured nonqualified plan allows the employer to tax deduct the benefits, as a business expense, when they are paid. Some nonqualified plans also provide survivorship benefits in the event of death or disability before or after fulfillment of the employer–employee agreement.

Nonqualified plans come in various forms, depending on the ingenuity of the people who create them. They are funded and paid out in varying ways. When they are actively funded, different vehicles are used to meet the end: stocks and bonds, annuities, life insurance, or combinations of these. Because of the size of these plans for the benefit of highly compensated employees, trust and investment services play an integral role during and after the funding period.

ESTABLISHING A RETIREMENT PLAN

Although they come in varying sizes and forms (corporate and individual, qualified and nonqualified), employee benefit retirement plans are highly structured; are subject to rules, regulations, and agreements; and are established carefully.

Once an employer begins to think about instituting retirement plans for the benefit of its employees, it is always best for the employer to seek the professional assistance of a retirement planning consultant. These specialists can be found in the accounting, law, insurance, actuarial, and banking disciplines. Bank trust departments are prepared to assist the employer with

- Determining the type of plan(s) to use
- Suggesting whether employee contributions be considered
- Adhering to plan qualifications
- Administering both qualified and nonqualified plans

The success of a retirement plan rests with its players: trustees, investment managers, actuary, administrators, and legal counsel. Many retirement plans use unbundled services—separate professionals or groups of professionals, each with skill in installing and administering a particular, specialized aspect of the plans.

Trustee

Except for employee benefit plans that consist solely of insurance contracts (that is, life, medical, and disability plans), ERISA requires that all the assets of an employee benefit plan be held by a trustee; hence the name **employee benefit trust.** Additionally, inherent throughout ERISA is the trustee's responsibility to act in the interests of the plan participants. Therefore, the trustee is the main player—the one who is ultimately responsible for getting the job done completely and correctly. The trustee can be an individual, a group of individuals (such as executives of the employer or members of the company's board of directors), a bank trust department, or a combination of these. Specific concern

USING TRUST PRODUCTS AND SERVICES
TO MEET CUSTOMER NEEDS

Karen was a highly successful executive specializing in the restructuring of large corporations that have been merged with or spun off of other corporations and companies experiencing financial problems. At age 53, Karen was asked to work for a company that recently broke away from a larger corporation. The spin-off caused financial strains, necessitating Karen's expertise.

Despite the company's generous fringe benefit package and the hefty salary they were willing to offer, the company needed to provide additional incentive to attract Karen. Both the company and Karen felt that additional compensation, geared to Karen's requirements and the company's ability, would provide the edge needed to attract her to the position.

The company offered a nonqualified deferred compensation package that would provide a $250,000 per year retirement payment to Karen, starting at age 65. In return, Karen was asked to stay with the company for a minimum of 10 years, which is the amount of time they felt was needed to put the company back in shape financially. The retirement package would pay the retirement benefit for 10 years (or in a lump sum, at the company's discretion); benefits would be paid at a 50 percent reduction to Karen's named beneficiary if she died after 5 years of employment. Of course, if Karen left the company before the 10-year commitment, she would receive nothing. In effect, this was a $2,500,000 promise to Karen.

Because of the company's bleak financial picture, Karen was concerned that the money would not be there 10 years from now. Karen said she would agree to the employment terms if the company would fund the promise today with $1,000,000 and make adequate contributions annually so the money would be there when she turned age 65. The company agreed to Karen's request.

Before execution of the agreement, Karen had some additional concerns: Where would the money be funded and how would the funds be invested? Although the company felt this was their call, Karen had reservations. Naturally, the company would not place the funds close to Karen's hands, but they understood her concerns about keeping the funds separate from the general assets of the company. The company suggested that together they meet with the company's legal counsel and their bank to discuss these points.

Unfamiliar with the nature of these arrangements—investments, employee benefits, and legal agreements—the company's commercial banking officer sought the assistance of the personal trust and investment management department. Following two planning meetings, it was suggested that Karen and the company enter into a trust agreement, which would contain the language of the employment agreement and provide an investment medium for the funds. Karen, the company, and legal counsel agreed.

Karen and the company (as cograntors) established a trust, which would be funded with $1 million (the corpus) plus the additional annual deposits; the bank (as trustee) would serve as investment manager—and referee between the two parties, so to speak—and provide payment of the benefits to Karen (as beneficiary) upon completion of the agreement.

should be given to choosing a trustee who can offer the fiduciary responsibilities of loyalty, impartiality, full administration, prudence, and accurate reporting. In addition, the trustee must possess skill in providing or overseeing investment activities and performance and ensuring that the rules of ERISA, the Department of Labor, the Department of the Treasury, the PBGC, the Federal Reserve Board, the FDIC, and the OCC are followed.

Although the laws and the beneficiaries differ between a personal trust and an employee benefit trust, the role of the trustee does not. The trustee qualifications discussed in Chapters 7 and 8 apply equally to employee benefit trustees.

As we discuss the players involved in an employee benefit plan, keep in mind that fiduciary responsibilities are not necessarily limited to specific players. The lines are not drawn. ERISA defines a fiduciary as

- Any person who exercises any discretionary authority or control over a plan's management or disposition of assets

- Any person who renders investment advice for a fee or other compensation with respect to plan funds

- Any person who has any discretionary authority or responsibility in the plan's administration

In light of the several retirement plan debacles witnessed in the past few years, a larger emphasis is being placed on *who is responsible* for the safety, administration, and performance of a qualified plan. No longer do participants—and the law— point the finger to one entity (the trustee). Other players are held to the same high standards expected of a trustee. Therefore, fiduciary responsibilities are a necessity of others besides the trustee.

If anyone involved with an employee benefit plan is responsible for any of the actions mentioned above, that player is held accountable as if he were in a fiduciary capacity. For example, when ABC Corporation retains XYZ Investment Management Company to serve as the investment advisor for its defined contribution plan, XYZ holds a fiduciary responsibility to manage the plan's assets consistent with the rules of investment prudence and in the best interests of the participants. Yes, ABC Corporation is responsible for the total management of the defined contribution plan, but its having that responsibility does not release the investment management company from its fiduciary responsibilities.

Investment Manager

Employees (who depend on investment returns of a defined contribution plan) and employers (who must maintain the investment performance of a defined benefit plan) depend heavily on the investment return of a retirement fund. Investment management is the responsibility of the trustee.

ERISA permits trustees and sponsors of retirement plans to hire outside investment managers (agents). Limited to banks, insurance companies, and registered investment advisors, investment managers can provide insured, trustee, and split-fund plans. Notice how the role of trustee and investment manager go hand-in-hand.

Insured Plan

An **insured pension plan** is a retirement plan provided by an insurance company that also serves as the plan's investment manager. Traditionally, these plans were funded with life insurance, annuities, and guaranteed interest contracts as the investment vehicles. A **guaranteed interest contract (GIC)** works on basically the same principle as a certificate of deposit (CD). The insurance company guarantees a minimum rate of return on the invested funds for a stipulated period of time. The insurance company may offer an option to pay higher returns, but never lower. As with a bond and a CD, risk is reduced, but the contract is still subject to fluctuating interest rates.

Trusteed Pension Plan

In a **trusteed pension plan,** the plan's contributions are placed in a trust, then invested and managed directly by the trustee in individual securities or the trustee's funds (bank trust department common trust funds or mutual funds). (Note that separate commingled—common trust—funds must be kept for personal trust and employee benefit trust customers.) The trustee may also hire an outside investment agent, depending on the trustee's level of investment management expertise or the investment objectives of the fund, as will be discussed in the master trust section below. When the plan's trustee is an individual or group of individuals, they will probably turn to professional investment managers—bank trust departments—to serve as the plan's investment agent.

Split-Fund Pension Plan

This type of plan involves the deposit of contributions into a trust, from which funds may be split among an insurance company (when life insurance or annuity products are used), separate investment manager, and trustee. The plan's trustee has the responsibility to manage, or delegate the management of, the retirement plan's assets profitably yet carefully, cautiously, and prudently, with due regard for the safety of the investments. The terms, considerations, and approaches to a $20-million retirement plan are no different from managing a $300,000 personal trust. Assets must be conserved and protected, assets must be diversified, and the risk of financial investment loss must be minimized—all professional concerns and qualifications of a trust department.

Trust departments come equipped to meet the checklist of requirements for investment managers:

- Past experience
- References
- Investment performance
- Reasonableness of fee structure
- Timely and understandable reports
- Asset allocation guidelines
- Financial condition and capitalization

Master Trustee

Depending on the size of the retirement plan, an employer may use several trusts and trustees, investment managers, administrators, and agents, each with a specific area of expertise. ABC Corporation may hire a separate trustee for each plan, separate investment managers with specialization in a specific area of investment expertise, a separate asset custodian, and an unrelated administrative manager.

Larger employee benefit plans may use a **master trust** arrangement, in which the master trustee uniformly coordinates a consolidated reporting of investment information and plan activity supplied by each individual investment manager, trustee and administrator or agent. The term *trustee* is used loosely in this section because this entity in most instances does not provide any fiduciary responsibilities; duties may be limited primarily to administrative activities. Then again, the master trustee may be charged with the overall fiduciary activities of all the agents and administrators.

Actuary

The discussion of defined benefit plans mentioned the concept of hitting a moving target in the future. The **actuary's** task is the mathematical calculations needed to determine what an employer's annual contributions must be year after year to provide a predetermined benefit in the future for each employee.

An employer may have hundreds or thousands of employees with varying income levels, varying years of service, and assorted ages. Employees may come and go (turn over), interest rates and stock performances rise and fall over time, **mortality rates/tables** (the frequency and number of employee deaths) and **morbidity rates/tables** (the number, frequency, and duration of employee disabilities) change, retirement ages come early and late, salaries change, and vesting formulas may be modified. It is a difficult task to actuarially (mathematically) determine year after year what will be needed to fund the plan to hit the target and provide to the employees what is promised.

Administrators

Many nonfiduciary and noninvestment management activities are associated with a retirement plan:

- Custody of plan assets
- Recordkeeping
- Processing checks to pension participants
- Producing required reports to the trustee, investment managers, employees, and the government

Although the employer itself can take on each of these responsibilities, more and more businesses look to outside professional plan administrators—again, trust departments—to provide these important services. (We will delve deeper into a trust department's duties as an agent for corporate services in Chapter 11.)

Legal Counsel

Concurrent with the type of plan chosen and the selection of trustees, investment managers, and administrators is selection of the trust agreement, which will guide the plan's trustee. The employee benefit trust can be drafted from scratch by legal counsel that specializes in this area. If the plan is meant to be qualified, the agreement must meet the rules and regulations set by employee benefit law.

After the trust agreement is designed and written, it must be submitted to the Internal Revenue Service for review and approval. IRS approval is given by way of a **determination letter,** which states that the plan meets all legal requirements for a plan to be qualified. Employee benefit laws change. Depending on the extent of change, employee benefit plans may require formal amendment to adhere to the law. In addition to the requirements that employers notify participants of changes in the law, employers may be required to submit the amendments to the IRS for continued qualification of the plan.

In some circumstances, an employer may want to change certain terms of the plan or terminate the plan totally. Depending on the changes, it may be necessary to receive a new determination letter from the IRS. If a plan is to be terminated, the employer must request from the IRS approval of the termination and a determination letter that reflects the approval. Trust departments have standardized plan language that is preapproved by the IRS. Rather than constructing a plan from the bottom up, many sponsors will use an IRS preapproved **prototype**. Prototypes also require IRS approval if they are amended or terminated, a task handled by the trust department as trustee.

SUMMARY

- Employee benefit programs are any benefit that an employer offers to employees over and above salary. Employee benefit programs are distinguished as welfare plans and pension plans.

- Corporate-sponsored employee benefit and retirement plans and Social Security have evolved and grown extensively since World War II. Retirement plans offer employers the opportunity to stabilize employment, enhance a hiring advantage, build corporate productivity, and supplement employee income today and tomorrow.

- Corporate retirement plans (deferred compensation) exist as defined contribution and defined benefit plans. To an extent, Social Security is also considered a corporate retirement plan in that retirement benefits come partly from employer contributions.

- In 1974 ERISA created IRAs—individual retirement accounts for workers who are not covered by an employer plan. IRAs are either contributory on a voluntary, annual basis or rollover—a medium for accepting and investing lump sum distributions from qualified plans.

- Employer contributions to a retirement plan are tax deductible if the plan is qualified. Qualification is achieved if the plan meets the rules set forth by ERISA, the IRS, and subsequent retirement laws. Qualified plans must provide plan exclusiveness, formal construction, nondiscrimination, contribution limits, active funding, plan disclosure, permanence, investment prudence, vesting formula, establishment of retirement age, and PBGC insurance.

- If a retirement plan does not meet qualification requirements, it is nonqualified. Nonqualified plans (supplemental employee retirement plans) are used by businesses to reward highly compensated employees on a discriminatory basis.

- There are several steps in establishing a retirement plan, most of which involve meeting the requirements for a plan to be qualified. Important to the establishment and maintenance of a retirement plan are the players: trustee, investment manager, actuary, administrator, and legal counsel.

REVIEW QUESTIONS

1. What advantages could you cite to an employer deciding whether to establish an employee benefit retirement plan?
2. What are some of the factors considered in determining an employer's contribution for a defined contribution plan and for a defined benefit plan?
3. Give three examples of how 401(k) and profit sharing plans differ.
4. Employee benefit plans are governed by ERISA. What does this acronym mean? List five of ERISA's provisions pertaining to qualification of a retirement plan.
5. What roles do trust departments play in employee benefit plans?

11

CORPORATE TRUST
AND AGENCY SERVICES

"Business? It's quite simple: it's other people's money."

Alexandre Dumas (1824–1895)

Everyone needs money for something. Bill and Anne want to buy a house, furniture, and cars; pay for their children's college education; and save for retirement. ABC Corporation and XYZ Company want to purchase machinery and raw materials to manufacture and sell more products. If Bill, Anne, ABC, and XYZ don't have the money in their checking or savings accounts to buy what they want now, they need to raise **capital.** *Raising capital* is jargon for using other people's money.

Bill and Anne can borrow indirectly by using their credit cards or borrow directly from a bank to purchase the car (through an auto loan) or house (with a mortgage). ABC and XYZ can also borrow money (raise capital) from their bank, or they can borrow from individual investors and institutional investors (other companies) by selling stock (equity) in their company and issuing bonds (debt). For businesses, **equity capital** is money supplied by stockholders who invest in the company. **Debt capital** is bond money supplied to a corporation through a loan made by others. A business's land, buildings, equipment, inventory, bank balances, and investments that develop from initial equity and debt capital are also categorized as capital.

As we can see, the financial needs of institutions are not all that different from the financial needs of individuals. They are bigger, though, and they need the services of our trust departments.

LEARNING OBJECTIVES

Personal trusts and agencies are established by an individual for individuals. Employee benefit trusts and agencies are established by corporations for individuals. But **corporate trusts** and **corporate agencies** are established by a corporation for the corporation. Just as trust departments are equipped to serve the trust and investment management needs of individuals, trust departments are equally prepared to serve institutions and corporations with similar trust and agency products and services. A trust department's opportunity to serve corporations is the subject of this chapter.

Upon completion of this chapter, you will be able to

- Describe how corporations raise capital
- Distinguish national banks from state banks
- Explain the various securities laws for issuing securities and protecting investors
- Relate the purposes of a corporate trust indenture to a personal trust
- List the various bond and stock agents that corporations use
- Define and use the terms that appear in bold in the text

CORPORATE HISTORY

The raising and use of capital date back to ancient Middle East empires and, to a larger extent, to the Roman Empire. Not until the Industrial Revolution did a system of capital—capitalism—become organizationally prevalent.

Capital Investment

From the latter half of the eighteenth century through the early 1900s, our country's expansive economic system was born. Individuals and businesses produced their products and services with the help of those who were willing to lend money (debt) and invest money (equity). Capital came from a bank, if it was willing to extend credit, or from non-bank lenders (bond investing). Capital also came from individuals and companies that in return received equity in the business venture—a form of ownership.

Business doesn't stand still—the need for capital does not stop. Corporations (both new and established) cannot survive if they don't grow and expand; if they don't acquire market attraction and dominance; if they don't keep current with research and development. These activities require capital. So too do municipalities and government entities need capital: to build schools, roads, and public facilities and to provide social programs. This acquisition of capital to increase the rate of return from investment is also referred to as **leverage.** Of course, the more leveraged a company is,

the more in debt it is. This is a risk an investor takes when "investing" capital.

Evidence of Investment

During the early industrial years, corporations (businesses) raised their capital and issued their own stocks and bonds. They did everything themselves. Once an owner convinced others to invest in his company or lend money, he dusted off the typewriter and prepared a stock or bond certificate, a piece of paper proving the investor's ownership (capital investment) in the company or the company's indebtedness to a lender.

Lenders and investors provided capital, businesses produced products and services, and consumers bought. But dishonest people disrupted this legitimate enterprise system. Fraudulent business entities convinced lenders and investors to supply capital to nonexistent ventures. Convinced of profit, lenders and investors were left with empty pocketbooks and worthless stock and bond certificates. Because of such incidents, investors became wary of investing in companies they suspected might not be real or would not perform as presented. Conversely, legitimate businesses suffered from inability to secure financing from wary investors.

As a result of the need to bolster investor confidence and to move away from do-it-yourself activities, capital investment was shifted to **centralized trading exchanges,** the physical marketplace where securities (stocks and bonds) are bought and sold. The exchanges required that securities be registered at an agency appointed by the exchanges.

New York Stock Exchange

Sometimes called the Big Board, the **New York Stock Exchange (NYSE)** was formed on May 17, 1792, when 24 businessmen banded together to provide an organized system for handling the general public's buying and selling of stocks and bonds. Initially, this group met each day at the same time under a large tree on Wall Street in New York City. Today, the NYSE has grown to 1,366 members, and each member is said to hold a seat on the exchange. The companies that are traded, or listed, on the NYSE must meet certain financial requirements with respect to earning power, net assets, number of shares, number of stockholders, and market value of the stock.

American Stock Exchange

Companies that do not have the financial size and strength to meet the NYSE's requirements use the **American Stock Exchange (AMEX).** The AMEX, as it is called today, began in the mid-1800s. Known originally as the Curb Exchange (because its members conducted their transactions each day on a curb at Trinity Place in New York City), the AMEX is the home of newer, smaller companies. Like the NYSE, the AMEX also requires that certain financial requirements be met for a company to trade or list on this exchange.

Regional Stock Exchanges

Below the two national exchanges are the **regional stock exchanges,** such as the Midwest Stock Exchange in Chicago and the Pacific Stock Exchange in San Francisco. Companies listed on the regional exchanges are not big enough to qualify for the larger national exchanges; the regional exchanges may also provide more convenient trading services for local companies.

Over-the-Counter

Not all public stocks are traded on the national and regional exchanges. An additional trading medium is the **over-the-counter (OTC)** market. The OTC is actually many times larger than the national and regional exchanges combined, measured by the number of issues traded. The OTC (sometimes called the Third Market) is not a physical trading place, but a system of phone lines and computers that connect buyers and sellers through the **National Association of Securities Dealers Automated Quotations (NASDAQ)** system. This provides ongoing, instantaneous quotations for nonexchange stocks (**unlisted securities**) and new issues. In 1998, NASDAQ acquired AMEX and now competes with the New York Stock Exchange in listing large, prestigious companies. During this early period of investments and capital production, and amid the regulations and marketplaces that serve investors, bank involvement and government intervention altered the picture.

BANKING DEVELOPMENT

Shortly after the creation of the Office of the Comptroller of the Currency (OCC) in 1863, authority was given to the OCC to charter and supervise banks under national regulations. (Refer to the discussion of the OCC in Chapter 4.) These **national banks** brought strength and credibility to the businesses that turned to them for their lending services. Businesses also appointed banks to issue (underwrite) their securities. The bank became a trusted intermediary to businesses seeking capital and investors looking for sound investments. New and existing companies were assured they would be taken seriously, and the investor could be assured she was buying into a legitimate investment endeavor. Both parties were supported by the regulated banking industry.

As our country grew, national banks did not expand into every metropolitan area. Just as regional stock exchanges served smaller local companies, smaller local banks developed outside the national banking system. As states grew and were admitted to the Union, state laws, which mirrored federal regulations, emerged to counter fraudulent investment activity. Thus, **state banks** cropped up.

Today, national and state banks differ only slightly. A national bank must include the word *National* or *N.A.* in its title. National banks are required to be members of the Federal Deposit Insurance Corporation (FDIC), which is discussed later in the chapter. It is rare to encounter a state bank that is not an FDIC member. National and state banks no longer differ by location and size, and each is capable of managing trust and agency accounts.

SECURITIES LAWS

To protect capital production and investment activity from fraudulent securities and investment schemes, state and federal laws were established to protect the investing public.

Blue Sky Laws

In the late nineteenth century and into the early twentieth century, fraudulent securities became known as pieces of the blue sky. The sky was the limit with respect to offering and selling securities. Looking fine when presented, many apparent companies and securities offerings were nonexistent. Their worth was equal to a handful of blue sky. In conjunction with the federal government's controls, individual states enacted laws to protect matters within their boundaries. In the early 1900s, many states (Kansas being the first in 1911) became active in regulating the securities industry on a local level by passing **blue sky** laws. These laws were designed to control the issuance of false securities and provide a process to prevent dishonesty, self-dealing, and conflicts of interest. These state laws supplemented federal safeguards to protect the individual investor.

Despite trading-exchange requirements, the early enactment of federal banking legislation, and blue sky legislation enacted by the states, the securities industry overall was subject to very little regulation. "Buyer beware" became the guiding principle to the individual investor.

Federal Laws

During the post–World War I boom, more companies emerged, more capital was created, more loans were made by banks, and more investors entered the market. But with every high tide comes the ebb: the Stock Market Crash of 1929 and the Great Depression.

Truth in Securities Act

Congress stepped forward, passing the **Securities Act of 1933.** This antifraud act attempted to safeguard the public from misrepresented securities. A filing process was developed that required all new securities to be fully disclosed, properly registered, and clearly described through offering literature or a registration statement, more commonly known as a **prospectus.** A prospectus must show the company's intent to issue the securities, disclose and describe the securities, and provide full financial data regarding the company.

Federal Banking Act

Also in 1933, Congress passed the Federal Banking Act, which came to be known as the **Glass–Steagall Act,** after the legislators who introduced the law. This was the government's attempt to restore public confidence in investment practices and in banks.

The overnight growth of the banking industry in the early 1900s led to investment problems of its own. Following the crash of 1929, closings, insolvency, and loss of credibility took their toll on many national and state banks. Recent historians have laid the responsibility for the closing of banks on the depth of the depression itself, which caused the value of real estate and other investments to fall, causing problems for bank loans. At the time, though, analysts argued that much of the banking industry's problems occurred because of conflicts of interest that developed when a bank served a business or individual on both sides of the fence, issuing a company's securities and providing its banking (loan and deposit) services. From this analysis came what is called the **Chinese wall,** a policy that places a barrier between a trust department and the rest of the bank, and the concern about **insider information,** which will be discussed in Chapter 12.

The Federal Banking Act separated commercial and investment banking functions. **Commercial banks** were prohibited from underwriting securities, except for general obligations of municipalities. **Investment banks** (also known as **underwriters,** or institutions that directly underwrite corporate securities) were prohibited from accepting deposits and making loans. (We will visit investment banks again later in this chapter.)

The Gramm-Leach-Bliley Act of 1999 repealed most of the provisions of the Glass Steagall Act of 1933 that separated commercial banking from investment banking. The Gramm-Leach-Bliley Act repealed the blanket exemption of banks from the definitions of broker and dealer, but it retained most exemptions for longstanding trust and securities services offered by banks. As this text is being written, the specific regulations are still in development.

Federal Deposit Insurance Corporation

Another part of the Federal Banking Act of 1933 established the **Federal Deposit Insurance Corporation (FDIC)** to protect and insure bank customers' deposits.

Despite its many years of existence, FDIC coverage (currently at $100,000 per depositor per institution, but not per account) is misunderstood by many customers and bank personnel. Frequently, customers erroneously believe that FDIC insurance extends to trust department assets.

When a bank customer deposits money into the bank, the customer's money becomes a bank asset; the customer is a creditor to the bank. (It can be said that the customer lent his money to the bank.) In turn the bank lends the customer's money to other customers (borrowers). The interest paid to a depositor is less than the interest charged to a borrower. The difference in these rates is what the bank uses to pay its overhead: employee salaries, utility bills, the cost of computers, insurance premiums, furniture, rents, employee benefit plans, and so on. Of course, banks earn money in other ways—from the fees they charge for products and services, both on the banking side and the trust side. Banks have existed this way, under watchful regulatory eyes, for a long time. In the event a bank becomes insolvent and its assets (deposits) are at risk, deposits are protected by applicable FDIC insurance coverage.

In contrast, when a trust customer places money into a trust department account, the bank does not lend this money to others. These funds do not become assets of the bank; they belong to the trust customers. For this reason, trust assets are not shown in the bank's annual report to stockholders. It is not uncommon for a bank trust department to be managing many more dollars' worth of assets than the size of the bank's asset base.

Because assets in the trust department are not bank assets, FDIC protection does not extend to them unless they are placed in a bank account. Insolvency of a bank does not affect trust assets because of their separation from bank assets. The FDIC addresses the safety of trust assets in the Federal Deposit Insurance Act of 1950. In summary,

- The assets of trusts, estates, and agency accounts within a trust department are held physically separate from the bank's securities.

- Accountability for these assets is maintained on separate accounting systems.

- Separate controls preclude any creditor of the bank from attaching trust department customers' assets.

- These controls are enforced by the OCC and the FDIC.

- Missing, lost, stolen, or counterfeit securities are protected by standard and supplemental bank insurance coverage.

- In addition to receiving regulatory examinations and audits, trust department assets are audited by internal auditors; a trust audit committee is established by the bank's board of directors (no member of the committee may be an officer of the bank). This committee ensures that audits of the trust department are conducted at least annually.

- Opinion letters are available from the audit committee and the bank's outside public accounting auditor.

Securities and Exchange Act

Congress addressed problems pertaining to new and existing securities by passing the **Securities and Exchange Act of 1934,** which formed the **Securities and Exchange Commission (SEC).** The SEC, a five-member board appointed by the president with the consent of the Senate, has three basic responsibilities:

- To require companies that offer their securities for sale in interstate commerce to register with the commission and provide complete and accurate disclosure information to investors

- To protect investors against misrepresentation and fraud in the issuance and sale of securities

- To oversee the securities markets to ensure they operate in a fair and orderly manner

Because of the separation of commercial and investment banking, the SEC has but limited jurisdiction over the banking industry and several other investment-related matters. The SEC does not have control over

- Bank-initiated IRAs, which are under the control of the OCC, the Federal Reserve, and state banking authorities

- Government-issued securities, which are regulated by the Bureau of the Public Debt

- Commodity futures contracts, which are addressed by the Commodity Futures Trading Commission

- Registration of individual broker representatives, which are regulated by the National Association of Securities Dealers (NASD)

- Private pension (retirement plans), which are regulated under the Pension and Welfare Benefits Administration within the Department of Labor and ERISA

- Commercial sales practices, which are governed by the Correspondence Branch of the Federal Trade Commission (FTC)

- Taxes and tax shelters, which are regulated by the Internal Revenue Service

- Insurance, which is regulated by state insurance departments

The SEC, through its headquarters office in Washington, D.C., and nine regional offices—New York, Boston, Atlanta (with a branch in Miami), Chicago, Ft. Worth, Denver (with a branch in Salt Lake City), Seattle, Los Angeles (with a branch in San Francisco), and Philadelphia—provides investment guidelines to assist the general public. Registration of securities with the SEC does not imply that the commission approves the issue or has found the registration disclosures to be accurate. Nor does registration insure investors against loss of their investments. But registration does provide information on which investors may base an informed and realistic evaluation of the worth of securities.

Trust Indenture Act

In the opinion of students of the history of banking, the industry's phenomenal growth in the early years of the twentieth century, the problems many banks had during the Great Depression, and Congress's subsequent passage of banking laws left a scar on the banking industry. Yet a close look at history shows that the majority of banks kept their doors open and remained not only solvent but also solid following the stock market crash and the financially lean years of the Depression. The laws provided additional strength, protection, and guidance to the banking industry and the general public. For years businesses relied on banks to issue their securities. The involvement of the banking industry gave credibility to a company's capital-raising efforts. With the enactment of the Glass–Steagall Act, banks were removed from this process of selling (underwriting) securities, yet companies continued to use banks for servicing securities once they were issued. In fact, in 1939 Congress acted again, passing the **Trust Indenture Act of 1939,** which was meant to demonstrate the government's belief in the banking industry. Again the public turned to banks and their trust departments. The act stated in part,

> Every bond or other debt security which is offered to the public by use of mails or the channels of interstate commerce must be issued under an indenture which has been qualified by the Commission.

An **indenture** is a trust document that defines the specifics of a bond issue. An indenture establishes a trust department's responsibilities with respect to the relationship between the company issuing a bond (referred to as the obligor) and the bondholders who purchase the bond.

In essence, the Trust Indenture Act states that for an indenture to be qualified,

- An independent trustee, not associated with the obligor, must be appointed to provide safeguards in order to protect the lender's (bondholder's) interests, and

- The responsibilities of the borrowing company and the trustee must be specifically delineated.

Obligors could once again turn to the stability of the trust profession with the assurance that it would carry out the duties of the indenture trustee:

- Make payments of interest and principal

- Represent the bondholders in the event of a bond's default

- Resolve any conflicts between the company and the trustee or between the underwriters (sellers) of the issue and the trustee

- Provide reports to the bondholders on the rating of a bond issue and any securities pledged against the bond, if applicable; if a bond is not secured, it is called a **debenture.**

Additional Laws

In 1940 the federal government reached out again by passing the Investment Advisory Act and the Investment Company Act. These laws targeted individual investment counselors and investment consulting firms, basically by regulating the mutual fund industry. Although these laws do not protect the individual investor directly, they require mutual funds companies to register with the SEC, including disclosure of the company's financial condition and investment policies, the bank custodianship of the company's assets, the shareholder participation and notification of the company's investment activities, and its adherence to the Securities Act of 1933. Trust department common trust funds do not fall under these laws despite their similarity to mutual funds. But with the emergence of bank mutual funds, banks must adhere to this legislation. (The mutual fund industry will be visited again in Chapter 12.)

Throughout the development of these laws, the banking and trust industry evolved, providing valuable services to corporations and their investors. As the personal trust and employee benefit trust lines of business grew, the corporate trust side of the business increased its involvement and growth as well, with specific trust and agency services.

CORPORATE TRUST SERVICES

Today's entrepreneurs function similarly to the budding companies of the early 1800s. But the size of present-day ventures, the magnitude of capital required, and the need to adhere to laws cause businesses to turn to others for help. Just as John Doe turns to his bank and trust department for investment services because he doesn't have the time, desire, or capability to deal with them himself, ABC Company will turn to us for the same reasons.

Investment Banker

An investment banker advises companies and works with them by finding ways for them to raise capital. After a company decides whether to raise debt capital or equity capital, the investment banker, armed with a rating (for the company and the potential securities) obtained from Moody's or Standard & Poor's, initiates a process to determine the amount of capital needed, the type(s) of securities to use in raising the capital, and the approach needed to underwrite (sell) and distribute the securities to the investing public.

Stocks and bonds offered to the public for the first time—new issues—do not qualify to be listed with centralized trading exchanges. The investment banker therefore creates a **primary market** through NASDAQ, a sales medium that offers newly issued securities to investors. Existing securities are resold through the **secondary market:** the trading exchanges.

In a typical underwriting, the investment bank buys the entire new issue from the company. In turn, the investment bank sells the issue to the investing public at a small markup. The difference is the fee the investment bank earns for its services. If the investment bank sells the entire issue to investors, it is called a fully subscribed issue. If an issue is too large or risky for one investment bank to handle, the bank may enter into an arrangement with several other investment banks to conduct the transaction jointly (an underwriting syndicate).

In some situations a new issue may be sold in its entirety to one investor, such as an insurance company or venture capital fund. This is a private placement. An investment banker may be involved in this type of transaction, or the company may sell the securities directly to the investor.

With a bond issue, the investing public is not interested in seeing its money go into the company's pocket without some guarantees that they will get their semi-annual interest check and also receive 100 percent of their principal when the bond matures. Providing such reassurance does not fall within the activities of the investment banker; this is where a bank trust department enters the picture.

Trust Department's Role

The Trust Indenture Act of 1939 set the stage for trust departments by requiring the establishment of an indenture trust and the use of an independent trustee to safeguard the interests of the bondholders, lenders, and investors. Using the five ingredients of a trust from Chapter 7, the company (grantor) establishes an indenture (trust agreement) naming a bank (trustee) to protect the interests of the lenders (beneficiaries) by providing guarantees that payments will be made. Perhaps the trust relationship will be backed by collateral (corpus), such as the company's physical equipment purchased with the funds provided by the investors or a guarantee of payment from the borrower's bank in the event of default.

Trust's Chain of Events

Loosely presented, following an investment banker's activities, the corporate trust indenture development looks something like this:

- Just as John Doe has a personal trust prepared for him by his attorney, so does the company turn to legal counsel to have a similar document (the indenture) prepared.

- The bank trust department reviews the document for acceptability. Can the bank fulfill its responsibilities, based on the trust's wording, to the bondholders? Is the bank representing a stable company that can meet its financial obligations to the bondholders? Does the bank have a **conflict of interest** by accepting a trust from a company with which it has a commercial banking relationship?

- The legal staff of the corporate trust department must review and pay special attention to the aspects of the trust that give the trustee the authority to act on the provisions of the agreement. For example, what actions can the trustee take to meet an obligor's (grantor's) failure (default) to make interest or principal payments?

- If the bond issue is secured with collateral, the trustee usually takes title to the collateral (although not in a legal sense, which we will address shortly) or ensures that the collateral is maintained suitably.

- Once the indenture is reviewed and each party agrees to its provisions, the issuing corporation and the trustee, acting on behalf of the investors, sign the indenture document.

- The trustee is responsible for delivering the securities to the investors and guaranteeing authenticity. For example, as an investment banker personally buys or arranges for the sale of the securities, the money (capital) may flow through the trustee, or the trustee ensures direct transfer from the investors to the company. The trustee, as an intermediary, also delivers or arranges for delivery of the money to the obligor (the borrower) and also effects the physical delivery of the securities to the lenders (bondholders).

Additional Duties

In most instances the trust department provides administrative agency duties for the grantor in addition to the fiduciary responsibilities to the beneficiaries (investors) by protecting their investment interests. For example, the bank trustee, if asked, will make payments of interest to the lenders as it receives money from the grantor; it is the trustee's responsibility to get this money from the company. The trustee also provides the payment of principal when the bond matures. If the company defaults on its payments (in other words, it does not provide money to the trustee to be distributed as interest or principal to the bondholders), the trustee is again responsible to the bondholders. The trustee either takes physical possession of the collateral (if such exists) to satisfy the company's financial obligations to the lenders, or the trustee takes the necessary legal steps to provide satisfaction to the bondholders (beneficiaries). The trustee also keeps tabs on the company's financial position and any changes in the bond's rating, which must be reported to the bondholders.

Is an Indenture Truly a Trust?

Although trust departments are playing dual roles—fiduciary and agent—in an indenture arrangement, some authorities question whether this truly is a relationship of trust or an advanced agent, based on the following facts:

- Remember (from Chapters 1 and 7) that trust ownership of assets has a legal side and an equitable side. In a corporate indenture trust relationship, the trustee never really takes legal title to the property involved. Unlike a personal trust, in which John Doe gives his stocks and bonds to the trustee, an indenture trustee may never take physical possession (custody) of the property.

- A trustee's responsibilities are legally weighted toward the beneficiaries (bondholders), whereas there is more equal representation and division of tasks for both grantor and beneficiary in a personal or employee benefit trust. For these reasons, some writers feel that the indenture does not really create a true trust relationship.

- The indenture trustee and the obligor often do not know who the beneficiaries are, especially because they change so often with the sale of bonds from one entity to another, making it difficult for the trustee to keep up with whom the lenders really are.

For these reasons, this indenture relationship is sometimes viewed as a glorified escrow arrangement, whereby the trustee is charged with a set of duties (such as payment of interest and principal) to carry out between the principal and an agent.

Although an argument can be made that a corporate trust relationship is truly not a fiduciary arrangement, trust departments are nonetheless charged with important duties that transcend the agency services discussed in the next section.

CORPORATE AGENCY SERVICES

The administration and maintenance of a company's stock and bond issues involve many behind-the-scenes tasks that investors never see. Although some companies maintain these activities with in-house staff, more and more companies, big and small, turn to the experienced, automated services of a bank trust department to save time, personnel, and money. In many instances, however, to avoid any potential conflict of interest, fiduciary and agency services are obtained from separate institutions. Where one trust department may serve as indenture trustee, another trust department in a bank down the street may provide the agency services.

The financial needs of institutions are not all that different from the financial needs of individuals. The agency terms and services described in Chapter 3 come alive again with respect to serving corporations. The services discussed here take on the same agent–principal relationship: The trust department (as an agent) acts on behalf of the corporation (as the principal). (It may help you to review the investment concepts in Chapter 2 before you read the following sections.)

Bond Agencies

Trust departments provide bond agency services to corporations in several ways.

Paying Agent

With respect to registered bonds, more and more corporations use the streamlined systems of bank trust departments as **paying agents** to distribute semiannual interest payments and repayment of principal upon maturity or a call. Both corporations and municipalities use bank trust departments for this service. Government issues are handled exclusively by the Federal Reserve banks.

A small percentage of bearer bonds still exists. Although just about any bearer bond owner can present the bond's coupons to any bank for payment, one specific bank is appointed by the obligor to act as an agency clearinghouse (paying agent) for all coupons. Mrs. Jones, the owner of a bearer bond, may present a timely coupon to her bank to receive her interest payment, although a separate bank may be the official paying agent for the bond issue. Mrs.

Jones's bank may receive reimbursement from the paying agent for its services, which comes from the fee the paying agent collects from the obligor. Or Mrs. Jones may be directly charged a nominal handling fee by her bank. In most instances Mrs. Jones's bank will provide this transaction free of fees as a service to her as a customer.

It is the responsibility of the paying agent to have sufficient funds from the issuing company to pay the bondholders. Such arrangements are made between the paying agent and the issuing corporation. If the funds are not forthcoming, the paying agent can turn to the indenture trustee to enforce collection of money sufficient to pay the bondholders.

Bond Registrar

As mentioned, corporations and trustees usually do not know who their lenders and beneficiaries are and how much they own. Someone must know this information, however, in order for interest and principal payments to be made. This is the **registrar's** job. The trust department, as registrar, also keeps tabs on transfer of ownership, in the event of the sale of a bond from one investor to another. The registrar is also used when an obligor decides to call a bond issue before maturity (assuming this can be done). The registrar notifies the lenders of this action and effects the payment of principal and collection of the bond certificates.

Exchange Agent

For convertible bond and stock issues, an **exchange agent** effects the administrative services needed for exchanging (converting) bonds to stocks and stocks to bonds.

Additional Bond Agency Services

Trust departments also provide corporate bond agency services for

- Paying principal upon a bond's maturity or call
- Processing defaults

- Safekeeping collateral for a secured issue

Stock Agency Services

Currently an average of 1.5 billion shares of public stock are traded in the United States daily. This represents the total of the NYSE, AMEX, OTC, NASDAQ, and the regional exchanges throughout the country. Five years ago, trading volume was a third as much. With the astronomical amount of activity associated with the related administrative tasks of handling stocks, it is no wonder that corporations turn to trust departments to do the paperwork. Although the following text presents agency functions individually, many of these activities cross lines from one type of agent to another. For example, a paying agent may do some of a transfer agent's duties and the transfer agent may perform a stock registrar's duties. The extent of an agent's services depends on the needs of the principal. Most bank trust departments generically call their stock agency duties *shareholder services*.

Dividend-Paying Agent

When a company declares a dividend (votes to pay a dividend), the **dividend-paying agent's** job is to distribute the dividend to each stockholder according to the number of shares she owns. The dividend may be cash or additional shares of stock, depending on the company's decision or a stockholder's decision in cases where a company offers a **dividend reinvestment program (DRIP),** in which the stockholder may direct the company (or its dividend-paying agent) to use cash dividends to purchase additional shares of stock.

Dividends are usually declared once a year, but they are distributed to stockholders on a quarterly basis. If a stock is valued at $50 and a 4 percent dividend ($2) is declared, the company provides sufficient funds to the dividend-paying agent to distribute a 50¢ dividend per share per quarter to each stockholder of record.

Stock Registrar

Like a bond registrar, this agent is responsible for keeping track of who owns how many shares of stock that a transfer agent (discussed next) has issued, canceled, and reissued.

Transfer Agent

Of all agents, a **transfer agent** has the most activity. It is called on to do the following:

- Issue stock certificates. We previously discussed the requirements that corporations face when selling new stock. Once the stock has been approved by the SEC, the corporation is given written authority to issue stock. The corporation's **board of directors** then appoints a transfer agent, who engages in printing the certificates. The certificates are signed by the officers of the corporation, the transfer agent, and the stock registrar, if one is appointed. Issuance can then begin.

- Record change when stock ownership transfers from one owner to another. If Jill sells 1,000 shares of XYZ Company to Jack, the transfer agent collects the stock certificates from Jill, corrects the ownership records, and issues new certificates to Jack.

- Disburse dividends, as checks or additional shares, if a separate paying agent is not used.

- Provide custodial services and safekeeping of unissued stock certificates.

- Replace certificates that are lost and keep records of such occurrences.

- Provide prompt, correct answers to stockholder inquiries.

- Provide information to the corporation regarding its stockholders; for example, the company may be considering expansion on the West Coast and therefore may want to know how many stockholders live west of the Mississippi River and how many shares they own individually and as a whole.

- Send corporate information to stockholders, such as annual reports, notice of stockholder meetings, and **proxies**, which are written authority for a stockholder to vote on company matters.

- Keep accurate and timely records of stockholders' names, addresses, tax identification numbers, certificate numbers, number of shares per holder, and dates of issuance (Jill's 1,000 shares of XYZ Company may have been bought at different times and prices, and the transfer agent keeps track of Jill's individual certificates and her total ownership). A sample record appears below.

In 1985, Congress passed the Shareholder Communications Act, which mandates that companies effectively disseminate literature—such as annual reports, notice of stockholder meetings, and proxy material—to the beneficial stock owners, meaning those who actually own the stock shares. Because companies and their

Number of Shares	Date Purchased	Acquisition Cost	Certificate Number
100	03/08/72	$36.25 per share	1234
250	01/15/85	$40 per share	2345
250	06/10/86	$38.75 per share	3456
200	10/02/92	$34.50 per share	4567
200	12/30/93	$37 per share	5678

agents don't always know who the stockholders are, the act established a system for communicating between the issuers of stock and the owners, and it directs the SEC to develop a set of rules that outline policies to be followed for distributing materials to the specific owners, even if the stock is held in nominee name.

Assume that ABC Bank manages an investment agency account for Sally Smith; ABC is the agent and Sally is the principal. Assume that ABC purchases 1,000 shares of Federal Express (FedEx) stock for Sally's account. It is also safe to assume that ABC Bank may have purchased FedEx stock for other individual agency accounts, personal trust accounts, and employee benefit trusts and agencies. To facilitate purchases, sales, dividend collection, recordkeeping, and the dozens of other tasks associated with this stock and all other stocks, ABC lists itself as the **nominee** for all the FedEx stocks throughout all of the bank's accounts. This means that ABC is listed in FedEx records as the registered owner for all the stock it maintains for the actual beneficial owners of the various individual accounts the bank serves.

In a way, it can be said that the true, beneficial owners of the stock (Sally Smith and all the others) nominated ABC to be listed as the registered owner to help facilitate investment activity (buys, sells, dividend collection, and so forth). This way, ABC can conduct business with FedEx and its agents on an economical, collective basis, rather than by individual accounts.

ABC, as well as other investment managers, will use this nominee principle to conveniently transact business as a whole for many individual accounts. Because the stock is listed (registered) with the FedEx stock registrar or transfer agent, showing "ABC, as nominee" as the owner, FedEx cannot be aware of the actual, individual beneficial owners. This is where the Shareholder Communications Act and the SEC enter the picture to ensure that information is filtered down to the actual owners, including Sally, rather than being lost in the shuffle of nominees.

Agent for Stock Splits

Periodically a company splits its stock, which increases the number of shares of stock without actually selling more or increasing the value. For example, if a corporation whose stock is valued at $80 per share does a 4-for-1 split, each share of stock becomes four shares, each worth $20. Nothing new has been sold, and the value of the total holdings has not increased. Nothing has been added other than more shares and more paperwork.

The **stock split** agent either issues three new shares or collects the existing one share and issues four new ones. As shown below, the dividend proportionately decreases per share, but stockholders still receive the same total amount: a $2 annual dividend per share before the split becomes a 50¢ annual dividend after the split.

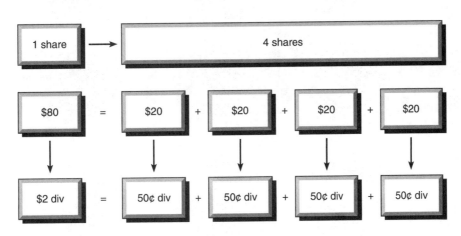

USING TRUST PRODUCTS AND SERVICES
TO MEET CUSTOMER NEEDS

Assume that FedEx declares a $4 per share dividend (to be paid $1 per quarter) to its owners of record. FedEx's transfer agent's records show that ABC Bank is a registered owner (nominee) for 50,000 shares of FedEx. FedEx's dividend-paying agent makes a quarterly dividend payment of $50,000 to ABC, as nominee. ABC then distributes the money to the respective accounts it manages.

FedEx provides dividend money to

↓

Dividend-paying agent, who distributes dividend checks to owners of record

↓   ↓   ↓   ↓

ABC Bank, as nominee, distributes dividend money in turn to

↓

$2,500 to the John Doe trust (ABC, as trustee), which holds 2,500 shares of FedEx

$25,000 to the PDQ, Inc. profit sharing plan (ABC, as investment agent),
which holds 25,000 shares of FedEx

$2,000 to the Sally Smith investment management account
(ABC, as investment agent), which holds 2,000 shares of FedEx

$3,500 to the Jim Dwyer custody account (ABC, as custodial agent),
which holds 3,500 shares of FedEx

$1,500 to the estate of Nancy Burrows (ABC, as executor),
which holds 1,500 shares of FedEx

$15,000 to the XYZ, Inc. 401(k) plan (ABC, as trustee),
which holds 15,000 shares of FedEx

$500 to Mr. Sullivan's guardianship account (ABC, as guardian of the estate),
which holds 500 shares of FedEx

Why do corporations bother to split their stock? The biggest reason is to bring the price per share down to a more reachable and reasonable price. Would an investor be more inclined to buy a $250-per-share stock or a $50-per-share stock? Investor psychology over the years has leaned toward the latter.

Although not seen very often, some companies do reverse splits. Rather than increasing the number of shares, a company decreases the number, for example, a 1-for-20 split.

Additional Stock Agency Services

Trust departments also serve as agent for the following:

- **Tenders:** ABC Corporation buys XYZ Company for cash. Owners of XYZ must tender (give up) their stock in exchange for cash from ABC. Or ABC may buy XYZ for stock, in which case XYZ stock is converted to ABC stock. The latter example may involve the services of an exchange agent.

- **Mergers:** ABC and XYZ merge into one company. ABC stock and XYZ stock are converted into a new, uniform class of stock. For example, when First Chicago Bank merged with National Bank of Detroit (NBD), the new entity converted its individual stock into a new "First Chicago NBD" stock.

- **Subscriptions:** This happens when a corporation wants to sell new stock but offers it to existing stockholders first.

- **Buybacks:** There are financial reasons why a company may buy back some of its outstanding stock (stock owned by outside investors); either the stock is retired or the company retains ownership.

- **Rights:** Corporations periodically authorize additional shares of stock to be issued. Common stockholders usually have a pre-emptive right to purchase all or a portion of the newly authorized stock. The price for the stock is set at the time of the new offering. Rights are typically exercisable only for a brief period. During the time an offer is open, the rights can be exercised, not exercised, or traded (sold) by the shareholders in the general marketplace.

- **Warrants:** Similar to rights, a warrant is a certificate (attached to a new stock issue or new bond issue, as a "bond sweetener") that permits the purchaser of the new issue to buy a set number of shares of stock at a specific price at any point in the future prior to the expiration of the warrant. The time period is usually fixed (say, 5 years) or it may be perpetual (no expiration). When a warrant is issued to a company's employee, it is called a **stock option.** Stock options are not tradable in the open market like rights and warrants.

- **Options:** An option contract, usually between individuals, gives an investor the right to buy (a **call**) or sell (a **put**) common stock at a certain price within a designated period of time.

SUMMARY

- Long gone are the simple days of raising capital, issuing securities, and keeping in direct touch with investors. Today's world of investments and related investment transactions has evolved into a frenzy of regulations and complex activities.

- Both individuals and institutions need money (capital). How capital is raised depends on the amounts needed and the purposes for the funds. Capital is either debt capital or equity capital. Evidence of ownership in a company (as a stockholder or bondholder) is the stock or bond certificate issued.

- In the 1800s, because of the volume of capital investing, centralized trading exchanges developed to facilitate the trading of securities. During this time national banks and state banks entered the picture as institutions that provided typical banking services, the underwriting (selling) of securities issues, and investment and deposit safety through creation of the OCC in 1863.

- Because of investment fraud, individual states and the federal government passed a series of securities laws designed to protect investors from false investment schemes. Individual states passed blue sky laws to regulate investment activities within each state. In 1933 Congress passed the Truth in Securities Act (which provided for the registration of securities) and the Federal Banking Act (the Glass–Steagall Act, which separated commercial and investment banking activities) and created the FDIC to protect bank customer deposits. In 1934 the Securities and Exchange Act created the SEC; in 1939 the Trust Indenture Act set guidelines for the use of a trustee in bond securities offerings.

- Investment banks (as opposed to commercial banks) work with companies by determining what type of capital to seek and by creating a primary market in which securities are sold to the investing public.

- An indenture trust is a trust document that defines the specifics of a bond issue. Trust departments serve as trustee by providing corporate trust services. The trustee is responsible for several administrative duties on behalf of the grantor (the company seeking capital), and it protects the financial interests of the bondholders (the beneficiaries) as a fiduciary in the event of interest or principal default.

- In addition to providing indenture trust services to companies, trust departments offer bond and stock agency services. Bond agencies are paying agent, bond registrar, and exchange agent. Stock agencies consist of dividend-paying agent, stock registrar, transfer agent, and agent for stock splits. Additional agency services are provided for tenders, mergers, subscriptions, buybacks, warrants, and options.

REVIEW QUESTIONS

1. Describe the difference between equity capital and debt capital.
2. Briefly describe the purposes of the Securities Act of 1933, the Federal Banking Act of 1933, and the Trust Indenture Act of 1939.
3. What are the basic responsibilities of a bank trust department in administering a corporate bond trust?
4. Name three bond agency services provided by trust departments and briefly describe their duties.
5. Name five stock agency services provided by trust departments.

12

SELLING, MARKETING, AND COMPETING

"The difficulty lies, not in the new ideas, but in escaping from the old ones, which ramify, for those brought up as most of us have been, into every corner of our minds."

John Maynard Keynes (1883–1946)

Once upon a time almost everyone bought an American car; household goods were purchased with cash, not credit; and military service was common. Things are different today, although many time-tested attitudes remain relevant: "Life is 10 percent what happens to you, 90 percent how you react to it"; "Progress is a given when you adapt, improvise, and overcome"; "Taking charge and taking responsibility breed success."

As we move through the closing pages of this text—from the established facts and definitions to the challenges of selling and marketing—it is vitally important that you determine up front whether your glass of water is half-full or half-empty. A negative or blasé approach will never bring customers in your door. Keep in mind that an action plan does not come prepackaged and ready to go. Selling, marketing, and competing are strictly "assembly required"; the instructions aren't always clear, parts may be missing, and others don't fit perfectly.

LEARNING OBJECTIVES

Although there really are no right or guaranteed answers or ideas for marketing, selling, and competing, those your trust department chooses may determine the fate of its business.

Upon completion of this chapter, you will be able to

- Explain what future-fee business is and why it is important to trust departments
- Explain why customer service is vital to trust departments
- Profile cross-cultivation between banking and trust departments
- Define a sales culture
- Compare internal and external referral programs
- Profile the competitors faced by trust departments

SELLING IS NOT A DIRTY WORD

"If I wanted to sell, I would have gone to work for an auto dealer" is the view of many trust professionals. "Our products and services are precious commodities that sell themselves" is another common belief. But a customer won't rely on you for his sense of financial stability, comfort, and being cared for just because you hang a sign in front of your place of business. Trust professionals have to take our story to the street.

What the Insiders Say

Although they appeared in print some time ago, the words of Maribeth Rahe, former senior executive vice president of personal and commercial trust and investment services at the Harris Bank in Chicago, are still true:

- Customer service is not old-fashioned.

- We must sell ourselves to the public by telling our customers how good we are.

- The amount of wealth in our country is enormous; nonbank competition is threatening the personal trust business.

- Trust departments need to become more aggressive with their marketing and selling programs and with developing cost-efficient, innovative products and services.

- Our knowledge and experience should enable us to educate our customers about how good we are as investment managers.

These are key sales concepts, and we will keep them in mind throughout this chapter.

What the Outsiders Say

A personal trust department recently conducted a mailing to its base of future-fee will and trust customers. The officer responsible for the mailing knew several of the customers personally. Three weeks after the mailing went out, a customer (let's call him Les) telephoned the trust officer to respond to the mailing and to renew an old friendship. During the phone conversation, Les (now an established M.D.) mentioned that his medical practice was recently sold. Taking a wild stab, the trust officer asked, "Les, did you ever think you would be a millionaire?" Les admitted to the magnitude of his assets since the practice was sold. "Who is managing your money, Les?" the trust officer asked. Les said he was referred to a local investment management firm. He expressed his pleasure with the manager, how they kept in close contact with him, and how strongly they had been recommended. Nothing was mentioned about fees and performance. "Why didn't you call us, Les?" the trust officer asked. Raucous laughter filled the line for several seconds. Les then replied, "Why would I want to talk with your trust department? I haven't died! Besides, what do trust departments know about managing money?" The trust department is not laughing.

Trust departments cannot ignore Rahe's words. We cannot allow prospects, referral sources, and customers the opportunity to say what Les said. Our marketing and selling efforts must inform customers about what trust departments do, express confidence in our ability to do it, and demonstrate concern for our customers.

FUTURE-FEE BUSINESS

Future-fee (potential-fee) business results when a customer names a bank as executor in a will and trustee in a trust. This is business that will mature (develop into fees) upon the customer's death. Since the early 1970s, the generation, record-keeping, and serving of future-fee will and trust business has had its ups and downs in just about every trust department across the United States. Though periodically encouraged, production of future-fee business is soon subordinated to the production of active-fee (current-fee) business.

In essence, future-fee business hobbles along as an unwanted orphan. It does not bring in fees today, and it may not see fees tomorrow. In addition, it costs time and money to maintain something so uncertain. Seen as the room in the basement that holds the junk the homeowner cannot bring himself to throw away, the plans for future-fee business often hang around, out of sight and out of mind.

Defining the Problem

Hot-and-cold attempts to sell and serve future-fee business stem from changing management, merger interruptions, and loss of interest in supporting a program that costs, but does not pay, at least in the early stages of the game. Admittedly, a potential-fee customer base does not generate income today. Maintaining a program of selling, servicing, and record-keeping for a will and trust client is difficult when the revenue will not be realized until later. But can the trust industry afford not to devote attention to future-fee business? If we ignore it, it is easy for customers to go elsewhere.

At a recent state trust convention, a senior-ranking trust manager from a large bank touted the size of her personal trust department's potential-fee records. "We have a storeroom with 18,000 files. When you factor in that a file can contain a will *and* a trust for Mr. Customer *and* Mrs. Customer, imagine the base magnitude of our potential business." Her small audience was impressed until a listener began to ask questions.

"Exactly how many wills and trusts and Mr.-and-Mrs. files are there?" (The answer was, "I don't know.") "How many of the wills and trusts name the bank in a primary, as opposed to secondary or contingent, capacity?" (Again, the trust manager couldn't answer.) "Do you have a program in place to keep in contact with and to service your customer base?" (The answer was, "Why? This business doesn't generate fees. How can we justify spending dollars, energy, and personnel's time on something that doesn't bring fees in the door?") When pressed about the actual percentage of executor and trustee appointments the department acted on after notification of a customer's death, she responded that it was 14 percent.

Where did the other 86 percent go?

Samuel Witting, former chairman of the Trust New Business Committee of Chicago Banks and Trust Departments, addressed this issue many years ago in the results of the committee's studies of the trust industry. Witting found that trust departments give little attention to serving future-fee customers once will and trust appointments are sold. Because this business is overlooked, a substantial percentage of it lapses.

Witting thought equal emphasis should be placed on maintaining future-fee business and selling it because it grows each year as customers' wealth increases. Because most trust departments do not have organized programs to serve their future-fee customer base, these departments have no idea what the value of their will and trust file is despite the considerable amount of money spent to generate potential-fee business.

Witting's timely take on the problem appears in *The Evaluation of New Trust Business,* published in 1934. His concerns persist today.

As trust professionals we know personal trust department revenues depend on customers' fees from the generation of new active-fee business (investment management, guardianship, IRA rollover, custody, and living trust accounts) and from matured business, meaning executor (nonrecurring) and trustee (recurring) fees following a customer's death. As long as a trust department emphasizes the sale of active-fee business, revenues should persist.

What happens, however, when the sale of future-fee business diminishes? Future revenue won't be there because there won't be business to mature. Furthermore, if future-fee customers are not served, the future revenues they represent will also lapse.

Retention Program

Recognizing the decline in will and executor and trust and trustee appointments, and the subsequent decrease in matured fees, a particular trust department designed an incentive bonus program to encourage the development and sale of future-fee business. The department was aware of the potential yet unknown cost of selling "that which does not generate fees now," but it was willing to spend the time and money necessary today in order to harvest increased fees tomorrow.

This sales effort was developed in 1975. Twenty years later, management questioned why matured fees had not increased despite two decades of increased sales efforts. Where the department fell short was in not developing a consistent and active program to service the newly developed estate plans. In essence, the department had no idea of the status of its future-fee (will and trust file) base of customers.

Mailings

After an initial cleanup of its files, the department launched a maintenance mailing to learn where customers were, whether they still named the bank in their wills and trusts, and whether their records were accurate. Over a 1-year period, the trust department conducted two separate mailings to its 6,500 customers. The department was astonished at the large number of inaccurate addresses, nonreplies, and responses that informed the department that the bank was no longer named in the customer's estate plan. Can any business afford to find out that it doesn't know where 26 percent of its customers are, that 21 percent don't respond, and that 24 percent no longer do business with it?

Support Program

What the department learned from its maintenance mailings was the need to develop a personal, structured, and continuous customer-contact program. Each segment of the program resulted in a beneficial outcome.

- *Ongoing mailing programs.* In addition to departmental welcome letters (when a new estate plan was sold) and annual anniversary letters (to remind customers of their estate plan), ancillary mailings were developed to provide will and trust customers with general financial information, product and service introductions, and tax updates when applicable.

  Result: Retention of future-fee business and matured fees increased.

- *Regular, periodic mailing program to the file's professional advisors.* This program assisted customers' advisors (attorneys, accountants, and insurance advisors) in maintaining contact with their clients, besides raising advisors' awareness and opinion of the trust department.

  Result: Referrals from outside sources increased in both future-fee and active-fee business.

- *Active face-to-face calling program.* Personal visits enabled department staff to review the level of executor and trustee appointments and to reintroduce the importance of the trust department's role in the customer's estate plan.

  Result: Secondary (successor) fiduciary appointments were upgraded to primary appointments.

- *Will and trust file customer seminars.* These seminars focused on tax law changes, banking and trust products and services, and estate planning considerations.

  Result: Referrals from the customer base, upgrade of fiduciary appointments, and the sale of active-fee products and services increased.

- *System to work closely with department personnel.* Both administrative managers and portfolio managers were encouraged to sell active-fee business to the will and trust file and to sell future-fee business to their base of current-fee customers.

  Result: Active-fee sales grew from the future-fee customer base, and vice versa.

- *Program of product and service training sessions.* These sessions provided nontrust personnel with the knowledge of and confidence in the department's products and services to help foster additional active-fee and future-fee business.

  Result: Cross-selling of personal trust and investment management and commercial and personal banking products and services increased.

SERVICE, MORE SERVICE, AND THEN SOME MORE SERVICE

Servicing a future-fee retention program takes time, money, and energy, but these costs bring win–win results to the bank and customers.

When customers pay thousands of dollars per year in fees for a trust, rollover, or investment management account, do they get more than a quarterly statement, a semiannual call from the portfolio manager, and a holiday greeting card? Are they called and visited regularly, thanked constantly, and sent items of special interest? Relationships must be given more than minimal service. For example, one successful trust department pays close attention to its customers by constantly asking them, through service programs, to be on the watch for reasons they shouldn't continue their accounts with the bank. This reminds the customers about the department's commitment to excellent service while controlling the quality of the department's efforts. If reasons to discontinue accounts are found, they are fixed immediately.

Marketing

Selling a product or a service is a two-step process: getting the prospect to say yes, then keeping the prospect-turned-customer from saying no. Selling is therefore a continuous process.

Marketing is first cousin to selling. It determines to whom to sell, what to sell, and how to serve the sale to keep the product or service sold. It isn't a complicated science, and it won't tell you *how* to sell, but it vitally supports the sales process. Let's look at some examples of marketing services.

- When an individual establishes an account with Merrill Lynch, two of Merrill's key concerns are keeping the customer and selling more. One successful marketing tool is an 80-page, leather-bound planning document for customers. Called *Financial Foundation,* this document covers estate planning, asset allocation, and risk tolerance. It also discusses life insurance, trust planning, and investment direction. This book will not improve an account's investment return, but it does improve customer retention. By giving customers more than a monthly statement, the name of an account representative, and a toll-free phone number, Merrill proves it can make its marketing pay off in new and repeat business.

- According to information reported in a *Fortune* magazine article, affluent customers look for service, confidentiality, a sense of interest on the part of their advisor, and trust. A solid referral by a trusted colleague or business advisor, personal contact, and a solid reputation were most important, and investment performance and fees placed last. Interestingly, if a customer's self-perceived needs are met, substandard investment performance and sloppy statements are overlooked. High-quality service is showing customers you care.

- The International Association of Financial Planners concluded from a survey that investors are twice as concerned about the honesty of a financial advisor as they are about the quality of service. Trust and ethical behavior outrank good advice and making money for the client as important characteristics of a financial advisor.

As financial service providers, trust departments can easily determine what a customer wants merely by asking. Remember, business is driven by customers. Ask them what they want and, more importantly, listen. The answers are golden.

Customer Surveys

Many trust departments use customer surveys to measure their customers' level of satisfaction with the bank's personal trust and investment management products and services. Primarily, these surveys address

- Account officer/support staff performance
  - Availability and responsiveness
  - Knowledge and professionalism
  - Personal attention and courtesy
  - Frequency and modes of contact
- Service evaluation
  - Response to inquiries
  - Accuracy and timeliness of statements and disbursement of funds
  - Investment performance and fees
  - Account officer turnover

As a trust professional, you must be constantly vigilant about meeting customer needs and weighing your strengths (and using them to your advantage) and your shortcomings (and correcting them).

The new wealth of the baby-boom generation has begun to trickle into the financial stream. Trust departments would be wise to develop innovative marketing and sales techniques, and responsive products and services, to meet the baby boomers' changing needs, perceptions, and financial expectations before this trickle becomes a torrent.

CROSS-CULTIVATION

ABC Bank & Trust Company's head of trust (Tom) and head of banking (Jerry) sat next to each other many times on the train home from work. Their chit-chat always centered on nonwork topics: the grandkids, Sunday's football games, and politics. One evening as they left the train and made their way to their cars, Tom commented, "Jerry, seldom do we talk about the bank or our departments." Jerry nodded in agreement and suggested they do so some day.

Tom and Jerry met for breakfast two days later. They talked for three hours. These men had combined working careers of 52 years at ABC Bank & Trust Company, but this was the first time they had spent this much time together, one-on-one, in a single sitting. Clearly something was wrong with their departments' lack of interaction. For example, one of Jerry's young bankers had told him he didn't know the bank had a trust department; one of Tom's trust administrators had never heard of a letter of credit. Concerned, Tom and Jerry hired an outside consultant to look at each department, learn what personnel thought of their respective and opposite departments, find common ties, and identify ways to improve interaction. Here is what the consultant found.

Banking View of Trust

Poor investment returns
"Vanilla" products and services
High fees
Frequent personnel turnover
Little knowledge of banking
Mysterious
No concern for customers
Poor trust leadership
Poor incentive to sell trust products
Weak sister
No effort to sell banking products
Little visibility
Doesn't provide training
Not knowledgeable
Inaccessible
Aloof

Trust View of Banking

Little commitment from bank management
  to the trust department
No resources and budget strength
Inexperienced banking management
Little coordination and contact with the
  banking department
No sales and service culture
Absence of referrals
No image or visibility
Minimal training
No cross-cultivation
No incentive to sell banking products
Constant reorganization
Won't make customer accommodations
Possessive of customers

These perceptions are not rare. This state of affairs exists in many institutions. But in successful institutions, banking and trust departments train and educate each other, sell together, prospect to and from the other side, mutually call on and serve their individual and common customers, and of course share profits. Compare this collaboration to a military exercise when ground, naval, and air units coordinate their individual and combined logistics and activities and support each other.

Tom and Jerry concluded that cross-prospecting, cross-selling, cross-calling, cross-serving, and cross-profiting would never occur if

- The trust officer doesn't know what a letter of credit is, what mortgage points and interest rates are, or what checking account minimum balance requirements are.

- The banking officer doesn't know his bank has a trust department, what an IRA is, or that the custodian department is not the same as janitorial services.

Tom and Jerry and their staffs needed to spend more time together, teaching each other what they do, how they can help each other, and otherwise breaking down the walls and false barriers that kept two strong departments from making one institution stronger.

CREATE A SALES CULTURE

As recent as twenty years ago, bank trust departments enjoyed a monopoly in the arena of asset management. Selling was treated as order-taking and customer service was relegated to hand holding. Since then, nonbank competitors have grown stronger. Recognizing the opportunity for business, nonbank competitors created products, services, and sales programs to serve customers with modest assets today who have the potential to amass wealth tomorrow.

The trust industry did not lag in designing and developing products and services; lately, it has developed a broader spectrum of products and services for a variety of customers. But it *has* lagged in selling them. It is imperative that bank trust departments continually improve their sales techniques to retain and regain market share.

Successful trust departments create a total institutional sales culture in which everyone is *sales-minded*. Everyone is cross-educated, cross-trained, and financially rewarded to recognize a prospect and a sales opportunity. It should be common for bank employees—not just for senior management, but also for a teller, a personal and commercial banker, a bank guard, and a telephone operator—to identify prospects and refer them to the proper desk.

Not everyone wants to be a salesperson, and not everyone should sell. An institution that pressures everyone to meet a sales quota jeopardizes employee harmony and overall production. Trust departments must complement their sales culture with a dedicated, trained, well-managed, financially motivated sales force. Yet many institutions believe that anyone with drive will qualify.

Perhaps our industry should look to the successful sales trainee programs developed in other industries that depend heavily on sales. Consider the life insurance industry. The vast majority of the salespeople hired by insurance companies have little or no previous sales experience or background in financial services, have never envisioned being "an insurance person," and seldom move from one company to another. The insurance industry makes great efforts to recruit and train its sales force. Its year-after-year sales records prove this. So does the comment of a very prominent estate planning attorney: "I've worked with Chartered Life Underwriters (CLUs) who can sell, talk, and advise circles around most of the trust officers I know."

GENERATE REFERRALS

The most difficult part of the sales process is neither the actual sales presentation nor the closing; it's finding prospects.

Who are a trust department's prospects? Business owners, executives, professionals, retirees, lottery winners, insurance claimants, someone who has inherited a sizable estate, a bank customer with large deposits, an investor with a large portfolio, someone who has sold her business—anyone who has accumulated assets.

Where and how are prospects found? Each institution should ask all employees to prospect as part of the overall sales culture, and it should provide incentives for employees to refer qualified prospects to the trust department.

The importance of prospecting and referral sources to a trust department is indicated by statistics gathered from VIP Forum studies by the Washington, D.C.–based Advisory Company.

- In a typical commercial bank, 50 percent of the trust and private banking prospects come from the bank's current customer base; 20 percent come from retail and corporate sectors of the bank. Outside prospecting is minimal: 30 percent from third-party professionals, cold calls, and direct mail.

- When accountants refer business to a bank, the close ratio for sales is 67 percent. Percentages from other sources are 39 percent from attorneys, 35 percent from internal leads, 25 percent from customer referrals, and 3 percent from cold calls. Third-party referral sources help prequalify the prospect.

- Third-party referral sources generate larger accounts and larger fees than do internal referrals: Attorneys from a targeted city account for $1–8 million average relationships with average annual fees of $17,700 (compared to internal referrals for $0.5–1.5 million average relationships with fees of $5–10 thousand).

- Affluent customers seldom cite trust department personnel as their financial advisor; 67 percent of customers use an attorney, 65 percent use an accountant, 63 percent use a broker, 39 percent use a financial planner, 38 percent consult a family member, 37 percent use an insurance agent, 31 percent use a private banker, 23 percent use a regular banker, 23 percent consult friends, 19 percent use a retirement counselor, and 17 percent use an asset manager.

- Many trust professionals feel it is difficult to obtain third-party referrals. This is because outside referral sources perceive high turnover among banking and trust officers, absence of referral reciprocity, and lack of attention to cultivating friendships with the professionals. In addition, referral sources claim that too often trust departments give them little or late feedback following a referral, sometimes attempt to steal their clients' business, and blunder more often than they should when providing service (for example, by being inaccessible and unresponsive).

- To improve referral relations, professionals refer to providers they know and trust; personal friendships are at the core of a referral relationship; developing these friendships takes time, effort, and persistence. Attorneys and accountants expect feedback on clients they refer; they view subsequent, ongoing communication as professional treatment and a matter of courtesy. Rewarding referrers is an absolute necessity; reciprocity and delivery of satisfied clients is hailed as the best, if not the only acceptable, reward for a referral.

The successful sales force has a plethora of prospects. Internal referrals through an established referral program are important in building internal relationships, yet external referrals (as shown in the study) provide larger, prequalified business.

MEET THE COMPETITION

Every business, every individual, faces competition. Without competition, free enterprise would collapse and monopolies would persist. To beat the competition (in a sports event, a military skirmish, or a sales situation), we must be aware of our competitor's strengths and weaknesses as well as what we are capable and incapable of doing.

One way of meeting the competition is to promote our profession's high-quality people, technological resources, marketing knowledge, and investment track record. Without doing so we may sit on our assets and continue to lose them to nonbank competitors like these:

- Full-service and discount brokers
- Mutual funds
- Insurance companies
- Investment counselors
- Certified Financial Planners
- Attorneys and accountants
- Brokerage trust companies
- Mutual fund trust companies
- Independent trust companies
- Individuals (families and friends)
- Family offices

- Other departments in the bank (bond departments, bank brokerage, and bank mutual funds)

Regulations as a Competitor

Throughout this book we have encountered many rules, regulations, and laws governing the banking and trust industries. The series of securities laws enacted in the 1930s (see Chapter 11), including those that spawned the Chinese wall practices, constrained bank activities and therefore favored the nonbank competition. The securities laws limited the services banks could provide and barred banks from entering the lucrative mutual fund and insurance businesses. Alan Greenspan, an advocate of financial deregulation, described the banks' plight as a regulatory strait jacket.

In 1982 the American Bankers Association and the accounting firm Coopers & Lybrand conducted a nationwide survey among banks regarding the separation of banking and trust services. The extensive report, "Synergy in Banking: A Strategic Assessment of Trust Banking Opportunities in the Eighties," suggested that trust departments were at a disadvantage compared to their competitors and that various departments of banks should share and integrate functions. When the ABA shared this report with the regulatory agencies and requested clarification of the Chinese wall, the regulators responded that misunderstandings about the appropriate degree of separateness between trust departments and commercial banking had been harmful to the public interest. As a result of this clarification, trust departments were allowed to implement the recommendations of the study without violating trust regulations. This synergy between trust departments and commercial banking, as desirable today as it was in 1982, provides an opportunity for trust departments to scale the Chinese wall and meet outside competition on an equal footing, yet still provide safe, regulated services to customers.

Although regulations have been relaxed over the past decade, some trust professionals still describe these regulations as a tourniquet on the trust industry. But regulations are intended to protect consumers. When faced with a prospective customer, trust professionals should emphasize how these regulations make trust departments a safer, more responsible, more prudent—but no less productive—choice than nonblank financial services providers.

Brokerage Houses

Merrill Lynch, Fidelity, Vanguard, and Schwab are among the nonbank competitors that have moved into our neighborhood. These brokerage firms have established multi-billion-dollar personal trust departments, retirement counseling centers, and home mortgage loan arms. But that wasn't always true. Not long ago, brokerage houses concentrated on investment buy-and-sell transactions to bring commissions in the door. Derided for "churning" customer accounts to earn commissions, these nonbank competitors turned to fee-based investment management—the trust industry's stalwart way of doing things. To this service the brokerage houses added one-stop shopping for estate and financial planning, wealth transfer analyses, investment research, and banking services. They also instituted loans, electronic bill payment, credit cards, ATMs, and online access to client accounts. The brokerage business also entered the qualified and nonqualified retirement plan business (including the lucrative IRA market) and personal trusts. Almost overnight, while many in the trust industry stood virtually still, the brokerage industry rose like the phoenix to become multi-billion-dollar trust and banking conglomerates.

Unlike many banks, brokerage houses aggressively spend time and money recruiting customers. Annual marketing and advertising budgets range in the tens of millions of dollars. Merrill Lynch alone devoted in excess of $50 million in 2000 toward its sales efforts. In contrast, the Bank Marketing Association reports that marketing expenditures for banks are a small fraction of what brokerage firms spend, and these expenses have been shrinking over the past five years.

Brokerage houses treat marketing and selling as the name of the game. And once a prospect is sold, the customer is cross-sold additional products and services in anticipation of the customer's bringing all of his business to the brokerage. Brokerage houses don't know something we don't—they *do* something we don't.

Life Insurance Companies

During the past 20 years, numerous insurance companies have experienced deep financial problems, including occasional bankruptcies and receiverships. Of the existing 1,600 companies, only 10 percent have acceptable ratings from the rating services (Moody's, Best, Standard & Poor's, and Duff & Phelps). Nonetheless, many reputable insurance firms aggressively and successfully sell their products as investment vehicles. How big is this business? One of the top-15 U.S. insurance companies, the Minnesota Mutual Life Insurance Company of St. Paul, Minnesota, boasted $18 billion in assets under management and mutual fund sales close to $485 million in 2001—all in addition to in-force life insurance plans in excess of $295 billion.

Very few banks can boast numbers like these. How do life insurance companies do it? Traditionally, the industry manages to grab such a large share of the overall financial markets by using a professional, aggressive, and knowledgeable sales force.

Financial Planners

Comparable to the independent investment management firms that have grown by 600 percent over the past 20 years while tripling their work force, a new generation of financial planners has emerged. From the conglomerate financial planning institutions to the one-person shops, financial planners (or Certified Financial Planners [CFPs], for those who have gained the designation through class work and exams via the College of Financial Planning in Denver, Colorado) have developed into yet another source of competition. Acting on the theory of providing holistic guidance—of being an estate and financial planning architect—on investments, insurance, taxation, and estate and retirement planning, these planners are varied in their approach and structure.

Twenty-five percent charge by fee only (the fee can vary immensely depending on how much or little the planer offers a customer), 25 percent earn income solely from commissions on products they sell (life insurance, mutual funds, pension plans), and the remaining 50 percent offer a fee and commission structure or receive a flat salary from their employer.

Many people migrate to financial planners, attracted by a one-stop planning service. It is good business practice for trust professionals to know the competition well enough to be able to explain to their customers how the competitions' services compare to those provided by trust departments in banks. We should try to help customers decide what they really want from a financial planner. The place for the customer to start is by checking a planner's training and experience. Is the planner a CFP, CLU (Chartered Life Underwriter), ChFC (Chartered Financial Consultant), or CTFA (Certified Trust and Financial Advisor)? Is the planner a member of the International Association for Financial Planning? The customer should look into a planner's experience and performance record and his or her knowledge of estates, trusts, real estate, and investments. The search for a financial planner may not produce a financial hero who can step in and solve every financial concern. Yet it is very likely that the customer will find the right professional planner—right in the bank's personal trust department.

Mutual Funds

Many people think of mutual funds as a relatively new way of investing, but mutual funds began in 1924 when Massachusetts Financial Services, a Boston investment company, formed the Massachusetts Investors Trust mutual fund. In 1960 there were 161 mutual funds; today the number is in excess of 10,000. In 1980 only 6 percent of households invested in mutual funds; today, more than 45 percent of householders invest in mutual funds, totaling in excess of $500 billion. In 1975 the mutual fund industry boasted $50 billion under management. Today, despite the 2000–2002 stock market tumble, the mutual fund industry manages more than $1.5 trillion—a 3,000 percent growth with an average annual growth rate of 110 percent.

Prospectus

When an individual elects to invest in a mutual fund, the fund (investment company) is required by securities laws to provide the investor with a prospectus, a written description that discloses details about the fund (investment objective, date of inception, minimum deposits, holdings, size, performance, and fees).

Absent a fund's formal prospectus, a quick guide to costs, investment objectives, and performance is the *Wall Street Journal's* quarterly mutual fund report, which is included in a daily issue within the first week of each calendar quarter. In addition to general investment articles, the report lists over 8,000 mutual funds and shows each fund's minimum initial and subsequent investment amounts, size, sales charges, annual expenses, performance, and investment objectives.

Mutual Funds in Banks

Many people think of mutual funds and bank trust departments as oil-and-water—they don't mix. This was true at one time. Securities laws did not allow banks to distribute (underwrite) mutual funds. The slow relaxation of the securities laws—and more progressive and pro-competitive interpretations of the laws—provided that banks could engage in such securities activities as providing agency services (investment management, custody, transfer agent, fund accounting) to mutual funds. This gave banks the opportunity to provide their customers with access—directly or indirectly (whichever way you want to look at it)—to the mutual fund industry.

The Financial Services Modernization Act of 1999 altered the laws that kept banks from competing with other financial institutions and services—mutual funds included. The act repealed provisions of the older securities laws by dismantling the walls that separated banking, insurance, and securities activities. (Refer again to Chapter 11.) The legislation created a new financial services structure, the "financial holding company," that may engage in any activity deemed to be financial in nature. As a result, banks may now affiliate with securities firms and insurance companies within the same financial holding company. Banks may even merge with or purchase securities firms and insurance companies. This opportunity to affiliate has inspired banks to offer a broad array of financial products and services apart from traditional banking and trust products, including all forms of insurance and administration and distribution of mutual funds.

Interestingly, a large percentage of the growth of mutual funds is due to banks' use of mutual funds for customers' portfolios (personal and institutional). As an example, Bank One's "One Group" family of mutual funds consists of a complex of 48 mutual funds totaling more than $100 billion under one investment roof. Bank One's funds are the third largest bank-advised fund family and the seventeenth largest fund family overall in the mutual fund industry.

Fees and Performance

Surprisingly, many people think that mutual funds do not charge fees because there is no bill for the fund's services. But there is a fee. It is either deducted directly against the investor's account or, in most instances, taken off the top, meaning the fund's return or balance is net of fees.

Your customers should be made aware that mutual funds' fees may be expensive. Although mutual funds are required to disclose their fees, many fund managers find ingenious ways to do so, leading investors to believe that their mutual funds are competitively inexpensive. Some critics of mutual funds' fees have gone so far as to say that many mutual funds hide their fees, thereby giving investors the false impression that costs are nonexistent or low. As a result, the SEC has mandated that a clear, concise disclosure of fees be printed on the inside cover of mutual-fund prospectuses.

As a trust professional, you need to keep in mind that mutual funds can charge one or more of the following fees:

- Annual expense or management fee: charged to cover the fund's annual investment advisory staff expenses

- 12B-1 fee: fee for registering the fund and for marketing and distribution costs, named after an SEC regulation

- Front-load fee: entry fee (basically a sales commission) assessed to a customer to enter a fund

- Back-load fee: an exit fee; in some funds this fee disappears after 5 to 10 years; at times this fee is structured to decrease on a sliding basis, depending on the amount of time an investor stays in a fund

- Reinvestment fee: charge for the fund to reinvest bond interest or stock dividends

- Brokerage fee: assessed to pay the broker or advisor who sold the customer into a fund

- Withdrawal and transfer fee: charges to withdraw money from one fund and transfer to another

- Service fee (maintenance fee): administrative fee for bookkeeping, asset custody, auditing, legal, and indescribable other expenses

In a mathematical equation, what is done to one side must be done to the other side to maintain equilibrium. Such is also the case, so to speak, when comparing the performance of mutual funds to that of individually managed investment services. A mutual fund's performance must be judged from a net perspective: gross performance minus fees. The same is true for the performance of a trust department's individually managed investment advisory services: gross return minus advisory fees.

Where fee-and-performance calculations get warped is when layers are attached—to the negative and to the positive. For example, many independent financial advisors use mutual funds as their way of providing customers with investment management services. There is nothing sinister about this. Mutual funds are viable investment vehicles, and the advisor is most likely assisting the customer in choosing those funds that will meet the customer's investment objectives and risk tolerance. But doing this is also likely to cause a double fee—the advisor's and the fund's. This is a negative.

The competition has volleyed in return that a similar double fee occurs when a trust department uses mutual funds for a customer's account. In some instances this is true, and this makes salespeople hesitant to discuss fees, believing that the talk of cost scares customers away. Never be defensive about what time, products, and services cost. Contrary to popular belief, the combined fund-and-department fees of bank trust departments are quite competitive to those charged by nonbank competitors.

Being confident in our offerings and prices requires knowledge of the competition. If your products and services are less expensive, be proud. If your products and services are more expensive, show the extras (what the nonbank competitors do not have) that justify the expenses:

- Tax and retirement planning
- One-on-one personalized service

- Dedicated administrative and portfolio managers
- Estate analysis
- Risk and asset allocation determination
- Banking products

Often—and surprisingly to the competition—a trust department's fees combined with its mutual funds' fees are eyeball-to-eyeball with nonbank competitors' fees. What a fine way to meet our foes: offer competitive fees and then top the cake with a frosting filled with extras. This is a positive.

WE SHALL OVERCOME

To some critics the picture painted in this chapter is one of doom and gloom—that banks and their trust departments have not fully accepted the competition's challenge.

The picture really isn't gloom and doom; however, clearly, bank trust departments must strive continually to recognize their shortcomings, eliminate the negatives, accentuate the positives, and overcome complacency in their practices. Bank and trust departments must market and sell more specifically, and more often, in order to show customers and prospective customers

- Our personalized, value-added products
- Our competitive investment performance
- Our personal service
- Our efficient fee structures

As trust professionals, we must counter the customer's belief that trusts and investment management services are only for older, wealthier clients and that our products and services are only for the incapacitated and dying. We are not just guardians of a final stage of life, but also advisors to our beginning and midcourse customers.

We must educate ourselves, our customers, our referral sources, and our competition. It is imperative that we do more than simply read about marketing and selling, attend seminars, or ponder industry studies. Without action, our growth and performance will stagnate. Unless we put our size and strengths to work, the competition will continue to invade our territory and threaten our survival.

Customers are not ignorant. We may become so if we don't pay attention to them. Trust departments that ignore customers' demands are wrong to do so. In a December 2000 Trust and Wealth Advisory Industry Trends teleconference "Through the Client's Eyes—What They Want and What They Are Willing to Pay For," Roy Adams stated:

> Clients expect and need their lawyer to work with others to achieve their goals, including accountants, financial planners, life insurance agents and consultants, private bankers, trust officers, investment advisors, and brokers. They expect and require cooperation (not competition); and they want improved results through a team effort, much like the results which the team approach has achieved in medicine.

Should trust professionals be any different? Woe be the trust department that does not recognize:

- Customers are willing to pay for what they want. We won't get those fees unless we show and prove we have what they are looking for.

- Customers won't pay unless they know we are willing and capable to help. We must live with the advice that a renowned medical professor gives to his students: "You must prove to your patient how much you care before you impress them with how much you know."

- An institution's innovative products and services will never bring growth if personnel are not capable of marketing, selling, and providing attention and diligence toward servicing prospects and customers.

- Before and after the sale, customers demand to know that the people they are talking to can demonstrate sophisticated knowledge and background. Despite what we may think, customers will exercise due diligence. In addition to researching performance, products, and fees—and assuring themselves that attention will be given to their needs—customers will look closely at their provider's credentials before they will take the risks associated with turning their money over to someone they don't know.

Are we ready?

SUMMARY

- Selling trust and investment services is vital to the survival of the trust industry. It is time to promote our products and services and to inform customers that we do manage money, that we are good at it, that we are efficient and approachable, and that we are the best place for sound investment management.

- Because future-fee business does not generate fees today, trust departments tend to overlook this customer base as a strong source of revenue. Proactive trust departments are addressing this omission by developing formal will and trust file retention programs to serve potential-fee business and to use this base of customers to prospect for active-fee business.

- Trust departments are learning the importance of providing service to all customers regardless of their account relationships. Marketing plans are being developed, and customer surveys are being conducted to find better ways to serve customers.

- Banks and their trust departments are working together today to increase business across the spectrum of all departments and products. Various departments are cross-selling, cross-training, cross-calling, and cross-profiting for the good of the institution as a whole.

- Trust departments are building a sales culture that encompasses all employees. Programs are in place to promote the department's products and services through marketing, a dedicated sales force, bonus and referral programs, and effective sales management.

- Trust departments are learning the value of prospecting and generating referrals inter- and intradepartmentally and from third-party referral sources.

- Trust departments face fierce competition for customers' money. How we meet the competition depends on knowing who the competition is, what they provide, and what their strengths and weaknesses are. The trust industry faces competition from regulatory bodies, brokerage houses, life insurance companies, financial planners, and mutual funds.

- Our tasks are to
  - ▲ Recognize our shortcomings and eliminate them
  - ▲ Promote our personalized service, value-added products and services, and competitive investment performance
  - ▲ Take our story to the street
  - ▲ Educate the public that we are not a business reserved for widows and orphans

REVIEW QUESTIONS

1. How has the promotion of trust services changed over the last few decades?
2. What is future-fee (potential-fee) business and how does it benefit a trust department?
3. What characteristics are evident in banks that exhibit a strong sales culture?
4. How can external referrals to the trust department be improved?
5. Name five nonbank competitors of the trust industry.

Appendix 1:
Confidential
Personal Statement

FAMILY DATA

Full name

    Date of birth _____

    Social Security # _____

    Place of birth _____

    Health status _____

Home address and phone

_____

_____

_____

_____

Spouse's full name_____

    Date of birth _____

    Social Security # _____

    Place of birth_____

    Health status _____

Date of marriage _____

Divorces _____

_____

Children

Name	Date of Birth	Health	Occupation
_____	_____	_____	_____
_____	_____	_____	_____
_____	_____	_____	_____
_____	_____	_____	_____
_____	_____	_____	_____

Adoptions

_____

Grandchildren

Name	Date of Birth	From Whom
_____	_____	_____
_____	_____	_____
_____	_____	_____
_____	_____	_____

Other Dependents

Name	Date of Birth	Relationship
_____	_____	_____
_____	_____	_____
_____	_____	_____
_____	_____	_____
_____	_____	_____

Father living? _____ Age _____ Health _____

Mother living? _____ Age _____ Health _____

Parents' financial status

_____

Spouse's father living? _____ Age _____ Health _____

Spouse's mother living? _____ Age _____ Health _____

Spouse's parents' financial status

_____

EMPLOYMENT

Employer_____

Address and phone

_____

_____

    Position _____

    How long_____

    Anticipated advancement _____

    Possible change of employment_____

Are you a veteran?_____

Spouse's employer_____

Address and phone

_____

_____

    Position _____

    How long_____

    Anticipated advancement _____

    Possible change of employment_____

INCOME STATUS

	Self	Spouse
Salary	_____	_____
Bonus/commissions	_____	_____
Dividends	_____	_____
Taxable interest	_____	_____
Tax-exempt interest	_____	_____
Pension/profit sharing	_____	_____
Trust income	_____	_____
Annuities	_____	_____
Real estate	_____	_____
Social Security	_____	_____
Other (identify)	_____	_____
Total	_____	_____

How dependent are you on your income?

_____

_____

What is your tax bracket?

_____

_____

Do you follow a particular saving or investment plan at the present time? Explain.

_____

_____

What is the purpose?

_____

Special personal assets, property, and collectibles (describe)

_____

_____

Do you or your spouse have any substantial liabilities?

_____

_____

Do you or your spouse expect any inheritances?

_____

_____

Are you now, or do you anticipate, establishing a special fund in order to:

Purchase or start a business _____

_____

Accumulate college funds _____

_____

Other _____

_____

ASSETS

	Husband	Wife	Joint
Liquid assets			
Cash on hand	_____	_____	_____
Checking accounts	_____	_____	_____
Savings accounts	_____	_____	_____
Annuities	_____	_____	_____
CDs	_____	_____	_____
Receivables	_____	_____	_____
Insurance cash values	_____	_____	_____
Other	_____	_____	_____

	Husband	Wife	Joint
Marketable securities*			
Corporate stock (1)	_____	_____	_____
Mutual funds (2)	_____	_____	_____
Corporate bonds (3)	_____	_____	_____
Government securities (4)	_____	_____	_____
Municipal bonds (5)	_____	_____	_____
Other (6)	_____	_____	_____

* Please describe particulars (names, where and when bought, initial value, current value)

1 _____

_____

2 _____

_____

3 _____

_____

4 _____

_____

5 _____

_____

6 _____

_____

Are you entirely satisfied with the investment results you have achieved during the past 5 years? If not, why not? _____

_____

_____

Are there any investments you feel tied to for past performance, family or social reasons, or indecision? _____

_____

_____

BUSINESS INTERESTS*

	Husband	Wife	Joint
Sole proprietorship (1)	_____	_____	_____
Partnership (2)	_____	_____	_____
Closely held corp. (3)	_____	_____	_____
Restricted stock (4)	_____	_____	_____

* Please describe particulars (business, purpose, etc.)

1 _____

_____

2 _____

_____

3 _____

_____

4 _____

_____

Do any of your business entities have any particular business continuation plans, stock redemption plans, or buy-sell agreements? _____

REAL ESTATE

	Husband	Wife	Joint
Equity in home(s) (1)	_____	_____	_____
Income-producing (2)	_____	_____	_____
Unimproved realty (3)	_____	_____	_____

* Please describe particulars (locations, description, when acquired, initial cost, present market value, etc.)

1 _____

_____

2 _____

_____

3 _____

_____

What provisions have you made for the ongoing management of your properties in the event of a serious disability or death?_____

_____

LIFE INSURANCE

(indicate whether it is personal, group, business, or pension)

	Husband	Wife
Company	_____	_____
Amount	_____	_____
Type	_____	_____
Loans	_____	_____
Owner	_____	_____
Beneficiary	_____	_____

How was the amount of your insurance portfolio determined? _____
_____
_____

Do you understand your insurance coverage? _____
_____
_____

What are the most appealing and nonappealing aspects of your insurance program?
_____
_____

Major medical insurance (Individual? Group? Benefits? Company?) _____
_____
_____

Are you a participant in an employer medical reimbursement plan? _____

DISABILITY INCOME (SALARY CONTINUATION) INSURANCE

You:

	Individual	Group
Amount	_____	_____
Waiting period	_____	_____
Benefit length	_____	_____
Paid by whom	_____	_____

Spouse:

	Individual	Group
Amount	_____	_____
Waiting period	_____	_____
Benefit length	_____	_____
Paid by whom	_____	_____

RETIREMENT BENEFITS

(indicate husband's or wife's and state particulars such as vested amounts, anticipated benefit at retirement, and beneficiary)

Pension _____

_____

Profit sharing _____

_____

Stock options_____

_____

Savings/thrift _____

_____

401(k) plan _____

_____

Keogh_____

_____

IRA/ESOP/other _____

_____

Deferred compensation _____

_____

Have you established a retirement date? _____

In order to feel that you have been a financial success, how much monthly income do you feel is necessary to have following your retirement? _____

ESTATE PLANNING DATA

Do you have a will? _____   Date of will _____

State will drafted in _____   Date last reviewed _____

Drafted by_____

Any special changes in your estate or family since your will was drafted/reviewed?

_____

_____

Location of will?_____

_____

Who is the named executor? _____

_____

Who is named as successor? _____

_____

Guardian for minor children? _____

_____

Successor guardian? _____

_____

Does your will include trust provisions? _____

_____

Please provide the same information regarding your spouse's will: _____

_____

_____

_____

_____

_____

Do you have a living trust? _____

_____

Date of trust _____

_____

Trustee _____

_____

Cotrustee _____

_____

Successor trustee _____

_____

Trust particulars _____

_____

Please provide the same information regarding your spouse's trust: _____

_____

_____

_____

_____

Power of attorney _____

Do you have a power of attorney for healthcare? _____

Particulars: _____

_____

Do you have a power of attorney for property? _____

Particulars: _____

_____

Please provide the same information regarding your spouse.

_____

_____

_____

_____

_____

Any special family needs (child support, alimony, special education, dependent support)? _____

_____

ADVISORS

Attorney_____

_____

Accountant _____

_____

Insurance counselor _____

_____

Personal banker/name of bank _____

_____

Safe deposit box location and number_____

_____

Key location _____

Owned jointly? _____

Have you instituted any sporadic or systematized charitable giving or gifting program?

_____

_____

Have gift tax returns been filed? _____

_____

GENERAL QUESTIONS

Do you have any lifetime objectives before or at retirement?_____

_____

Are there any specific objectives at your death for your spouse with minor/adult children? _____

_____

Are there specific objectives at your spouse's death with minor/adult children?

_____

_____

What is financial success to you? _____

_____

_____

Do you foresee any financial problems in the next 5–10 years? _____

_____

_____

UPON YOUR DEATH . . .

Will your widow/er continue to live in the family home or move to a smaller home?

_____

If he/she stays where he/she is, and if there is a mortgage on your home, do you want the mortgage to be liquidated at the time of your death? _____

_____

How familiar are you with the benefits accorded to you by OASDHI (Social Security)?

_____

_____

When was the last time you verified your Social Security benefits through the Social Security Administration? _____

_____

If tomorrow you were mentally or physically incapacitated, or died, would your spouse know the procedures for obtaining everything for which you are eligible from:

    Social Security Administration _____

    Veterans' Administration _____

    Employment programs _____

    Insurance companies _____

Have you prepared a list for your family of all documents and records, together with a description of their use, and their location? _____

_____

Could your spouse locate your list and does it contain the following:

Income tax returns and supporting paperwork for 5 years _____

Deed and mortgage documents to all real property _____

Necessary title to all personal property _____

Will and trust agreement _____

Birth certificates of every family member _____

Marriage certificate _____

Names and addresses of advisors _____

Veterans' papers _____

Cemetery deed of ownership _____

ATTITUDE TOWARD FINANCIAL MATTERS

Rate your degree of concern on a scale of 1 = slight to 10 = high.

Tax advantage: To what extent are you concerned about
getting all of the tax relief to which you are legally entitled?   _____

Leverage: To what extent are you comfortable with using
borrowed money to make money in larger amounts than
would otherwise be possible?   _____

Safety: How concerned are you about being sure you could
get back your own money during a protracted recession?   _____

Liquidity: How concerned are you about having cash available
at once to meet emergencies or opportunities?   _____

Diversification: How concerned are you about
hedging big losses by spreading your risks?   _____

Expert management: How desirable is it for you to use others'
expert know-how for your investing, leaving you free to
concentrate on your own career?   _____

Current income: How concerned are you about getting maximum
income from your savings and investments this year and next?   _____

Self-completion: To what extent are you concerned about
your investment program not being harmful or unwieldy
for your widow/er?   _____

INVESTMENT OBJECTIVES

Choose the statement that best describes your objectives.

A. I am very conservative and am more interested in conserving capital than in making it grow. I am willing to accept moderate income and nominal capital gains potential in exchange for minimum risk.

B. I am interested only in high-quality investments and will be quite satisfied with a reasonable current return and some growth potential.

C. I want primarily a liberal cash return and then some chance for future capital appreciation.

D. I can accept a lower level of income now in order to aim for capital appreciation over the years and growth of income in the future.

E. I am willing to accept high risks in exchange for the possibility of high profits.

From an investment viewpoint, what is your opinion of the current economic outlook?
_____
_____

Do you have a different opinion for a longer range of the next 5 years? If so, how does it differ? _____
_____

Who decides on your investments? You? Joint decision? Other?_____
_____

Do you consider yourself a good money manager? Why?_____
_____

Are your beneficiaries good at managing money and to what extent? _____
_____
_____

What is the largest amount of cash your spouse (or other immediate family members) has ever handled at one time?_____
_____
_____

Is there any other information that would be helpful in evaluating your present and future financial situation? _____
_____
_____
_____
_____
_____

APPENDIX 2:
PRINCIPLES OF ESTATE PLANNING

There are several ways to get from point A to point B. A traveler can walk, ride a bus or train, fly, or drive by car. Why point B rather than point C? Why choose one mode of transportation over another? Why go at all? Choosing where to go, planning how to get there, and setting the objectives to obtain once there are all-important considerations to the individual traveler.

Estate planning has its similarities. Where to go? How to get there? Where to go for help? In simple terms, an estate plan—the process of estate planning—is the effective accumulation, preservation, and disposition of one's assets, during life and at death, for oneself and others. Estate planning encompasses everyone—the older, established generation and the younger, growing generation, the wealthy and the not so wealthy.

The need for estate planning today is greater than ever. Consider that today's senior citizens are widely regarded as the wealthiest generation of Americans to date. It is estimated that they will leave 8 to 10 trillion dollars to their heirs over the next 20 years. Despite this massive amount of wealth, most of those in this generation are still in dire need of planning their estate. For example, according to the American Bar Association, only 30 percent of Americans currently have a will—the most basic building block of an estate plan.

THE ESTATE PLANNING PROCESS

Estate planning is both an art and a science—yet neither discipline taken alone. Estate planning involves having family and financial affairs in order for the present and well planned for the future. An estate plan involves concern for one's self and for others, and it encompasses the estate planner, the planner's assets, and the planner's family. Estate *and* financial planning—perhaps a more apropos term—includes wills, investing, retirement planning, taxes, gifting, insurance, and trusts.

Estate and financial planning must focus on the aspirations and needs of the estate owner. Only the estate owner can decide what route to take to build and conserve the estate, what dispositions to make of property, to whom such dispositions will be made, and when and how they are to be made. A person planning his estate must evaluate the intellectual, moral, and physical strengths, weaknesses, and needs of self and intended beneficiaries, and he alone must decide how willing and able he is to develop a meaningful program. Therefore, the estate owner is the most important participant in the estate planning process.

Estate planning is erroneously viewed as benefiting the wealthy, the elderly, and the sophisticated. Adequate estate planning is equally and extremely important for smaller, younger estates where there can be no margin for loss because of taxes, neglect, or error. The wealthy *and* the not-so-wealthy benefit from estate planning. Regardless of a customer's financial stratum, an estate planner can help her define where she presently is, where she wants to get, and how to get there. In today's demanding society, everyone planning an estate must make the time, set the objectives, and build the commitment to follow the planning without trepidation.

Estate planning may hinge on an individual's desires and goals, but creating an estate plan is not a solo trek. The epicenter of activity is the estate planning team—an interdisciplinary, cooperative core of professional helpers: an attorney, insurance counselor, investment manager, trust officer, and accountant. Even so, among all the players, the most important ones are the spouse and family, for whose benefit the plan is being devised. The family must never be left out of the planning. A good trust professional will prepare, involve, advise, communicate, and consult continually with the family. Remember that the family must live with what was planned.

A healthy beginning to understanding estate planning is answering . . .

WHAT IS ESTATE PLANNING?

Let's start backwards. What is *not* estate planning?

- It is not meant primarily as an activity undertaken because of death. Estate planning is done for the same reason life insurance is bought—not because one will die, but because others will continue living.

- It is not an activity reserved solely for the elderly and rich. Smaller estates leave less room for the mistakes made by not doing estate planning.

- It is not an activity of keeping up with the Joneses. We accumulate estates for ourselves and our family, not for impressing the next-door neighbor.

- It is not an ugly, onerous, and traumatic activity wrought with the potential to raise blood pressure. Yet it may become all these things for families when it is not done or is not done well.

So, what is estate planning? Some refer to it as tax engineering, financial management, shaping one's financial environ-

ment—social work for the rich. One wealthy individual stated that "estate planning is a way of constructing a perfect inheritance, one that gives enough money to the beneficiaries so they can do anything, but not so much that they can do nothing."

To many people, estate planning is very objective . . . cold and prickly . . . so centered around shaping one's financial horizons that death, taxes, and investments preoccupy the planner's thinking. These are important aspects of planning an estate. But, as a trust professional, be careful that this predilection doesn't become overweening. Estate planning is also subjective. It has its "soft and fuzzy" elements, and at its best it provides for both the business and the personal, non-tax benefits—the family's complete well-being.

Estate Planning and Taxes

There have been arguments for many decades as to whether transfer taxes should exist. Financial planners have espoused, "No taxation without respiration . . . grave robbery . . . an attempt to tax dead people." (We'll leave the arguments for others.)

Yes, taxes are inevitable, but we should be mindful of the oft-quoted words of Judge Billings Learned Hand (1872–1961), frequently referred to as one of the greatest judges of the twentieth century never to be appointed to the Supreme Court:

> Anyone may arrange his affairs so that his taxes shall be as low as possible; he is not bound to choose that pattern which best pays the Treasury . . . there is nothing sinister in so arranging affairs as to keep taxes as low as possible . . . nobody owes any public duty to pay more than the law demands; taxes are enforced exactions, not voluntary contributions.

Let's go further. There is a positive duty (if not to ourselves, then to our families and those whom we favor) to maximize tax-saving opportunities.

WHAT AN ESTATE IS

An estate is everything that a person owns. *Own,* though, is a very big word. It means having title to, interest in, and power over assets (property). Let's look at some examples.

A *title* is a document (bill of sale, receipt, or deed) that evidences ownership of the property. An automobile, as an example, is accompanied by a title—a piece of paper naming the owner. Many assets (property) do not have formal titles or deeds—ownership papers. Simple examples are clothing, golf clubs, and stamp collections. The estate owner knows he owns these assets because he bought them, yet there may not be a receipt (ownership documentation) to say so.

To have *power* over an asset is to have the authority or right to do something with the asset. For example, if a person has the power to change the beneficiary of a life insurance policy or surrender it, he has authority to do so. This power (authority) causes the estate owner to own the life insurance policy; therefore, the life insurance cash value is an estate asset, and the death proceeds will be part of the estate owner's gross estate at death.

Here's another way to look at ownership. Think of ownership as a person's ability to attach a string to the asset. If the asset can be controlled, directed, or pulled back, then it is "owned." This is an important aspect to remember as an estate planner.

WHO SHOULD DO ESTATE PLANNING?

Simply, the estate owner. Although the owner may consider himself to be a layman to the technical aspects of estate and financial planning, he is the only person entitled to decide what to do with his estate; what risks to take to build it; what measures to take to preserve it; how much to make available for the education of children; how much to be available at retirement; who is to get what, and when and how they are to get it. Trust professionals are vital to the process, but they offer assistance to the estate owner rather than make decisions for him.

WHEN SHOULD ESTATE PLANNING BE DONE?

Yesterday. But, of course, hindsight has 20/20 vision. So, encourage your clients to start today. And remind them that estate planning is a lifetime action—an evolution—across generations. Planning is dynamic—not static—and it is a combination of bits and pieces.

Why don't people do estate planning—or not do it now? Many don't know where to start. Or, they superstitiously believe that to plan an estate is to plan for death and disability, thereby inviting it. Some people have the uneasy feeling that the signing of estate planning documents—such as a will and a trust—is an omen that the grim reaper is right around the corner. The reaper could be hovering in the wings, but the mere preparation of an estate for loved ones does not invite death. In contrast, some people seem to be unaware of their mortality and therefore of the inexorable passing of time. Another common excuse is: "I'm too busy!" Some build prejudices toward the professionals who assist in the estate planning process. And all too often, "It's too expensive!" Part of the trust professional's job is to show clients that dollars spent planning today seldom hurt an estate tomorrow.

WHY IS ESTATE PLANNING DONE?

Depending on the size of an estate, the impact of gift and estate taxes can be horrific.

Very few people go without insurance that protects their house from the possibility of burglary, fire, and damage. Interestingly, these perils may never occur, but nonetheless homeowner's insurance is bought "just in case." Without it we feel financially naked and unprepared. But think about it: how many houses in your neighborhood have burned down?

Schools and businesses conduct fire drills . . . military personnel prepare for battles . . . towns test tornado sirens—all in preparation for events that may never occur. Why? Just in case. Death and taxes *are* inevitable—they will happen. While most people prepare for the *just-in-case* occurrences, many do not prepare for that which will happen.

HOW IS ESTATE PLANNING DONE?

When a patient sees a physician, the physician takes a complete history and physical (H&P). The physician cannot prescribe a drug, surgery, therapy, or whatever unless he knows what's going on. So, let's work with a premise: A trust professional cannot help a customer plan her estate—and the trust professional cannot eliminate mistakes in the estate planning process—until the customer has identified what she wants to accomplish.

General descriptions of estate planning make sense in a macro way, but they are empty without specifics. A healthy start is to ask your customer to gather information about his estate—an estate H&P. What assets and liabilities does your customer have? Complete disclosure is a must. There are myriad forms that can assist the estate owner in accomplishing this inventory.

In conjunction with asking your client to list his assets, ask him the following questions and share with him some of the reasons for asking them. They will help the customer sidestep pitfalls in the estate planning process:

- *Have you assembled financial information about yourself and your family and analyzed your assets with respect to income and liabilities? Have you taken an in-depth inventory, and do you know your estate's exact worth?* Too many people have their estates tied up in bricks and glass, with little liquidity.

- *Have you considered transferring assets or arranging ownership to*

minimize future liabilities and problems? For example, joint tenancy ownership of property is called the poor person's will; it may be the wrong path for your customer.

- *Do you have a systematic savings and investment program? Because financial emergencies may come at any time, where will the assets come from to meet them when income cannot meet the liabilities? Who will manage your investments when you cannot do so?* Remember your financial responsibilities to family first. Save, then spend. Invest prudently.

- *Do you have a will? Is it current? Does it truly express your wishes? Have you named the right guardian for your children if both you and your spouse die? Are you comfortable with the executor you chose?* Failure to make a will guarantees that your estate will die with you.

- *Have you taken advantage of charitable giving now and at your death?* There are positive tax consequences of having a charitable heart.

- *Does your estate planning provide an education fund for your children? Do you know how much a four-year college education will cost? Where will the funds come from?* Tomorrow is viewed with binoculars, yet it comes around the corner quickly.

- *Are your salary continuation and life insurance plans adequate in the event of a long-term disability and death? Are the plans the right kind? Do you understand your insurance coverage? Does the right person own your plans?* Most people dread talking about insurance, but no widow has ever complained that her husband owned too much life insurance.

- *Is your estate planning team in place? Are the team members qualified? Can they work together with your best interests in mind, now for you and later for your family?* Never under use professional advisors; a planning dollar spent wisely today will save several tomorrow.

- *Have you designated someone to manage your financial affairs when you are incapable of doing so? Is she the right choice?* Living wills and powers of attorney are not scary things; be fearful if you don't have them.

- *When was the last time you seriously analyzed your employee benefit package? Is it a minimal stopgap? Is it broad enough to meet the future?* The costs of medical and dental care have skyrocketed. It is better to examine your plan today than after you are discharged from the hospital.

- *Do you have a succession plan in place for your business? Should your family maintain control of the business in the event of your death or long-term disability? Can it? Should the business be sold?* Today's pearl-necklace business may be tomorrow's noose without a continuation or disposal plan.

- *Have you taken advantage of tax laws in order to reduce taxation (income taxes, inheritance taxes, and estate taxes) upon death?* Remember what Judge Learned Hand stated, "Anyone may so arrange his affairs that his taxes shall be as low as possible; he is not bound to choose the pattern which will best pay the Treasury; there is not even a patriotic duty to increase one's taxes."

- *How well have you prepared yourself and your family in the event of retirement? Are your funds sufficient? Do they provide adequate survivor benefits? Have you taken advantage of both individual and employer plans?* Never assume that the funds will be there; this type of planning will make

you dependent on Social Security and employer-sponsored retirement benefits. There is no such thing as too much retirement funding.

- *Do you regularly review your estate plan and keep its provisions up to date?* Tax laws, families, and objectives change. If you review as often as you repaint your living room, you should be fairly safe.

- *Have you considered the use of a trust? Do you have one? Have you funded it? Do you understand it? Should it be revocable or irrevocable? Have you picked the best trustee? Is the trust flexible?*

Honest answers to these questions will help the trust professional assess how healthy an estate plan is or how best to create one. And, although no element of an estate planning checklist is insignificant, certain aspects may have higher priority than others, depending on estate size, family circumstances, and objectives.

By no means is this list all-inclusive. It is a means of getting the estate owner started down the path of estate planning. The estate owner may not understand some of these questions or may not have ready answers, but that is okay because asking the questions opens an avenue of communication between the estate owner, his planners, and his family.

The difficult inventory is the soft facts—the ones that may be relevant to one member of the family and irrelevant to another one. Here is where the estate owner's misconceptions and preconceptions are brought to the surface. The estate owner may be proud that he has prepared for his family by purchasing a million-dollar life insurance policy. But has he considered how the insurance is to be owned? Should it be part of a trust? Are the proceeds to be paid lump sum? To whom should the proceeds be paid? How does the estate owner feel about family? Should some members of the family get more than others?

As said earlier, estate planning is an objective and a subjective process. Dollars are objective . . . what to do with them is subjective. By communicating with customers, trust professionals can improve the odds that the estate owner will provide for the complete needs of his family.

WHERE CAN ESTATE PLANNING HELP BE FOUND?

No one professional should handle all aspects of planning a complex estate. Encourage your client to build an estate planning team, an interdisciplinary collection of qualified, specialized professionals who will assist the estate owner. A good estate planning team tells it client what can be done, not what *should be done*. In addition, professional estate planners should offer compassion and uncompromising personal commitments to the needs of the estate owner's personal and professional life and the needs of family. It is not uncommon for a professional planner to be a psychologist with a vast base of estate-planning knowledge.

Since the estate owner is the focal point of estate planning, the estate owner is responsible for preparing for the process. Homework here is the word. Although no one would expect the estate owner to *read it all,* the following is a list of reference guides that will introduce one to sources of information.

The Complete Estate Planning Guide
Kathleen Adams and Robert Brosterman
A Mentor book published by the Penguin Group
New York, NY
(This inexpensive paperback provides the estate owner with a solid background in estate planning terminology and techniques.)

The New Book of Trusts
Daniel B. Evans, Stephen R. Leimberg, Russell E. Miller, and Charles K. Plotnick
Leimberg Associates
Bryn Mawr, PA
(This book is devoted solely to describing virtually every kind of trust there is.)

Tax Facts
Volumes 1 and 2
The National Underwriter Company
Cincinnati, OH
(These are Q&A reference books that address any tax question you can think of. The books are quite technical and they include references to Internal Revenue Code sections.)

The National Underwriter Company also publishes a series of books devoted to specific topics:
   The Tools and Techniques of Employee and Retirement Planning
   The Tools and Techniques of Estate Planning
   The Tools and Techniques of Financial Planning
   The Tools and Techniques of Life Insurance Planning

Beyond the Grave: The Right Way and the Wrong Way of Leaving Money to Your Children
Gerald M. Condon and Jeffrey L. Condon
2001, Harper Business, New York

Internal Revenue Service:
Publication 559	Survivors, Executors, and Administrators
Publication 590	Individual Retirement Arrangements (IRAs) (Including Roth IRAs and Education IRAs)
Form 706	Estate (and Generation-Skipping Transfer) Tax Return
Form 709	Gift (and Generation-Skipping Transfer) Tax Return

GLOSSARY

"There will be a time when you believe everything is finished. That will be the beginning."

Louis L'Amour (1908–1988)

abatement: The reduction of a gift (bequest) in a will because the estate's assets are insufficient to satisfy all the gifts after the estate's debts, claims, and taxes have been paid; all gifts of the same class abate proportionately unless provided otherwise.

abstract of trust: A document that briefly outlines a trust's key provisions and existence.

accounting: 1. The recording of transactions within an account. 2. The submission of account records by a fiduciary to a court or to the beneficiaries of a trust or estate.

actuary: A statistician who calculates life insurance, disability insurance, and pension rates and premiums based on experience tables (i.e., mortality and morbidity frequencies).

ademption: The act of a testator that causes an extinguishment or withdrawal of a legacy in a will because the asset does not exist at the time of death.

adjudication: The decision of a court with respect to matters of dispute; used most often with regard to judgment of incapacitation or incompetence.

administration: The management of an estate by a trustee, guardian, or personal representative.

administrative provisions: The terms of a will or trust that define the duties and powers of the executor or trustee with respect to management of the property.

administrator: An individual or institution appointed by a court to administer and settle the estate of a person who died intestate.

administrator with will annexed: An individual or institution appointed by a court to administer and settle the estate of a person who died testate if an executor has not been named in the will, or if the executor is incapable of acting, refuses to act, resigns after appointment, or is not appointed by the court.

administratrix: A seldom-used term for a female administrator.

affidavit: A document signed before a notary pertaining to a specific statement.

affidavit of trust: See *abstract of trust*.

after-born child: A child born after the execution of the parent's will; to be distinguished from posthumous child.

agency: An account relationship between two parties: a principal and an agent. Title to and ownership of the property, which constitutes the agency, remains with the principal; the agent acts on behalf of the principal and is charged with certain duties with respect to the property.

agent: A person or institution acting on behalf of another (the principal); the principal's written authority controls and dictates the agent's actions.

agreement: An understanding or arrangement between two or more people or institutions. Also see *contract*.

agricultural real property: Farm land.

alternate valuation date: A date 6 months following the decedent's death; an estate is valued by its executor as of the date of death or the alternate valuation date; the alternate valuation date can be chosen only if the estate's value at that time results in a lower federal estate tax.

amendment: An addition, deletion, or modification to a legal document; this term is used primarily with respect to trusts.

American Stock Exchange (AMEX): See *centralized trading exchange.*

ancillary: (adj.) Auxiliary (in conjunction with) or subordinate (lower than) to someone or something, as in *ancillary administration, ancillary guardian, ancillary trustee.*

annuity: A fixed or variable amount payable annually or at regular intervals for a given period, such as for a stated number of years or for the life of the annuitant (the one receiving the annuity payment).

antenuptial agreement: See *nuptial agreement.*

anticipation note: A short-term municipal bond (comparable to commercial paper). Also called a municipal note.

appoint (v.)/**appointment:** The formal approval by the court of the executor nominated in a will.

apportionment: The division, distribution, or disbursement of property among two or more accounts or individuals, as between principal and income.

appraisal: The valuation of property; the value arrived on a specific date is the appraised value.

appreciation: The increase in value of property; the opposite is depreciation.

approved list: A statutory or nonstatutory list of authorized investments that a fiduciary is permitted to acquire.

asset: Something of value (tangible and intangible) that is owned by a person, a person's estate, a trust, or a business entity.

asset allocation: A method of determining the percentages assigned to various investment classes (i.e. stocks, bonds, cash) within a fund or portfolio dependent on one's investment objectives and risk tolerance.

assignment: The transfer of the title of property in writing from one person to another; this may be done as a gift or as a satisfaction of indebtedness.

attest: (v.) To serve as a witness, as to a will.

attestation clause: The part of a document containing the formal act of witnessing; in a will the clause follows the testator's signature.

attesting witness: A person who testifies (attests) to the authenticity of a document.

attorney at law: A person who is legally qualified and authorized to represent another in legal proceedings.

attorney in fact: A person, acting as an agent, who is authorized in writing to act and transact business for another outside court. Also see *power of attorney.*

bankers acceptance: A time draft (bill of exchange) drawn on and accepted by the bank on which it was drawn; it usually arises from international trade transactions where there is an obligation to a buyer to make payment to a seller at some future date; bankers acceptances are created when payment is made by a letter of credit; the bank accepting the draft assumes the obligation of making payment at maturity on behalf of the buyer or the buyer's banks.

bearer bond: A bond that is not formally registered in the name of the owner; payment of interest is facilitated by coupons attached to the bond; title of the bond vests in the one who physically possesses the bond; title passes to another upon delivery.

beneficial ownership: See *equitable ownership.*

beneficiary: The one to whom the benefits of an insurance policy, annuity, will, or trust are paid.

bequeath: (v.) To give property by will.

bequest: The property given by will; also called a legacy.

bill of exchange: See *draft.*

blue chip stock: The stock of a company that is a leader in a major industry; the stock has a consistent record of earnings during good and bad economic times, has an unbroken record of dividend payments, and has a definite indication of solid future performance.

blue sky laws: State laws, as opposed to federal regulations, that pertain to the issuance and registration of securities.

board of directors: The people elected by a corporation's stockholders at the corporation's annual meetings to guide the operations of the company; directors make corporate decisions such as choosing management personnel, declaring dividends, and looking after the best interests of the stockholders.

bomb clause: A provision in a trust that provides direction for the distribution of a trust's corpus upon the death of the last of the grantor, grantor's spouse, and all descendants.

bond rating: An evaluation and classification by a rating company (such as Standard & Poor's and Moody's) as to a bond issuer's financial strength and ability to meet its financial obligations (payment of interest and repayment of the principal upon maturity); the rating also measures the probability that a bond will default.

bonds: Interest-bearing securities (a certificate of indebtedness) issued by a corporation, municipality, or government.

book entry: A method for registering and keeping record of government securities without issuing a physical certificate to the bondholder.

budget: (v.) To set aside funds in order to meet future needs. (n.): The statement of revenues and expenditures for an individual, estate, or business entity; in a probate estate, the statement of funds needed to pay claims, taxes, and cash bequests.

buyback: A corporation's purchase of its own stock from its stockholders, either directly from the stockholders or in the open market; the corporation may retain ownership of the stock within the company or retire it. (v.): To repurchase one's own stock.

call: 1. The right of a corporation to repurchase its bond obligation or stock; if the securities are stock, the corporation may retain the stock or retire it. 2. An option to buy shares of a certain stock within a given period of time and at a specific price set in the call contract. (v.): To exercise an option.

callable bond: A bond that is payable by the debtor before the bond's maturity according to the terms of the bond indenture; the bond issue may be called completely or partially.

capital: The amount of funds invested into a company on a long-term basis; these funds may come from borrowing from a bank or from bond debt (debt capital), and funds may come from issuing stock (equity capital).

centralized trading exchange: A physical marketplace for conducting the purchase and sale of securities; the major exchanges are the New York Stock Exchange (NYSE) and the American Stock Exchange (AMEX); smaller regional stock exchanges provide trading services for smaller, local companies.

certificate of deposit (CD): A certificate issued by a bank to a depositor, indicating the amount of money deposited, the rate of interest to be paid, and the maturity of the deposit.

chancery court: See *probate court.*

charitable bequest: A gift of property by a will to a legal charity.

charity: An organization formed for the educational, religious, medical, or scientific benefit of others.

charter: A formal permission given to an institution to engage in the trust business; this charter is granted after proper application is made and accepted by the applicable authorities; future examination of the institution determines whether the charter remains active.

child's award: See *family allowance.*

Chinese wall: The popular name for the barrier between the commercial banking department and trust department of a bank, designed to prevent the sharing of information between the departments, which may cause conflicts of interest that may influence the trust department's fiduciary and investment roles.

churning: (n. or v.)The creation of an excessive amount of investment transactions (buys and sells) for the benefit of creating sales commissions.

civil law: The legal system that originated from ancient Rome and now exists in nearly all non–English-speaking countries; it is the basis for property ownership in community property states. Also see *common law*.

claim: A right to a debt or the possession(s) of another; a demand on an estate by a creditor for a debt owed by the decedent at the time of death.

closed-end fund: An investment fund that allows only an original prescribed number of shares to be distributed; a closed-end fund raises substantially all of its funds at the time the fund is established; its stock certificates are traded on stock exchanges.

closed-end investment management company: See *closed-end fund*.

closely held business: A corporation that is owned by one or a few persons, such as a family; this business is not traded on any organized exchange, such as the New York Stock Exchange.

codicil: An amendment to a will that modifies one or more parts of the will; it possesses all the legalities and formalities of a will.

collateral: Specific assets formally set aside by a borrower as a promise from the debtor for the repayment of a loan that may not be paid.

collective investment fund: See *common trust fund*.

commercial bank: An institution that accepts demand deposits (i.e., savings accounts and checking accounts) and makes personal and business (commercial) loans; to be distinguished from investment bank.

commercial paper: Short-term certificates of indebtedness from a corporation; the corporation promises to repay the principal (the face amount of the certificate) plus interest at the end of the period of debt; maturities usually do not exceed 1 year.

commercial real property: Property used by an owner for business purposes, such as a factory or office building; this property is considered rental real property when rented to tenants for income-producing purposes.

commingled fund: See *common trust fund*.

common disaster: A sudden event that causes the simultaneous or near-simultaneous death of two or more closely associated persons, such as a husband and wife or business partners. Also see *simultaneous death*.

common law: The legal system that originated in England and now exists in the British Commonwealth and the United States; it is the basis for property ownership in common law (non-community) property states. Also see *civil law*.

common stock: The ordinary ownership shares of a corporation; this class of stock carries stockholder voting rights. Also see *stock* and *preferred stock*.

common trust fund: A pooled fund of money or securities maintained by a bank trust company for the common and exclusive investment of assets of several trust, estate, and guardianship accounts; these funds are governed by the rules and regulations of the Comptroller of the Currency; also called a pooled fund, commingled fund, collective investment fund, and personal investment fund.

community property: A form of property ownership recognized in all civil law countries and certain states of the United States; when property is acquired after marriage, husband and wife (because of their marital status) each own a one-half interest in the property regardless of who purchased it.

compliance: The act of conforming to (obeying) laws that are in place; for example, trust departments must comply with statutes set in place by regulatory bodies, such as the Comptroller of the Currency, in the conduct of their business as a fiduciary.

compound interest: A method of computing interest in which the rate of interest is applied to principal for a specific period and then is applied in subsequent periods to the principal plus previously earned interest.

Comptroller of the Currency: See *Office of the Comptroller of the Currency.*

conflict of interest: A situation in which an action taken by an individual or institution in an official capacity may benefit that individual or institution personally; a situation in which an individual or institution may be representing two or more parties with contradictory interests.

conformed copy: Not an original document; a copy of an original document on which the signatures, seals, and other written features are typed or handwritten, therefore indicating the document's originality.

conservator: An individual or institution appointed by a court to care for and manage the property of an incompetent individual who is not a minor.

constructive receipt: Income not yet physically received but set aside or available to an individual, allowing the individual to draw on it at any time; once available the income is taxable regardless of whether it is actually taken.

contest of a will: A legal action taken to prevent the probate of a will or the distribution of the property according to the will's provisions.

contingent: (adj.) Dependent on; for example, a contingent beneficiary is one who will become a beneficiary based on the occurrence of a future event, such as the death of a prior beneficiary.

contract: A legally binding and enforceable agreement between two or more persons or institutions; not all agreements are contracts, but all contracts are agreements. Also see *agreement.*

contract ownership: A form of ownership in which one person owns property (similar to sole ownership), but the property (such as life insurance and employee benefit plans) does not pass through the owner's probate estate upon death due to the property's beneficiary designation.

contribution: An amount paid by an employer or employee to an employee benefit plan for the benefit of the employee.

contributory IRA: An individual retirement account into which eligible individuals may make annual contributions with the benefit of tax deferral on the investment earnings of the contributions.

conversion: The change of property from one form to another (e.g., from real property to personal property); this is a physical change of the nature of the property, not an exchange.

convertible securities: Securities with the provision for exchange from one type to another (e.g., from a stock to a bond) perhaps at a specific time and at a specific price.

conveyance: The transfer of the title, by act or document, of real property from one owner to another.

corporate agency: A relationship in which an institution performs for corporations such services as paying dividends for stocks and interest for bonds.

corporate bond: An evidence of indebtedness sold by a corporation for the purpose of raising money; the bond may be secured (collateralized) or unsecured (debentured).

corporate trust: A trust created by a corporation, as grantor, in order to secure a bond issue.

corporate trustee: A corporate entity that serves as a trustee.

corporation: A business organization that is treated as a single legal entity and is owned by its stockholders, whose liability is generally limited to the extent of their investment; the ownership of a corporation is represented by shares of stock that are issued to people or to other companies in exchange for cash, physical assets, services, or goodwill; the stockholders elect a board of directors, which then directs the management of the corporation's affairs.

corpus: The assets of a trust; also known as res, principal, and trust estate.

coupon: A certificate, attached to a bond, that represents the interest payment; the coupon states the amount and date of payment; when the payment date comes due, the coupon is clipped and presented to a paying agent for payment.

creator: See *grantor*.

creditor: One to whom money is owed by another.

creditor's notice: A notice of a person's death (not an obituary notice) published in a local newspaper for a required period of time; this announces the death, who the executor or administrator is, and where claims should be presented for payment; also called notice to interested persons.

credit risk: See *risk*.

current yield: The interpolated yield (greater or smaller than coupon yield) of a bond in relationship to the bond's discount or premium purchase price.

custody account: An agency relationship in which the foremost duties are to safekeep and account for the property in the custodian's care; duties also include performing the contractual administrative duties as directed by the principal; a custodian is not responsible for investment management.

death certificate: A legal document prepared and authenticated by a coroner or hospital official confirming an individual's death.

debenture: An obligation, such as a bond, that is not secured by collateral.

debt: A sum of money owed to another (person or institution).

debt capital: See *capital*.

debtor: One who owes money to another.

decedent: A deceased person.

decline/declination: (v./n.) An action in which an individual or institution, named in a will as an executor or named in a trust as a trustee, refuses to accept the nomination; also known as renunciation.

deed: A written instrument evidencing the transfer of ownership of real property from one owner to another; the owner(s) may be individuals or institutions. (v.): To transfer the property.

default: The failure of a bond issuer to make interest or principal payments when due. (v.): To fail to make the payments.

defensive stock: A stock that tends to resist general stock market declines.

deferred compensation: The contractual postponement of payment for services rendered until a future date; used more commonly with respect to retirement benefits (qualified or nonqualified) paid in the future.

defined benefit plan: A plan that ensures the payment of a specified, predetermined pension benefit at the time of retirement; the plan requires annual contributions that are actuarially determined to meet the benefit.

defined contribution plan: A plan that provides a nondetermined pension benefit at the time of retirement; the benefit depends on the fixed, annual contributions, gains or losses, and expenses.

demise: death.

depositary: A person or institution that receives and safekeeps money, securities, or other property.

depository: A place where something is placed (deposited), such as a vault.

depreciation: A decrease in the value of an asset; the opposite is appreciation.

descendant: One who has descended in a direct family line from another, even if remotely, such as a grandchild or great-grandchild.

determination letter: A letter of approval from the Internal Revenue Service regarding the qualified status of a retirement plan or approval of a plan's termination.

devise: A gift of real property by will.

directed trust: Also called a nondiscretionary account; the investment decisions in this account are made by someone other than the trustee; the trustee is accountable for carrying out the directed investment instructions.

disability: The physical conditions or deficiencies of not being able to manage certain physical, living activities; this is distinguishable from incompetence.

discount: The amount or percentage below par or face value at which securities are bought or sold; the opposite is premium. (v.): To reduce the price below par.

discretionary account or powers: The investment responsibilities and powers of an account vested in a trustee (under the terms of a trust) or an agent (under the terms of an investment management agency).

discrimination: When used with respect to employee benefit plans, this is where contributions or benefits are unfairly lopsided to favor officers, directors, or highly compensated employees of a corporation; discrimination causes a plan to be nonqualified.

dispositive provisions: The terms of a will or trust regarding the distribution of its property.

distribution in kind: The disbursement of the actual property (the "kind"), as opposed to converting the property to cash and then disbursing the proceeds.

diversification: The spreading of investments within a fund or a portfolio as to type of securities; further diversification occurs within the class of securities, as in mixing industries among common and preferred stocks and determining the types, ratings, maturities, and taxability of bonds.

dividend: A distribution of a company's profits, either as cash or additional stock, made by a corporation to its stockholders in proportion to the number of shares of stock owned.

dividend-paying agent: An agent of a corporation given the responsibility for making dividend payments to the stockholders from funds supplied by the corporation.

dividend reinvestment program: A plan in which dividends declared to be paid to a shareholder are not paid in cash; the payable dividend is used to purchase additional shares of stock.

domicile: A place that a person considers his or her permanent home; one's domicile is not necessarily one's residence. Also see *residence*.

domiciliary: Relating to the place a person regards as his permanent abode; with respect to an executor, this is the personal representative located in the decedent's state of legal residence (domicile).

domiciliary letters: See *letters testamentary*.

Dow Jones Industrial Average (DJIA): A daily measurement (done daily since 1884) of the stock market's performance based on the cumulative average price changes of 30 industrial stocks.

draft: Also known as a bill of exchange, a signed order by one party (the drawer) addressed to another (the drawee) directing the drawee to pay at demand or at a definable time in the future a specified sum of money to the order of a third person (the payee); drafts are basic financial instruments used in international trade to buy goods or services from abroad in a similar way that a check is used in domestic trade. Also see *bankers acceptance*.

durable power of attorney: See *power of attorney*.

election against the will: An action taken by a surviving spouse allowing the survivor to challenge the deceased spouse's will in order to receive a fixed, statutory share of the estate contrary to the will's dispositive provisions; also known as renouncing the will, right of election, forced heirship, taking against the estate, and widow's election.

emancipation: The transition from being of minor age to being of majority age. Also see *majority*.

employee benefit plan: A plan established by an employer in which fringe benefits are provided to the employees; examples of these benefits are pension or profit sharing plans, medical, sickness, dental and disability benefits, life insurance, and sick pay.

employee benefit trust: A trust established to manage the assets of an employee benefit plan.

employee identification number (EIN): See *tax identification number (TIN)*.

Employee Retirement Income Security Act of 1974 (ERISA): A federal law governing the management of employee benefit plans; the law sets minimum standards, regulation of the plan fiduciary's conduct, and the guarantee of payment (vesting) of benefits from retirement plans.

employee stock ownership plan (ESOP): A qualified retirement plan in which all or a majority of the plan's assets are securities of the employer.

equitable ownership: The beneficial interest a person has in property, such as a beneficial right to the assets of a trust; the legal ownership of the property vests in another, such as a trust; also known as beneficial ownership.

equitable title: A right to the benefits of property, enforced in a court of law. Also see *legal title*.

equity: 1. Another word for stock; the value of a stockholder's interest in a corporation. 2. The market value of real property minus any mortgage or indebtedness. 3. Total assets less total liabilities equals equity (net value or net worth).

equity capital: See *capital*.

escheat: Reversion of real or personal property (depending on state statutes) of a decedent's estate to the state or county in which the decedent was domiciled in the event the decedent is not survived by any legatees, heirs, or next of kin. (v.): To revert.

escrow account: An agency relationship in which securities or assets are deposited by two or more persons or institutions with a third party to be delivered in the future contingent on a certain event.

estate: 1. The total interest in property that an individual owns. 2. The property of a decedent.

estate administration: The management of a decedent's estate by an executor or administrator; an estate may be managed under the watchful eye of the probate court (supervised administration), on a non-court-supervised basis (independent administration), or quickly for small estates (summary administration).

estate plan/estate planning: An arrangement for the ownership and the accumulation, preservation, and disposition of one's property during life and at death, with an emphasis on tax planning and the use of wills and trusts.

estate settlement: The final reporting and distribution of an estate by an executor or administrator.

euro: The recently developed common form of currency adopted by a majority of European countries; the euro replaces the separate currencies of individual countries.

eurodollar: A deposit in any branch or bank outside the United States, but especially in Europe, denominated in U.S. dollars and providing a readily available short-term source of funds to banks.

exchange agent: An agent that receives one kind of security and delivers a different one in its place, such being the case with convertible securities or during a corporate acquisition when stock of the company acquired is replaced with stock of the acquirer.

exchange risk: See *risk*.

exculpatory language: A provision of immunity in a will or trust that attempts to or actually does relieve the executor or trustee from liability for breach of its fiduciary duties.

execute: (v.) To sign a document or to carry out the terms of the document.

executor: An individual or trust institution nominated in a will and appointed by the court to settle the estate of a decedent.

executrix: A seldom-used term for a female executor.

face value: The amount stated on the face of a security certificate; also called par value.

fair market value: The amount arrived at by a willing buyer and a willing seller. Also see *market value*.

family allowance: The amount from a decedent's estate provided by statute or by court approval for the children's living expenses during the period of estate settlement; also called child's award. Also see *spouse's allowance*.

family limited partnership: A limited partnership made up of family members (owners related by blood or marriage) and created to limit certain partners' control over the partnership; the partnership is used to consolidate management of the assets of the family and pass property to junior family members, thereby effecting a reduction in certain partners' value in the partnership via valuation discounts.

Federal Deposit Insurance Corporation (FDIC): A federal agency that insures customers' deposits in member commercial banks in the event of the bank's insolvency; the member banks pay an insurance premium for this coverage based on the amount of bank deposits; individual accounts are insured to a maximum of $100,000 per depositor. All national banks are required to provide FDIC insurance; most state banks and savings and loan associations subscribe to FDIC coverage.

fee: The amount charged or received by an individual or corporate agent or fiduciary for the services rendered.

fee simple: An estate of inheritance without limitation to any particular class of heirs and with no restrictions on alienation; a fee simple is the largest interest or estate in real property a person may own; fee simple is sometimes equated to sole ownership of real property.

fiduciary: An individual or institution charged with the duty of acting in good faith and fairness on behalf of and for the benefit of another within the definition of the relationship, such as the relationship between an individual and trustee, executor, or guardian in whom trust and confidence are placed.

final report and petition for distribution: A report given to the court by the executor following completion of the administration of an estate; this report summarizes the executor's activities during the probate proceedings and requests approval from the court for the final distribution (settlement) of the estate's assets.

five-and-five power: A provision in a trust allowing a noncumulative annual distribution from the trust of the greater of 5 percent of the trust's value or $5,000.

fixed income: A term for securities whose income stream (dollar amount or percentage) is constant, such as bonds or preferred stock; in most instances the principal of the investment is also fixed.

forced heirship: See *election against the will.*

401(k) plan: A qualified retirement plan in which an employee's income is reduced (as opposed to a deduction) in order to provide for a contribution to the plan; the employer may or may not match the employee's contribution.

403(b) plan: A qualified retirement plan (similar to a 401(k) plan) established for educators, healthcare workers, and employees of religious institutions and nonprofit organizations.

fringe benefit: See *employee benefit plan.*

fund: A group of assets segregated or commingled for a specific investment purpose. See *mutual fund and collective investment fund.* (v.): To place assets into a trust or retirement plan.

general obligation bond (GO): A municipal bond that is secured by the full faith and credit of the issuer rather than by specific property.

general partnership: A partnership created by two or more persons who agree to place their money, efforts, and skills in a business and to share profits and losses; general partners are responsible for the management of the business; all partners are subject to unlimited joint and several liability, both personally and for the actions of other partners.

general power of appointment: See *power of appointment.*

general power of attorney: See *power of attorney.*

Glass–Steagall Act: The Federal Banking Act of 1933, which separates the activities of commercial banks and investment banks.

goods and chattels: A term used to describe one's tangible personal property.

government bonds: U.S. government debt securities (bills, notes, or bonds); also referred to as Treasuries.

grantor: A person or institution that creates a trust; also called a creator, settlor, or trustor.

growth stock: Stock that is characterized by its potential increase in value (appreciation) rather than by its dividend payment.

guaranteed interest contract (GIC): Used in retirement plans, a contract issued mainly by insurance companies in which the interest paid on the funds is guaranteed for a given period of time, as in a certificate of deposit.

guardian: An individual or institution appointed by a court to care for the property (guardian of the estate) or the person (guardian of the person) of a minor or an incompetent adult; in some states guardian pertains to a minor and conservator pertains to an incompetent adult.

guardian of the estate: See *guardian.*

guardian of the person: See *guardian.*

heir: A person who inherits from a decedent's estate; an heir is a beneficiary who is not necessarily a family member, descendant, or next of kin.

holographic will: A will written entirely in the handwriting of the testator and not witnessed.

homestead: Land and buildings on the land occupied by the owner(s) as a home.

improved property: Land that is enhanced beyond being merely vacant; minimally it may be accessible and have utilities (e.g., water and electricity) or it may be highly developed, such as having a multicomplex commercial building on it.

imputed income: Income received in a form other than money, such as the growth of a zero coupon bond from the time of purchase to maturity.

incapacitation: The legal term for a person's inability to act on his or her own behalf because of medical reasons, minority, addiction to drugs or alcohol, imprisonment, mental illness, or disappearance.

income: Opposite principal, this is the return received from property, such as interest, dividends, and rental income.

income stock: Common or preferred stock known for its high dividend payments.

incompetence: The legal inability of a person to manage his or her financial affairs due to mental, as opposed to physical, inability.

indemnification: An agreement to compensate or reimburse an individual or other legal entity in the event of a loss.

indenture: The document that establishes a corporate trust.

independent administration: See *estate administration.*

independent executorship: Also called independent administration; see *estate administration.*

individual retirement account (IRA): A retirement plan established by an individual (as opposed to a company retirement plan) for his or her own personal retirement purposes; contributions and their tax deductibility depend on whether the individual participates in a corporate plan and what the individual's income level is; the earnings of the plan grow tax-deferred and may be taken without penalty at age $59\frac{1}{2}$.

individual trustee: An individual (person) who serves as a trustee.

inflation risk: See *risk.*

inherit: (v.) To receive property from a decedent's estate whether by will or intestacy; the property received is called the inheritance.

insider information: Information about the financial status of a company that is gathered or known only by a few persons close to the corporation, giving them an opportunity to profit unfairly from their knowledge, as opposed to being properly disseminated to the general public.

insolvency: A condition that exists when the liabilities, debts, taxes, and claims of a decedent's estate exceed the estate's assets.

insured pension plan: A retirement plan provided by an insurance company in which the benefits and earnings are guaranteed by life insurance, annuities, and guaranteed interest contracts (GIC). Also see *trusteed pension plan.*

intangible property: Personal property that cannot be physically distinguished by the senses; property that represents something else (e.g., a stock certificate is not the property itself, yet it represents ownership in a company that cannot be physically sensed).

interest: An amount paid by a borrower (debtor) to a lender (creditor) in exchange for the use of the lender's money for a stipulated period of time; interest is paid on loans or on debt securities (i.e., bonds) either at regular intervals (e.g., every 6 months) or as a lump sum payment when the issue matures (e.g., a zero-coupon bond).

interest rate risk: See *risk*.

in terrorem clause: A provision of a will or trust agreement intended to frighten a possible beneficiary into doing or refraining from doing something with the consequence of forfeiting his possible benefits, such as a provision that would disinherit any named or potential beneficiary who contested the will. Also called a no-contest clause.

inter vivos trust: A trust created during the grantor's life; also called a living trust or trust under agreement; this type of trust is distinguished from a testamentary trust, which is created in one's will and does not go into effect until after the grantor's death.

intestacy/intestate: (adj.) Dying without leaving a valid will. Opposite of *testate*.

inventory: An accounting and valuation of the assets of a decedent's estate accomplished by the executor or administrator.

investment: An asset acquired for the purpose of earning interest, dividends, or appreciation.

investment bank: An institution that effects the issuance and sale of new securities issues to the general public; also called an underwriter; to be distinguished from commercial bank.

investment management account: An agency relationship that provides investment advice and portfolio management to individuals and institutions for a fee.

irrevocable trust: A trust that cannot be revoked (terminated) or amended by the grantor.

issue: A term describing those who descend from a common ancestor; this extends beyond immediate children.

joint tenancy: Ownership of property by two or more persons, related or not; upon the death of the first owner, by act of law the survivors take possession of the property absent probate proceedings; joint tenancy property is not controlled by the dispositive provisions of a tenant's will; the ownership of the property converts to sole ownership when there is only one surviving tenant.

joint tenancy with rights of survivorship (JTWROS): A term equivalent to joint tenancy.

junk bond: A bond which possesses an extremely low bond rating and is, therefore, considered very risky due to its high default potential.

kickout clause: A clause in a personal trust that permits a trustee to terminate the trust and distribute the assets to the beneficiaries once the principal of the trust falls to a certain amount stipulated in the trust agreement.

kin: See *next of kin*.

kind: See *distribution in kind*.

land trust: A form of trust in which the corpus is solely real property; what distinguishes this type of trust from a personal trust is that both the legal and equitable title are vested in the trustee; the trustee has no duties other than to deal with the real property as directed by the beneficiary or sell the property upon the trust's termination; all rights of management and control of the property vest in the beneficiary; although the corpus of the trust is real property, the beneficiary's interest in the property is characterized as intangible personal property.

lapse: (v.) The failure of an event to happen, such as a powerholder's failure to exercise a given power of appointment.

last will: The very last will document executed by a testator before death; any will automatically revokes all prior wills, yet the word *last* is used to emphasize the fact that it is the latest will and is thereby the effective will of the testator.

last will and testament: A legal document that expresses a person's intents regarding the distribution of his estate upon death; wills do not pertain only to financial matters; a will can provide burial and organ donor instructions and the naming of a guardian for one's minor children; wills are revocable and amendable by a codicil; a testator must have testamentary capacity to execute a will.

law of descent and distribution: See *statutes of distribution*.

legacy: See *bequest*.

legal ownership: The legal interest a person has in property; legal ownership rests in an individual under all forms of property ownership except in a trust, in which the legal ownership vests in the trust, and the beneficiary possesses equitable ownership.

legal title: A right to the ownership of property, enforced in a court of law. Also see *equitable title*.

legatee: The person who receives a gift or legacy.

letter of credit: An agreement between a bank and bank customer that stipulates that the bank will honor demands for payment on behalf of the customer in compliance with the conditions specified in the credit; when the credit is exercised, a loan occurs; the credit is predicated upon the customer's credit standing and ability to pay the future loan if and when the credit is exercised.

letters of authority: See *letters testamentary*.

letters of guardianship: A certificate of authority, given by the court to the appointed estate guardian, which evidences the guardian's authority to act.

letters of office: See *letters of guardianship* and *letters testamentary*.

letters testamentary: A certificate of authority given to the appointed executor or administrator by a court to settle the affairs of a decedent's estate.

leverage: The use of borrowed money to increase investing power.

life insurance trust: A living trust consisting primarily of life insurance policies that will fund the trust by way of beneficiary designation upon the insured's or grantor's death.

limited liability company: A corporation that is taxed as a partnership for federal tax purposes; profits and losses are passed through to the owners (members); similar to a limited partnership, the members are limited as to liability.

limited liability partnership: A form of general partnership in which the general partners are provided limited liability protection.

limited partnership: A type of partnership composed of one or more general partners who manage the business and are personally liable for the partnership's debts, and one or more limited partners who contribute capital and share in profits but who do not take part in management and incur no liability for the partnership's debts beyond their contributions to capital.

limited power of appointment: See *power of appointment*.

limited power of attorney: See *power of attorney*.

liquidity: A measure of how quickly (how marketable) an asset can be converted to cash.

liquidity risk: See *risk*.

living trust: See *inter vivos trust*.

living will: A document that states a person's desires regarding the use or removal of life-sustaining or death-deterring procedures in the event of a terminal illness or injury. Also see *power of attorney for healthcare*.

load: A commission, charge, or fee paid by a buyer for participation in an open-end mutual fund.

load fund: A mutual fund that sells its shares through an agent that acts as a middleperson and charges a sales commission.

lump sum distribution: A single payment of the total benefits available from a retirement plan; the single payment may qualify for special income tax treatment and may be eligible for rollover into a rollover IRA.

majority: (adj.) Of legal age.

market risk: See *risk*.

market value: The price at which an investment will sell within a trading center. Also see *fair market value*.

marshal: (v.) To collect and arrange the assets of a decedent's estate or a ward's estate.

master trust: An arrangement whereby one trustee uniformly coordinates the administration and accounting of the assets of possibly many trusts, retirement plans, multiple custodians, and several investment managers; this is found primarily within large employee benefit plans or situations that entail multiple, related corporations.

maturity: The date on which the principal of a bond or a certificate of deposit comes due and is to be paid or returned to the bondholder or depositor.

merger: The combination of two or more business entities; if the entities are corporations, the transaction involves the exchange of securities or issuance of new ones.

minor: A person who is not of legal age.

money market: A bank account or mutual fund that consists solely of short-term securities, thereby giving a customer instant availability to deposits and withdrawals from the fund.

Moody's Investor Service: An investment advisory service that is a subsidiary of Dun & Bradstreet; this service analyzes corporate and municipal securities, as well as preferred stocks and some common stocks; the securities that are analyzed are also rated as to their creditworthiness and risk potential.

morbidity rates/table: A statistical study showing the number of people at any age that will become disabled within the next year; the table can also establish how long a disability is expected to last depending on the type of disability and age of onset.

mortality rates/table: A statistical study showing the number of people of any age that will die within the next year; these tables can also establish the life expectancy of a person at any given age.

mortgage: A written instrument evidencing an indebtedness on real property; the borrower (mortgagor) borrows from the lender (mortgagee) for the purpose of buying real property (e.g., a house); the property is collateral against the loan; the borrower uses the property during the period of loan repayment; once the loan is satisfied, the collateral is removed.

municipal bond: A bond issued by a municipality, such as a state, city, or county; these bonds are also called tax-exempt bonds because the interest paid on these issues is exempt from federal income taxes and most state and local income taxes.

municipal note: See *anticipation note.*

mutual fund: An investment company that pools its shareholders' money into various investment funds; each fund has its particular investment objective, which determines the types of securities bought in the fund; the owners of a fund own a proportionate share of the fund and are taxed proportionately depending on the amount of their investment in relationship to the size of the fund; funds are priced on a daily basis; a fund may charge a front-end load (a cost to the customer to invest in the fund), a back-end load (a cost to exit the fund), or an annual expense charge (fee).

National Association of Securities Dealers Automated Quotations (NASDAQ): An automated price quotation service for over-the-counter securities.

national bank: A commercial bank chartered under federal authority and regulated and examined by the Office of the Comptroller of the Currency (OCC); the word *National* or initials *N.A.* (national association) must appear in the bank's name; a national bank must be a member of the Federal Deposit Insurance Corporation (FDIC).

natural guardian: The parent of a minor; as the parent, the natural guardian is the guardian of the person but not necessarily the guardian of the estate.

net asset value (NAV): The market value of all securities plus other assets, minus liabilities, divided by the number of shares outstanding; NAV is used to compute the price of a share in an open-end investment company (mutual fund).

New York Stock Exchange (NYSE): See *centralized trading exchange.*

next of kin: Those who are the closest, living blood relatives to a decedent.

no-load fund: A mutual fund with no sales charge for executing transactions.

no-contest clause: See *in terrorem clause*.

nominate/nomination: (v./n.) The naming as opposed to the appointment; for example, a testator can name an executor in her will, but the court appoints the executor.

nominee: A person or corporation in whose name registered securities are held for the benefit of another.

noncallable bond: A bond that cannot be called by the bond issuer (e.g., the corporation) for the purpose of redemption or conversion.

nondiscretionary account: 1. An account in which the management and responsibility of investment decision making remains with the grantor (for a trust) or principal (for an agency). 2. With respect to an investment management agency, this is an account in which the investment agent cannot carry out investment changes (e.g., sells or purchases) without first receiving approval from the principal.

nonqualified retirement plan: A supplemental, deferred compensation retirement plan established by an employer for certain select employees; employer contributions to the plan are not currently taxed to the participant(s); the plan's earnings before distribution may be taxed to the employee, depending on how the plan is structured; based on how the plan is structured, the assets may or may not be subject to the claims of the company's creditors. Also called a supplemental employee retirement plan.

notary/notary public: An authorized public officer who attests (certifies) the authenticity of deeds, documents, and contracts; for wills the notary is present to attest the signatures of the testator and the witnesses.

notice to heirs/legatees: A notice given by the executor or administrator of a decedent's estate to the rightful takers of one's will or estate.

notice to interested persons: See *creditor's notice*.

nuptial agreement: An agreement between spouses, made before their marriage (prenuptial) or after their marriage (antenup-

tial) with respect to their property and its disposition during life and following death.

obligor: The one who is obligated to repay a loan or debt; for example, a corporation is obligated to repay the loan created by a bond issue sold to investors.

Office of the Comptroller of the Currency (OCC): The office of the U.S. Treasury Department that is the chief regulator, supervisory agency, and examiner of national banks.

open-end fund: A mutual fund that sells new shares to new and existing investors and redeems shares at the market price when investors wish to sell.

open-end investment management company: A mutual fund; a registered investment management company; "open-end" means that the fund's capitalization increases whenever it sells new shares to the public and decreases when the shares are redeemed.

option: An agreement that permits an investor to buy or sell something within a designated period of time according to the terms of the agreement. Also see *call* and *put*.

order of distribution: Within the probate process of settling an estate, this is the court order that directs the final distribution of the estate's assets.

ordinary court: See *probate court*.

orphan's court: See *probate court*.

over-the-counter market (OTC): A computerized web of a large number of small investment brokers and dealers who deal with stock issues not listed on the larger organized stock exchanges; the issues are called unlisted securities; business is not transacted in a physical location.

ownership in the severalty: See *separate property*.

participant: An employee who takes part in an employee benefit plan.

partition: A division of property between or among two or more persons or institutions who are entitled to fractional interests of the property; this pertains mainly to real property (which is owned by parties with unallocated interests, as in joint tenancy), when it must be sold or divided to satisfy indebtedness or settle a divorce action. (v.): To divide the property.

partnership: An association of two or more persons for the conduct of an enterprise other than in corporate form; the rights, duties, and responsibilities of the people so associated may be covered in a partnership agreement; if not, law determines them.

par value: See *face value*.

payable on death (POD): A beneficiary designation associated primarily with bank accounts owned by one person; the asset does not pass through probate and is paid directly to the pre-arranged beneficiary. Also known as *transfer on death*.

paying agent: An agent whose duty is to receive money from an obligor in order to pay bond interest and maturing bonds or stock dividends from a corporation.

Pension Benefit Guaranty Corporation (PBGC): A government corporation that provides insurance programs to guarantee payment of basic retirement benefits to participants of defined-benefit pension plans in the event the plan does not have sufficient funds to pay all benefits.

per capita: A term used when the distribution of property from a trust is to be made to a group of surviving beneficiaries equally ("by the head") as opposed to per stirpes ("by the branch"). For example, assume John Doe's family looks like this (the brackets indicate that this family member is not alive at the time of distribution):

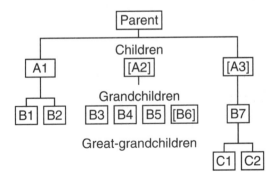

Per capita distribution of John's $900,000 trust would be equal payments of $100,000 to each of the nine living beneficiaries: A1, B1, B2, B3, B4, B5, B7, C1, and C2.

personal effects: With respect to a decedent's estate, these are the assets of a personal nature such as clothing and jewelry.

personal investment fund: See *common trust fund*.

personal property: All property that is not real property; personal property is either intangible or tangible.

personal representative: A generic term for an executor or administrator.

personal trust: A trust established by an individual (grantor) for the benefit of oneself or others (beneficiaries), as opposed to an employee trust, which is established by a corporation for individuals, or a corporate trust, which is established by a corporation for a corporation.

per stirpes: A term used when the distribution of property from a trust is among survivors of generations ("by the branch") as opposed to equally per capita ("by the head") among all surviving family members. For example, using the family structure from the per capita definition, the distribution of John's trust would be $300,000 to A1, $300,000 split among B3, B4, and B5 ($100,000 to each) as survivors of A2, and $300,000 to B7 as survivor of A3. B1 and B2 do not receive a share because A1 is alive, and C1 and C2 do not receive a share because B7 is alive. If A2 (who predeceased John Doe) did not have children, the share that would have gone to A2 (if he or she were alive) would be split equally along the A1 and A3 branches; this would be so because A2 did not have any children, meaning that the A2 branch ended.

petition: A written request to a court. (v.): To ask/request; for example, a person can petition the court to appoint a particular person or institution to serve as guardian of the estate for a minor or incompetent adult; based upon the request and the facts, the court will make its decision and appointment.

pooled fund: See *common trust fund*.

portfolio: A collection of one's (individual or institution) investments.

posthumous child: A child born after a father's death; to be distinguished from after-born child.

pourover: The transferring of property from an estate or trust to another estate or trust; this occurs according to the terms and conditions of the first instrument (estate, will, or trust). (v.): To transfer the property.

power of appointment: A right given to a person to dispose of property he does not own. For example, A in his trust gives B, as a beneficiary, the power to say how and to whom the trust's property will be distributed based on the trust's provisions and a future contingency, such as B's death. A general power of appointment gives B the right to distribute the property as B sees fit; a special (or limited) power of appointment limits B as to whom the property can be distributed (e.g., B as a surviving spouse may be limited to distributing the trust's assets only to the children of A & B's marriage).

power of attorney: A document that authorizes a person (the attorney in fact) to act as an agent for the signer of the document; if the document permits the agent to act in all matters, it is a general power of attorney; if the document limits the agent to certain matters, it is a specific (or limited) power of attorney; if the document allows the agent to continue acting during the powergiver's incapacitation, it is a durable power of attorney; if the document states that the power is effective only upon a future contingency, it is a springing (or standby) power of attorney. A power of attorney is generally called a power of attorney for property. Also see *power of attorney for healthcare.*

power of attorney for healthcare: A power given to an agent to make healthcare decisions on behalf of another who is unable to make his or her own decisions; this power can include life support decisions. Also see *living will.*

power of attorney for property: See *power of attorney.*

prefect's court: See *probate court.*

preferred stock: Stock that pays a fixed dividend and has preference over common stock with respect to payment of dividends and to any claim made against the corporation in the event of liquidation; preferred stock usually does not carry any voting rights, so preferred stockholders do not have any voice in the management of the company. Also see *stock* and *common stock.*

premium: The amount or percentage above face value at which securities are bought or sold; the opposite is discount.

prenuptial agreement: See *nuptial agreement.*

present value: The value today of a single payment, or a stream of payments to be received, over a specified future period, discounted at a specific rate of interest.

primary beneficiary: A beneficiary of a trust who is entitled to immediate benefits from the trust, before others, regardless of whether the benefits are income or principal.

primary market: The market in which newly issued securities are sold by a broker, investment banker, or underwriter.

primogeniture: The position of being the first-born child, or the eldest child, or the eldest living son, depending on the historical context.

principal: 1. The amount of a deposit, investment, or loan exclusive of interest. 2. The one who employs an agent. 3. Property/corpus of an estate or trust as opposed to income.

probate: For an executor or administrator, the process of gathering assets, paying debts and taxes, and distributing the assets of a decedent's estate. 2. For a guardian, the process of managing the financial affairs of a minor or incompetent adult. (v.): To administer and settle a decedent's estate.

probate court: The court that has jurisdiction over the settlement and administration of an estate, whether under a valid will or because of intestacy; depending on the state, this court may also have jurisdiction over guardianships and adoptions; also called prefect's court, orphan's court, surrogate court, chancery court, and ordinary court.

profit sharing plan: An employee benefit plan in which an employee receives a share of the net profits of a business; these shares can be received currently (annually or periodically) or accumulated for the employee in a deferred retirement plan.

property: Assets subject to ownership; property is classified as personal or real.

proration: (v.) A proportionate division.

prospectus: A document required by the Securities and Exchange Commission (SEC) that gives information stating the formation, purpose, and intention to issue securities; the prospectus also describes the business of the issuer, the issuer's financial condition, and how the shares will be offered; a mutual fund prospectus must be given to any prospective investor in the fund; this prospectus must also disclose any costs related to the fund.

prototype: A written, standardized pension or profit-sharing plan document that is preapproved (prequalified) by the IRS before its adoption by an employer.

proxy: 1. A person given a power by another to act as an agent in order to vote shares of stock. 2. An instrument evidencing the agent's power to vote stock.

Prudent Investor Rule: A rule enacted in recent years by several individual states that sets investment guidelines to update the Prudent Man Rule.

Prudent Man Rule: A rule stated in 1830 in the Supreme Judicial Court of Massachusetts in *Harvard v. Amory,* which has set the example for a fiduciary's investment parameters. In 1974 ERISA set into place prudent man rules for persons and institutions dealing with pension and retirement plans.

put: An option to sell shares of a certain stock within a given period of time and at a specific price set in the put contract. (v.): To exercise the option.

qualified plan: An employee benefit plan that qualifies under the Internal Revenue Code rules and regulations; qualification entitles the employer to deduct its contributions to the plan and allows certain income tax benefits that are outlined in the code.

quitclaim deed: A simple and quick form of conveying real property; the grantor conveys the property without guarantee of title, and the grantee receives only the title that was vested in the grantor; this form of deeding is seen primarily between family members when a situation requires a quick transfer of property.

real estate: The title or interest one has in real property as opposed to the property itself.

real property: Land and anything permanently attached to the land or considered a permanent part of the property.

redemption: 1. The repayment of the principal amount of debt securities, plus any accrued interest, on the maturity date or when a call is exercised. 2. The removal of money from a fund by an investor.

refinancing: The retirement of existing securities, or the repayment of a debt from the proceeds of new borrowings.

refunding: The issuance of new debt securities to replace an older issue. Also see *refinancing*.

regional stock exchange: See *centralized trading exchange*.

registered bond: A bond in which the owner's name is on record with the obligor and paying agent for the purpose of determining ownership, and for paying interest and principal (upon a call or maturity).

registrar: For bonds, this is the agent that maintains records of ownership with respect to registered bonds; for stocks, this is the agent that places its signature to the stock certificates for the purpose of preventing overissuance of the company's stock.

remainderman: The person or institution that receives the corpus of a trust (according to the trust's dispositive provisions) following a prior or primary beneficiary; a remainderman may be a secondary beneficiary.

renounce: (v.) To decline taking from the decedent spouse's will according to the will's dispositive provisions, therefore causing the surviving spouse to take from the decedent spouse's estate according to statutory rules.

renouncing the will: See *election against the will.*

rental real property: Noncommercial property from which income is gained from tenant rents, such as a residential apartment building.

renunciation: See *declination.*

repurchase agreement: A sale of securities with a simultaneous agreement to buy back the same securities at a stated price on a stated date; a repurchase agreement (known as a "repo") is the most common form of overnight investment of corporate funds; repos are sold in large minimum denominations (for example, $1 million) and they are supported (collateralized) 100 percent by securities from the borrower or more commonly by Treasury bills.

res: See *corpus.*

residence: A place where one lives permanently or temporarily; a residence is not necessarily one's domicile. Also see *domicile.*

residential real property: A primary (permanent) or secondary (temporary) residence.

residuary clause: A provision in a will or a trust that provides for the disposition of the estate's or trust's property following the payment of debts, taxes, expenses, and distribution of specific bequests; that which is left over is called the residue or residuary estate.

resign/resignation: (v./n.) The voluntary act by which an individual or institution, after being appointed as a fiduciary, declines to continue acting in its capacity.

restatement: An amendment to a trust that alters (changes) all provisions of the original trust and any previous amendments; whereas a revocation totally cancels a trust, a restatement does not cancel the original trust; it serves as a rewriting of the trust, thereby leaving the original trust date intact. The pourover provision of a will, asset titling, and beneficiary designations of employee benefit plans and life insurance do not have to be changed to reflect the restatement because the restatement does not cancel the original trust.

retired stock: Stock of a corporation that is canceled; the stock can be retired before being issued (due to oversubscription); or, if owned by stockholders, it can be retired once back in the corporation's hands following a buyback or a call.

return: What an investment pays an investor; return can be interest from a bond, the difference between buying a bond at a discount and the payment of face value upon maturity (or a call), dividends from a stock, or stock appreciation; also known as yield.

revenue bond: A municipal bond issued to finance an income-producing project such as a tollway or an energy-generating facility; the bond is secured by the income that will be generated from the completed project.

revocable trust: A trust that can be terminated (revoked) or amended (changed) by the grantor.

revocation: A complete cancellation (termination) of a will or revocable trust or parts of a will or trust.

right: A pre-emptive privilege of the existing shareholders of a company to purchase additional shares of stock when approved and issued by the company.

right of election: See *election against the will.*

risk: An uncertainty that an investment vehicle will earn an expected rate of return or that a loss may occur; types of risk include interest rate risk (risk that interest-bearing securities, such as bonds, will decline in value as market interest rates rise), liquidity risk (the risk that the attractiveness of securities will fall, therefore affecting their liquidity), exchange risk (the possibility that a loss will occur because of the appreciation or depreciation of a foreign currency in relationship to the U.S. dollar), credit risk (a risk that a bond rating will fall due to the obligor's financial condition or the possibility of default), inflation risk (the possibility that an increase in the rate of inflation will affect the relative return of securities), volatility risk (a risk associated with the erratic rising and falling of a stock's price over a period of time), and market risk (the risk that an entire market may fall).

rollover IRA: An individual retirement account (IRA) into which is deposited total or partial lump sum distributions from qualified retirement plans; the amount that is rolled over avoids immediate payment of income tax; the principal of the rollover and its earnings remain on a tax-deferred basis until distributions are made from the rollover.

rule against perpetuities: A rule that prohibits an estate or a trust from lasting perpetually; known as "lives in being plus 21 years," this rule generally states that when an estate is created or a trust becomes irrevocable, the estate or trust must terminate no later than 21 years after the death of the last beneficiary; the beneficiaries are determined at the time the estate or trust becomes irrevocable.

safe deposit box: See *vault*.

safekeeping account: An agency account in which the agent's duties are limited to accepting the principal's property, assuming responsibility for (safekeeping) it, and returning it to the principal when requested.

secondary beneficiary: A trust beneficiary that follows a primary beneficiary; a secondary beneficiary is sometimes called a remainderman.

secondary market: Any market that deals in the resale of existing securities, such as a centralized trading exchange and the over-the-counter (OTC) market.

secured: (adj.) Backed by collateral.

secured bond: A bond that is guaranteed by the pledge of collateral; opposite is debenture.

Securities Act of 1933: An antifraud act passed by Congress requiring registration of securities intended for sale to the public; the issuer must disclose financial information to the SEC by way of a registration statement; disclosure to the public is done by a prospectus.

Securities and Exchange Act of 1934: An act passed by Congress establishing the Securities and Exchange Commission (SEC), an independent agency that enforces federal securities laws; the act extended the registration and disclosure requirements of the Securities Act of 1933 to all companies with securities listed for sale on a national exchange; the act also required disclosure of proxy solicitations; in addition, the act required registration of brokers and dealers and exchanges in the over-the-counter (OTC) market.

Securities and Exchange Commission (SEC): See *Securities and Exchange Act of 1934*.

securities: Intangible personal property such as stocks, bonds, notes, and fixed-income instruments.

security: The property or asset that is given, deposited, or pledged as collateral to ensure the fulfillment of an obligation.

self-declaration of trust: A revocable living trust in which the grantor is also the beneficiary and trustee of the trust.

separate property: 1. Property that is owned solely by only one person, as opposed to joint tenancy, tenancy in common, or tenancy by the entirety in which the property rights or control is shared by others; also called ownership in the severalty. 2. Property owned in common law states by one or more persons.

settlor: See *grantor*.

share: A unit of ownership in a business; synonymous with stock and a certificate of stock.

shareholder: See *stockholder*.

siblings: Children of the same parents.

simultaneous death: The death of two or more persons under such circumstances that the order of their deaths cannot be determined. Also see *common disaster*.

situs: A physical place.

small estate affidavit: Also called summary administration; see *estate administration*.

sole ownership: See *separate property*.

sole proprietorship: An unincorporated business owned and operated by one person.

sound mind: See *testamentary capacity*.

special power of appointment: See *power of appointment*.

specific power of attorney: See *power of attorney*.

speculative stock: Stock of a company that is small or new and may be struggling financially; this type of stock may provide a healthy return (mostly with respect to appreciation), but it also poses the risk of failing.

spendthrift clause: A provision in a will or a trust that prevents a beneficiary from disposing of his interests by way of assignment to creditors or to alimony claims.

split: (n./v.) The conversion of securities from larger units into smaller ones (e.g., the changing of 1,000 shares of stock into two 500-share units); this may be done for the purpose of selling a portion of the stock or for a distribution in kind to several legatees.

sponsor: An employer who establishes an employee benefit plan.

spouse's allowance: An amount from a decedent's estate provided by statute or by court approval for the surviving spouse's living expenses during the period of estate settlement; also called widow's award. Also see *family allowance*.

spray clause: See *sprinkle clause*.

spread: The difference in the rate of return of one bond compared to another, each of the same quality and maturity; this comparison may be made between similar taxable bonds and similar tax-exempt bonds; when comparing a taxable bond to a tax-exempt bond, applicable income tax rates must be taken into consideration.

springing power of attorney: See *power of attorney*.

sprinkle clause: A dispositive provision of a trust that gives the trustee the discretionary power to distribute income or principal unevenly among the beneficiaries depending on their particular needs. Also called a spray clause.

Standard & Poor's (S&P): An investment advisory service (a subsidiary of McGraw-Hill) that supplies security ratings for corporate and municipal bonds (similar to Moody's Investor Service), commercial paper, and common and preferred stock; S&P also publishes investment guides and compiles market indices, the best known being the S&P 500, a daily stock market index measurement of 500 domestic stocks, which are representative of the overall U.S. stock market.

standby power of attorney: See *power of attorney*.

state bank: A commercial bank chartered, regulated, and examined by state banking authorities; state banks are not required to be a member of the Federal Deposit Insurance Corporation (FDIC), although most are.

statement: An account listing provided to a customer on a regular periodic basis (e.g., monthly or quarterly); statements can be consolidated or broken into separate ones, such as a statement of property held (listing stocks, bonds, and other property to include cost basis, market value, plus dividend and interest rates) and a statement of transactions (what was bought or sold, dividend posting, interest crediting, and fees charged).

Statute of Uses: A 1536 English law that directed that the legal and equitable title to land held for the use of a person vested in that person; this statute was an early precursor to the development of trusts as we know them today.

statutes of distribution: Laws that govern the distribution of property in the event of a person's intestate demise; also called laws of descent and distribution.

statutory: (adj.) Pertaining to the rules of law; these rules may be federal, state, local, or those contained in the Internal Revenue Code.

stock: A certificate or share that evidences ownership in a corporation; stock may be either common or preferred; stockholders share in the profits of a company, but they are subordinate to the claims of creditors and bondholders in the event of liquidation.

stock certificate: A printed, signed certificate that evidences proof of an investor's ownership of an equity portion of a corporation.

stock dividend: A dividend payable in stock as opposed to cash.

stockholder: The owner of stock of a corporation; also called a shareholder.

stock option: An employee's right to purchase stock of the employer; a stock option is usually limited to a specific number of shares, at a specific fixed price, and within a certain period of time.

stock split: A division of the total shares of a company's stock that increases or decreases the overall number of shares outstanding without decreasing or increasing the capitalization of the company or the value of a stockholder's holdings.

subscription: A term applied to the order for the purchase of new securities.

successor: One who follows another, such as a successor trustee who steps in following the initial trustee in the event the first dies, resigns, or is incapable of acting.

summary administration: See *estate administration.*

summary plan description: A written document that describes the pertinent elements of a qualified retirement plan; this document is required by law and must be furnished to employees (participants) upon their request.

supervised administration: See *estate administration.*

supplemental employee retirement plan (SERP): See *nonqualified retirement plan.*

surety: An individual or company that is responsible for the performance of an action that is required by another (e.g., A is required to carry out a task for B; in the event A does not carry out its task, the surety is responsible).

surety bond: A guarantee given by a bonding or insurance company (the surety) to be responsible for the debt or default of another; for example, a guardian of an estate may be required by a court to post a bond to ensure that the guardian's financial responsibilities to the ward are met.

surrogate court: See *probate court.*

sweep: (n.) An investment function of an accounting system provided by financial institutions to customers whose accounts receive funds that temporarily await reinvestment; such funds are swept into an interest-bearing account until the reinvestment occurs. (v.) To temporarily invest funds in an interest-bearing account until the funds are reinvested.

taking against the estate: See *election against the will.*

tangible property: Personal property that has a definite, distinguishable physical feature to it; this property is identified by the senses (e.g., an automobile, which can be seen and touched, as opposed to a stock certificate, which is evidence of company ownership that cannot be discerned by the senses).

tax-exempt bond: See *municipal bond.*

tax identification number (TIN): A number assigned by the Internal Revenue Service for tax purposes; for an individual this is a Social Security number; for a trust or a business it is an employer identification number.

temporary administrator: An individual or institution appointed by a court to serve as an administrator for a finite period of time or for a given purpose; this may occur until a permanent administrator is appointed; a temporary administrator may be appointed because of a lawsuit pertaining to the estate, which requires the expertise of an administrator with specific talents, or when probate is delayed or interrupted.

tenancy by the entirety: Recognized only in certain states; this is a form of property ownership similar to joint tenancy; it exists only between spouses.

tenancy in common: A form of property ownership between two or more individuals or institutions in which each tenant owns a divided percentage interest in the property; each tenant can deal with their interest as he or she sees fit to sell, gift, or bequeath it.

tenant: A person, trust, or institution that owns legal interest in property; this can be a sole tenant (see *separate property*) or a joint tenant (see *joint tenancy, tenancy in common,* and *tenancy by the entirety*).

tender: The selling of stock that is owned in a company that is being purchased by another company or due to a merger or buyback. (v.): To sell the stock.

testamentary capacity: The mental ability (sound mind) to make a valid will; this includes a testator's ability to know how much property he owns, knowledge that he is making a will, knowing who his family members are and how they will benefit from his estate, and knowledge of the consequences of the will being signed.

testamentary guardian: A guardian, for a minor or an incompetent adult, nominated in a will.

testamentary trust: A trust established in a will; a trust of this type is not operative or funded until one's death; also called a trust under will.

testate/testacy: (adj.) Dying with a valid will. Opposite of intestate.

testator: The person who creates a will.

testatrix: A seldom-used term for a female testator.

title: The legal right to ownership of property; the title to property is the document received when the property is bought and needed when it is sold; the document could be a bill of sale, a receipt, a deed, or any specific document that evidences ownership of the property.

Totten trust: A trust created when a person deposits money in his or her own name as a trustee for another; title vests in the trustee/donor who during his or her life holds it in a revocable trust for the named beneficiary; upon the depositor's/trustee's death, the property passes to the beneficiary.

transfer: The formal change of ownership of securities from one person to another by canceling the old certificates and issuing new ones. (v.): To change ownership of an asset from one owner to another owner.

transfer agent: An agent whose responsibility it is to transfer ownership of securities from one owner to another; the agent may be responsible for stock transfer, bond transfer, or both.

transfer on death (TOD): See *payable on death.*

Treasuries: A shortened, generic name for U.S. government bonds.

Treasury bills: Marketable fixed-income U.S. government securities with a maturity of less than one year.

Treasury bonds: Marketable fixed-income U.S. government securities with a maturity greater than 10 years.

Treasury notes: Marketable fixed-income U.S. government securities with a maturity ranging from 1 to 10 years.

trust: A fiduciary relationship created by a grantor in which a trustee agrees to hold legal title to property (corpus) for the benefit of another (beneficiary).

trust account: A term applied to any account managed by a trust institution, whether fiduciary in nature (estate, trust, guardian) or an agency (safekeeping, escrow, custody, investment management).

trust administration: The management of the assets of a trust account.

trust agreement: The formal written document between a grantor and a trustee that sets forth the terms of the trust; this is a set of instructions for the trustee. Also see *trust instrument.*

trust company: A corporation that manages trust accounts.

trust compliance officer: An officer of a trust department charged with ensuring that the department follows policies and procedures to ensure it is obeying all federal and state laws and regulations.

trustee: An individual or institution that holds legal title to property for benefit of another (beneficiary).

trusteed pension plan: A pension plan in which the assets are placed in a trust; the trust's assets are invested in vehicles other than those secured by an insurance company. Also see *insured pension plan.*

trust estate: See *corpus*.

Trust Indenture Act of 1939: Federal legislation that requires that bonds be issued under an indenture qualified by the SEC; the indenture trustee's role is to safeguard the bondholders' interests.

trust institution: A trust company, state or national bank, or other corporation that engages in the trust business; the institution must be chartered to carry on its trust activities.

trust instrument: Any written instrument that creates a trust; this can be a will, trust agreement, or order of court. Also see *trust agreement*.

trust investment committee: A committee made up of bank directors or officers of a trust institution who oversee trust investments, other than those directly related to investment activity.

trust investments: The property in which trust assets are invested.

trustor: See *grantor*.

trust under agreement: See *inter vivos trust*.

trust under will: See *testamentary trust*.

turnover: The activity that measures the frequency, percentage, and number of stocks bought and sold in a portfolio over a given period of time.

underwriter: See *investment bank*.

undue influence: When one person has enough influence over another person to prevent that person from exercising free choice; this is seen primarily with respect to the formation and amendment of a will or a trust in which the dispositive provisions of the document are not the creator's intentions.

unimproved property: Vacant land on which no facilities exist, such as ready access to roads or utilities (e.g., water and electricity); also called vacant real property.

unit: A single piece or share that an investor owns of a fund.

unit value: The price per unit, or amount of money needed to buy one unit (share) of a fund.

unlisted securities: See *over-the-counter market*.

unsecured: Not backed by collateral.

unsupervised administration: Also called independent administration; see *estate administration*.

vacant real property: See *unimproved property*.

valuation: The estimation of a property's worth.

valuation date: The date on which a decedent's estate is valued; this is either the date of death or the alternate valuation date.

vault: A guarded area of a bank or nonbank depository used for the storage of cash, securities, and other valuable assets; this area is protected from theft, fire, and water; a vault can be used by bank personnel only or by bank customers on a rental basis, such as a safe deposit box in the safe deposit vault.

vesting: With respect to qualified retirement plans, this pertains to a point in time in a participant's employment when the employee's benefits in the retirement plan become partially and eventually fully nonforfeitable; the vesting formula used in the plan determines at what point the benefits are fully or partially forfeitable or completely nonforfeitable regardless of whether the employee leaves.

volatility risk: See *risk*.

voting right: The right of a common stockholder (and sometimes a preferred stockholder, depending on the class of the stock) to vote on corporate issues and to elect the corporation's board of directors.

ward: A person who is under the protection of a court or a guardian because of minority or incompetence.

warrant: A certificate attached to a new securities issue that gives a stockholder the right to buy a certain number of shares of stock at a specified price within a certain period of time

widow's award: See *spouse's allowance*.

widow's election: See *election against the will*.

will: See *last will and last will and testament*.

yield: The annual rate of return from securities expressed as a percentage; also see *return*.

yield curve: A graphic representation of varying bond maturities and their respective returns; each graph measurement is done for one particular type of bond; the vertical axis plots the rates, and the horizontal axis plots maturities; different graphs (e.g., a government bond vs. a AAA-rated corporate bond) can be compared to determine spreads; yield curves are positive if the graph line slopes upward as maturities increase, flat if the graph line is a straight horizontal one, or inverted if the line slopes downward as maturities increase.

yield to maturity: A bond's average annual rate of return over the life of the bond, calculated with respect to the difference between the purchase price and the sale or maturity price and the bond's stated yield.

zero coupon bond: A taxable or tax-exempt bond that is bought at a deep discount from its par value; this bond does not make annual interest payments, but it pays the full face amount at maturity; although interest is not actually paid, it is imputed each year, making the market value of the bond increase.

INDEX

STUDENT SURVEY

Thank you for participating in this American Bankers Association/American Institute of Banking course/seminar. Your responses on the following evaluation will help shape the structure and content of future courses. After completing the evaluation, please fold, staple, and mail this postage-paid response form.

TELL US ABOUT YOURSELF:

Name _____ Phone # _____

Title_____ E-mail_____ Fax no. _____

Department_____ Bank/Company _____

Address _____

City _____ State _____ Zip _____

Your education ❑ high school   ❑ some college   ❑ BA/BS degree ❑ advanced degree _____

TELL US ABOUT YOUR EMPLOYER

Your employer's business is in ❑ banking ❑ other
(specify)_____

Number of years you've worked for financial services industry:
❑ 0-2   ❑ 3-5   ❑ 6-10   ❑ more than 10

Your employer's asset size: ❑ up to $250mm
❑ $251mm - $500mm   ❑ $501mm - $5 B ❑ $5 B plus

Number of employees:
❑ up to 100   ❑ 101 to 300   ❑ 301 to 1,000   ❑ 1,001 plus

Does your employer have an in-house training department?
❑ yes   ❑ no

If the answer is *yes*, who manages that department?
Name: _____
Title: _____

TELL US ABOUT YOUR AIB EXPERIENCE

Number of courses/seminars taken in last 3 years:
❑ 0   ❑ 1-2   ❑ 3-5   ❑ 6 or more

AIB course taken through (please check all that apply):
❑ Local ABA Training Provider
❑ AIB online program
❑ AIB correspondence study
❑ other (specify _____)

Are you working on another degree? ❑ yes ❑ no
(specify)_____
_____

Are you working on an AIB certificate/diploma program?
❑ yes (please specify)   ❑ no
❑ Bank Operations   ❑ Banking & Finance
❑ General Banking   ❑ Bank Marketing
❑ Performance Training Series Certificate
❑ Lending Diploma [❑ Commercial ❑ Consumer ❑ Mortgage]

Please list any other training providers you have used and the courses/seminars you have taken.

_____
_____
_____

TELL US YOUR OPINION OF THE COURSE MATERIALS

Please indicate your degree of agreement with the following:

	Strongly Disagree			Strongly Agree
Materials covered all important topics.	1	2	3	4
Learning objectives were clear.	1	2	3	4
Graphics well illustrated course content.	1	2	3	4
Theory and practical applications were well balanced.	1	2	3	4
Examples/case studies helped achieve learning objectives.	1	2	3	4
Exercises gave ample opportunity to apply learning.	1	2	3	4

Overall, how would you rate the following?

	Poor			Excellent
Course/seminar materials	1	2	3	4
Your experience with the course/seminar	1	2	3	4

Did your instructor use any supplemental materials to teach this course/seminar? ❑ Yes (What? _____)❑ No

TELL US WHAT OTHER SUBJECTS IN THE FINANCIAL SERVICES INDUSTRY YOU WOULD LIKE TO STUDY

Are there other banking areas you want to learn about? Please specify: _____
_____
_____

What course(s) would help you improve your performance in your current job? Please specify: _____
_____
_____

What type of courses best suit your needs?
❑   Instructor led classroom training
❑   Courses presented over the Internet
❑   Courses presented on CD-ROM multimedia
❑   Printed correspondence courses
❑   Other (please specify):_____

_____

Please provide additional comments about the course/seminar, the materials, other training topics, ABA/AIB, and/or your training needs so that we may better serve you in the future:

_____
_____
_____
_____
_____
_____
_____
_____

TELL US WHAT INFORMATION WE SHOULD SEND TO YOU (check all that apply)
❑ AIB diploma programs ❑ ABA conferences ❑ AIB online programs
❑ ABA schools ❑ ICB certification program ❑ other products and services (describe: _____)
May we contact you about courses/seminars under development for your input? ❑ yes ❑ no

Thank you for completing this survey.
For more information about the ABA/AIB, please visit our Internet Web site at **www.aba.com** or call our Member Service Center at **1-800-BANKERS**.

- - - - - - - - - - - - - - PLEASE FOLD ALONG DOTTED LINE - - - - - - - - - - -